YALE PUBLICATIONS IN THE HISTORY OF ART, 35

GEORGE L. HERSEY, EDITOR

THE ARCHITECTURE OF THE

ROMAN EMPIRE

II AN URBAN APPRAISAL

WILLIAM L. MacDONALD

NEW HAVEN AND LONDON

YALE UNIVERSITY PRESS

Frontispiece: Anjar, part of the tetrakionion

Designed by John O. C. McCrillis and Sally Harris
and set in Garamond type by
The Composing Room of Michigan, Inc.
Printed in the United States of America by
Halliday Lithograph, West Hanover, Mass.

Library of Congress Cataloging-in-Publication Data
(Revised for vol. 2)

MacDonald, William Lloyd.
    The architecture of the Roman Empire.

    (Yale publications in the history of art ; 17, 35)
    Includes bibliographies and indexes.
    Contents:—v. 2. An urban appraisal.
    1. Architecture—Rome. I. Title. II. Series.
NA310.M2 1982   772'.7   81-16513
ISBN 0-300-02818-0 (v. 1)
ISBN 0-300-03456-3 (v. 2)
ISBN 0-300-02819-9 (pbk. : v. 1)
ISBN 0-300-03470-9 (pbk.: v. 2)

The paper in this book meets the guidelines for
permanence and durability of the Committee on
Production Guidelines for Book Longevity
of the Council on Library Resources.

10 9 8 7 6 5 4 3 2 1

for F. E. B. and S. D.

CONTENTS

PREFACE

The critical evaluation of ancient classical architecture lags well behind that of most subsequent western architectural periods. Ancient buildings are so often discussed as isolated entities or as members of typological or regional groups that contextual implications and overall formal and thematic relationships are frequently undervalued. I believe that studying Roman buildings primarily as urban elements can help bring classical architecture into clearer focus and at the same time advance our understanding of the imperial town, the paramount artifact and image of Roman civilization.

An early attempt at such a study proved inadequate. Further research and travel, as time and resources permitted, as well as editorial and other work on the Princeton Encyclopedia of Classical Sites, *broadened my knowledge and helped me see the shape of the book more clearly; the new draft that followed was the basis for this book. The discussion is still tentative in some respects, but it is unlikely that further effort on my part would improve it appreciably.*

Although attempting a synoptic view of so large a subject makes mistakes and frequent qualification inevitable, the risks seem to me worth taking. The book is offered with the same awareness, and in the same hope, that Haverfield expressed in 1913 in his Ancient Town-Planning, *when he said that although "completeness and certainty are often unattainable and errors fatally easy, {the} results may nevertheless contain some suggestions and may help future workers." That the text has fewer mistakes and infelicitous features than it had as I composed it is due chiefly to the knowledge and generosity of friends who read the manuscript and gave me the benefit of their advice and criticism. Ramsay MacMullen and Bernard M. Boyle kindly pointed out various weaknesses and obscurities, and Sterling Dow gave the work the same painstaking attention he gave to my undergraduate course papers almost forty years ago. I am much indebted to them for their help, as I am also to Judy Metro of the Yale University Press for her advice and patience.*

Among those who helped me in other ways, Francesca Wiig has my warmest thanks for making the Dean William Emerson Fund available; her generosity helped defray the cost of work at Hadrian's Villa and of several forays from Rome into the provinces. I deeply appreciate also the assistance of the archaeologists and custodians who took the time to facilitate visits to their sites as I crisscrossed the empire over the years. The content of the book rests largely on direct study of buildings and of sites large and small, attended or not; many were examined at length and visited repeatedly. But I regret that I have not been to Albania, Bulgaria, Hungary, Romania, or the easternmost districts of Turkey. Elsewhere there are also sites I know only from publications, for example (and inexplicably) Lugo, or Apamea. Some were unreachable—Dura Europos, for instance—because travel permits could not be obtained. Two or three, such as Gemellae, simply refused to be found, though later I discovered that Gemellae is a kilometer or so from where I had finally come to a halt, peering Sahara-ward.

For help on various points I wish to thank Wilhelm Alzinger, Herbert Benario, Lorne Bruce, David Buck, George Dimock, Karin Einaudi, Paul-Albert Février, Alfred Frazer, Ann Gilkerson, Charles Henderson, John Hoag, Renata Holod, John Humphrey, Spiro Kostof, Yani Makridis, Lucilla Marino, John Pinto, David Rupp, Myles Weintraub, Fikret Yegül, and the Syrian scholars who organized the Ninth International Congress of Classical Archaeology. The names of the late Richard Goodchild, Ernest Nash, Henry Rowell, and John Ward-Perkins belong here also. I am indebted to those who made the drawings and to those who kindly provided me with photographs; their names appear in the credits for illustrations.

Above all I want to record my gratitude to Boris Bittker, Sterling Professor of Law in Yale University, for the gift of a splendid trip with him through Morocco and Algeria and for his company during other explorations, and to the distinguished scholars whose unfailing support and generosity, of many years' duration, are gratefully but inadequately acknowledged in the dedication.

W. L. M.

Washington D.C.
December 1984

THE ARCHITECTURE OF THE ROMAN EMPIRE

II

AN URBAN APPRAISAL

The plans, drawings, and models are on the whole only general guides to the ancient states of sites and buildings. Different place names inevitably appear in different languages; traditional English versions are often used. The examples cited are not intended to be inclusive. All dates are A.D. unless otherwise indicated. The adjective "Roman," used without qualification, refers to imperial times. Phrases like "Roman Pergamon" indicate complete ancient cities and towns of the empire insofar as they are known, not just their structures of Roman date.

I

INTRODUCTION

IN THE HISTORY of Western architecture, Roman forms and themes persist in style after style. The quantity of evidence for this is incalculable. There are historical explanations for it, but the intrinsic reasons are obscure because our understanding of Roman design is incomplete. We know that interior space was mastered and that the orders were interpreted and deployed in new ways. Some social needs were answered effectively, and primary structural advances were made. But the most conspicuous achievement of Roman architecture was its dominant role in creating, rebuilding, and expanding hundreds of cities and towns—its urban instrumentality. The results are impossible to take for anything but work of Roman times; clearly they do not belong to other periods. We need to know more about why this is so and about the enduring inherent qualities of Roman architecture that were put squarely in the way of future architectural evolution on three continents. These qualities are studied here from a city-oriented point of view.

The underlying premises are that mature Roman design was shaped largely in response to urban needs and civic ambition, and that empire-wide principles proved stronger, on the whole, than regional impulses. Public buildings are discussed both as interdependent parts of their extended urban context and as entities in themselves. Visual, allusive, and associative qualities are stressed, for the book derives more from the history of architecture, from the study of forms and their meaning, than from archaeology or the history of city planning.

Programmed to locate visible Roman sites, a scholars' satellite would transmit data whose graphic mode would closely match the map established by research and archaeology. The transmission resulting from instructions to describe the sites, on the other hand, would reflect the realities of imperial urbanism in its heyday poorly because of the amount of destruction and change wrought over the centuries. Were the computer asked to combine the two classes of data and display relative degrees of preservation across the empire, the results would show that the existing tangible evidence for reasonably complete cities and towns is heavily concentrated in a few areas. For many sites, including some large ones, we have only a ruined building or two, if that. Details of a situation now apprehensible only in general terms would become vividly clear, and the patterns and significance of the distribution of the evidence could be assessed and put to work. Awareness of the lack of such advantages is essential: in spite of its quantity, the evidence is woefully incomplete, and its distribution does not record the original architectural geography of the empire.

The majority of relatively well-preserved sites are in North Africa and the Near East, where many were never built over to a significant degree. There is an intermittent band of them along a fishhook-shaped arc of 5500 km. extending from Morocco to eastern Libya and from Jordan north and then west to the Aegean. In some areas—northeastern Algeria, Tunisia, western Syria, and along Turkey's Mediterranean coast—there are heavy concentrations; here and there, as in Cyrenaica and inland Turkey, significant clusters. [1]

The situation in Europe is different. There most Roman cities and towns were completely built over, though some monumental structures survive. Once in a while an abandoned site makes systematic excavation possible, but only a small fraction of the huge number of European sites have been explored sufficiently to give a sense of their original appearance. The partial recovery of many military camps and towns along the northern frontiers of the empire ameliorates this situation. Throughout Europe much ingenuity has been applied to the problem of obtaining coherent results from bits and pieces of evidence scattered through densely populated areas, and this exacting work, as well as excavation at less restricted sites across the empire, continues. Still we have a more detailed view in the south and the east of relationships between buildings and their urban setting than in the north and the west, however promising our inferences.

But the relative lack of thorough excavation of European sites is not so much a barrier to urban architectural analysis as might be thought. The evidence for individual buildings and for some city quarters and building complexes in Europe is often extensive and detailed. It shows that the architectural principals involved, with respect to buildings as urban instruments, are much the same there as across the Mediterranean. In other words, there is enough evidence in Europe of enough different kinds to compensate largely for the lack of complete sites. For example, it is clear that although many European towns began as military foundations or were heavily influenced by military planning and traditions (as were some sites in Africa and the east) and thus started out as rather spare and austere places, they gradually acquired enough of the essential architectural features of properly imperial towns to bring them broadly into line with urban practice across the empire. This could not be known from just a few sites.

Gradual acquisition must be stressed because fully formed cities and towns, the finished products of a lengthy synthesis of Roman formulations with Hellenistic and other potent forces, are the principal subject here. The period emphasized is that from Trajan through Constantine, the period of Roman urbanism at its zenith, when cities and towns were nearing or had reached full growth. Even the most modest boasted examples of structures so readily associated with Roman urbanism—arches, basilicas, fountains, spacious baths, and the like. The discussion is based largely on this accumulated evidence (whatever the dates of individual structures) as it appears today, and on what may be deduced from it about style and meaning. Questions of origins, of the degree of dependence on earlier achievements in Italy or elsewhere, are little pursued. The evidence is taken by and large on its own terms, restoration and all, in order to study imperial architecture more as it was known and experienced in its day than as the result of various evolutions and developments.

This is Roman architecture far removed from the conservative, nostalgic world of Vitruvius, whose attitudes are summed up in his sentence about the proper way of founding towns: "I cannot insist too strongly upon the need to return to the old ways."[2] It is an architecture of another age, one of hundreds of prosperous market towns, of administrative centers, port cities, veterans' colonies, religious foundations, and three or four very large metropolitan areas. These chapters attempt to show that there is a wholeness to it, an apposite homogeneity of form and intent across the whole range of evidence. The objectives are to suggest that the cities and towns all belong to the same architectural community and to propose reasons why this is so.

Each city and town is seen as formed around a clearly delineated, path-like core of thoroughfares and plazas, which for convenience can be called an armature, that provided uninterrupted passage throughout the town and gave ready access to its principal public buildings (chapter II). This core, or armature, consisted minimally of a high street wider than the other streets, plazas (the forum or agora might in the smallest places be the only one), civic buildings, and open structures marking junctions or intersections, or providing amenities, along the way. To be truly Roman, towns had to have at least the rudiments of armatures; those of large cities were highly elaborated. Only incidentally the products of city planning, they were formed gradually, in part by somewhat haphazard accumulation. Their principal elements are as follows:

> open spaces—high streets and major plazas—linked together, an architecture of connection (chapter III)
> constructions partly or wholly open to connective architecture, such as arches or fountains, that marked stages or segments of it, an architecture of passage (chapter IV)
> public buildings—civil, religious, social, and commercial (chapter V, where they are considered as instruments of urbanism; dwellings, well studied elsewhere, are omitted)

These essential public constituents of Roman towns were bound together visually by architectural forms based partly on Hellenistic precedents revised and augmented. Roman orders and compositional themes are familiar, but their manner of use, both functional and symbolic, needs scrutiny. A new kind of classicism, distinct from that of the past, was combined with traditional motifs to give the cities and towns their communal formal character (chapter VI). Roman classicism was not a matter of mindless repetition, but of quite sophisticated architectural modalities and images following empire-wide principles loosely but in unmistakably Roman ways (chapters VII and VIII). Some implications of the argument overall are discussed and summarized at the end (chapter IX). The aim is to interpret imperial architecture by analyzing its urban purposes and content.

MAPS

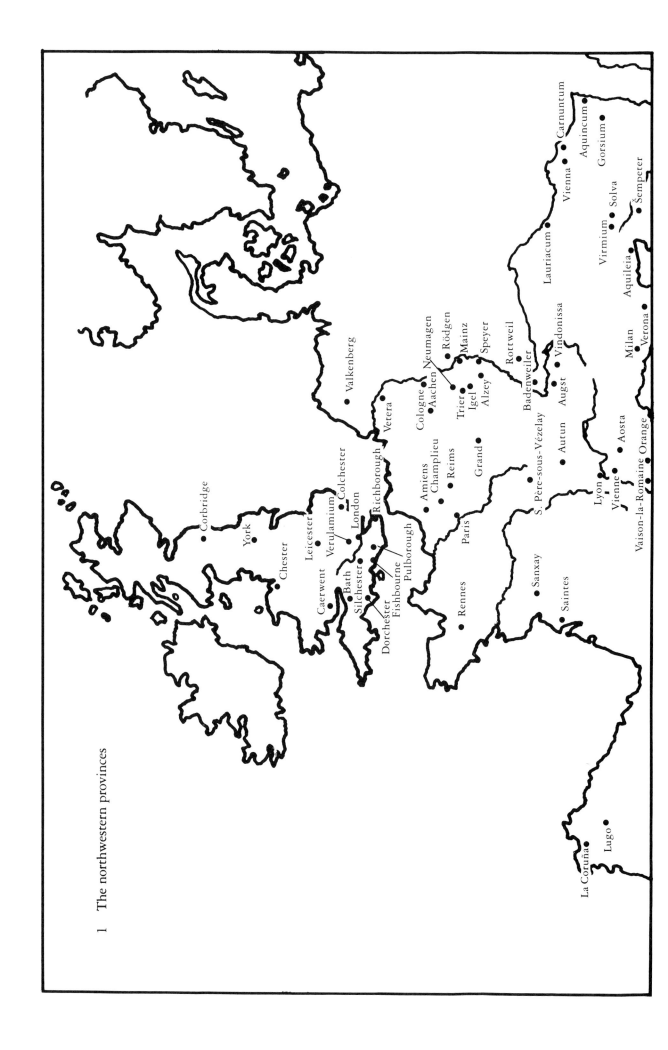

1 The northwestern provinces

Corbridge
York
Chester
Leicester
Caerwent
Verulamium
Bath
Silchester
London
Colchester
Dorchester
Fishbourne
Pulborough
Richborough
Valkenberg
Vetera
Amiens
Champlieu
Reims
Grand
Paris
Rennes
Sanxay
Saintes
Cologne Neumagen
Aachen Rödgen
Trier Mainz
Igel Speyer
Alzey
Rottweil
Badenweiler
S. Père-sous-Vézelay
Autun
Lyon
Vienne
Vaison-la-Romaine Orange
Augst
Vindonissa
Lauriacum
Carnuntum
Vienna Aquincum
Virmium Gorsium
Solva
Šempeter
Aquileia
Milan
Verona
Aosta

La Coruña
Lugo

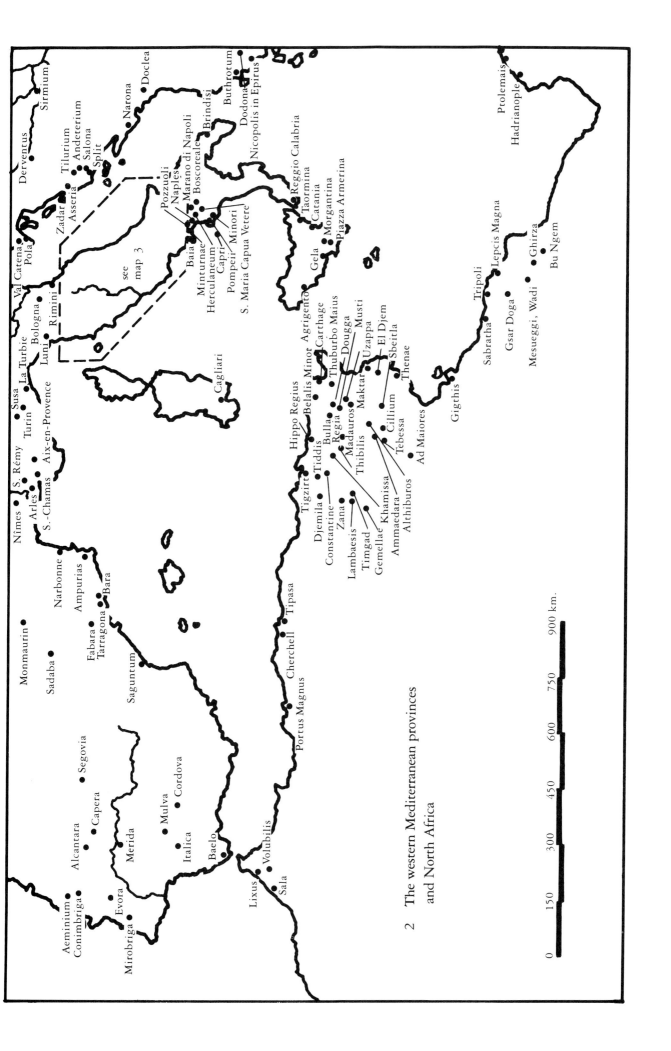

2 The western Mediterranean provinces and North Africa

Aeminium
Conimbriga
Evora
Mirobriga
Monmaurin
Sadaba
Alcantara
Capera
Segovia
Fabara
Tarragona
Bara
Merida
Italica
Mulva
Cordova
Baelo
Lixus
Sala
Volubilis
Saguntum
Ampurias
Narbonne
Nîmes
S. Rémy
Arles
S.-Chamas
Turin
Susa
La Turbie
Aix-en-Provence
Bologna
Luni
Rimini
Pola
Val Catena
Zadar
Asseria
Tilurium
Andeterium
Salona
Split
Narona
Derventus
Sirmium
Doclea
Buthrotum
Brindisi
Dodona
Nicopolis in Epirus
Pozzuoli
Naples
Marano di Napoli
Boscoreale
Baia
Minturnae
Herculaneum
Capri
Minori
Pompeii
S. Maria Capua Vetere
see map 3
Cagliari
Reggio Calabria
Taormina
Catania
Morgantina
Piazza Armerina
Gela
Agrigento
Carthage
Thuburbo Maius
Dougga
Musti
Uzappa
El Djem
Sbeitla
Thenae
Belalis Minor
Hippo Regius
Bulla Regia
Madauros
Thibilis
Maktar
Cillium
Tebessa
Ad Maiores
Tiddis
Djemila
Constantine
Zana
Lambaesis
Timgad
Gemellae
Khamissa
Ammaedara
Althiburos
Tigzirt
Tipasa
Cherchell
Portus Magnus
Gigthis
Tripoli
Sabratha
Lepcis Magna
Gsar Doga
Mesueggi, Wadi
Ghirza
Bu Ngem
Ptolemais
Hadrianople

0   150   300   450   600   750   900 km.

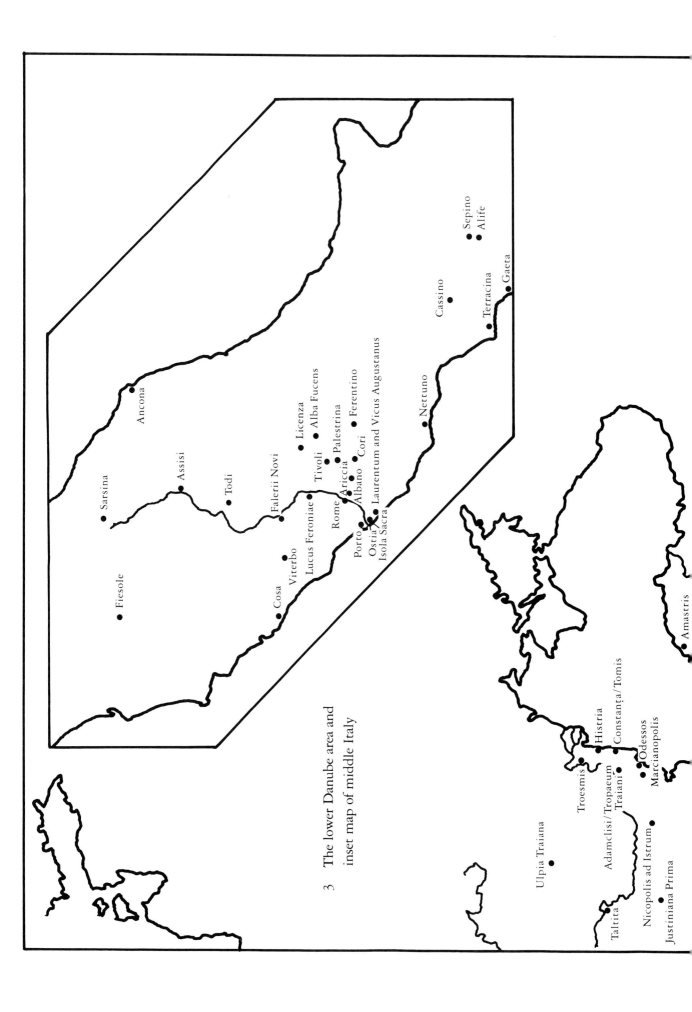

3 The lower Danube area and
   inset map of middle Italy

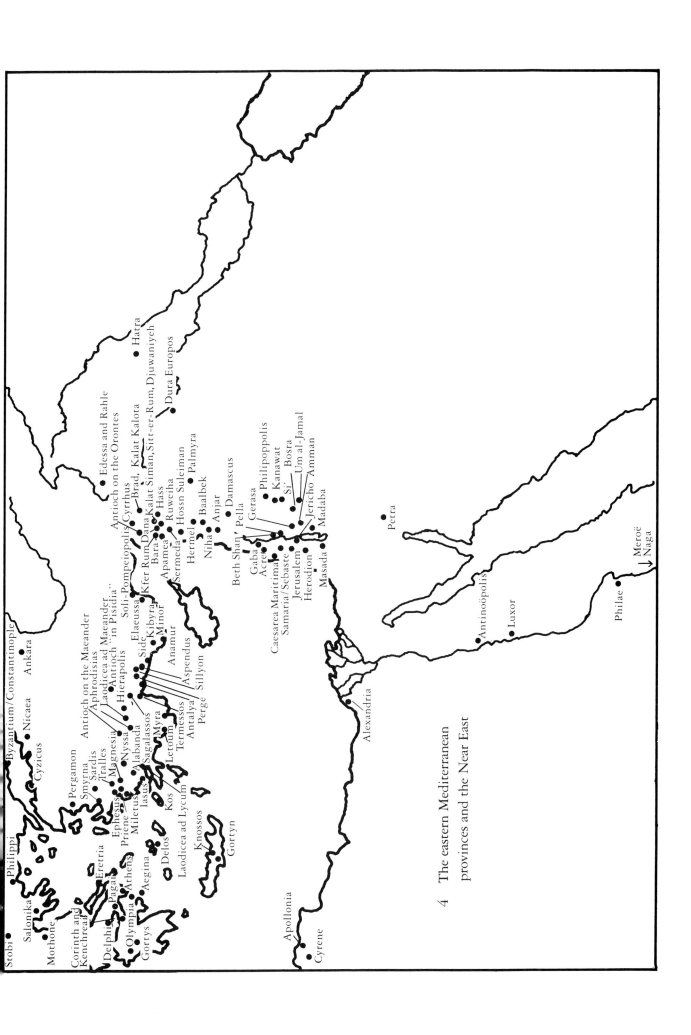

Stobi

Salonika

Mothone

Corinth and
Kenchreai

Delphi

Pagai

Olympia

Gortys

Apollonia

Cyrene

Philippi

Eretria

Athens

Aegina

Delos

Laodicea ad Lycum

Knossos

Gortyn

Byzantium/Constantinople

Nicaea   Ankara

Cyzicus

Pergamon

Smyrna

Sardis

Tralles

Magnesia

Antioch on the Maeander

Aphrodisias

Laodicea ad Maeander

Antioch "in Pisidia"

Hierapolis

Soli-Pompetopolis/Cyrrhus

Ephesus

Priene

Miletus

Iasus

Sagalassos

Kos

Letoüm

Myra

Termessos

Antalya

Perge

Sillyon

Aspendus

Anamur

Nyssa

Abanda

Kibyra

Elaeussa

Side

Minor

Pergamon

Antioch on the Orontes

Edessa and Rahle

Kfer Rum

Brad, Kalat Kalota

Dana Kalat Siman, Sitt-er-Rum, Djuwaniyeh

Hatra

Dura Europos

Bara

Hass

Ruweiha

Sermeda

Apamea

Hossn Suleiman

Hermel

Niha

Baalbek

Palmyra

Anjar

Damascus

Beth Shan, Pella

Gerasa

Philippoppolis

Kanawat

Si'   Bosra

Um al-Jamal

Gaba

Acre

Jericho Amman

Caesarea Maritima

Samaria/Sebaste

Jerusalem

Herodion

Madaba

Masada

Petra

Alexandria

Antinoöpolis

Luxor

Philae

Meroë

Naga

4   The eastern Mediterranean
     provinces and the Near East

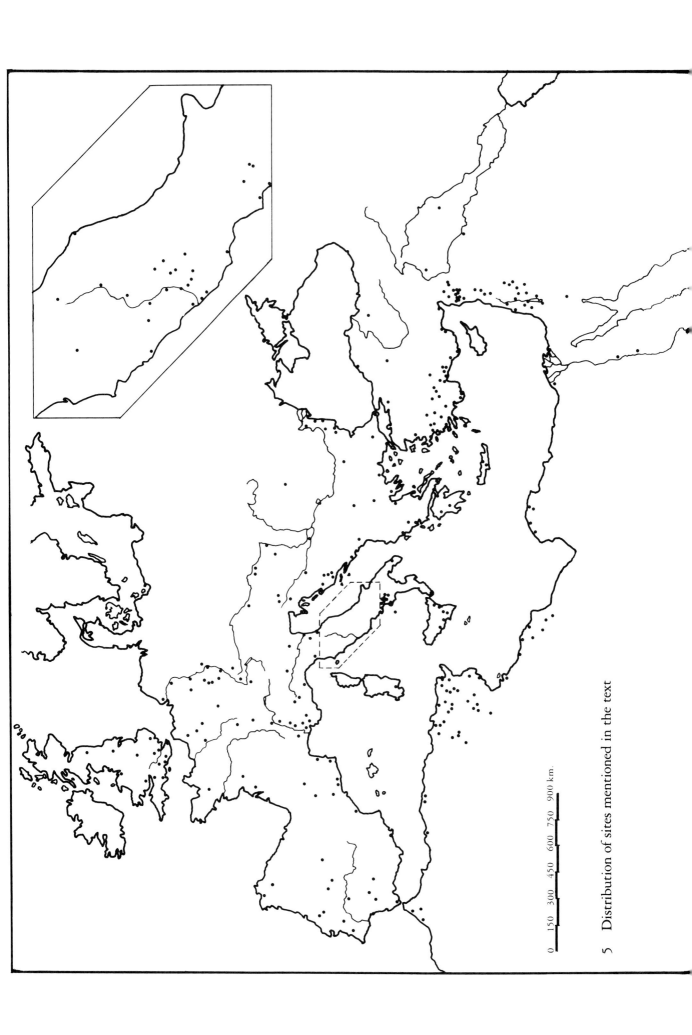

5 Distribution of sites mentioned in the text

0   150 300 450 600 750 900 km.

II

URBAN ARMATURES

ARMATURES CONSIST OF main streets, squares, and essential public buildings linked together across cities and towns from gate to gate, with junctions and entranceways prominently articulated. They are the setting for the familiar Roman civic building typology, the framework for the unmistakable imagery of imperial urbanism. As the central arenas of public activity, they are integrated functional and symbolic wholes. Their dominant characteristic on the ground is directional and spatial unity, an indivisibility underwritten by fluid, unimpeded connections. Though they differ widely from place to place in size and plan and in degree of formal complexity, they are all conceptually and schematically analogous, and are made up of elements and motifs from the same architectural repertory.

CHARACTERISTICS

The armature of Djemila, a town in western Numidia, is typical. Founded at the very end of the first century, in mountainous country, Djemila began as a small settlement of 1, 2 about seven hectares (seventeen acres). The town walls, of polygonal plan, enclosed high ground on a defensible spur sloping downward to the north. Most streets meet at right angles, but as they are short, they do not form an overall grid. As a result the civic and residential blocks that have been uncovered are of different sizes, producing an impressionistic, relaxed orthogonality common in Roman planning. The central street runs northwest–southeast more or less along the crown of the spur from one main gate to another; it takes eight or ten minutes to traverse it at a leisurely pace. A change of direction, slight but decisive, takes place somewhat south of its midpoint, and this 10° 3 angle and the angles of the perimeter wall account for the non-rectilinear shapes of several city blocks. A spacious forum was built along the east side of the main street, and soon a basilica, a curia, temples, a public fountain, a market, and a bath building were added beside or near the forum, forming a contiguous civic center occupying nearly a tenth of the total area of the town.

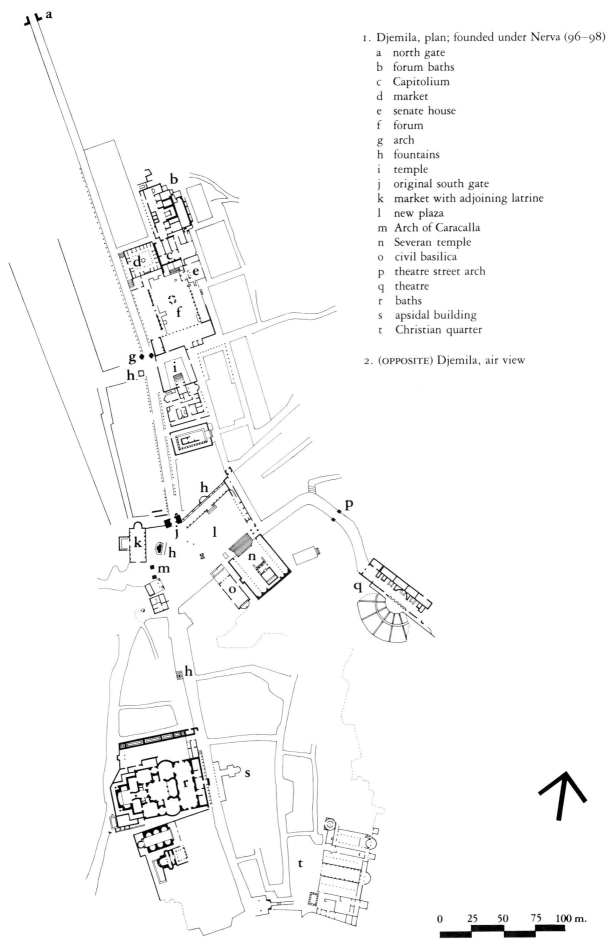

1. Djemila, plan; founded under Nerva (96–98)
   a north gate
   b forum baths
   c Capitolium
   d market
   e senate house
   f forum
   g arch
   h fountains
   i temple
   j original south gate
   k market with adjoining latrine
   l new plaza
   m Arch of Caracalla
   n Severan temple
   o civil basilica
   p theatre street arch
   q theatre
   r baths
   s apsidal building
   t Christian quarter

2. (OPPOSITE) Djemila, air view

3. Djemila, principal street, looking south

Djemila prospered and grew. During the second century the southeast wall was partly dismantled and the land beyond, where the spur widens into a broad hill, was largely built over, chiefly with new houses. To the southeast a theatre, seating perhaps three thousand, was built, its cavea fitted against the steep northeast slope of the hill. Toward the end of the century a monumental arch was erected astride a wide, curving street leading down to the theatre. In due time the original main street was extended up the hill to the south well beyond the original south gate, almost doubling its length. Beside it, close to the summit of the hill, a grand, sophisticated bath building, 55 by 70 m. overall, was built in the 180s. Just outside the original south gate, between the old and new quarters, an extensive plaza in the form of a loose parallelogram about 45 by 80 m.

was laid out, perhaps shortly after 200, on the site of an extramural marketplace. Embellished with colonnades on its northwest and northeast sides, with fountains, and, on its open southwest side, with a triumphal arch, this ample, paved space slopes downward from west to east. Adjacent to its lowest or southeast corner, where a pair of arches opens onto the street passing down to the theatre, a temple to the Severan family was erected in 229. This rises from a lofty artificial terrace occupying about the same area as the forum plaza of the original settlement. Beyond the temple to the south the hill was gradually built over; urban construction ended in the fifth century with the addition of a sizable Christian complex—basilicas, a baptistery, a bishop's palace, and several auxiliary buildings. The Roman town is last mentioned in contemporary records as having been represented at a church synod in Constantinople in the mid-sixth century.

As originally planned, Djemila conformed to Roman tradition in having a main street traversing the entire town, gate to gate, and leading undeviatingly to the forum. As the town expanded this street was connected by way of the new south plaza to the other principal streets, a normal enough development. The result, a flowing chain of thoroughfares linking the principal buildings and squares, made up the skeleton of an 4 armature of avenues and public spaces and their adjoining public buildings. There are no barriers to the flow of pedestrian or wheeled traffic and no abrupt changes of direction. But because other telling features of urban design are present, the armature is more subtle and effective as the definitive frame of the town's formal essence than the uncomplicated nature of its general layout suggests. For example, junctions are thoughtfully articulated. In addition to the six arches already mentioned (including those of the original north and south gates), there are a number of others; all are strategically located where changes of direction are required or offered, bringing them to life in three dimensions while offering no bar to one's path.

An instructive example is the transverse arch set precisely at the 10° angle in the main street. It divides the street into two parts, each of apprehensible scale, and composes

4. Djemila, sketch plan (see legend for ill. 1)

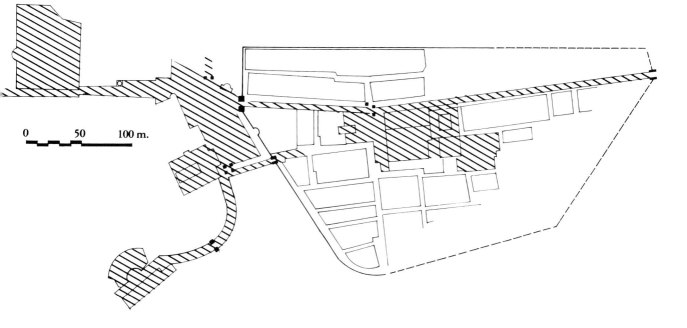

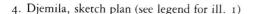

0   50   100 m.

5. Djemila, principal street, looking north

slightly off-center vistas suggesting rather than revealing the projection of the town's frame. It quickens the sense of directional shift, and as its shape is in harmony with the city gates that once stood at either end of the street, it is an effective broker of the traverse between them. On the west side of the street, just south of the arch, is a public
5   fountain; across the way, an arched opening to a temple precinct. This second arch, which because of the slope of the street stands on higher ground than the transverse one, was designed so as to bring the springing lines of both to almost the same height. Thus when approaching the ensemble from the south the two openings are in comfortable accord, similar portals opening off a major communal space, and the resulting suggestion of equality of choice is nicely calculated.

Other means served to mark and emphasize nodal points. Changes in level received close attention; stairs were usually carefully thought out by Roman architects and builders. There is an example of this outside the north corner of the central plaza, where
6   the stair access from the street below both to the elevated plaza and to its still higher portico is composed effectively. The entrance is arcaded soberly but not meanly. The stairs are readily visible through the arches; the purpose of the complex and its changes in direction and level are immediately comprehensible. The plaza proper is good
7   evidence for the play of small-scale elements against large that can be seen throughout
8   the town: the large temple atop its platform is set off against both its own flanking lower
9   colonnades and the columns of the nymphaeum portico directly opposite. The south-easterly slope of the paving, emphasized by both the high temple terrace and the raised

6. Djemila, east wall and arches of the new Severan plaza, looking south

7. Djemila, the Severan temple; ca. 200

8. Djemila, side colonnade of the Severan temple terrace

9. Djemila, colonnade opposite the Severan temple

10. Djemila, the new Severan plaza, looking east; late second or early third century

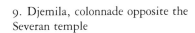

porticos, transports an invisible armature axis diagonally down and across the plaza to the pair of arches marking the beginning of the theatre street, where the space drains away and is funneled down the eastern slope.   10

There are other working parts of Djemila's armature. Public fountains are one example. The presence at strategic points of open basins of water (supplied, wherever possible, more or less continuously from open pipes) was a universal feature of Roman towns. Djemila's fountains range in form from unadorned stone tubs to a slim conoidal   11 monument beside the southern extension of the main street, whose piping carried water to its summit. The sound of running water and the attraction of accessible, brimming basins and pools, their light-struck surfaces usually in motion, were skillfully exploited by Roman city-makers. Along an urban armature water was rarely more than a few blocks away and frequently considerably closer; it could confidently be expected at principal crossways and plazas.

By contrast, Djemila's two known monumental, freestanding arches might seem useless. Necessary trappings of empire, they were effectively located. The eastern arch announced the proximity of the theatre and joined with it in a mutual declaration of the maturity and sophistication the inhabitants claimed for their town. The other, an honorific monument from the time of Caracalla, erected in 216, served two purposes.   12

11. (BELOW) Djemila, conoidal fountain

12. (RIGHT) Djemila, Arch of Caracalla; 216

First, it marked the location of the entrance to the plaza on its high, southeast side unmistakably. In addition, it focused on the equally elevated forecourt of the Severan temple standing near the opposite end of the square, affirming across the open space an ideological link between the two. Perhaps the plaza and its major buildings were designed as an ensemble.[3]

Djemila records the essential parts and schematic principle of the Roman armature: thoroughfares, plazas (for our purposes a forum or an agora is a variety of plaza), and municipal buildings, all joined together in a continuous, flowing system, with no single component isolated from the whole, and with the chief junctions, entrances, and changes in direction prominently and meaningfully articulated. Close to a hundred examples of armatures survive sufficiently complete to be read easily on the ground, and scores of others can be inferred from their outlines.

Literary images of the Roman city often depend upon references to major streets and public buildings, a topos that verges on describing armatures. Some examples:

> The whole civilized world lays down the arms which were once its ancient burden and has turned to adornment . . . this one contention holds them all, how each city may appear most beautiful and attractive. All localities are full of gymnasia, fountains, monumental approaches, temples, workshops, schools.
>
> [Aelius Aristides][4]

> For emperors such as ourselves, whose active concern is to found new cities, [and] to give back their ancient glory to those established long ago . . . this request [from the town of Orcistus in Galatia] is most welcome . . . the settlement has, for a long time, flourished with all the splendor of a town: it boasts magistrates . . . and civic dignitaries. . . . It is well placed at the joining of four highways, each provided with an official staging-post. . . . And water is abundant there. There are baths, public and private, and the town is decorated with statues of emperors past.
>
> [Constantine the Great][5]

> At Milan everything is admirable—abundant wealth, innumerable stately mansions, and men of quality who are eloquent and cheerfully disposed. And there is the setting of the place, enlarged by an additional wall; a circus, which the people love; and the wedge-shaped, walled-in mass of the theatre. There are temples, imperial seats, a rich mint, and the Herculian Baths, large like a city quarter. The colonnades are all adorned with statues, and the wall surrounding the city is like an immense earthern rampart. All these stand tall—rivals, as it were, in the grand scale of their construction—and the nearness of Rome diminishes them not at all.
>
> [Ausonius][6]

These passages—others could be cited—evoke images of proper cities by stressing important civic structures, including city walls.[7] Streets with monumental features such as colonnades or other grand fittings are sometimes mentioned, but fora and plazas turn up only infrequently and in less relevant contexts.

The pictorial evidence parallels the archaeological material closely. In almost every representation, selected primary elements are compacted effectively to produce a lively sense of urban density. Walls and city gates are emphasized, usually at exaggerated scales, whether the medium is sculpture, painting, coinage, or mosaic.[8] The master of _13_ the Column of Trajan, for example, wishing to bring out efficiently the civilized, Roman nature of a town, represents its chief buildings behind a gated wall, pressing them close to each other and concentrating on their most prominent and therefore most recognizable features.[9] The result, though not abstract, approaches the allusive power and mnemonic grip of an ideogram. Thoroughfares are usually missing because streets are difficult to represent in sculpture without obscuring their identity, though oversized _45_ city gates, doing double duty, can assure their presence, as do the implied divisions between rows of buildings.[10] Roman sculpture includes a large number of such views— immediately comprehensible impressions of the unmistakable core silhouette of the Roman town created by crowding together images of the lofty bulk of familiar municipal building types behind their indispensable encircling walls.

13. Gerasa, church of S. John the Baptist, detail of a floor mosaic showing the city of Alexandria; about 530

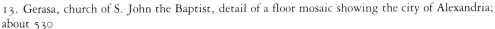

14. Rome, Tomb of the Aurelii, wall painting; first half of the third century

In painting and mosaic the same principles apply, with the same results. Aerial
views, set out in rough perspective, are not uncommon. In painting as in sculpture, the
Roman use of simultaneity of viewpoints is frequently present—walls seen head-on at
their own level, for example, with parts of the city behind them seen at an angle from
above. Streets appear more frequently than in sculpture, and often come through
clearly. When that happens the principle of simplification, carried through by selecting
essential elements and compacting them together, produces views of armatures. Many
late antique and early medieval manuscript vignettes of cities and towns continued this
tradition, albeit in increasingly stylized and abstracted forms, as in the Notitia Dignitatum or the technical literature of surveying and land allotment.[11] At their simplest,
these are little more than sketches of walls and gates with a few emphatic lines marking
direct traverses between them. Yet they clearly belong to a tradition of representing
urban centers by focusing on their most prominent public elements. So it can be said
that writers, and artists in particular, often envisaged the architectural essence of
Roman urbanism as inhering in the primary architectural features of the armature.
Given the familiar realities of the cities and towns themselves, readers and viewers
would take the interconnections among these features and the implied fluidity of
movement for granted.

At one level this evidence is unremarkable, since cities were and are often represented by widely reproduced architectural symbols. But in the present context it takes on considerable importance. First, there is broad general agreement among the various categories of material as to the kind of thing emphasized and, in the pictorial evidence, the manner of emphasizing it. Second, each example is without exception a composite, a selective assembly of various structures. We are looking at evidence that is closely related to the realities of Roman urban architecture, in contrast to unitary symbolic representations of cities such as the crowned personifications, the seated city deities of the Tabula Peutingeriana. [12] Third, each pictorial example is different from the others. No routine formulas appear. This is not to say that there are no conventions, for there are—the kinds of pictorial shorthand that appear throughout much of ancient art. Nor is it to claim that each example was the result of close observation of an individual city; thus far there are few identifiable views such as that of Ancona on Trajan's Column. [13] But no two examples are alike even on the imperial columns; true repetition appears only in early medieval times.

Across the whole range of the relevant pictorial evidence building types are juxtaposed variously, scales differ, skylines vary, and the number of buildings shown shifts greatly; these views are based with a few exceptions on reality of a general, not a specific, kind. Variety flourished, but the results never pass the bounds of the recognizable because the shapes and forms always portray the familiar town core. The evidence makes it clear that the armature is not a modern conceit, an analytical device conceived after the fact and then imposed on the data. The carvings and paintings all sprang from the same conceptual principles; paler versions appear now and again in the texts. And since these representations and descriptions follow the archaeological testimony closely, it seems certain that what today can be called an armature was recognized far and wide in Roman times as the indispensable, and therefore representative, nucleus of urban experience.

SIGNIFICANCE

The path or road leading inward from the periphery of a primitive town to an open space used as a market and meeting place was the ultimate source of the armature. City planning hardly entered into the matter at all, though the ancient market street tradition was given rational form both in Hellenistic ("Hippodamian") planning and in the overall rectilinear formula adopted for Rome's colonial foundations. The use of this formula, which joined fora and main streets orthogonally and embedded them in extended grids, dwindled rapidly following the death of Augustus and all but ceased after the end of the first century. Thus the only effect of Hellenistic and Roman rectilinear planning on the empire-wide evolution of finished armatures was that orthogonal axes were sometimes already in place, ready to carry the often modest examples that would appear in the planned towns of the west as well as the more sophisticated versions in Hellenistic lands. But of the factors making up an armature, this largely unwitting provision of pre-existing axes is the only one derived from city planning, and even it is limited to sites with overall orthogonal patterns. Armatures were not created consciously and all at once within the controlling requirements of comprehensive city plans. Nor were they conceived of from their beginnings as entities in themselves. Instead, they evolved over time through gradual elaboration and, quite often, extension. They were finished only when and because no more changes or additions were made to them. The cumulative, composite results have patterns and shapes so varied that no evidence of a universal, generative plan type can be found in them. Studying city plans is not the same as studying armatures.

Although the market street tradition underlies all armatures, its metamorphosis into what can be seen, for example, at Djemila required the passage of considerable time and the development of substantial interaction across the complex architectural geography of classical lands. Growth to maturity took place as distinctive features of regional architectural modes increasingly lost ground to the pressures of Roman dominion or were absorbed into Roman practice. Eastern and western ideas combined to form new morphologies and to create the high recognition factor echoed by the pictorial evidence. Though the process was complicated and only the outline of part of it can be discerned, there can be no doubt that it took place. The end result, the urban cores of the second and third centuries, was neither Greek nor narrowly Roman, but thoroughly imperial, in a sense an architectural counterpart to the Antonine Constitution, or of the productive marriage of themes and forms of divergent origins seen in sculpture after early imperial times.

In order to use the concept of the armature effectively, some brief historical background is needed. Walls and gates fixed the extremities of embryonic armatures in space, and together with public squares and an avenue or two formed their frames. A high road, coming from another town, sometimes by way of a difficult mountain or desert route, joined the next town at a major gateway, the threshold of urban, civilized life unequivocally marking the end of a stage of wayfaring. Inside the wall, the road was transformed into a thoroughfare passing through densely built-up ground to the forum or agora. Irrespective of its topographical position on a measured plan, this plaza was the center of the town, not only because of its functions and symbolic prominence, but also because of its direct, unimpeded connections with the main gates and the larger world beyond.

In one sense merely convenient perforations in the walls, gates also fastened the lines of the main streets in position, as staples anchor lines of wire. Gates helped give the armature a clear and separate identity by distinguishing it from the surrounding urban fabric: a street with its own gate, especially a principal gate, is a ranking one. Of course the gates also marked profoundly the transition from one side of the wall to the other. By contrast with the wall's blank impenetrability, they intimated to arriving travelers the shape of the expected journey beyond, assuring them that the heart of the town would quickly and easily be found. Walls and gates provided not only security and an appearance of strength, but a fitting dignity as well, for they were the proper, expected dress of classical towns, which can be defined schematically as walled enclosures pierced by one or more trunk roads leading directly to the main square.

15. Timgad, approaching the town on the Lambaesis road, looking southeast

Whatever their degree of complexity, armatures in imperial times were all descended from this archetypal pattern. Civic pride, and the building rivalry it engendered, furthered elaboration of the kind seen at Djemila, a tendency aided by the prosperity that helped give magnates and municipal councils the wherewithal to sponsor works they naturally erected at important, busy locations. The architecture of these additions often reflected the prestige of monumental buildings in Rome and the half-dozen largest provincial cities, a centrifugal process strengthened through the widespread contribution by the central government of major structures to the cities and towns, for these buildings too reflected metropolitan fashions.

But no two armatures are alike; they are as different as the cities and towns (the monotonous regularity sometimes attributed to Roman towns is a myth with respect to the empire, for though some Republican and Augustan colonies had been planned according to a generalized formula, subsequent expansion and the almost inevitable addition of the familiar but varied imperial amenities relaxed the formula's rigidity.[14]) Elaborate versions were not limited to the grander municipalities by any means. And if many towns lacked the glitter of a Palmyra or a Lepcis Magna, the armature's basic   16, 17

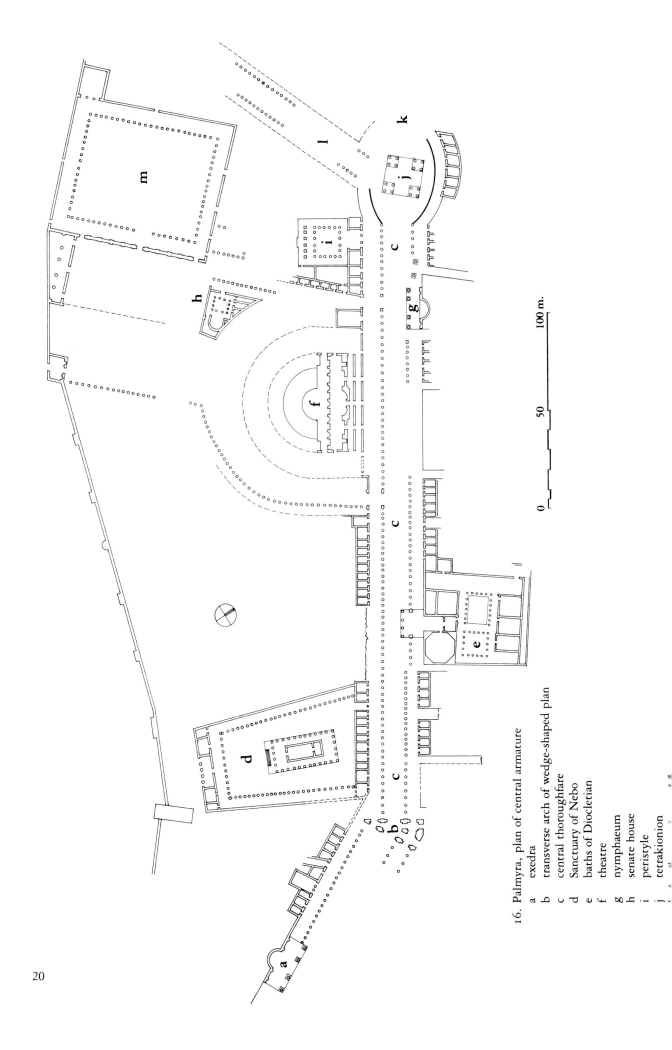

16. Palmyra, plan of central armature
a   exedra
b   transverse arch of wedge-shaped plan
c   central thoroughfare
d   Sanctuary of Nebo
e   baths of Diocletian
f   theatre
g   nymphaeum
h   senate house
i   peristyle
j   tetrakionion

20

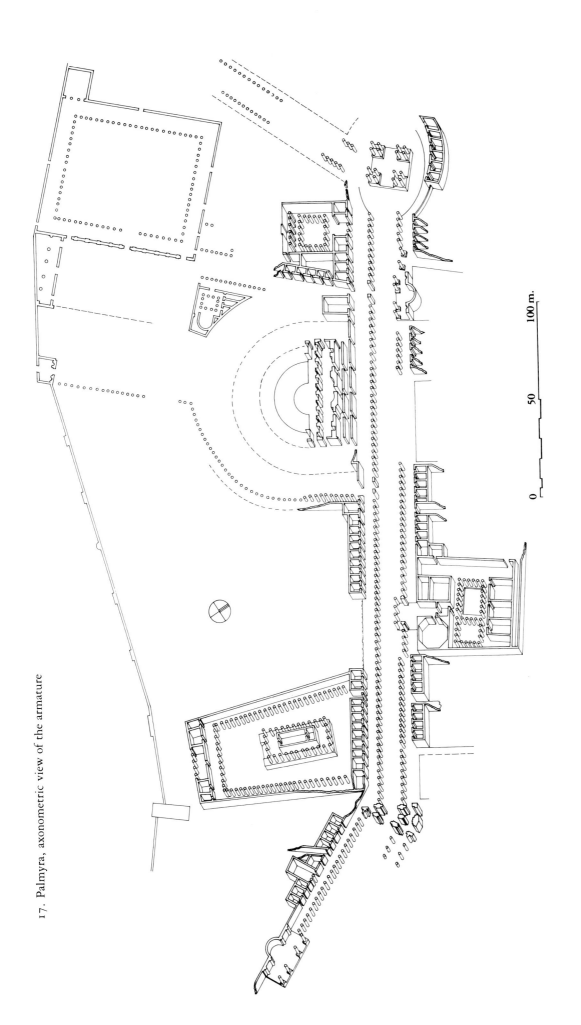

17. Palmyra, axonometric view of the armature

21

features were present, usually with a touch or two of sophistication—diluted versions of fashionable appointments found in grander places. Studying armatures complements traditional studies of Roman architecture, which usually do not reveal much about the effects on design and planning of enchaining public structures across a town, or about formal and functional relationships among them. Because of their practical basis and symbolic importance, armatures constitute a significant methodological tool: they encompass more facets of architectural design and meaning than a single building, building type, or regional mode. Analyzing them offers several promising opportunities.

Sequence. Visualizing and comprehending an armature ideally requires inspection building by building—column by column if possible. Attempting this suggests the seriality of experiences, the sequences of visual and kinetic effects, in a fashion approximating that known in Roman times. True scale is suggested both with respect to people and to differences among various structures, and one's sense of the three-dimensionality of a town is improved. Continuities are effectively evoked. Even if it is pursued only on paper, this procedure may improve our understanding of Roman architectural forms.

Context. Interconnections among public structures become clearer. Since passing along a street, or from a street into a square or building, is the essence of town activity, understanding architectural contexts is essential. Extended, serial juxtapositions make up armatures, which in turn bind towns together, helping to make them whole. The design and detail of streets and squares, of fountains, exedras, and triumphal arches, become as important as those of basilicas or temples or bath buildings, because almost the whole public typology of Roman architecture is inextricably connected in fully developed armatures.

Single buildings. The juxtaposition of buildings is emphasized as much as the individual buildings themselves. Given the number of monuments that survive bereft of their original surroundings—especially in Rome, the first subject of scholars—the strength of single-building studies is understandable, and we are fortunate in having the results of many detailed investigations. They are indispensable; more are needed. This tradition, however, should not discourage synoptic views, especially as some hold that Roman architects designed major buildings independently of their settings, with the implication that context counted for little.[15] There are pitfalls in studying buildings independently of their surroundings when those are known or can be surmised. Buildings carry on effective dialogues with their neighbors simply by being there; examining armatures reveals some of the complexities inhering in such relationships.

Typology. The study of building typology has drawbacks. Because it is based on functions, it cannot readily accommodate the problem of the stylistic variety that often exists within one type. And because it tends to rely heavily on plan studies, the volumetric realities of the buildings proper sometimes all but vanish from view; in a discipline frequently dependent upon a course or two of stones outlining a building's plan, this is understandable. Along the armature, most public building types were prominently displayed, so that as its measure was taken, no one type was gathered into an artifically isolated group. Stylistic connections among types can often be refined, and now and then functional differences are revealed as less prominent than had been thought.

Regions. Regionalism does not affect the conceptual principles of the armature. Highly visible as a few regional modes may be, from an empire-wide point of view they are subsumed under an architectural interdependence that is a central theme of this book. The surprising thing is not so much that clear-cut regional preferences existed, but that imperial architecture was sufficiently consistent stylistically to project every-where an urban image recognizably Roman.

City planning. City planning came first and plenary armatures later. Planning evolved from theory and the application of technical knowledge, but armatures were the result of a comparatively disorderly accumulation of components, a process energized by the forces of the imperial synthesis. The two are not much related; the common character of armatures was not derived from a ubiquitous two-dimensional system. Plans of finished armatures, recorded and transcribed today, are not based on an ideal configuration, a   18, 19, 20

18. Antioch on the Orontes, sketch plan
- a palace area
- b circus
- c quadrifons or tetrakionion
- d Campus Martius
- e nymphaeum
- f street of Herod and Tiberius
- g wall of Seleucus I
- h east gate
- i Daphne or Golden Gate
- j amphitheatre
- k theatre
- l location of Valens' Forum

0   500   1000 m.

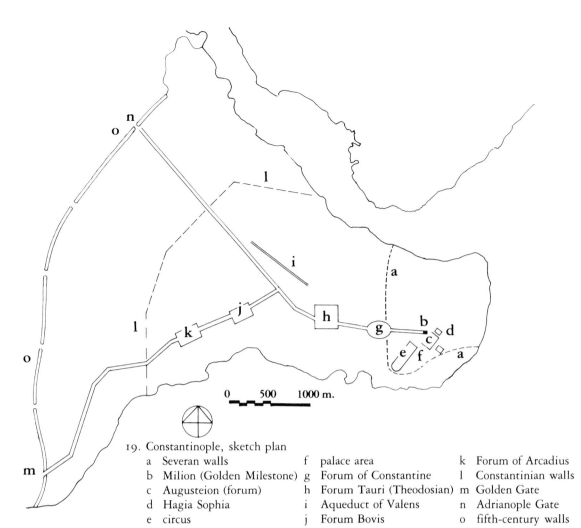

19. Constantinople, sketch plan

a	Severan walls	f	palace area
b	Milion (Golden Milestone)	g	Forum of Constantine
c	Augusteion (forum)	h	Forum Tauri (Theodosian)
d	Hagia Sophia	i	Aqueduct of Valens
e	circus	j	Forum Bovis
k	Forum of Arcadius		
l	Constantinian walls		
m	Golden Gate		
n	Adrianople Gate		
o	fifth-century walls		

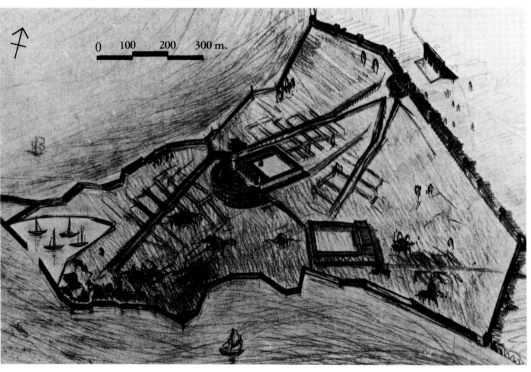

20. Side, sketch plan

conscious model upon which distances and locations, fixed by surveying and arithmetic, were based. So although such a plan is part of a city plan, it is rarely the result of city planning consciously practiced. It is more a flowchart of an architectural course, an urban arterial diagram. Though an armature plan represents finite dimensions, it cannot convey substantial reality; like all plans it is a miniature, if seductive, abstraction. City planning is a comparative study, but armature analysis is the opposite, for it starts with essential comparisons already made—the presence of common qualities and features—and proceeds to the investigation of their several levels of relationships.

Contrasts between city plans and armatures are revealing. Planning places things, whereas armatures, with their architecture of connection and passage, identify them and tell where they are. Planning is applied all at once; armatures are the products of the passage of time, of a process energized not by the work of a corps of professionals but by the imperial synthesis. The contrast throws the heavy concentration of planning studies on orthogonal patterns of Republican and Augustan times into sharp relief and emphasizes the fairly rapid disintegration of the orderly principles of early times. True orthogonal planning dwindled as erratic street patterns appeared ever more frequently. New or rebuilt quarters were often deliberately laid out with more or less parallel streets that met their cross streets at odd angles, and beside long-established towns of orthogonal plan, new districts sprang up willy-nilly, entirely unplanned. The taste for precise reticulation almost disappeared in the high imperial age, and the elaborated armature, flexible and adaptable and with no set plan, flourished. Even austere early foundations, where military and land-allotment considerations had often come first, were freed somewhat from the grip of the surveyors' inelastic decrees.

To examine the familiar plan of Timgad in light of the town's architectural history is 21 instructive. Although the plan is now enshrined as a textbook example of Roman 22 theory, when it was laid out in the year 100 it was almost an anachronism. Its twelve and 23 one-half hectares (about thirty acres, slightly larger than the Baths of Caracalla overall) soon proved inadequate, and the town expanded rapidly, largely patternlessly, beyond its original four-square walls. Architectural evidence soon appeared there of the empire-wide urge to urban competition and improvement that carried all before it. This construction—the walls were largely demolished and replaced by streets—included large baths, markets, and an enormous Capitolium, the kinds of buildings a self-respecting town had to have. In this way Timgad, the gridded town par excellence, was girdled with some of the principal elements of an armature. These elements could not easily be fitted into the original plan to augment the spare orthogonal armature already established. That original plan, so alluring to the eye, does not tell this story. Nor does it convey a proper impression of the terrain, which is hardly as featureless as is sometimes implied. Several streets slope considerably, and most of the southeast quarter is on 24 a hill, against which the theatre is set. Small, two-dimensional diagrams, lacking contour lines, do not indicate these differences, which on the ground ameliorate somewhat the monotony the founders' plan suggests.

On the western side of the town a revealing pattern of streets and buildings mate-

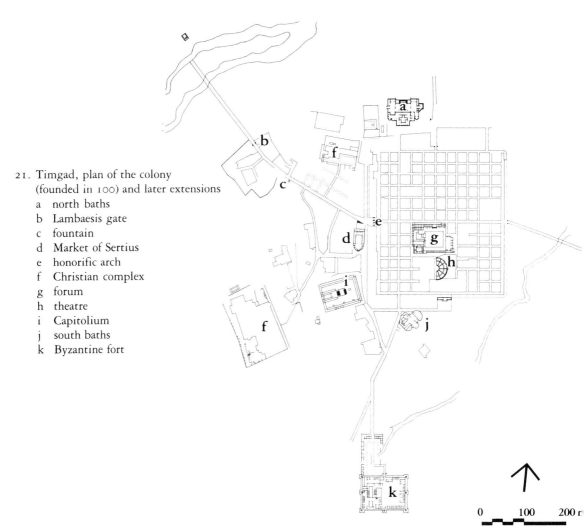

21. Timgad, plan of the colony
    (founded in 100) and later extensions
    a   north baths
    b   Lambaesis gate
    c   fountain
    d   Market of Sertius
    e   honorific arch
    f   Christian complex
    g   forum
    h   theatre
    i   Capitolium
    j   south baths
    k   Byzantine fort

0   100   200 r

22. Timgad, looking west to the Capitolium

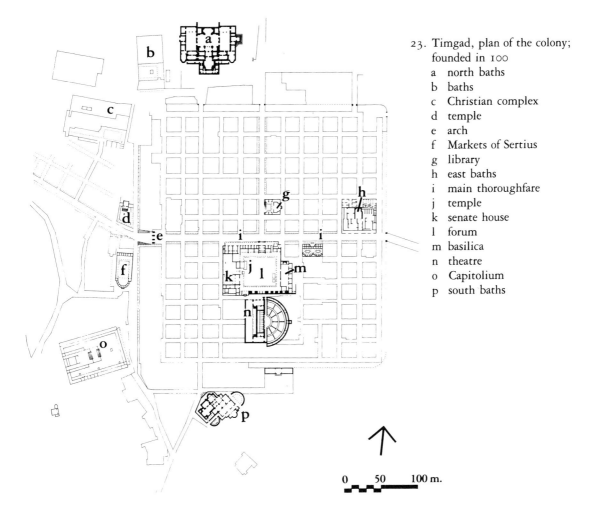

23. Timgad, plan of the colony;
founded in 100
a north baths
b baths
c Christian complex
d temple
e arch
f Markets of Sertius
g library
h east baths
i main thoroughfare
j temple
k senate house
l forum
m basilica
n theatre
o Capitolium
p south baths

0   50   100 m.

rialized. Just east of the site of the original west gate a three-bayed honorific arch was
built, and the space between it and the original town perimeter was cleared to make a   25
large, nearly rectangular plaza. From there a broad avenue leads northwest to an
elaborate gate 300 m. distant that marks the beginning of the high road to Lambaesis.
About two-thirds of the way between the plaza and this new gate a public fountain
stands beside the avenue. Immediately beyond the plaza, on the right-hand side of the
avenue, a temple stood in a precinct; facing it, across the way, was a large market
building behind its own spacious, accessible plaza. Both buildings are flanked on the   26
east by the north–south street that replaced the original line of the wall. This street
intersects the Lambaesis avenue at the edges of both plazas to form the major junction,
the nodal point, of an extramural armature bounded by the triumphal arch and the
Lambaesis gate. The Capitolium is just west of the wall-street. An inn was built nearby.   27
Immediately north of the avenue the planning was partly orthogonal; to the south, as
elsewhere, it was all askew. To say that Timgad is a late example of Roman orthogonal
planning is correct only with respect to the original foundation. To fail to add that as the
town grew the grid concept was quickly abandoned for other, more disorderly configurations suspends an unfinished venture artificially in time.

24. Timgad, air view, looking east

25. Timgad, air view, looking southeast

We should not concentrate on Timgad's orthogonality at the expense of the equally important information the site, as effectively as any, so plainly conveys: plans alone did not give imperial towns their character, and armatures would not be denied. What might be called armature-plan studies are needed, analyses combining the two subjects that would include the dimension of time and a consideration of such essentials as the nature of typological distribution and the architecture of connection and passage. We need a better understanding of the architectural composition of the fully formed Roman town—of what was seen and how it was used. And we need to reflect on the manner of its perception in the mind's eye, and why its buildings almost never seem to be out of place stylistically. With respect to city planning, the evidence suggests that non-orthogonal patterns of the kind composed of straight streets intersecting at various angles were as common and important as orthogonal ones; surely not all of them can have derived from the orientation of pre-existing routes and property lines. But whatever their plans, towns gained in cohesion and coherence through their armatures, which drew activity to themselves centripetally as they passed through different quarters and wards.

36, 57, 203

In framing and facilitating much of the business of town life, armatures were a success. Inscriptions and sculpture were displayed in them on all sides, the lion's share erected by local magnates; among them at least civic pride abounded. These often ostentatious and hortatory works, like armatures Roman to the core, were essential constituents of urban life and its badges of civilization. This art and architecture and formulary language certified where one was, not only in the immediate sense of place, of

26. Timgad, Markets of Sertius, model; early third century (apsidal roof form uncertain)

27. Timgad, Capitolium; ca. 160

perceived location, but also in the sense of affirming that one's town belonged to the interlocking mosaic of communities making up the Roman world. Though little can be known of how people felt about such things, the High Street and forum/agora with their monumental appendages surely were firmly fixed in everyone's awareness. The rest of the town was not unimportant, but it was not the center, not downtown in our sense, not the part by which the quality and station of the place would be judged.

Without the essentials of an armature, a town, whatever its rank or the ethnic origins of its inhabitants, was not complete. The armature was a physical counterpart of Roman rule, a mainstay of imperial urbanism and the bedrock of its architectural unity. Like the empire itself, an armature had many parts, each readily apprehensible on its own terms; when joined together, the parts formed a recognizable, functional whole. Throughout the Roman world the parts of armatures remained much the same, but their number and manner of assembly and the resulting patterns always varied. Since Rome offered a rich array of symbolic monuments local communities could imitate, it played an important role in armature-making. It has often been observed that Rome, the great plan-giver, was unplanned, a statement true of pre-imperial times. Early Rome first coalesced and then grew around a primitive armature that later generated much of its early imperial center. The prestige of the capital stimulated provincial authorities and builders to recall, in a general, reductive way, the most impressive and memorable parts of the city. Simulacra of famous structures appeared far and wide, their origins recognizable irrespective of intrusions of regional features.

It was largely by armatures that Roman cities and towns were organized physically and visually and were given a common identity clearly different from that of cities and towns of other historical periods. The practice persisted to the end, when Constantine and his successors vastly expanded Severan Byzantium in one of the most impressive exercises in city-making ever undertaken. Almost all of Roman Constantinople has disappeared, but what is known of it from texts, archaeological fragments, and a few precious vedute, is primarily its armature: fora and grand plazas with their linking boulevards and imposing civic buildings, all behind awesome, gated walls. The planners and architects made considerable use of Rome as a schematic model, as others had earlier for many less important sites. The pictorial imagery of that model outlasted antiquity, and the armatures themselves have had, all things considered, a high survival rate. If the modern plan of the remains of a Roman town does not reveal an armature, extensive digging, were it possible, almost certainly would.

Armatures were sophisticated responses to the universal urban need for an architecture of connection and passage—for unimpeded movement and casual assembly appropriately channeled and tellingly marked out, and for ready access to public places effectively identified. In summary, they

> pass unimpeded through their towns
> vary in configuration and numbers of parts within the frame of an empire-wide
> > conceptual order

are not derived overall from city planning, largely because they are emphatically three-dimensional

are composed of public structures only

are perceived as Roman chiefly because of an appropriate architecture

were formed gradually by addition and extension.

III

CONNECTIVE ARCHITECTURE

PROPERLY URBAN BUILDINGS must have streets and squares in order to function; without streets and squares, they are not urban at all; streets and squares alone, of the kind that can be traced today on the abandoned ground of failed subdivisions, are just lifeless patterns. Streets approach, bound, and fix the locations of buildings, linking them together and displaying them. Buildings give streets part of their character and identity as well as their reason for being. The surviving work of Roman architects and builders shows they were acutely aware of these familiar but complex relationships, of how streets and buildings define each other. Public squares were conceived as architecture. Main avenues, whether bordered or not by colonnades or porticos, were given architectural presence by civic buildings and the devices of the armature. Thoroughfares and plazas were functional spaces formally treated, as much architecture as the buildings they led to and adjoined.

The fundamentals of this architecture of connection were constant across the empire. Thoroughfares and plazas were at once linear or one-dimensional (plazas had entrance-exit axes), planar or two-dimensional (the pavement surfaces), and volumetric or three-dimensional (because of their vertical borders), each modality having its own function and effects. Every stretch of avenue, each public square, was joined with one or more additional components of an armature. Unless the city or forum gates were closed for curfew or defense, streets and plazas were never isolated from each other or from the main roads beyond the walls. All avenues and squares, save for any pavement camber, were right-angled in transverse section. Obvious as this is, it needs to be said. Clarity inheres in simple rectilinearity, and inside closely built-up places, artificial horizon lines with some intersecting vertical coordinates are essential to human orientation.[16] The architecture of connection provided continuous linear frames of reference reinforcing those of the edge-lines of the surrounding buildings. These fixed outlines implied stability, an effect strengthened by solid construction as well as by the repetition of architectural features, whether parts of streets and plazas or of buildings along the way.

All these uncovered connective spaces were bounded by the closely pressing facades of bordering buildings or covered walkways. And all of them, in a given town, were linked together as continuous conduits, narrow or wide. Framed by verticals meeting the pavement at right angles, they determined and channeled individuals' progress, revealing the urban core and its public buildings. What was seen and experienced of the architecture of connection in any given location did not differ substantially from that to come. There were few abrupt changes of formal ambience once the main gate had been passed. From time to time the directional forces of an avenue might be dissipated temporarily across a plaza, only to be captured and redirected on the opposite side by an archway or some other instrument of the architecture of passage signaling their resumption. Finally, these constructions were accommodated to pedestrian locomotion— rarely more than a kilometer every fifteen or twenty minutes—by manipulation of scale and proportion and by effective repetitions of elements of design.

THOROUGHFARES

The minimum requirement for a street to be a thoroughfare is that it connect a main gate with a cardinal plaza. It need not be wider than other streets, though it usually is, nor be adorned with arches and amenities, though by the end of the third century very few were not. The list that follows is a general guide to the formal categories of Roman streets. The first type rarely turns up as a thoroughfare, but the rest do so regularly.

1. The pavement meets the walls of its flanking buildings directly.   28
2. Sidewalks appear on one or both sides of the pavement.
3. One side of the street has covered porticos, each no more than a block long,   29 carried on columns or piers and interposed between the pavement and the buildings.
4. The same as type 3, but with porticos on both sides of the street.   30
5. The same as type 3, but with a continuous colonnade at least several blocks long.
6. The same as type 5, but with colonnades on both sides.   31

Mixtures are common. Thoroughfares not infrequently change from one type to another over their length; those that do not are sometimes the result of unifying reconstruction programs. Porticos of types 3 and 4 are often spaced intermittently, having been added independently of each other. The porticos and colonnades of types 3–6, with the walkways they shelter, are almost always elevated above pavement level, sometimes quite noticeably. Some carry superstructures, as at Alesia or Herculaneum, and once in a   46 while one is arcaded.   32, 43

Again, early Timgad is instructive. Almost all of the original town has been re-   21–25 covered, and its thoroughfares and their surroundings are largely intact (only an eroded, non-armature segment of the original town, in the southeast quarter, is missing; it can confidently be restored on paper). Since Timgad was a provincial showcase set down for the military toward the close of Rome's long history of founding colonies, it records

28. Ostia, Via della Fontana

29. Vaison-la-Romaine, streetside walkway, with house entrance, left, and shops beyond, looking north; later first century

30. Timgad, main east–west thoroughfare, looking west

31. Ephesus, the thoroughfare (the Arkadiané) leading west to the harbor; fourth century

32. Damascus, arcaded approach to the Sanctuary of Zeus, detail; begun early first century

traditional urban practices. So its orthogonality is an advantage: its armature features had to conform to the plan. As they were clearly singled out and identified under these conservative—not to say retardataire—circumstances, the working hypothesis set out in the preceding chapter for all the cities and towns is strengthened.

23   First the streets, then thoroughfares as a special class of them. A glance at the plan will show how roomy Timgad is, how much space there is between blocks, in com-

1, 33, 34 parison, say, to Djemila, Verulamium, or Trier. The circumscribing square of walls and the grid of streets are less constricting than the plan concept suggests. A third of the space within the walls is taken up by streets alone. If the forum is included, the figure approaches two-fifths. When public buildings are added it becomes two-thirds or thereabouts, the balance being given over to blocks of housing. Perhaps the generous provision for streets was meant to balance the lack of any public square except the forum or to improve air circulation during hot weather, but whatever the reason, the proportion of open space is exceptional. In comparison with other sites, using two-fifths of the

48   total town area for public spaces is very unusual; at Pompeii, for example, where about three-quarters of the area within the walls has been excavated, the comparable figure is less than half that much, 17.7 percent.[17]

Timgad's approximate 1:3 street-to-site area ratio is surely at the upper limit for such figures empire-wide, which probably average less than 1:5. It follows that the figures for Timgad's connective architecture (about 2:5) and for public works (about 2:3) are also exceptionally high. On the other hand, the total length of the streets, about 7 km. within the original 355 m. square of walls, is much closer to general practice; it works out to a little less than 2 km. per hectare. These figures, rough but serviceable for comparison, suggest that although Timgad's streets were not overly numerous for its size, they were comparatively wide for the time.

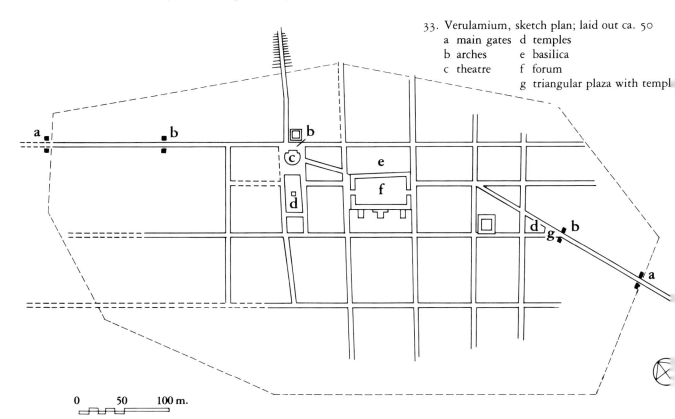

33. Verulamium, sketch plan; laid out ca. 50
a main gates   d temples
b arches   e basilica
c theatre   f forum
                g triangular plaza with templ

0   50   100 m.

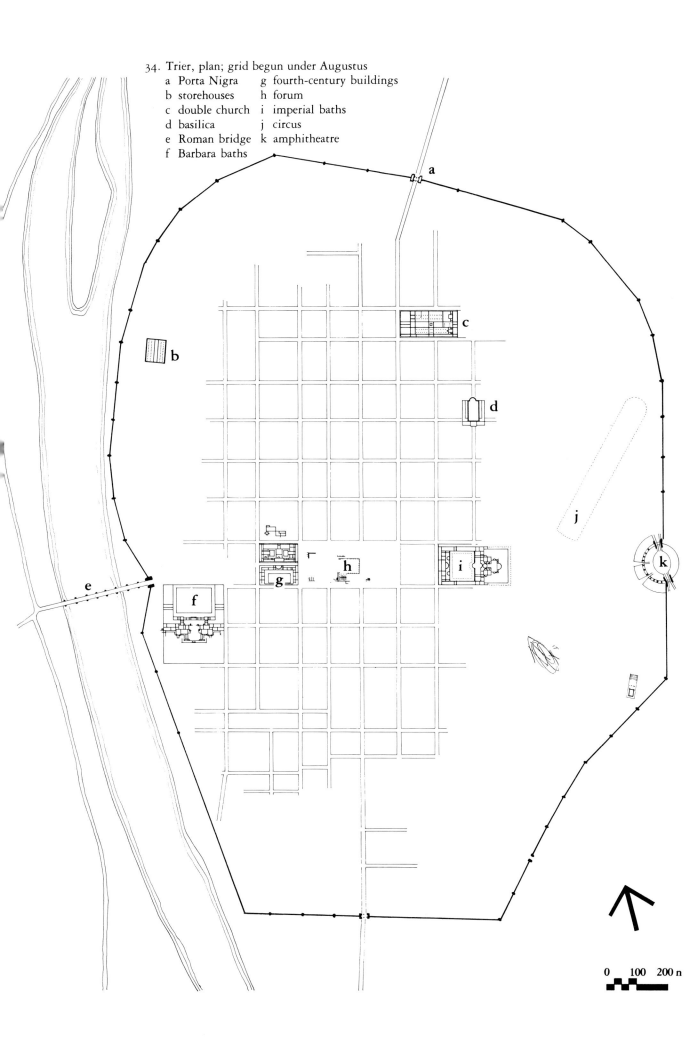

34. Trier, plan; grid begun under Augustus
a Porta Nigra g fourth-century buildings
b storehouses h forum
c double church i imperial baths
d basilica j circus
e Roman bridge k amphitheatre
f Barbara baths

0   100 200 n

All the streets save one are 5 or 6 m. wide. The avenue that runs through the center of the town between the east and west gates is somewhat wider (7 to 8 m.) and is lined with porticos on both sides (type 4). Each of these is 2-1/2 to 3 m. deep, giving the street a maximum overall width of about 14 m. or some 50 Roman feet, about half again as wide as the pavement of an ordinary two-lane city side street today. From its center point, at the middle of the north flank of the forum complex, another main street, half the length of the first, leads downward gradually to the north gate. Its pavement is about 6 m. wide, and it too was lined continuously with porticos. The main connection from the wide east–west thoroughfare to the south is displaced three blocks west of the grid's north–south axis because of the central position of the forum complex. This connecting street is also about 6 m. wide, with porticos here and there. So Timgad's crosstown thoroughfare and its northern connection were given continuous, differentiating architectural treatment; no other streets were. Both led directly to the main, north entrance to the forum area with its paved, colonnaded plaza and its rostrum, curia, temple, city offices, and civil basilica: an elementary armature mobilized by its thoroughfares.

When town plans are reasonably complete, main thoroughfares are obvious. In the north and west, because of colonial grids, they are usually straight as at Timgad. But skewed angles do occur, in colonies and elsewhere (Amiens; Damascus). When a thoroughfare and a main gate are not aligned, an oblique line must be followed either for some distance (Verulamium; Augst) or for a short, adjusting stretch (Trier; Tropaeum Traiani; Gerasa, from the oval plaza to the south gate). In the east, the legacy of Hellenistic planning produced straight thoroughfares of considerable lengths (see table). Curves, relatively rare, are usually due to steep slopes (Djemila, from the new plaza to the theatre; Tiddis; Mirobriga; Aspendus) or to pre-existing patterns (Dougga). Grids were sometimes laid over precipitous terrain regardless, and bridges carried many major streets—and an occasional plaza—across water and ravines (Alexandria; Antioch on the Orontes; Gerasa; Jerusalem; Nysa; Pergamon, the court in front of the Red Hall; Salona). These considerations, as well as extensions and alterations over time, account for a wide variety of configurations. Thoroughfares broken up into two or more sections, usually by the interposition of plazas, are common in the southern and eastern provinces (Lepcis Magna; Antioch on the Orontes; Palmyra). Some alter direction autonomously, without plazas or other features at the points of deflection (Side; Perge; Stobi). There is no common orientation for thoroughfares, though orthogonal towns east and west were often aligned with the cardinal directions. Overall widths, which frequently vary along a single thoroughfare (Caerwent; Doclea; Petra), range from a few meters in small towns to 12 m. at Herculaneum, to 29 m. at Antioch, with its grand, doubled colonnades, rising to 42 m. for the arcaded boulevard at Lepcis Magna connecting the nymphaeum plaza and port (the Champs Elysées, from the Rond Point to the Etoile, are about 75 m. wide; Fifth and Park avenues in New York are 30 and 43 m. respectively). Few thoroughfares seem to have been named.[18]

Flat, straight, gate-to-gate examples, precisely laid down with neatly parallel sides and symmetrically built-up flanks throughout, are fairly rare. Uneven levels and some-

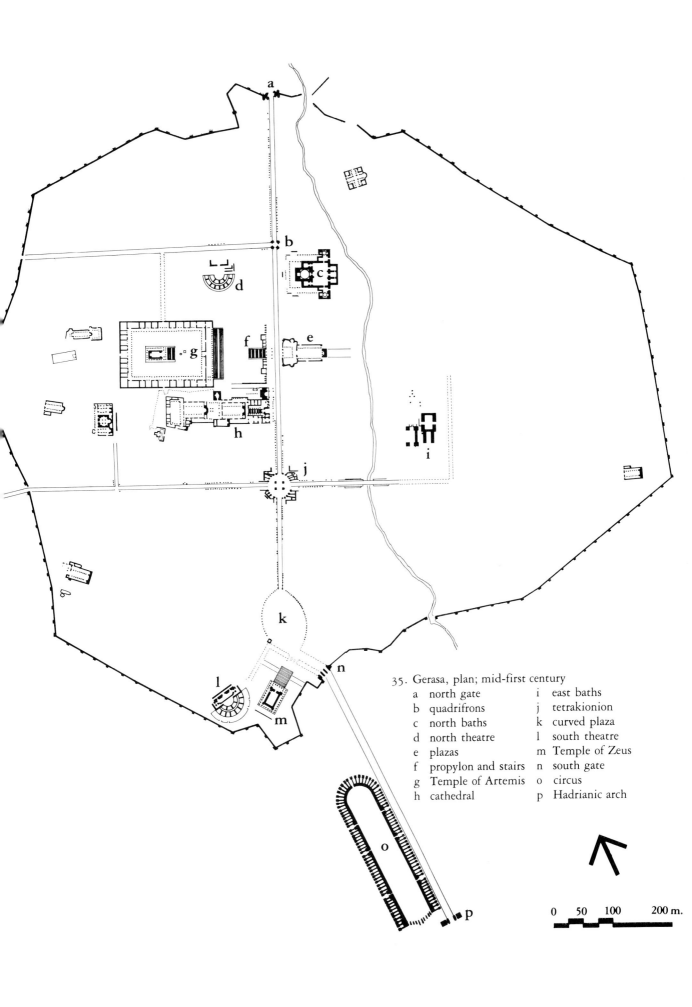

35. Gerasa, plan; mid-first century

a north gate
b quadrifrons
c north baths
d north theatre
e plazas
f propylon and stairs
g Temple of Artemis
h cathedral

i east baths
j tetrakionion
k curved plaza
l south theatre
m Temple of Zeus
n south gate
o circus
p Hadrianic arch

0   50   100   200 m.

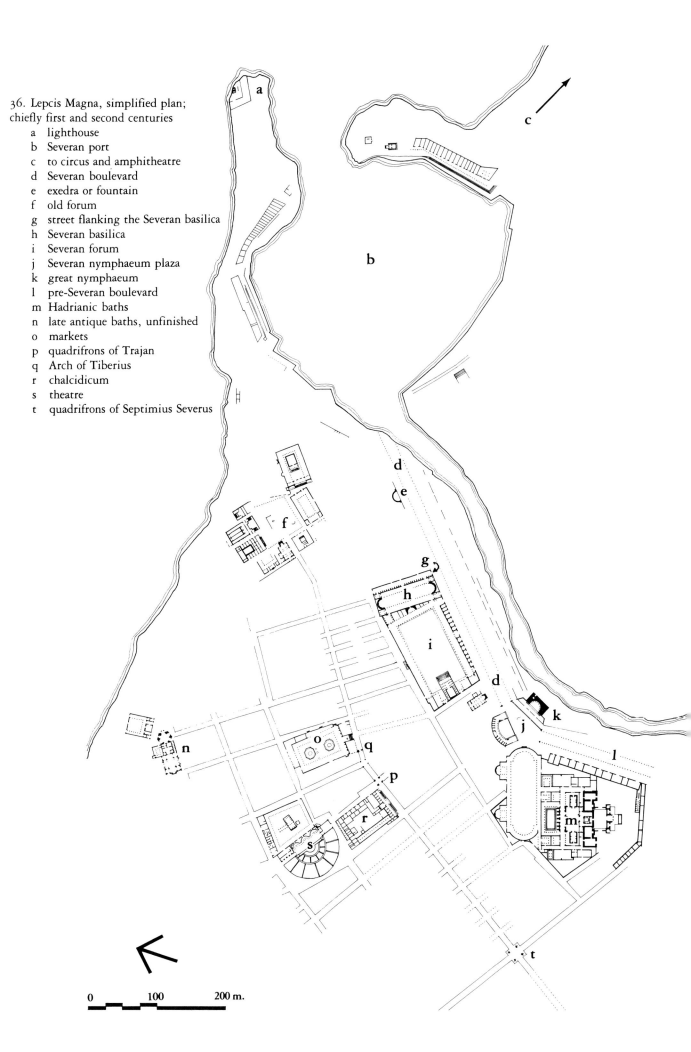

36. Lepcis Magna, simplified plan;
chiefly first and second centuries
- a   lighthouse
- b   Severan port
- c   to circus and amphitheatre
- d   Severan boulevard
- e   exedra or fountain
- f   old forum
- g   street flanking the Severan basilica
- h   Severan basilica
- i   Severan forum
- j   Severan nymphaeum plaza
- k   great nymphaeum
- l   pre-Severan boulevard
- m   Hadrianic baths
- n   late antique baths, unfinished
- o   markets
- p   quadrifrons of Trajan
- q   Arch of Tiberius
- r   chalcidicum
- s   theatre
- t   quadrifrons of Septimius Severus

0   100   200 m.

what sketchy plans are common, as are dissimilar borders—flanking buildings, porticos, or colonnades unmatched left and right. Many man-made irregularities caused by faulty surveying or arbitrary rebuilding or additions stand out on the ground. These tendencies to informality were augmented by the partial open-sidedness of many Roman streets, created by the entranceways of shops set row on row. Along the grander avenues 37 there was the additional volumetric presence of covered walkways screened by files of columns or piers. Either way, workaday street spaces were expanded transversely to a greater or lesser degree along much of their length. In public quarters, the larger entrances to civic buildings and the open volumes of fountains and exedras increased the 38 sense of spatial release and expansion.

Thoroughfares Compared
(approximate dimensions in meters; minimum/maximum)

City	Illustration numbers	Type (given in list, p. 33)	Length if straight or nearly so (approx.)	Segment lengths and totals (approx.)	Width
Amman		6		410 550/ 960/	/9
Ammaedara		2?	1150		9?
Antioch	18	6		1600 650 590 2840	/29
Apamea		6	2000		23
Apollonia (Cyrenaica)			400/		7?
Augst, NW–SE		4	670/		14
Bosra, E–W		6	860		19
Bosra, N–S		6	400		19
Caerwent		2	460		11
Constantinople, Augusteum to Golden Gate	19	4 and 6		400 600 500 1000 2500 5000	
Djemila	1, 4	mixed		600	6/7
Doclea			400/		15/
Ephesus, Embolos	104	mixed	300	(curved)	8/9
Ephesus, Arkadiané		6	520		23

City	Illustration numbers	Type (given in list, p. 33)	Length if straight or nearly so (approx.)	Segment lengths and totals (approx.)	Width
Gerasa	35	6	810		22/24
Hierapolis (Phrygia)		6	1700/		16?
Lepcis Magna	36, 51	6	400		42
Ostia	44, 203	mixed		720 400 ——— 1120	8/10
Palmyra	16, 17	6		300 320 560 ——— 1180	/27
Paris, rue Saint-Jacques, etc.			1800/		
Perge		6		110 400 630 ——— 1140	/28
Pompeii, NE–SW	48	2		620 450 ——— 1070	7/14
Ptolemais (Cyrenaica), E–W		4	1320		15
Rome, Via Flaminia		4	1750		21
Philippopolis, N–S		6	440		13
Side, Great Gate to Port	20	6		340 500 ——— 840	20
Silchester, N–S		2	750		9?
Timgad	21, 23	4	350		7/8
Trier, N–S	34	2		1000 100 950 ——— 2050	/9
Verulamium	33	2 and 3		230 140 40 360 ——— 770	6/7

By late Antonine times scores of cities and towns had colonnaded streets of various kinds. Clearly they were found not only practical, but were considered the pinnacle of architectural refinement as well; Jerusalem's appears, seen through a gateway, in a S. Maria Maggiore mosaic. In this sense the popular image today of the colonnaded street as typical of sophisticated Roman avenues is not far wrong. But the photogenic files of columns one sees at many sites and in widely reproduced illustrations are misleading with respect both to the original appearance of these elaborate thoroughfares and to their function as urban elements. Their walkway roofs are gone, and often their bordering buildings too, losses that the preservation of portions of entablatures cannot make good.   29, 30 The sense of structural and formal context is missing, for the columns appear not as conjunctive parts of a larger concept but as independent entities lined up for their own   31, 49 sake. But since in fact a street colonnade made up the street-pavement side of a covered passageway, it was an inseparable part of a volumetric rather than a linear structure, which it screened in the usual fashion of orthostyle architecture. The effects produced by these shaded corridors, the servants of both the streets proper and their flanking buildings, have vanished forever. Even when the facades of the buildings have been preserved the light is always wrong. It can be difficult to envision the reality of these long stoa-like, perforated passageways. Their geometry was often enlivened by a pronounced entasis of their column shafts, originally experienced in sharp contrast to the fully lit avenues alongside.

In discussions of the possible origins and genealogy of the colonnaded thoroughfare, some say they began with Rome's early porticos (types 3 and 4); others, with late Hellenistic colonnades in the east.[19] It has also been said that one of the earliest monumental examples, if not the first, was built at Antioch on the Orontes for Herod   18 about 30/20 B.C., but this is unlikely. The main street there was paved at Herod's

37. Perge, north–south colonnaded thoroughfare, shop entrances; second century?

38. Lepcis Magna, northwest–southeast thoroughfare, entrance to a major building

order, but the roofed colonnades beside it were probably built in the time of Tiberius.[20] By the end of the first century it is certain that colonnaded thoroughfares had caught on, with porticos predominating in the west (types 3 and 4) and colonnades in the east (types 5 and 6). But the assertion that colonnades were almost entirely limited to eastern provinces is not correct, as the remains at many western sites show (Stobi; Lepcis; Timgad; Djemila; Vaison-la-Romaine; cf. Schwartzenacker).[21] In establishing the architectural geography of the column-lined thoroughfare, much depends on whether only type 6 is defined as a true colonnaded street or whether the presence of any kind of covered, street-lining walkway, continuous or not, is a reasonable and proper criterion of "colonnaded-ness." For present purposes the broader sense is preferred because in urban analysis the important thing is the presence of walkways—on one or both sides of the street—evidence that a considerable attempt has been made to give the street special character by providing it with its own volumetric borders. No doubt many portico streets (types 3 and 4), built late, were inspired in part by colonnaded streets proper (types 5 and 6). The effect, for all practical purposes, was much the same for type 3 as for type 5 and for 4 as for 6.

39   Architectural treatment varies greatly. The Corinthian order is very common, the Ionic fairly rare (Perge). An unusual case of the use of engaged Doric columns occurs along the facades of buildings lining part of the colonnaded thoroughfare of Hierapolis 40 in Phrygia. Apamea's great north–south street has a stretch of spirally fluted shafts, the direction of revolution alternating column by column. Now and then, as beside the 41 street flanking the northeast wall of the basilica at Lepcis, there is a colonnade tight to a building, without a walkway or continuous entablature, reminiscent of the parietal colonnades of the Forum of Nerva and perhaps the Templum Pacis in Rome or the facade 42 of Hadrian's Library in Athens. Columns are by no means always the same height throughout a street, sometimes because entrances to major buildings needed the emphasis taller orders supplied. In the smaller western towns, piers are sometimes mixed in with columns, or are placed at the corners of blocks, in types 3 and 4 (Timgad; Djemila). 32, 163 Arches on columns are rare, though all of Lepcis Magna's grand colonnaded boulevard 43 was arcuated; arches on piers are somewhat more common, but are still scarce in contrast with traditional colonnades. Some important streets were wholly or partly roofed over (Sabratha; Ephesus; Ostia, Via Tecta; Antioch "in Pisidia"), but few can confidently be called thoroughfares. A cryptoportico—a long, sunken, vaulted corridor lit by small, 112 raking windows—lay alongside part of a Bosra thoroughfare and functioned marginally as connective architecture; the more familiar, better lit, versions found along the edges of broad civic terraces were essentially ambulatories.

    Consistency of treatment alongside an entire street was less common by far than inconsistency. As always in classical urbanism, there is little evidence of standardization. But there was a significant common feature: thoroughfare pavements were sunk a step or more below their bordering features. Other streets might be, but thoroughfares always. Of course these curbs or steps facilitated drainage and cleaning, but those were not their only functions. They gave avenues greater definition and individuality, for

39. Palmyra, main thoroughfare, colonnade seen from the tetrakionion, looking southeast; third century

40. Apamea, main north–south thoroughfare, file of spirally fluted columns; second century

their three-dimensionality was emphasized. With continuous lateral steps, streets became broad, shallow troughs, more stable and solid than they would appear to be without this modeling and channeling. Edge-lines and shadows accentuated this. The kinetic implications of the steps themselves made a thoroughfare an outdoor building, more architectural and more in keeping with the forms of the surrounding buildings, than streets undifferentiated from the floor levels beside them. Continuous steps are part of that gathering of extended, parallel lines, real or implied, that give a long, straight, colonnaded or porticoed avenue so powerful a sense of focus and directional control.

Thus identified and given a separate and particular character, thoroughfares contrasted sharply with lesser streets. Though there were exceptions, most cities and towns were packed tightly with buildings largely placed on narrow streets and alleys. In contrast to these dense urban regions, where the continuity and fluidity of armatures was unknown, thoroughfares provided spatial ventilation, some elbowroom or breathing space, augmented at larger sites by intermediating tributaries. By pulling a town together and making its several quarters mutually more accessible, thoroughfares

44, 45
104, 203

41. Lepcis Magna, street beside the Severan basilica; ca. 200

42. Athens, Hadrian's Library (132). Above, model; below, a portion of the facade

insured urban cohesion. Their success, their partial intrusion into even the most obdurately orthogonal plans, should probably be explained largely in these terms. Thoroughfares' functions and effects were neatly reciprocal, for they were equally practical and symbolic, making essential locations available while establishing the framework for a common imagery of cultural and political allegiance.

That imagery sprang in part from the essential thoroughfare qualities of continuity and seriality. Short streets would not do, nor would streets without their own architectural borders, save in the smallest towns. Even if those borders changed form along the length of a street, it was no matter so long as they did not disappear. Scores, sometimes hundreds, of columns set in line gave many thoroughfares a pulsating, metronomic presence of great power. Regular column spacing relates to human ambulation, giving pace to a street or plaza by its suggestion of the potential of regularity in walking, of an ideal rhythm of steady steps. Porticoed and colonnaded streets, like loose palisades largely consistent in their rhythms, provided stable backdrops for town life. The continuous lines of entablatures above and curbs and steps below traced the limits of these metered settings. Because of this, many thoroughfares suggested the existence of an ordered world against which the chaotic untidiness of life might be measured; in some ways their architecture expresses an ideal order. Such statements may read more into the evidence than the original inhabitants might have been willing to concede. But it is true that a long, well-made colonnade or arcade is a systematic, regular kind of architecture, in sharp contrast with the agitated movement of town life.

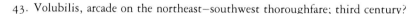

43. Volubilis, arcade on the northeast–southwest thoroughfare; third century?

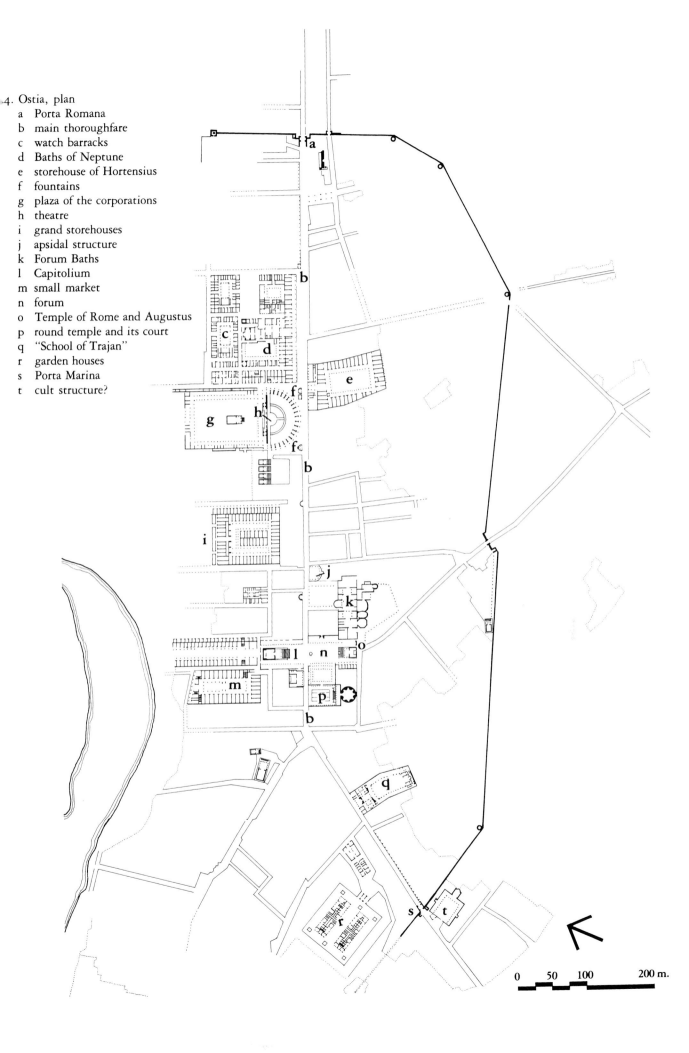

4. Ostia, plan
- a Porta Romana
- b main thoroughfare
- c watch barracks
- d Baths of Neptune
- e storehouse of Hortensius
- f fountains
- g plaza of the corporations
- h theatre
- i grand storehouses
- j apsidal structure
- k Forum Baths
- l Capitolium
- m small market
- n forum
- o Temple of Rome and Augustus
- p round temple and its court
- q "School of Trajan"
- r garden houses
- s Porta Marina
- t cult structure?

0   50   100   200 m.

To the uses and meaning of these avenues, found empire-wide, must be added the dimension of time, for by nature they are creatures and consumers of time. They should not be thought of as static architecture but as having always a past, a now, and a future; that is, from the user's point of view and memory, before-and-afterness. One's position along a thoroughfare changed, but the street form itself remained much the same. This was a factor vital to the thoroughfare's function of helping to bring cohesion and unity to a town because it was little affected by the architectural particularities of the different quarters it traversed. In due time various structures encroached on rights of way—bath
16, 17   buildings, for example, as at Palmyra. But the evidence at excavated sites strongly

45. Avezzano, cast of a relief once in the Museo Torlonia, Rome; second century

46. Herculaneum, Cardo IV, looking south

suggests that thoroughfares were not blocked until drastic measures for defense, common in late antiquity, were taken. Until then these avenues continued to function.

Before imperial times, grand avenues with architectural borders were built chiefly by dynasts for ceremonial purposes. Roman thoroughfares were the first truly arterial streets built for whole communities and their public business throughout an entire commonwealth. Only short stretches of Roman streets seem to have been restored, as at Jerusalem (the "cardo") or Herculaneum, and none for any distance. Modern streets in   46 Tripoli, Leningrad, Rome's E.U.R. suburb, or the rue des Colonnes in Paris, vaguely suggest the effects of elaborate Roman avenues. But the traditional porticos of southern Europe, such as those in Bologna and various Lombard towns or in western Spain, as at Santiago da Compostela, are closer to the scale and purposes of antiquity.

PLAZAS

With their bordering, shaded walkways and rows of shops, plazas were the centers of Roman cities and towns. Most were all-purpose places with a busy commercial life, though some were first conceived as open spaces for their own sake. Large cities might have one or more plazas set apart for the sale of particular classes of goods, just as there were streets for similar purposes. The forum, though more formal, also tended to be multifunctional and commercial to a degree, but as the seat of authority with official buildings and municipal offices, it surely differed from other plazas in people's minds. In the east the Hellenistic tendency to regularize the agora, to give it clear geometric boundaries, became more pronounced over time, and sometimes an agora took on a western cast as traditional Latin features were added. Growing towns east and west constructed new plazas, sometimes by clearing spaces within built-up areas, sometimes   63 starting afresh outside the walls. Modest plazas appeared next to major city gates both inside and out. And capacious forecourts of civic buildings, temples included, provided plaza-like spaces here and there beside main streets.

Very few plazas of consequence are independent of thoroughfares. Broadly speaking there are two kinds of plazas, those lying across thoroughfares without blocking them, and those standing beside thoroughfares and connected with them by large, clearly marked entranceways or through open colonnades. The perimeter continuities of the first type are interrupted where they meet intersecting thoroughfares; secondary streets may also abut these plazas and further fragment their perimeters. If this kind of plaza is set across an avenue's extended axis it may appear to be a temporarily broadened segment of that avenue, especially if the avenue's colonnades or porticos accommodate the wider   47 plaza without interrupting their rhythm and then resume their parallel track on the opposite side. A plaza of the second category, one that stands not athwart but beside a   1, 23 thoroughfare, will have a less discontinuous perimeter and a greater sense of enclosure. Its minor exits will insure that it is no cul-de-sac, but it will not function as an expanded segment of a thoroughfare offering through passage to heavy traffic. Such a plaza is almost always bordered in part by internal colonnades or arcades, frequently interrupted

47. Gerasa, curved plaza and thoroughfare; late first century?

by projecting buildings and sometimes by a monumental entranceway. Often though by no means always fora are of this second kind.

Rectilinear plans are common east and west, though many are slightly askew with not quite parallel sides. Vitruvius prescribes a ratio of 2:3 for the width and length of fora.[22] That precise relationship does not often turn up; oblongs of 1:2 or broader were usually preferred. Fora range from fairly long and narrow (Assisi; Pompeii; Tarragona) through more Vitruvian shapes (Conimbriga; Timgad; the Severan forum at Lepcis Magna) to nearly square (Paris; Thuburbo Maius) to actually square (Doclea; Nicopolis ad Istrum). Other kinds of rectilinear plazas run through about the same range of shapes, including squares and near squares (Side; Perge; the hectare-sized lower market at Ephesus; the courtyard of the Templum Pacis in Rome). Plazas of approximately triangular shape can be found (Verulamium—tiny, but triangular; Perge; Bosra); they are usually small. Many others, large and small, including some fora, have asymmetrical or irregular outlines (Dougga; Thibilis; the old forum at Lepcis Magna; Stobi; Lauriacum; Perge; the plaza of the two bridges at Antioch on the Orontes). Of course in the choice or formation of a plaza's shape much might depend on terrain, or the nature of an existing city plan, or changes wrought over time. But whatever their plans, plazas are basic evidence for the form and character of the architecture of Roman urbanism. Solidly built, located at busy intersections, they were as important to town life as any other public structures.

Among the scores of plazas that can be seen today, another distinctive class is characterized by rounded borders. Large public spaces of curved outline go back at least

48. Pompeii, air view

to the fifth century B.C.; one thinks, for example, of the southerly Argive exedra beside
the Sacred Way at Delphi, some 13 m. across. The monumental paired exedras of the
fora of Augustus and Trajan, about 40 m. wide, continued this tradition, as did similar
forms found at sanctuaries and temples (Palestrina; the Temples of Caelestis and of
Augustan Piety at Dougga; of Asklepios at Lambaesis; the temple at Hössn Suleiman).
It is difficult to say when the first planned piazzas of curvilinear shape appeared. The
date of the larger curved plaza at Gerasa is debated; that at Bosra must have been built   49
after 106.[23] The one at Antioch on the Orontes seems to have been inserted in the fourth   18
century. No doubt the popularity of these forms came late, flowering in the fourth

century—an important urban development as yet little investigated. Whatever the chronology, the appearance of curving plazas was part of a vigorous Roman interest in rounded shapes. Baths large and small, round temples, palace halls, villas, and huge structures for public entertainment kept curved design before the architect's eye, and it is not surprising that during the high empire large rounded public spaces began to appear.

Fully rounded plazas have not yet been found in the western European provinces, partly because of the prevalence of closely knit orthogonal patterns filled in with first- and second-century buildings. But they should be mentioned briefly because they form a significant subchapter in the history of urbanism. They are found in the east, the Balkans, and North Africa with different-shaped plans. There are circular plazas, as at Gerasa, Bosra, and Antioch on the Orontes. Others were built at Jerusalem and Justinian Prima, and one was planned for Lepcis Magna. Then there are oval shapes and oval-like shapes, figures usually not proper ellipses but four-center constructions made up of arcs of circles often somewhat inexactly laid out. Two examples are found at Palmyra, and there is a famous asymmetrical one at Gerasa.

Sometimes plaza plans are based on circles diminished by parallel chords placed equidistant from the center of the circle, producing a conformation often found in bath

49. Gerasa, curved plaza colonnade; late first century?

buildings, that intimates an oval (the plaza of the Harbor Baths at Ephesus); a variant
may have existed at Jerusalem, where about a third of a continuously curving figure was
cut off by a single straight side. More or less semicircular plazas were built at Bosra and
Perge, and also at Stobi (about 28 m. wide, an example of what might be called an
exedra-plaza). Finally, there are plazas with segmental or semicircular curves at one or
both ends (Dougga; Troesmis; the Forum of Nerva at Rome). Some curved examples are   65
known only from texts (the oval Forum of Constantine, Constantinople), and this list is   19
not complete.

The radial character of curved plazas gave planners and builders a useful device for
emphasizing important street intersections while relieving congestion. Circular plazas
could de-emphasize the sharp-edged geometry of orthogonal crossings, and radial
shapes made it possible to bring together non-parallel streets in a rational way. Curved
plazas were particularly effective when located so as to prevent several converging streets
from intersecting at awkward or inconveniently sharp angles, in the manner of the
quasi-oval of the obelisk-centered Piazza del Popolo in Rome (the proposed nymphaeum
plaza at Lepcis; the plaza inside the Neapolis gate at Jerusalem). This surface use of
radiality has its vertical analogy in the deployment and forms of monumental archways
and gates. It can be seen in buildings where otherwise clumsy relationships caused by

50. Thuburbo Maius, courtyard of the Temple of Baalat; early second century?

unaligned axes or non-parallel borders are brought into satisfactory adjustment. They receive two or more such axes along the radii of a single curving form or along the perpendiculars to polygonal facets (the courts of the Temple of Baalat at Maktar, and of the Episcopal Basilica at Stobi; the apse on the north side of the Severan Forum at Lepcis Magna; and both the entrance court and the shorter ends of the main courtyard fountain at Piazza Armerina).

Because of their radiality, curved plazas properly located can accept centered axes from numerous directions, reducing their directional force and individuality while tying them together inside broad common spaces. Regular polygons have similar qualities (the hexagonal court at Baalbek; the octagonal atrium of the Domus Aurea; the harbor at Portus; numerous freestanding monuments such as those at Tropaeum Traiani and Ammaedara). The chief disadvantage of curved plazas, especially noticeable when they are set into rectilinear street patterns, is their effect on surrounding structures, whose forms must be adjusted accordingly; Gerasa is perhaps the only case where the results are adequately known.

The nymphaeum complex at Lepcis Magna is an instructive example of Roman plaza-making, curved or otherwise, with features typical of the grand imperial manner. Before

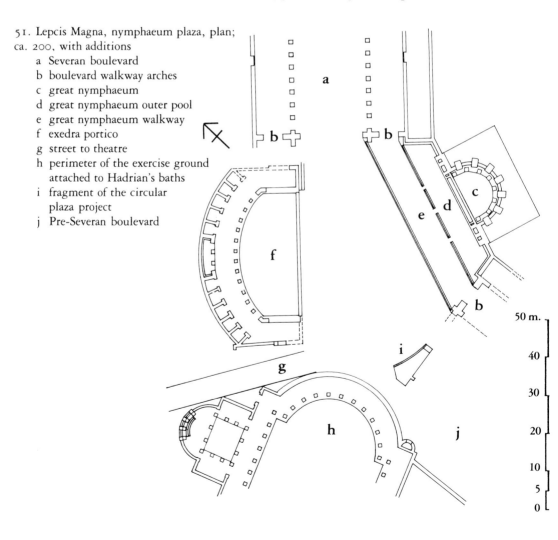

51. Lepcis Magna, nymphaeum plaza, plan;
ca. 200, with additions
  a Severan boulevard
  b boulevard walkway arches
  c great nymphaeum
  d great nymphaeum outer pool
  e great nymphaeum walkway
  f exedra portico
  g street to theatre
  h perimeter of the exercise ground
     attached to Hadrian's baths
  i fragment of the circular
     plaza project
  j Pre-Severan boulevard

Severan times a colonnaded thoroughfare had been built running north to a point just beyond the Hadrianic baths, about even with the end of their exercise court; its details are unknown. In Severan times an extension of this thoroughfare was built, but on an axis 50° further toward the east. A vast circular plaza was begun in order to mediate this change of direction as well as to accommodate, somewhat tangentially, a secondary street leading northwest to the theatre. But this project was never completed. Some foundations, and perhaps the outer curving wall and arcaded portico of what is now the segmental exedra on the northwest side of the plaza, were put in place. The curved plan was changed to an open-ended triangular one dominated by a huge nymphaeum 40 m.   53 wide whose axis of symmetry bisected the 130° angle between the two streets. Had the original circular scheme been finished, it would have been about 75 m. or 250 Roman feet in diameter (that of Hardouin Mansart's sadly mutilated Place des Victoires in Paris is about 60 m.; the circular Rue de Viarmes nearby is nearly 40 m.; for the scale of the Lepcis nymphaeum, compare the Trevi fountain, about half as wide).

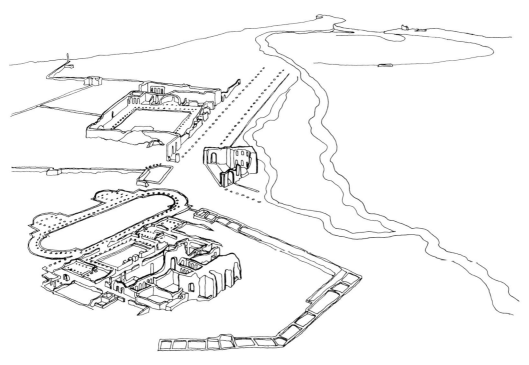

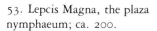
52. Lepcis Magna, sketch of the central district seen from the air, looking north

53. Lepcis Magna, the plaza nymphaeum; ca. 200.

Though the pre-Severan thoroughfare has not been excavated, some details of its junction with the new plaza—which may never have been quite finished—are clear. Walkway traffic passed through arches in line that cut across the end of the street at right angles to it; if a higher central archway was erected over the paved roadway, it would have had an unusually wide span of some 17 m. The plan-line of these arches was parallel to that of the nymphaeum's outer wall, a configuration repeated across the plaza where the new Severan boulevard began. The plan of the plaza and nymphaeum was based on a spreading, V-shaped frame that kept the avenues from meeting. The result, as at all major Roman plazas, was that thoroughfares discharged traffic into a broad pool of open space where, for the moment, their powerful axial control was dissipated. One side of the Lepcis plaza was bordered by the nymphaeum's long, trapezoidal overflow basin (the parapet was added later). This shape and its interlocking relationship with the spreading space beyond are similar to the design and setting of the trapezoidal plaza, about 42 m. on its longest side, that lies across the street from the entrance to the Temple of Artemis at Gerasa; other monuments, such as the "Kalybé" at Bosra and the Amman nymphaeum, echo these dispositions, as does the polygonal Domus Aurea court, though more faintly.

The controlling feature of the Lepcis plaza was the unseen, mediating centerline of the nymphaeum. Composed of trapezoidal bands expanding in width toward the west, and with no closing feature symmetrically placed on its far side, the plaza is open-ended in the formal sense. The large segmental portico is not aligned with this geometry but with the Severan avenue (as the smaller but comparable Timgad market, with its segmental walls, curving porticos, and wedge-shaped stalls, is aligned with a grid). Thus, while the plaza is rationally planned with respect to the adjustment of the two

54. Lepcis Magna, the nymphaeum plaza, arch, and walkway
55. Timgad, eastern market, ca. 100?

56. Rome, street behind the Basilica of Maxentius, looking southeast; early fourth century

arterial axes, it is otherwise irregular. The convex end wall of the exercise ground may not have obtruded as much as it appears to in the plan, for it was not as high as the nymphaeum or the segmental portico. Still, as one came southeast along the theatre street, a heady mixture of forms loomed up, not dissimilar to late antique juxtapositions of planar and curved volumes that existed at Piazza Armerina (the irregular court [p] just north of the trefoil dining hall) and that can still be seen behind the Basilica of Maxentius and Constantine. But the primary features of the Lepcis plaza were the spreading arcuated extensions of the nymphaeum walls and the deep scenic apse of the fountain itself (the segmental portico was too wide, and its curve too shallow, to take command of the central space). With the future in mind, one can discern the lineaments of a sector of the octagon interior at Kalat Siman.

It would be helpful to know what the walkway roofs were like, how the walkways joined the walls with the transverse arches, and whether or not huge arches spanned the central roadways. Perhaps the oblique walkway in front of the nymphaeum was not roofed, while the curving portico opposite was. Of the two thoroughfares only the Severan can be described with any confidence. It was a true boulevard, arcaded in a straight line for some 400 m. from the plaza to the harbor; on the same axis, another 500 m. or so across the water, the lighthouse tower stood several stories high. On the left-hand side of the street were rows of shops and the entrance to the rectangular, arcaded Severan forum with its dynastic temple and adjoining basilica. Just beyond is the street

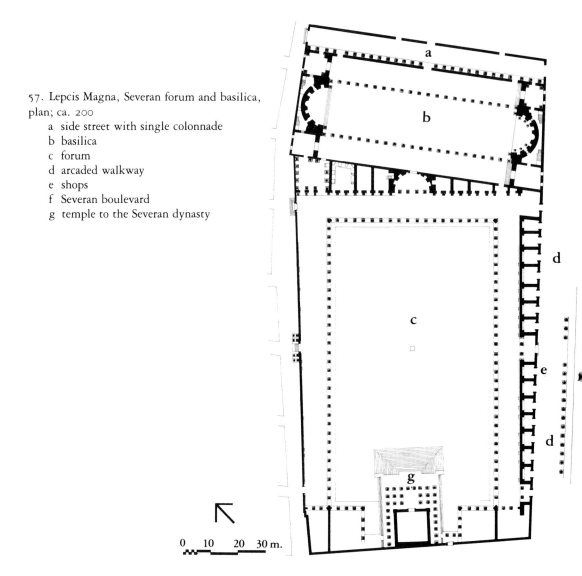

57. Lepcis Magna, Severan forum and basilica,
plan; ca. 200
    a side street with single colonnade
    b basilica
    c forum
    d arcaded walkway
    e shops
    f Severan boulevard
    g temple to the Severan dynasty

0   10   20   30 m.

with the parietal colonnade; beyond that, about halfway to the harbor, is a large exedra
beside the walkway. Baths stood on the boulevard's right-hand side, but they have not
been excavated. The architectural treatment of the junction of the boulevard with the
harborside installations is not known, but it may have been marked by a grand triumphal arch or gate as at Ephesus, Ancona, or Antinoöpolis. It seems probable that the
extended esplanade beside the harbor's southwest rim was connected with this end of the
boulevard. Taken together, these Severan structures form a monumental armature built
at a time when the accumulated experience and experiments of the past had been largely
digested. The plaza was the vestibule for the entire complex, fittingly scaled and
furnished to prefigure the scenic monumentality beyond.

    The capitals (called Pergamene—lotus and acanthus combined), the masons' marks
in Greek, and the circular project, presumably Syrian in origin, have understandably
caused these buildings to be characterized as essentially eastern.[24] No doubt this is
correct with regard to architectural carving and certain features of design, but the

58. Ancona. Above, Arch of Trajan (115);
below, representation of Ancona on
Trajan's Column, detail

59. Lepcis Magna, esplanade beside the port and steps up to the Temple of Jupiter Dolichenus

arcades, the plans of the forum temple and basilica, the deployment of the plaza arches, the form of the nymphaeum apse, and aspects of the underlying geometry of the plaza all seem rooted in western practice. But even that practice had been conditioned earlier by eastern influences. These works are imperial, eastern and western both, built when different artistic forces from around the Mediterranean were beginning to coalesce. Architectural change in the empire was probably energized more by this process of interaction among stylistic trends than by any other factor. The Severan work at Lepcis evolved from a creative synthesis of this kind, incomplete and awkward in some ways but no less instructive for that. To derive it, on the evidence of one or another group of architectural features, from a particular tradition or area, runs the risk of ignoring its stylistic totality. Detailed studies of architectural carving, for example, often useful tools for comparative dating and for revealing the movements or influence of schools and hands, should whenever possible be used in conjunction with an awareness of the underlying architectural forms the carving is attached to—plans, elevations, and the architectural forms they describe. The presence of capitals and entablatures of clearly Hellenistic provenience in, say, an elaborate vaulted bath building or western luxury villa does not alone say much about the style or origin of those buildings.

Prosperity, pride, and the need for appropriate, informal concourses encouraged plaza-building. Plazas other than fora were partly the creatures of streets, of their intersection, reconstruction, and extension. Though providing commercial and social community spaces, they were also crucial plan elements, mediating among street patterns and angles. They were often chronological hinges as well, interpolated between street construction of different periods, serving as important evidence of evolving architectural thinking. Plazas are dynamic hollows in the urban fabric, not just broad, fixed pavements.

But seen as nodal points transmitting yet slowing traffic while unmistakably marking off sections of avenues, their indispensable active role becomes apparent; they have more functions than any other major city element. A place with no plaza was an insignificant one indeed, with little memorable spatial character and no proper facilities for the social and commercial opportunities all towns promise. In colder climates, where there were few large cities, civic plazas were not so numerous. Fora, however, were always present.

Containing the civic and religious essentials of town life, often shops as well, the forum was the repository of the town's soul. It made an architectural statement, both functional and symbolic, of civic values and purposes. Because of this and its psychological and political associations with Rome, the forum was the focus of town activity in fact and in mind; it seems to have kept its aura to the end. There was no standardization, though a general scheme prevailed: a rectangular plaza lined on two or more sides by porticos, a temple (capitolium or not), and one or more municipal buildings, all composed in a systematized if distant version of dispositions in Rome. The temple might sit out in the plaza or beside it; the civic structures—basilica, curia, administrative offices—flanked and sometimes interrupted the porticos. Rostra and hydraulic amenities are fairly common, gatherings of statuary ubiquitous. Certain plan patterns were popular: placing the basilica lengthwise alongside the plaza (Caerwent; Leicester; St.-Rémy; the Forum of Trajan in Rome; Cyrene), or the temple on axis at one end of the plaza, inside it or not (Pompeii; the Forum of Augustus in Rome; Virunum; Paris; Thuburbo Maius). What might seem an obvious plaza arrangement, with porticos of equal depth all round in the Hellenistic manner, does not appear often in the west, where overall symmetry is frequently precluded by building shapes and arbitrary locations. It does appear in the east, in great forum-like squares built or refurbished in Roman times (Palmyra; Perge; Ephesus; eastern colonnaded plazas are often of Roman date). Some eastern towns built or rebuilt in Roman times may have had fora of the western type (Gerasa; Philippopolis).[25]

Portico design ranges from conservative (Cyrene, for example, with a sober Doric order) to near flamboyant (the arcaded Severan forum at Lepcis Magna). Plaza sizes can be very small (Tiddis; Solva?) or half a hectare and even larger (Rome; Lepcis; Cyrene; perhaps Gerasa). The porticos—very few fora lacked them—supplied the dignity Hellenistic orthostyle architecture embodies, and in cities and towns with colonnaded thoroughfares they extended the formal affinities of the armature. Sometimes a forum-temple complex is traversed by a thoroughfare (Ostia; Paris; Virunum; Zadar?). This was likely to be closed to wheeled traffic and sumpters, if not originally, then later (Augst). But the majority of fora stood beside their thoroughfares, connected by prominent entranceways. One turned off an avenue and passed through a gateway to enter a forum, gaining the plaza pavement directly or by stepping across a portico. This process would be unremarkable except that avenue and plaza levels are almost universally below those of entranceways, whether or not porticos intervene, so that in order to get to forum level one had first to go up, then down; plazas without an internal bordering step or two are rarely fora.

60

48

60, 61

44

62, 79

60. (TOP) Cyrene, forum and basilica from the air

61. (ABOVE) Cyrene, forum, detail; Hellenistic plaza modified in the late first century B.C.

62. (RIGHT) Maktar, entrance to the forum; early second century

63. Forum edges. Above, Maktar (early second century); right, Athens, the Roman agora, late first century B.C.

63   Because of these steps (which could double as seats), forum plazas were given stronger visual identities than they otherwise would have had. Pavements laid evenly from wall to wall level with portico floors were unsuitable because the central spaces would lack volumetric identity. The solution is in part the result of the classical architect's passion for architectural underlining, for defining and emphasizing basic forms and surfaces by replicating their edges with steps or mouldings. Circumscribing steps are to a plaza pavement as a raised frame is to a picture surface: a way of emphasizing the presence and shape of a flat and featureless rectangular expanse.

By such means thoroughfares and plazas were given an intaglio quality, were let into the earth, of which they seemed to become a more permanent part. This architectural channeling or chasing has much to do with their pronounced sense of place, their firm fixity of location. The edge of the shield-like oval of the Campidoglio plaza, sunk two steps below the encircling paving level, is similarly conceived. If marking out the oval figure had been the only need, a paving pattern like that used for the twelve-pointed star would have sufficed. But breaking the level creates a different and more emphatic sense of place, and the broad, low steps, with their shaded recesses, are effective in this out of all proportion to their scale. The work of Roman architects and builders is not as elegant or subtle as Michelangelo's, but it rests on the same principles.

Roman plazas were loose architectural containers, informal theatres for town business. They gave cities and towns spatial variety and change, increasing here and there the pedestrian's sense of transverse scale and the breadth of visible sky. Orthogonal towns with narrow streets needed them most and got the fewest, though expansion apparently guaranteed additions. The evidence is incomplete, but from the first century onward, the number of plazas apparently grew at a proportionately greater rate than the cities and towns they served. If this is correct, the ratio between open and roofed space changed perceptibly in many places, reducing building densities. Meanwhile plazas became more crowded, set about with statues on sizable bases and a variety of other permanent plaza furniture. For of the many places in a town to erect a memorial, self-serving or not, a plaza—above all a forum—was the most desirable.

STAIRS

Armatures include public stairs and steps. There are both short flights marking plaza
64   entrances and stairs that are part of streets (Tiddis; beside the Artemis sanctuary at
            Gerasa; Cyrene, beside the market theatre; at the southern end of the Lechaion road at
7, 70   Corinth). Grand stairs led to elevated precincts and monumental buildings, and long,
59   stepped esplanades were popular (Bulla Regia; Lepcis Magna). Because of a strong
126   interest in artificial terraces and raised building platforms, stairs were by no means always simply responses to sloping terrain. Though obviously functional, and thus easy to take for granted, they were essential links in the architecture of connection. Their kinetic import and strong, prismatic forms emphasized those junctions where differing levels require direct, efficient coupling. Their combined dualities of practical function

64. Tiddis, street of steps

and physical effect, of simultaneous horizontal and vertical movement, were exploited regularly, and armatures could not be traversed without going up or down from one part to another.

Thoroughfares interrupted by elevated platforms are fairly rare but do occur, as at Lepcis Magna, where the platform steps of the four-way Severan arch extend across major streets where they intersect, or at Sbeitla, where the avenue leading to the theatre is interrupted by an abruptly elevated plaza laid over it and is resumed by way of steps. The propylon plaza at Gerasa was set four steps above its surroundings. At Dougga, 65 passage from the theatre street to the forum involves two separate flights of steps. At Volubilis the quarter just south of the forum is reached by a short flight interrupted by a 66 curved landing; there are similar street-steps at Pompeii and Herculaneum. Steps leading to buildings beside thoroughfares, all but mandatory, sometimes adapt to 67 sloping streets or plazas. Now and then a flight of stairs will break in plan to accommodate lines of approach to its building (the steps to the main entrance to the north baths at 68 Timgad, facing their entrance plaza outside the north gate; Djemila, where the lowest levels of the Severan temple steps curl slightly outward in response to approaches from 7 the east). This tendency to deflect from a planning axis to accommodate traffic is not uncommon: the steps flanking the west plaza at Timgad, for example, make such an 25 adjustment, and similar arrangements can be found at Tiddis and Sbeitla. But most armature stairs connect thoroughfares and plazas with elevated terraces and platforms.

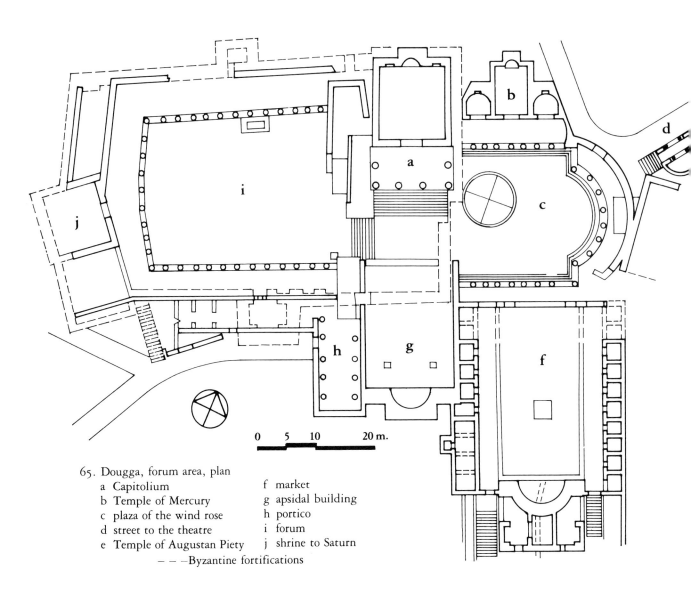

65. Dougga, forum area, plan
a Capitolium
b Temple of Mercury
c plaza of the wind rose
d street to the theatre
e Temple of Augustan Piety
f market
g apsidal building
h portico
i forum
j shrine to Saturn
– – –Byzantine fortifications

66. Volubilis, steps between the forum and the southern quarter.

67. (LEFT) Timgad, library steps; probably fourth century
68. (ABOVE) Timgad, steps to the north baths; early fourth century

Students of imperial architecture quickly discover the Roman predilection for artificial terrain, for large, neatly edged and leveled spaces, usually rectangular and
frequently used as plazas. Making them often involved cutting into and building up
from natural hillsides, as at Khamissa (the upper plaza or forum), or the Forum and   69
Markets of Trajan at Rome. But the creation by construction of elevated level expanses,
a practice evolved from the work of Hellenistic and earlier builders in the east, was
carried almost to the point of addiction. The number of vast terraces and parades, of the
kind seen at Palestrina, Aeminium, Baalbek, and on the Celian Hill at Rome, is large;
the quantity of smaller but still impressively spacious examples is almost limitless. Parts
of some cities were terraced (Tarragona; Tomis; the Constantinople quarter between the
circus and the Sea of Marmara), and the buildings of grand villas usually stood on
artificial, layered platforms. Major Roman building types were often elevated on ter-

69. Khamissa, upper terrace or forum; begun ca. 100?

race-like forms: temple heights could be further increased by tall podia, and large public baths were set upon functional, honeycombed platforms. These postures were echoed on all sides by innumerable plinths, pedestals, and other subordinate devices of elevation. All extensive, powerful substructures (their wrecks are a common sight) required suitable stairs. The more monumental the buildings, the grander the stairs, which, because of the strong Roman emphasis on principal axes, were usually symmetrically centered in front of their buildings' main entrances. The Romans built other kinds of important stairs: connecting terrace levels or terraces with the ground, as at Mulva and Djemila, or beside the long edges of esplanades, as at Sbeitla or Lepcis Magna. At Lepcis the upper flight led to the platform of the presumed Temple of Jupiter Dolichenus, and the lower one and its extension mark the southwest border of the port; there are six more steps down, now covered over.

What might be done with stairs is illustrated by the approach to the Temple of Artemis at Gerasa. Behind the propylaea that face the main thoroughfare there is a staircase almost 20 m. wide, whose forty-nine steps are separated into seven flights by landings; it has high walls on both sides but is open to the sky. The temple precinct was

70. Gerasa, steps from the Artemis precinct propylon up to the temple terrace; mid-second century

then approached by stairs apparently nearly 100 m. wide, made of three flights of nine steps each, and the temple itself, with a podium over 4 m. high, had an additional fourteen steps. Thus, to gain the temple porch, some 90 steps had to be climbed, spaced 127 over a horizontal distance of about 160 m. This dramatic display is echoed at lesser scales throughout much of the Roman world, where small towns with big temples were common—by the third century, temples appeared whose stairs took up as much space as 7, 27, 156 their cellas. Making broad, imposing flights of stairs was a very ancient tradition which did not flourish again until the Baroque age. Roman stairs were the result not only of ceremonial requirements, but also of a need for elevation, for declaring importance by means of height, for the quality of overlooking-ness. Even if the terrain assured these qualities, broad terraces were still likely to be built (for the Temple of Trajan at Pergamon, for that of the Divine Claudius in Rome).

The evidence indicates that stairs were frequently provided without strict regard for necessity. They were undoubtedly an important part of the imperial architect's repertory. Their size often exceeds any conceivable need. The large ones were a species of inclined plazas; the Spanish Steps, or the stairs in front of the Metropolitan Museum of Art in New York City, both of which in good weather are crowded theatres of urban life, come to mind as comparisons. Because stairs are so evenly and solidly layered, they suggest permanence and reliability. Their edges and iterated shadows draw parallel lines on the urban canvas: broad steps function as mouldings. At the same time they are purveyors of changes not only of locale but of meaning—from the street to the temple forecourt, for example, or from the street to the interior of the baths; they shift gears in urban transmission from one mode to another. Because they affect muscle sense more than streets or plazas, they reinforce the sense of arriving or departing, of gaining a goal or of leaving it behind for another phase of activity. There was some going up and down in a Roman town even if its site was flat, because stairs were significant connective devices. Part of this derived from the nature of monumental structures, but part resulted from the Roman interest in stairs as multipurpose instruments of urbanism. Behind this lay the grand stairs of earlier times, of the theatral kind seen at Knossos or Morgantina.

The attention paid to connective architecture produced public environments more cohesive than had existed earlier. The Greek designer had been less inclined to anchor his major buildings firmly in their urban architectural context, preferring to give them a greater degree of independence. With the exception of ceremonial ways, streets tended to remain paths until orthogonal planning took root. Hellenistic planners and architects organized cities tightly and strengthened the ties among public structures and spaces, but they were hampered by the rigidities of rectilinear planning. They seem to have had only a mild interest in developing the street as an architectural entity, though widened central avenues did appear. The degree of change after early Hellenistic times is difficult to judge. Alexandria is largely gone, and almost all the portions of Hellenistic cities we do have were extensively rebuilt in Roman times. But the growing tendency, from the first century onward, to treat towns as wholes in which the connection of one center of civic activity with another was regarded as important is confirmed by archaeological and pictorial evidence. There does not appear to have been any body of theory about this, but as we know little of what was taught in the classroom or about how the profession of architecture was carried on, certainty is impossible. [26] But apparently the elaboration of connective architecture was a Roman development carried out spontaneously. Its different versions were under local control in a process wherein inter-city competition and emulation played major roles.

That the cohesiveness of connective architecture throughout a town was due in great part to the repetition of familiar elements of classical design is more certain. The inspiration for some of these basic forms, especially for the orders and their trains of mouldings, was Hellenistic. This helps explain the clear sense of Roman identity the sites project today, because so many Roman building types and urban features are overlaid with those forms (on the orders in their Roman condition, see chapter VII, below). However wide the enlivening variety of design elements seen in thoroughfares and plazas, however novel or complex their Roman combinations or dispositions might appear in contrast to earlier architecture, no single, basic form would be unfamiliar, foreign to an individual's experience east or west. All stayed within the broad boundaries of an established formal tradition—column shafts, acanthus leaves, volutes, arches, mouldings and more mouldings—and few unrelated or bizzrre intrusions appeared. That this did not congeal into dead formalism was due to Roman inventiveness in devising new orchestrations of familiar elements, and in combining the results with their own architectural inventions.

When Tacitus bemoaned the loss of features of old Rome to the activities of Nero's post-fire planners and builders he recorded memories of a kind of urban context then fast disappearing—a city that preserved primitive structures and lacked the new wide streets (to which, as Suetonius adds, porticos were attached). [27] Rome's influence was enormous. Many details of its reconstruction can only be inferred, but building activities in the provinces are better known. There the cores of the cities and towns were elaborated, embellished, and extended, the connections among their public spaces strongly emphasized. This open and effective attachment of fixed locales of public activity to a flowing, architecturalized core or spine prefigures in some ways the achievements of late-fifteenth-century architects in Italy, who "began to think of single elements as a function of the whole—to regard a given environment not merely as a neutral repository for a [building], but as something that might be formed and controlled by the manipulation of voids and the co-ordination of masses." [28] Out of this came the concept for the renovation of the Campidoglio, with its several Roman features, and, subsequently, the city armature begun by Domenico Fontana for Sixtus V, both crucial events in the history of urban composition.

When Roman architects and builders so effectively enchained the settings of the chief public activities of town life, they broke new ground. That this may have happened haphazardly is not very important. What matters is that essential facilities were sharply defined within the context of the whole and were made readily accessible. By these means cities and towns became more apprehensible. Since this process took place across the empire, the sum of its effects was considerable. The frequent rhetorical use by contemporary writers of cities as images of empire, of the word city as a device to evoke the nature of civilization, appears in this light to be based solidly on reality. A step toward a kind of architectural democracy had been taken. Not that the Roman world was democratic, but rather that the architecture of connection made it clear that much of a city or town was given over to nearly classless public ground. Thoroughfares and plazas, the architectural equals of other public structures, were common property.

IV

PASSAGE ARCHITECTURE

ROMAN ARMATURES are intermittently punctuated and measured out by arches, way stations (such as exedras and fountains), and other apparently secondary structures. Unitary and discontinuous, in contrast to connective architecture, they are even so essential, articulative parts of finished cities and towns. At first they may seem randomly positioned, miscellaneous building types, some functional in a practical sense and some not. But they comprise a clearly defined group, an architecture of passage, that marked significant armature points and transitions and provided amenities along the way. Passage architecture is a proper urban building category, a basic constituent of urban public circuitry that also made cities and towns visually more apprehensible and vivid.

Passage buildings are found at armature junctions and deflections, at entrances and intersections, and alongside thoroughfares and plazas. They were not intended to be entered, to be used for any significant commercial, political, or religious activity, and so were rarely enclosed. Most lacked doors or barriers and were fully open on one or more sides, their volumes interpenetrating freely with the flowing core spaces of their armatures. Passage architecture was one of junctions and pauses, fashioning urban rhythms along the armature without impeding circulation. As it delimited urban areas or sections without separating them and offered respite for the moment in a public setting, this architecture enhanced and enriched streets and plazas and helped set off meaningfully the open-air diurnal activities that took place there.

No formal system, in the sense of a plan type or model, can be found in the site distribution of these buildings; locations were not often determined by city planning. Unlike such buildings as baths or theatres, they were not much intended to be major goals, places for specific activities, though some at central locations doubled as landmarks. Mostly they were inserted, in the course of time, into existing urban situations, amplifying and reinforcing any architectural directives already in place, or increasing the number of public amenities available. This additive process, so clearly recorded at Djemila and Timgad, contributed substantially to the formation of mature Roman urbanism. If an imperial town is envisioned without its passage architecture, without any civic or imperial arches, any fountains or exedras, it will appear comparatively impoverished and characterless, less identifiably Roman than in fact it was. And since much of this highly visible public architecture was as heavily freighted with meaning as any temple, it contributed powerfully to the assertive symbolic composition of the cities and towns.

ARCHES

After the column and the wall, the arch is the most common visible Roman building element. In monumental form it is probably the best-known image of Roman times. Its structural versatility and many functional and symbolic uses insured its presence empire-wide. Freestanding or as part of an extended structure, it is found in nearly every architectural context. Although the monumental triumphal arch (in fact usually honorary, not triumphal) comes to mind first, many other spacious arches appeared in the cities and towns. By imperial times gates and street or civic arches (*iani*) were essential to the Roman urban scene. Like the orders, arches are quickly assimilated by the eye and seem like simple formal concepts, but like the orders, they are not. They were deeply embedded in urban experience both functionally and symbolically, appearing at different locations for varying purposes while repeating overhead the same primary, unambiguous half-round shape.

Above all an arch is a mechanism of transit and transition. It sharply marks a division between two areas or places without sealing off either; in essence it is a large-scale perforation in a wall. The axis of its opening exerts powerful directional and organizing forces. The archway proper invites passage and suggests the presence beyond of a place different from that before it, of an experience in contrast to that of the present, near side. Archway axes organize space and traffic as funnels regulate flow. However chaotic that traffic or space may be, it is forced by the organizing forms and implications of the arch into more systematic patterns. Arches, similar to valves adjusted for flow and pressure, were not set about entirely at random. Placed at nodal armature points, large enough to be seen from a distance and thus impressed in advance upon one's awareness, monumental arches were powerful urban instruments. Because of their wide, unobstructed voids, outlined in formal sympathy with the spatial envelope implied by outstretched human limbs, they quickened the sense of passage and deepened its meaning.[29]

Monumental arches are ambiguous in several ways. They fuse localities while suggesting division, and though they may stand across a path they do not bar it. They first appeared as wall openings, as portals, but in mid-Republican times detached, freestanding versions appeared.[30] In a pragmatic sense these were paradoxical because they were openings one could walk around. In every archway, the radiality implied by its semicircular outline (so apparent if voussoir joints, real or applied, are visible) works in opposing directions simultaneously. It focuses down and in toward the curve's invisible center point, but at the same time suggests reciprocal extensions fanning outward and

71. Bara, arch of Licinius Sura; early second century

upward. The tension caused by this ambiguity is framed and regulated both visually and structurally by flanking walls or massive piers and by masonry piled up high above both the arch and its supports, a counterweight increased in many examples by buttressing orders and constellations of statuary. So a monumental arch is a complicated and in some ways subtle kind of building in spite of its massive, elemental forms. Clearly Roman architects and builders were aware both of this and of effects they could create by proper siting and appropriate decor.

80, 91 The most important quality of an archway is its transverse posture directly athwart the axis of a roadway or passage. It is this right-angled opposition of the lateral planes of a large opening to the path through it that makes an arch such an effective device. In the relationship between path and opening, it is important that the path is down on the ground and the arch high overhead, because this separation helps to dissipate the impact of their four-square confrontation and make the idea or impression of passage immedi-

3, 25 ately apprehensible. An archway declares or suggests a regional division that can be freely passed. But passage can occur only at a particular place which, because of the powerful contrast between the arched void and its palpable, solid enframement, is about as strongly located and marked as an empty opening can be. Arches are architectural forms that grant permission to proceed along a particular line, a quality also inhering in freestanding versions because they repeat the large-scale forms and therefore the meaning of city gates and of arcuated entranceways to enclosed public places. Overhead, an arch curves up, across, and down in one smooth, continuous figure tangent to its twin supports, avoiding the sense of rigidity and of the individuality of parts suggested by orthogonally shaped, trabeated openings. Thus archways are particularly suited to urban contexts, where unobstructed division and clearly marked axial directives are needed, and where a degree of visual coherence, brought about by iterating a single basic image (not necessarily at the same size), is desired.

Transverse arches were used liberally to call attention to thoroughfares, part of a predisposition, especially strong from the beginning of the second century, to add imperial and civic arches to cities and towns. Some minimal figures: Verulamium had two, Djemila seven, Thibilis two, Lepcis Magna seven, Timgad three, Athens one, Gerasa two, Ptolemais in Cyrenaica one, Pompeii four, Merida perhaps two, and Rome three across the Via Flaminia alone. A complete list would be very long. Most were erected over thoroughfares—at intersections, terminal points, or the angles of segments—a practice echoed in the countryside when arches were built to mark borders (Bara) or bridge crossings (Alcantara; St.-Chamas; Antioch on the Maeander). Thoroughfares and arches belonged to each other, the high, open frames advertising the paths of earthbound ribbons of streets. The locating, fixing quality first seen in the city gate was applied to thoroughfares repeatedly, as if they might otherwise lose their way. Even stair-streets could be anchored by arches (Tivoli). Avenues extending beyond original town walls sometimes terminated in monumental arches (Hierapolis; Gerasa; Sbeitla; Timgad). Arches in line, acting as a kind of scaffolding, sketchily intimated an invisible connecting vault overhead. They implied that the rising volume generated by a thoroughfare's three sides did not extend upward indefinitely while emphasizing the presence and significance of the street as no other device could (Pompeii; Thibilis; Ostia; Lepcis Magna; Gerasa; Rome).

71, 72, 73

74

Siting was crucial. When enough information is available, it is always worth considering what was seen through an archway—both along the extended passageway axis and from the sides of the approaching street or plaza. Roman designers often plotted the gradual revelation of monuments and architectural climaxes with care, as during the ascent at Palestrina, through the gates and courts of the great temple complex at Baalbek, or up the approach to the Temple of Artemis at Gerasa (whose stair systems were described in chapter III); the potentialities of the monumental gateway fitted this predisposition nicely. Even if some urban arches were placed without any conscious intention of framing a particular view, defining vistas remains an obvious result of putting up a large arch. What Roman architect or builder could have been unaware of this, of the widening angle of vision as an archway was gained?

72. Alcantara, Trajanic bridge; 104

73. St.-Chamas, bridge; late first century?

74. Arches in sequence along thoroughfares. Above, Pompeii, looking northwest from the forum along the Via del Foro; left, Lepcis Magna, looking southwest from the Arch of Tiberius to the quadrifrons of Trajan

In order to emphasize the principal functions of an arch—view-framing, penetration, entrance, passage, and transition—familiar design elements were used to articulate its structural surfaces. In a world of so much trabeated architecture these pilasters, columns, plinths, pediments, and mouldings brought civic and triumphal arches into harmony with their surroundings and enlivened them with strong patterns of light and shade. Symmetrically disposed, applied elements enframed the opening, often in an elaborate fashion, furthering the contrast between solid and void and helping to focus and fix the directive and organizing powers of the whole. And by being given traditional symbolic content, the unadorned basic forms were, so to speak, civilized.

Armature arches vary in type and location:

> Outside the walls, astride major roads leading to principal gates, freestanding arches of the imperial "triumphal"—usually honorary or commemorative—type
>
> Gates and portals in town walls
>
> Entrances to major public buildings and enclosures inside the walls
>
> Astride thoroughfares inside the walls, often but not always imperial arches. Those that are not, such as the walkway arches alongside the Lepcis Magna nymphaeum plaza or the arch over the angle of the main street at Djemila, are called here for convenience civic arches (though when dilapidated they cannot always be distinguished from triumphal or honorary arches, and the two categories can overlap)
>
> Astride intersections of internal thoroughfares meeting at right angles (the four-way or quadrifrons arch, with four piers set on a square plan), often imperial, sometimes triumphal monuments; these are discussed separately below.

Armature patterns were repeatedly anchored at these points. There were three arches in the forum at Pompeii, with two more across one of its approaches; at least ten of various kinds at Djemila; six in the original forum at Rome—seven if the Arch of Titus is included; at least four inside the walls at Bosra; and so on. In 1958 Pallottino published a list of 364 triumphal and honorary arches compiled from all sources (some are known only from inscriptions and coins); fifty years earlier, Curtis had listed and described seventy-nine standing ones.[31] There is much variation in size and the number of openings. The maximum height of imperial monumental arches is about 21 m. (the Arch of Constantine in Rome; the extramural arch of Hadrian's time at Gerasa); city gates rise to 29.5 m. (the Porta Nigra at Trier) and higher (the final, late antique state of gates in the Wall of Aurelian in Rome, such as the Porta Appia [S. Sebastiano]). Urban archways usually have from one to four ground-level openings, with one and three the most common. City gates may have arched openings above their passageways (Rome; Trier; Verona), but civic arches rarely do, imperial ones apparently never.

As urban elements, arches came into their own in Italy during the second century B.C. Arched city gates, as at Cosa and Falerii Novi (early and late third century B.C., respectively), or at Ferentino (the Porta Sanguinaria, second century B.C.), were a common sight. The first lengthy stretches of arches supporting an aqueduct channel were built in 141 B.C. (the Aqua Marcia), and by the end of the century arches and simple vaults were in use for both practical and aesthetic purposes. Doubled city gateways—two separate arched openings in line over an entrance axis—were built, as at Ferentino (the Porta di Casamari of the 70s B.C.). In 196 B.C., freestanding arches had been erected in Rome in the Circus Maximus and the Forum Boarium, and six years later one was raised on the Capitoline. In 121 B.C. a victory arch was built at the eastern end of the main Forum, spanning the Via Sacra next to the Regia. These lost arches, platforms or backdrops for statues and displays of booty, were Roman analogues of Greek columns crowned by statues of worthies. They were also the formal and symbolic antecedents of the Augustan monuments that insured the future success of the monumental imperial arch. So during two and a half centuries, as the influence of Hellenistic forms in Italy steadily increased, spare utilitarian structures evolved into the arches of Roman passage architecture.

75. Verona, Arch of the Borsari; probably late first century

This process was energized by the dominating image of the rounded, embellished city gate, the doorway to urban life and the peripheral anchor of the crosstown armature. The pictorial evidence, coins in particular, shows that city gates ranked with temples and altars as elements most often selected for representation.[32] Going back to the third century B.C., as we have seen, this image, combined with that of the city wall came to stand for the concept, the idea, of the city. By the time of Augustus, the arched city gateway had been fully metamorphosed into the type of arch commonly called triumphal. Its architectural treatment was modified subsequently, but the idea was well established by the beginning of the first century. The dozen or so Augustan arches sufficiently well preserved for analysis, taken together with the numismatic evidence, show that most forms found in subsequent imperial arches were in use by then.

Several kinds of monumental archways are found in the Augustan repertory. One opening, three and four openings, and the four-arched, square-plan quadrifrons all appear. There was much variety. The bulky, imposing imperial attic appears fully developed. The orders do not stand free, but ressauts and engaged pedestals are used to stress the presence and verticality of the orders. At Ephesus part or all of the triple gateway of Mazeus and Mithridates (4/3 B.C.) was two bays deep. The shorter sides of 76 the arch at Orange, perhaps erected in 20 or thereabouts, display arcuated lintels, features appearing in contemporary painting. These prefigure a powerful symbolic geometry of mature Roman architecture. The familiar triple archway appears there and elsewhere.

Whether or not it is correct to say that one erected in the Roman Forum in 19 B.C. 77 (the Parthian arch) was conceived as three single openings linked in the same plane, it was a triple gateway, the center void arched, the flanking ones trabeated.[33] It was very influential. The central opening was set in the usual way between powerful piers with a prominent attic above. The side gateways were trabeated, and pediments reached to a level just below the central arch's keystone. A coin of 17/15 B.C. shows statues of soldiers above the pediment peaks and a quadriga atop the attic. The orders rose from a common elevated level of plinths and pedestals; the inner ones of the side gateways overlapped with the central piers. The result was a highly articulated scenic tableau of imperial images symmetrically composed low-high-low from left to right. It was more scenic than some later triple archways contained in single massive blocks—a form inviting the additional articulative relief freestanding orders partially supply. This more common triple system is found at Orange, the first known one of its kind (if the customary early date is correct), though there the orders are engaged; such monuments are more like detached city gates than the Forum arch. Other triple structures of the period were built at Arles (6/4 B.C.) and at Antioch in Pisidia, as well as at Ephesus. Presumably the Augustan Porta Esquilina at Rome, replaced in the third century by the Arch of Gallienus, had three arches like its successor. Other city gates of more or less 78 Augustan date had four openings, a central, high pair flanked by smaller ones (Turin; the Porte St.-André at Autun).

So by the beginning of the empire monumental arches were already established as

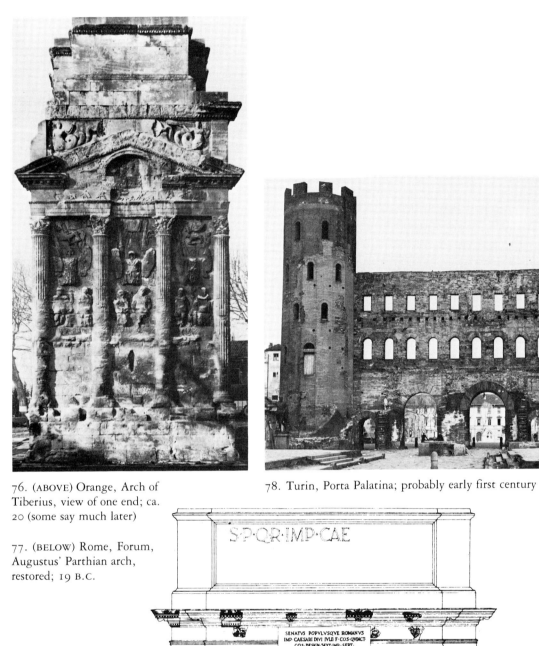

76. (ABOVE) Orange, Arch of
Tiberius, view of one end; ca.
20 (some say much later)

77. (BELOW) Rome, Forum,
Augustus' Parthian arch,
restored; 19 B.C.

78. Turin, Porta Palatina; probably early first century

S·P·Q·R·IMP·CAE

SENATVS·POPVLVSQVE·ROMANVS
IMP·CAESARI·DIVI·IVLI·F·COS·QVINCT·
COS·DESIGN·SEXT·IMP·SEPT·
RE·PVBLICA·CONSERVATA

symbols both of Roman rule and of Roman cities; the freestanding imperial arch, set apart from other structures, was well on the way to becoming a primary urban instrument.[34] To separate the city gate from its structural and functional context and reproduce it frequently in the cities and towns was, from the point of view of working toward urban cohesion and an apposite urban symbolism, an inspired process. Few other city forms deliver their message so directly and effectively as these formidable stone bowers, these working arches put into fancy dress and assigned new roles. Their inseparability from thoroughfares is essential to their function. Urban examples are never found apart from them. Even in the countryside they mark Roman lines of connection and division. Those that stand close outside city walls double the effect of the city gates they premonitor, while fixing armature thoroughfares relentlessly even before the gates are reached—the one at Gerasa and the city gate beyond were nearly twins. Some formed entrances to fora or sanctuaries (Maktar; Petra; Pompeii, at the northwest
79 corner of the forum; Sbeitla). Kähler established a limited typology of twenty-four variants based on the number of openings (one and three) and the patterns of architectural decor, excluding pediments (the four-square quadrifrons spanning an orthogonal intersection was not included).[35] Some city gates were given triumphal-arch form
80 (Rimini; Asseria; Baalbek).

79. Sbeitla, forum entrance; probably mid-second century

80. Rimini, Arch of Augustus; 27 B.C.

In unmistakable formal harmony with these prominent objects were the civic arches found along armatures, across street angles (Damascus had two) and beside thoroughfares—the last-named giving onto plazas (Khamissa; Lepcis Magna, the market), 81 stairs (Djemila; Gerasa) and side streets (Tiddis; Rome; Palmyra). There were also the innumerable arched entrances and internal passageways of public buildings and the intramural arches of aqueduct bridges (Segovia; Merida; Aspendus; Rome, across the 82 Via Flaminia and the "Via Trionfale"). Fifty-three monumental arches are known in the capital, about a half-dozen of them Augustan. In the year 19, two arches were placed in the Forum of Augustus, at right angles to the rear of the flanks of the Temple of Mars Ultor, an arrangement paralleled by the two at Ostia by the Temple of Rome and Augustus, and those abutting the pronaos of the Temple of Jupiter in Pompeii.

81. Khamissa, lower, newer forum, wit
arches; third century?

82. Segovia, aqueduct; probably first
century

83. Tiddis, arch of the town gate

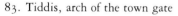

Building monumental arches, adding arched forms to established thoroughfares and
plazas, went on apace. No standard models were followed, for though imperial arches of
one or three openings were common, many variations were struck on the major theme.
These ranged from the Ephesus gate, a kind of transverse hall three bays wide and two
71, 83 deep, to the austere simplicity of the arch at Bara or the main portal at Tiddis, and from
the approximately catenary form of the Arch of Diocletian at Philae to the Doric gate of
Kibyra Minor.

84. Capera, quadrifrons; early second century

FOUR-SQUARE STRUCTURES

Right-angled thoroughfare intersections invited architectural emphasis. Influenced perhaps by Greek tetrastyle altars and the ancient, bronze-clad passage-shrine of Ianus Geminus in Rome, and beyond doubt by the rapid growth of interest in passage architecture, many cities and towns inserted four-square structures at armature junctions. There are two basic types, the roofed, baldacchino-like quadrifrons or four-arched building, usually but not always erected on a square plan, and the unroofed tetrakionion or four-unit monument, always of four elevated platforms set on a square plan, each usually carrying four columns, though sometimes apparently only one.[36] As usual, there was considerable variation in design and detail, though the basic characteristic remained the same: two armature axes, intersecting at the center of the structure's plan, were each framed symmetrically on either side of the intersection by arcuated or columnar architecture. The quadrifrons is found from Spain to Syria; known tetrakionia are, thus far, less common and confined to the east. At least one major quadrifrons, that at Carnuntum, was not empty, for it had a circular pedestal (presumably for a statue) at its center. The pavement of the Severan example at Lepcis Magna was raised three steps above the level of its intersecting streets (compare Richborough, paving core of a quadrifrons?). Small-scale versions of the form appear in non-armature settings, as at Lepcis Magna in the markets; others can be seen in funerary monuments, for example at

84
85

85. Palmyra, tetrakionion; third century?

86, 87 St.-Rémy; one from Ghirza is now in the Tripoli museum. At Vienne there is a smallish quadrifrons topped by a tall, slender pyramid (called "L'Aiguille," it embellished a circus spina).

    The *quadrifrons* generally stood free, though there were exceptions, as at Gerasa (the "north tetrapylon"), where the four piers block the walkways of both the thoroughfare and its intersecting avenue, and the four arches were approximately the same width as the street pavement; there were similar examples at Herculaneum, and perhaps at Milan. In some cases, two or all four faces were decorated with elaborate, honorific-arch fittings (Laodicea ad Mare, two faces; the Severan arch at Lepcis Magna and that of Caracalla at Tebessa, four). The oblong plan is not unknown (Laodicea ad Mare; Richborough?). Intermediate between the two-facade imperial arch and the quadrifrons are some arches that have both axial and subordinate lateral passageways, an arrangement hinted at but not carried through at Orange (the Arch of the Gavii at Verona;

88 Antinoöpolis; the east and central arches at Bosra). Although this kind of design probably did not influence the evolution of the quadrifrons, the two types are conceptually related. Quadrifrons arches at certain eastern sites were set in the middle of circular plazas (Jerusalem?; Bosra; Antioch on the Orontes).

35
    Tetrakionia had no piers to receive abutments and stood free in their plazas (circular at
16, 17 Gerasa, a truncated oval at Palmyra). At Anjar, which became an Omeyyad site, the
Frontispiece tetrakionion is a Roman creation upon which later construction was focused. At Ptolemais the evidence suggests that a single column was set upon each of four elevated platforms. The "tetracolumnar monument" of Diocletian's Camp at Luxor was located at the intersection of two colonnaded streets.[37] The size of the four platforms at Philippopolis and the wide spacing between them imply a tetrakionion, but their street-corner positions may suggest otherwise; the matter seems moot. Of related interest are
89 the blind tetrakionion tomb of the late 70s in the necropolis outside the Nocera gate at

86. (LEFT) St.-Rémy, monument of the Julii; early first century?

87. (BELOW) Ghirza, tomb (in the Tripoli Museum); fourth century

88. (BELOW LEFT) Bosra, east arch; second century

Pompeii, where the corners of all four tall piers are shaped as Corinthian columns three-quarters engaged, and the elaborate sixteen-column propylon (four files of four columns each), with its partially arcuated superstructure, found at Aphrodisias. The use of close-coupled columns carrying at most only entablature-enframed platforms can probably be traced to Hellenistic "extravaganzas" of the kind found for example at Delphi: two columns close together joined by a length of entablature carrying statuary. There were perhaps tetrakionia at Antioch on the Orontes (where there were at least three quadrifrons arches and probably several more), but the texts are not explicit on this point.[38] Tetrakionia are important evidence for the desire to create scenic architectural effects along the armatures of imperial cities and towns.

A four-square structure stands where the surveyor drove his stake or set up his sighting instrument, a point highly charged with meaning, a place holding a whole town or city quarter in fealty. From it a governing order was laid upon the earth roundabout through the agency of two intersecting, controlling lines. Four-square

84

89. Pompeii, tomb in the form of a tetrakionion; before 79

structures celebrate the location and significance of these spots, giving them spatial definition and visual character. The monuments themselves are elaborate and eye-catching, a complex architecture of perforation. As one's movement energizes the effects of parallax, the monuments' volumetric nature is displayed. Vistas through the arches are compound, in contrast to those seen through single-axis arches, creating a shifting, coulisse effect, and relationships among the sixteen columns of a tetrakionion appear to alter steadily. In sculpture and on coins, quadrifrons arches are often shown obliquely, 90 identifying them as such and emphasizing their powerful volumetric, three-dimensional qualities.[39]

At the root of these effects lie the implications of four-sidedness combined with perforation. These qualities change the single-axis effects of imperial and civic arches into something quite different, into palpable spaces suggesting more or less inhabitable volumes, covered or not. They are baldacchino-like armature houses, guarding points of intersection, marking important locations in the urban construct without actually

90. Rome, Vatican Museum, Tomb of the Haterii, relief of a temple-tomb and other structures; early second century

standing on them. At the same time they receive, note, and then transmit the directive forces of their streets. Like compass roses, they deal with matters well beyond the range of their immediate, tangible form. They express the tendency seen in imperial architecture to investigate the potentials of structures not largely bound by planar walls, to intermingle volumes, to broaden and enliven the received tradition. Housing and celebrating hallowed places with appropriate architecture had been a central generative force of that tradition, one adapted effectively to urban purposes in imperial times. As this took place, the transfer to secular functions of architectural forms and elements long associated with sacred localities was accelerated.

ARCH FACADES

The chief reasons for embellishing arch facades with carved architectural elements can be easily identified. City gates had been so treated since the third century B.C. That at Falerii Novi is a spare but handsome early example, its decor limited to strongly-defined impost mouldings joined to a semicircular archivolt traveling round the outer periphery of the voussoirs, a carved ornament at its summit. There are no orders, and the city wall proper and the arch supports are one. There was a strong need to relate arches visually to street and plaza architecture and to that of public buildings; a sufficient harmony of design with these dominating structures was essential. Finally, and perhaps most important, the symbolism of the naked arch-form needed to be associated unmistakably with imperial images found everywhere—symbolic statuary, framed niches or aedicules, the scenic imperial wall of orders and planes reaching forward and back, and attics with framed plaques carrying large, boldly-formed inscriptions.

80   The Rimini arch, erected in 27 B.C., the same year Octavian received the title Augustus from the Senate, is instructive. In addition to its honorific content, it was imperial also because it was a northern anchor of the Via Flaminia, the pendant of an arch by the Pons Mulvius in Rome where the road began, part of the extended interconnection of armatures of imperial cities and towns. Paired, engaged Corinthian columns are each topped by a full-bodied ressaut whose cymatium and corona form broad, plate-like projections similar to Brunelleschi's (S. Spirito). By contrast, the incipient ressauts

91   of the Augustan arches at Aosta (25 B.C.) and Pola (the Arch of the Sergii, 20/10 B.C.) are tentative and sedate, their outer sides continuous with the entablature returns of their flanks. Those at Rimini are of the fully-developed imperial kind with robust scroll modillions projecting abruptly from the wall face. Between them, only slightly forward from the wall face, is the outline of a pediment, its frieze and architrave almost entirely absorbed into the main structure. The pediment does not rest on the ressauts but, just touching them, is poised between them, a relationship seen on the quadrifrons at Laodicea ad Mare, in Pompeian painting (as in the scene of Iphigenia in Tauris in the House of Pinarius Cerialis), and incipiently at the Portico of Octavia.

The result is that the columns, with their projecting ressauts and bases, are strongly emphasized, suggesting that the pediment, frieze, and architrave are partly drawn back

91. Pola, Arch of the Sergii; late first century

into the solid structure behind. These are not to be thought of as forming part of a real building because in an architectural sense they are only sketched in, the pediment in a manner rather like that of open tent-flaps on Trajan's Column. These forms lie behind the paired columns literally and symbolically, suggesting both a greater depth than actually exists and the presence of proper urban structures behind. All together, these facade elements form an economical city image made up of imperial symbols—the arch, the Corinthian order, the ressauts, attic, appropriate sculpture (now gone), an inscription, and the ancient fastigium—an armature frontispiece, an abbreviated table of contents of that to come.

Their sculpture and sometimes their inscriptions apart, the great majority of imperial and civic arches seem to have had duplicate facades, though there were exceptions (Petra). Some had non-parallel faces such as the north gate at Gerasa and the angle arch over the great colonnaded street at Palmyra. Oblique roadway axes sometimes prevented front-and-back symmetry (the Porta Maggiore). Much detailed evidence has been lost, but if the familiar arches of Rome are representative (Titus, Septimius Severus, Constantine), triumphal structures were architecturally symmetrical. Even the best-preserved arches lack their original statuary atop their attics, forms that gave these huge blocks dramatic, flaring silhouettes. This effect can be seen now and then in a complete modern version, as at the Arc de Triomphe du Carrousel at the Louvre, whose architectural body is two-thirds the size of the Arch of Septimius Severus (compare the quadrigas atop the end pavilions of the Vittoriano in Rome). Texts, coins, and reliefs record the profusion of sculpture that arose from pedestals, ressauts, and above all from attics. The engravers of coin dies exaggerated the relative size of these creations, but the fact remains that honorific arches—and probably others as well—were intended to carry statues and that this silhouetted sculpture was large enough to remain prominent even in contrast with the massive forms below.

An attic usually rises from a corniced level not far above the centered crown of the 76 arch. Some attics are zoned horizontally (Orange), most are not. Attic-high projections 58 in the form of unfeatured, engaged piers are common. These are almost always centered 91 over the orders below, but there are exceptions (the Arch of the Sergii at Pola, which also has, unusually, a central projection; Orange, whose very broad side projections are not centered over the orders). Now and then an attic will be divided by engaged piers supported by corbels (Cillium). On honorific arches, the central flat surface usually carried an inscription, though sculpture was placed there sometimes (the Severan quadrifrons at Lepcis Magna; Orange again). Inscription plaques were framed by mouldings surrounding the formulary phrases, the letters sometimes cast in bronze and then attached, but usually cut into the stone (and then painted) in the stately V-trench forms that became common in Augustan times. They "truly revolutionized epigraphic writing and made possible the use of harder stones such as travertine and—with increasing frequency from the beginning of the Principate—marble from Luni," lettering that "came to appear as a characteristic instrument of the master race."[40]

The vertical sequence of form and of meaning in the honorific arch is significant. The archway rises from pavement level, flanked by engaged or freestanding orders that carry an entablature directly over the arch crown. Next comes the attic, a length of thick wall, with its official content. Centered above that was the main sculpture group, often accompanied left and right by statues of deities or worthies. In this graded hierarchy, rising from tangible, familiar ground through a region of framing architectural forms to a zone of exalted meaning, the attic played an important role. An attic is neatly packaged by horizontal mouldings and, usually, by vertical, pier-like projections. Normally it is at least as tall as the piers below are wide, its weight and position insuring the stability of the whole. It separates the arch crown or crowns sufficiently from the superposed sculpture, a division necessary for satisfactory proportions and visual effects; 92 compare the present condition of the arches at Reims and Aosta, which lack attics, or that at Susa, where the attic is perhaps a little low. One of the results of interposing attics between the arches proper and their crowning, freestanding sculpture is that the sculpture thus rose from stout, profoundly stable bases, above which it appeared outlined against the sky.

Honorific arches, including the quadrifrons type, were often crowned with horse-drawn quadrigas; judging from pictorial and textual evidence, elephant teams were not uncommon. If the pictorial evidence is reliable, the animals were not often all set parallel to one another; the outer two, or at least their heads, are seen turned out and away from the axis of the car. The single figures frequently found to the left and right anchor pyramidal, A-B-A compositions of the kind common in Roman design. Relief sculpture—rectilinear and round panels, victories (in the spandrels), wreaths, and swags—gave added vitality and content.

Just as important are the applied architectural elements found on every example. The first principle of this embellishment is the enframement, by means of orders and related devices, of the archway or archways. The second is symmetry: centerlines rule all, and left must equal right in every detail. These principles are obvious; less so are the varieties of means employed in applying them and the resulting effects. Both principles work toward the same end, focusing the whole composition on the empty, arched-over space at the middle (a few two- and four-arched designs are exceptions). In the simplest work, as at the single-opening, extramural arch at Philippi, all eight corners were encased in pilasters and the voussoir semicircle outlined by an archivolt; above, there was an entablature and a plain attic. In this way controlling lines were reinforced and their definition articulated, techniques found throughout the typology without exception. As the number of verticals and mouldings increased and niches and aediculas were added, the rhythms among the lateral distances between the various elements became more complex, culminating in the three-arched monument with two pairs of orders, each pair flanking a niche above a subordinate archway (Sbeitla). With the introduction of freestanding orders, definition by light and shade became more pronounced (Tebessa; 79

92. Reims, Porte de Mars; ca. 100?

Timgad; Petra; the Arches of Septimius Severus and Constantine at Rome). Highly scenic arches such as these are stylistically related to the incipiently baroque, push-pull wall systems of theatre stage-buildings and the marble halls of palatine and bath buildings.

Of the orders, the Corinthian predominated. Corners might be rounded, literally, by
92 columns three-quarters engaged; at Reims, pairs of engaged columns join at each outer corner. By such means enframement was made complete, and the simple forms of plain arches were turned into apparent buildings. When pediments were included—they had been placed over arched wall openings in Hellenistic buildings, as at the theatre at Letoum—the illusion was reinforced. They appeared on monumental arches across the empire, and though Hadrianic designers in particular may have favored them, there does not seem to have been any rule, typological or otherwise, for governing their use
93 (Orange; on the Haterii monument; Maktar; Uzappa; Athens; Baalbek; Gerasa; Alexandria [seen on coins, with a Doric entablature]; Antinoöpolis [with the same feature]). Various kinds appear, in different positions—the floating type of Rimini, the arcuated forms of Orange and possibly of the central arch at Bosra, the split, acutely pointed ones of the Severan quadrifrons at Lepcis Magna, the segmental ones carried by the pairs of
94 freestanding columns at Timgad, and those over the flank niches of the lost arch of Nero in Rome (also known from coins). These signs of diversity within the general type are

93. Rome, Vatican Museum, Tomb of the Haterii, relief of Flavian buildings; early second century

94. Timgad, honorific arch; ca. 200

paralleled by details such as the pulvinated frieze of the east arch at Zana and the cubical corbels under the attic pier-forms at Cillium.

Another feature of monumental arches is the niche or aedicula, common in three-bay honorific examples and seen on the quadrifrons as well (Tripoli in Libya; the Ianus Quadrifrons in the Forum Boarium in Rome). These recesses lessen the sense of ponderous weightiness, and, whether round- or flat-headed, relate their arches to the many similar forms of the urban architectural landscape. The round-headed variety implies the presence of sculpture in antiquity. The forty-eight arched niches of the Ianus Quadrifrons, small in relative scale, are unusual, probably unique; if they all contained statues, as the arches of the Flavian Amphitheatre apparently did, the building would have been vividly externalized. Sometimes recesses are placed low in the composition (Djemila; the Arch of Titus); sometimes, in triple arches, high (Timgad; the Forum arch at Sbeitla; the extramural arch at Gerasa; the angle arch at Palmyra); and sometimes, beside single archways, they are doubled high and low (the North Gate at Gerasa; the east arch at Bosra). In triple arches where recesses are centered above the lesser openings, and in single-opening arches where they are doubled vertically, the pilasters or columns rise up through two implied horizontal zones, and the result is in effect a two-story or colossal order; compare the treatment of the temenos wall and the inner propylaea face of the Temple of Bel at Palymra, the inner face of the propylaea of the Temple of Artemis at

12

79, 94

95

95. Palmyra, Temple of Bel, temenos detail; ca. 100

96   Gerasa, and the interior of the groma ("praetorium") at Lambaesis. In some examples
43   the impost moulding of the arch cuts right across the engaged orders (Uzappa; compare
157 the banded doorway columns of the Temple of Venus at Baalbek), and, in a few, orders
are placed one atop the other, joined at the level of the lateral extensions of the impost
moulding (Althiburos; Saintes, bridge arches paired on axis, moved from their original
location).

What these data describe is something of the wide variety of means employed to
obtain the same result: a composition whose balance and symmetry emphasized the
primacy of a centered, empty space—the archway or central archway itself. The range of
complexity is considerable, from the spare clarity of the Arch of Gallienus in Rome to
94   the proto-baroque intensity of Timgad and the staccato chiaroscuro of the entablature of
97   the Arch of Titus. Sometimes the detailing is slightly coarse but the massing splendid
62   (Orange); here and there the proportions seem ill-found (Maktar). In some examples the
designers doubled the enframing systems to create three centered devices: the arch, an
intermediate frame around it, and a still larger one embracing the whole (Uzappa;
Maktar; the Severan quadrifrons at Lepcis Magna). Enframements are almost entirely

96. (LEFT) Lambaesis, the groma, interior detail; probabl
mid-third century

97. (ABOVE) Rome, Arch of Titus, entablature detail;
early 80s

non-structural. If the orders are engaged or formed as pilasters, they are hardly more than limnings on the structural body of the arch; if they are freestanding they are too tight to that body to serve any practical purpose. Nothing was included that would threaten the compact, centered wholeness of these unitary, self-contained entities, but enough was included in each one to insure a ready mutual association among them in the mind's eye.

This then was the overriding significance of Roman civic and imperial arches, for whatever the details of their design they were omnipresent, mutually interrelated symbols of the times, wholly urban in origin. Their chief design characteristics gave them their ideological substance, a substance simultaneously invoking things sacred and temporal, traditional and imperial. These interlocking meanings were expressed by combining simple but powerfully evocative forms—rounded archways—with classical design elements. The results were seen in almost all cities and towns, along whose armatures arches rose repeatedly.

WAY STATIONS

Way stations—public fountains, exedras, porticoed courtyards—were also essential fixtures of complete Roman towns. Like arches, they were urban caesuras, marking off armatures into experiential segments of random lengths. Unlike arches, they were placed beside, not across, lines of communication. And unlike arches they were social structures, made for pausing or resting, an architecture of invitation, of the opportunity to quit, for the moment, the activity of the pavement. Often they were fitted with features for leaning and sitting—steps, ledges, stone railings, or seats—and in porticos there was strolling room.[41] Most were unwalled on the side or sides where they opened directly onto thoroughfares or plazas; some were entered through column screens or spacious gateways. Few were roofed over completely. Way stations were thus a species of half-building, their volumes, only partially defined, joining directly with those of contiguous streets and squares, ready to receive diversions from the traffic alongside.

The Roman habit of bringing water, often over considerable distances, to cities and towns through aqueducts from higher points made *fountains* commonplace. Conservative calculations for certain sites show that by any standards they were well provided with water by what Strabo calls "veritable rivers".[42] The daily per capita supply to Rome in the high imperial age was very roughly the same as that today to Cambridge, Massachusetts, an industrial city of consequence and thus water-hungry.[43] If aqueducts, or intramural springs (Buthrotum; Nîmes; Khamissa; Kasnakavo; Letoum) are found at a site, then there were fountains there. Public tubs of water could also be supplied from wells by buckets, enchained or not. If there is a large bath building, an aqueduct is very likely, though there are exceptions at riverain sites, and there were baths, such as the central ones at Herculaneum, that drew their water by bucket-chains from wells. Some towns depended entirely on wells. If appearances are correct, the remains of once continuously flowing fountains would probably be revealed if unrestricted excavation were possible (London).[44] Britain, where excavation is necessarily often piecemeal, to say the least, is instructive in this respect. About a half-dozen aqueducts are known there for certain (not the spectacular variety with their delivery channels carried on arched bridges over low terrain, but the more usual kind whose channels lie on or under the earth); perhaps half again as many are probable. But because of archaeological conditions only a few fountains are known (Corbridge; York; perhaps Verulamium). Yet these few aqueducts, given the hydraulic nature—indeed basis—of Roman urban culture, almost guarantee the presence in ancient times of other public fountains in Britain, however modest.

Djemila's armature fountains and the plaza nymphaeum at Lepcis Magna suggest the range of kinds and sizes. There are two basic types: the plain rectangular tub or basin, standing free or set against a wall, with or without architectural embellishment; and the type wherein a large basin is set off by an elevated architectural backdrop (major armature fountains are of the latter kind). They range from basins set against, or in, colonnades, single wall niches, or aediculas (Ostia; Side; Hierapolis), to hillsides lined

98
99
100

98. Ostia, fountain on the main thoroughfare

99. Hierapolis, fountain

100. Gerasa, fountain on the main thoroughfare

101. Tipasa, nymphaeum beside the main thoroughfare; ca. 300

102. Olympia, fountain of Herodes Atticus; 160

with repeated fountain niches (Todi; Taormina; the east flank of the Temple of the Divine Claudius in Rome), to the grand scenic water displays, with one or more rows of niches, orders, and statuary, rising behind the basin or basins. These last are found in major cities east and west (Tipasa; Olympia; Ephesus; Amman; the "Trofeo di Mario" in Rome). 101, 102

Some monumental structures, whose basins were often large, elongated pools, were essentially stretches of walls, however richly en-niched and decorated (Perge; the Septizodium in Rome). Such walls were frequently framed symmetrically by projecting spur walls (Side; two each at Sbeitla and Gortyn). In another important variation, the basin is set off by an architectural backdrop of curved or trapezoidal plan, the whole forming an exedra, vaulted or not (Vienne; Nicopolis ad Istrum; Bosra). Other variants appear. There were also important fountains that did not fit into either category (Timgad, the octagonal fountain; Ostia, the Ninfeo degli Eroti; Corinth, the Peirene fountain; Rome, the Meta Sudans; Khamissa, the great pools).

Exedras—curved demi-plazas or recesses of semicircular plan unwalled along their straight, open sides—appeared in classical architecture from at least the mid-fifth century B.C. (Delphi). They served many functions, commemorative and ritual among others. Exedra tombs were common (the Via dei Sepolcri at Pompeii), markets less so 103 (Timgad; Corinth). Exedras can be small, like those scattered around the agora at 55 Priene, or huge, as at the Fora of Augustus and Trajan, the Horti Aciliorum on the Pincian hill (about 120 m. in diameter), or as at Beauvais or the ceremonial forecourt of the Jupiter-temple complex at Baalbek. Larger ones were often porticoed (Stobi; the

103. Pompeii, exedra tomb

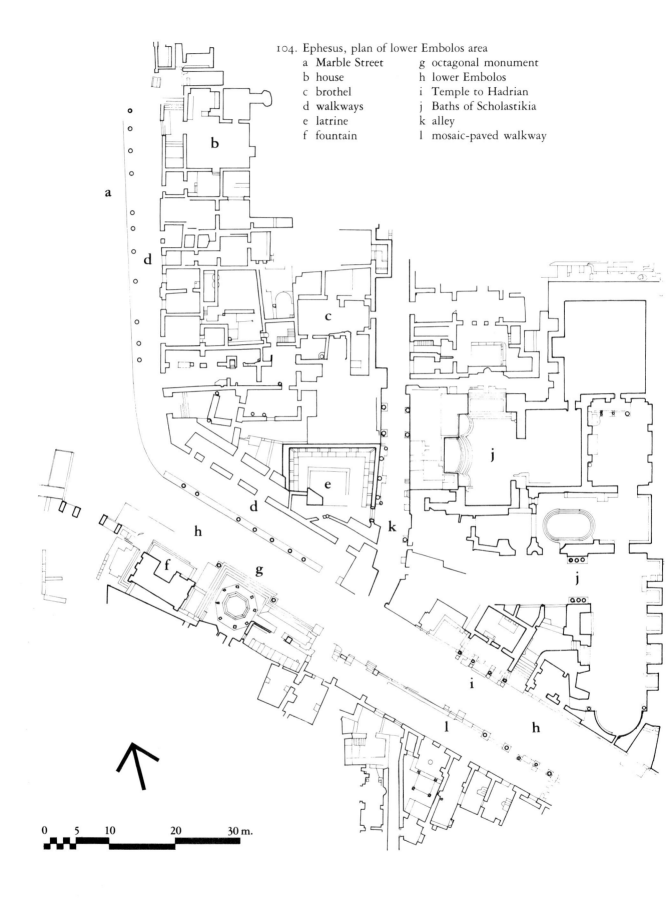

104. Ephesus, plan of lower Embolos area

a Marble Street
b house
c brothel
d walkways
e latrine
f fountain

g octagonal monument
h lower Embolos
i Temple to Hadrian
j Baths of Scholastikia
k alley
l mosaic-paved walkway

0   5   10   20   30 m.

nymphaeum plaza example at Lepcis Magna; the Porticus Absidata at Rome; the   51
truncated example beside the main thoroughfare of Ostia next to the Foro della Statua
Eroica). There were rectilinear ones, but they were not as common, and along major
Roman thoroughfares, curved plans prevailed (Bosra; Palmyra; beside the Severan   16, 17
boulevard at Lepcis Magna).   36

Not as common as fountains, exedras were nevertheless common and significant
enough to require consideration in any analysis of passage architecture. They helped
expand narrow and constricted spatial patterns, and they accentuated the amplified
volumes of grander systems. Propylaea functioned similarly. Porticoed courtyards,
more fully enclosed and therefore less immediately open to the thoroughfares they
flanked, had a comparable effect. Some were commemorative, erected by affluent locals
for general use (Thuburbo Maius; Palmyra), some were marked for such political
purposes as voting (Rome). Some were landscaped and planted. Finally, passage along
an armature was often marked by a variety of freestanding commemorative, honorific,
and jingoist monuments—statuary groups, cenotaphs, shrines, memorials, and freestanding columns and column-screens (along the Via Sacra, Rome, and the Embolos,   104
Ephesus; in the sanctuary and along the upper thoroughfare at Cyrene; Apamea; Brindisi; Ankara; Alexandria).

Much passage architecture was given to the cities and towns by their citizens.
Fountains were favored. One donor gave Sabratha twelve. Thirteen, several of them
gifts, are known along the thoroughfares of Ostia, where by the third century there was a
"positive mania" for them.[45] Frontinus records the presence in Rome of 39 ornamental
fountains and 591 basins.[46] Djemila had at least five public fountains along its armature. Locations were prominent and function unmistakable. Street intersections, and
the points where streets met plazas, were popular sites (Vienne; Laodicea ad Lycum;
Lepcis Magna; Hippo Regius; Bosra). By the end of the second century, apparently, a
thoroughfare without a fountain was unknown. So avenues and plazas were not only
spatially dilated and marked off by way stations, they were also enlivened and enriched,
not least by the sight and sound of moving water and the light reflected from its rarely
stilled surface.

Way stations were for pausing, for lingering, for gathering informally, stopping-off
places along a town's central circuit. Some, particularly those backed by benches or
walls, were a species of small theatre, their stages the busy streets and plazas alongside.   101, 103
Well placed for observing the human parade, with wide openings and angles of vision,   143, 204
they surely encouraged idling, though the provision of amenities answered practical
needs too. Because most way stations tended to be restorative, they were not empty
gestures but important servants of the urban symbiosis. Their variety of shapes and
functions is no impediment to placing them all in the same architectural category, for
they were all at the service of a single, clear need—relief both spatial and personal from
the constrictions and conditions of life along the armature. And they are good evidence,
as so much passage architecture is, for the readiness in imperial times to ignore associations of particular forms with specific functions, to apply formal solutions long associated with a single building type to various others.

105. Gerasa, nymphaeum beside the main thoroughfare; 191

Armatures were expanded and articulated here and there by these structures. Connective spaces in front of them lost something of their restrictive spatial character for the moment as two volumes, one of connection and one of passage, flowed freely into one another; places were not way stations if entrance was barred or inhibited. Recession was their common feature. Space was drawn off and away from the architecture of connection to be formed and shaped by continuous surfaces low or high. These boundaries might or might not be curved. The essential factor was that whatever their shapes, way station spaces were joined to connective spaces only, so that each way station was a pneumatic extension of its armature, an eddy in the stream of activity, formed where an armature border was temporarily widened. The necessary characteristic of this kind of architecture can for convenience be called concavity—a central, informing quality of imperial architecture. It was manifested in a way station building by the fact that one side was entirely open, a void. Behind and beyond that imaginary plane the boundary of the space receded from a viewer looking in from the street or plaza. The result was like the open-faced volume of a Moslem iwan, which, though subordinated to that of a much larger court, remains clearly defined even so.

101, 105

Because of these characteristics—concavity and incompleteness—most way stations, although wide open and immediately accessible, were yet partly enclosed. Thus they were embracing and sheltering places, in a sense protective, offering the harboring quality alluded to above. This effect was emphasized because, paradoxically, incompleteness implied completion. Large half-cylinders, or three walls joined at right or obtuse angles, suggested the condition of complete enclosure: not the fact of it, but the possibility of it, the hint of its shape. Because they were clearly differentiated locations to head for and stop at, way stations were topographic and social objectives. No traffic flowed through them, for they did not lead anywhere. They were less chaotic places than the streets and squares they served and, by comparison, were fixed and finite.

URBAN ARTICULATION

Passage architecture performed several interrelated functions, each crucial to the creation of a properly Roman city or town. It provided amenities while visually enriching the surroundings, adding formal variety to them (a partial antidote to the monotony of blocks set on a grid plan). In addition, it was a system of signs with both cultural (associative) and topographical (locational) content. Most important, it was articulative, partitioning armatures into comprehensible—and apprehensible—segments and so answering the need to be able readily to envision city quarters and districts in the mind; the sum of these impressions formed one's transportable, recallable image of a town's core, of a systematically linked whole. Combined, passage architecture's functions constituted a primary visual and practical component of the architectural definition of imperial urbanism, vying with connective works and the civic building typology in importance.

Passage architecture was to be expected at Greek sanctuaries that had grown and filled in slowly, such as Delphi or Olympia. The strength of its popularity can also be seen in civic settings, as at Priene, where the planner's scrupulously orthogonal agora came to contain at least nine exedras—two rectangular and the rest semicircular—in addition to a profusion of other urban furniture. In Roman times fountains were placed beside the Athenian Panathenaic Way, incidents in the long process of accumulation of monuments there. It was perhaps natural to add to cities and towns in this way, but it is important that each addition marked another point or place along an armature, and that with few exceptions the distances between passage structures were unequal. The result was a kind of artistic parataxis, the product, apparently, of an almost irresistible compulsion, one victorious over even inhospitable grids.

Since this process took place without benefit of rules, without the sanction of theory, it appears that a natural or cultural impulse toward a particular kind of diversified urban landscape was being implemented. The location of a monumental arch across a thoroughfare was far more likely to have been determined by visual and symbolic considerations of the town as a whole and its membership in the imperial system than in response to a planner's determination, from on high, that the right spot was thus-and-such a one because of accepted urban design theory. The apparently aimless distribution of passage structures resulted from the cumulative nature of urban growth. And physically and artistically a Roman town, its salient qualities based in the last analysis upon the buildings and symbols of its armature, was not a place where planners' decisions were

1, 25, 36, 44   regarded as sacrosanct (the evidence for this, inside and outside surveyors' grids, is entirely convincing). Passage architecture, a growth industry that would not be denied, persisted, grid or not. The results, with respect to positioning buildings, appear to be random and arbitrary, and though in an obvious sense that is correct, randomness has meaning.[47] Passage architecture is found in quantity throughout most of the empire and must therefore have been an essential component of the Roman urban ideal. It would probably be wrong also to dismiss minor passage structures as architectural or sculptural bric-a-brac, for they were suitable according to means and circumstances, their symbolism and to a degree their functional intent reflecting those of their grander relatives.

Passage structures were highly visible. They called attention to themselves not only because of function and location, but also because, freestanding or not, they were clearly differentiated from neighboring forms. They were not in the least neutral or passive, submerged in a continuous flow of buildings joining one city gate with another, but rather played leading roles in giving cities and towns individual identities and architectural character. Being both distinctive and set well apart, passage structures, by marking memorable, separate places, were points of reference in a complicated matrix which few, perhaps, could have envisioned entire. Spread about in casual patterns, arches and way stations established articulative urban frames, marking off segments of passage, of one length here, another there. As a result the whole could be grasped cumulatively, part by part, in a sequence of manageable portions. This was not division into discrete

172   districts (Hadrian's arch in Athens is a passage structure, not a barrier), but a system of reference points breaking up long stretches into convenient and readily comprehensible experiences. So in addition to their other functions, passage structures were aids to urban navigation, to comprehending a city's fabric, reassuring signals that the whole was made up of identifiable, apprehensible parts.

The net result was a cognitive system of largely functional units dividing urban texts into chapters and paragraphs. Each structure was a reliably fixed event in the complex weave of time, place, and motion that underlies all urban existence. Positioning was crucial. One has only to turn passage buildings (other than four-square ones) $90°$ in the mind's eye to appreciate how closely involved they were in the flow of traffic and the articulation of their armatures. The effectiveness and authority of many structures was enhanced by the cultural and historical meanings associated with their basic forms and sculptural and architectural decor. And though passage architecture was one of moments, of pauses, it was also one of structures and monuments in their own right, of forms that spoke in up-to-date terms of city-ness and that worked toward manifesting that quality effectively. It did this by accentuating the presence and individuality of main points and by increasing their visual interest while at the same time contributing forcefully both to the city's physical organization and its practical functions.

Since the primacy of interior space in imperial architecture has been emphasized so often, it is important to call attention to the open, exterior quality of passage buildings. They are doorways, always open, that embrace or lead to public spaces accessible to all. They say a lot about the expressive power of half-formed architectural space, about its potential for suggesting the existence of shapes and places that in physical fact are not there. It is this openness, inconclusive with respect to boundaries but unambiguous regarding position and its implications, that as much as anything explains why passage architecture so effectively articulated Roman armatures. Because these structures are open to all they are in a sense public dwellings, not only as places for stopping or resting but also as receptacles, storage places, for traditional sentiments and convictions. A monumental arch, for example, stands over special if not hallowed ground; the act of erecting it made this so, consciously or not, by celebrating a collective Roman belief held nearly everywhere. The nymphs of the springs inhabited civic fountains, however ethereally, and throughout cities and towns buildings were touched by ancient meanings. Loosely held in the open volumes of passage buildings, such meanings were essential to the symbolic nature of armatures and thus to their success.

Quite a few stretches of armatures, together with remains of their passage architecture, are well preserved. Those at Djemila and Timgad, and parts of the ones at Lepcis Magna and Dougga, have already been described, and others were mentioned in the discussion of way stations. That at Palmyra was unusually long and perhaps unusually 16, 17, 39 scenic, but it was typical in all respects nevertheless. Almost 2 km. from end to end, including tributaries leading from the main thoroughfare to the agora and the Damascus Gate, it connected the sanctuary of Bel with the western quarter of the city. The southeasternmost portion of the thoroughfare, leading northwest away from the sanctuary, was never finished; our knowledge of the route begins about 200 m. along the way, where there was an exedra whose four-columned porch extended into the central pavement. Further along was the double archway of wedge-shaped plan that accommodated 106 a 25° shift in direction toward the west. From there the thoroughfare drove some 350 m.

106. Palymyra, double arch of wedge-shaped plan across the main thoroughfare, northwest face; second century

to the tetrakionion set in the oval plaza, where there was another, but slight, change of direction. Between the arch and the tetrakionion were baths, a second sanctuary, a theatre, and a nymphaeum; beyond the tetrakionion another exedra. In all, there were six passage structures, exclusive of any on the tributaries. The entire thoroughfare, and its tributaries as well, were colonnaded on both sides; changes in level overall were very gradual.

At Petra a central portion of the armature is known. A colonnaded street ran from a nymphaeum to a triumphal arch, and a temple propylaea with stairs was among the major building complexes alongside. There were similar arrangements at Corinth (the southern portion of the Lechaion road) and Pergamon (the Asklepieion approach); compare Perge and the Hallenstrasse at Ephesus.

Salonika and Herculaneum are rewarding, as are Volubilis and Tipasa. Ostia and Pompeii preserve primary evidence. There are many hints at sites such as Perge, Side, Salona, Vaison-la-Romaine, Verulamium, and Sbeitla, and the number of identifiable passage structures whose contexts have disappeared or still lie buried is very large. There is perhaps no better place to sense the full original effect than at Gerasa, where the 400 m. axis running from the west side of the sanctuary of Artemis to the crumbling piers of the north bridge over the Chrysorhoas displays nearly every element of the mature Roman armature system: intersecting colonnaded thoroughfares, a grand propylon, monumental stairs, steps, fountains, and an intermediating plaza, all lined up between a huge temple set in one of the largest Roman enclosures known and an honorific arch with three openings.[48] Four structures are passage buildings. Levels change frequently, and the whole was richly scenic. The sequence included structures with plans shaped by segmental curves and semicircles as well as by rectangles, was screened and lined by more than two hundred columns, and contained an unknown quantity of statuary.

There would once have been many other such sequences studded with the architecture of passage. The huge scenic nymphaea of Pella, Acre, and Hadrianople, for example, known from coins, surely could not have existed in isolation, nor could the many monumental arches and propylaea known only from the same source.

Envisioning a familiar site without its way stations suggests how much visual and formal variety they contributed, how much more lively and humane they made the urban experience. Miletus, say, or Apamea, had they lacked them, would have been all right angles, places of unrelieved, perhaps grim, efficiency. But traversing Roman armatures almost always meant going under arches and passing fountains, whatever the original town plan. Though way stations were fewer, and smaller, in cities and towns in the Rhine-Danube provinces and the far north and west, they were there nevertheless, unmistakable reflections, however thinly spread, of appointments in great cities and prosperous towns to the south and east. They were essential to those distinct architectural formations that make imperial sites immediately recognizable. And because they articulated spaces clearly different from those adjoining and were disposed in varied patterns from place to place, they as much as anything else formed each town's architectural personality.

V

PUBLIC BUILDINGS

PUBLIC BUILDINGS are the Roman structures known best and studied most. To describe and analyze them in detail, type by type, would duplicate much already in print. But as they were joined inextricably to the architecture of connection and passage to form armatures, their contributions to urban coherence and identity were not limited to their purely typological characteristics. Here, although some of those characteristics are reviewed briefly, the emphasis is on the roles of these buildings within the armature structure, on such factors as distribution and visibility—evidence for the predisposition in imperial times toward an empire-wide urban architectural system.

TYPOLOGY

The primary types, largely exclusive of connective and passage architecture, are these:

amphitheatre	* religious buildings
* basilica (municipal sense)	* capitolium (in the west)
* bath	* temple not a capitolium
circus	* cult building
* cistern	* senate house (curia)
concert hall (odeum)	* shop (taberna)
cryptoportico	stadium
* latrine	* storehouse (horreum)
library	theatre
* market	

The starred buildings were indispensable to a proper town. Ranking places had many religious buildings, several baths and storehouses, and shops by the score. Some types were not normally accessible to the general public but were essential to town life (cisterns, storehouses, senate houses; cult buildings, only marginally civic, were ubiquitous). Other significant structures were appropriate only to particular kinds of towns—barracks, palaces, or lighthouses, for example. Of the primary types, certain characteristics are relevant here.

Amphitheatres. Nearly 400 amphitheatres are known or suspected; some, perhaps many, of the suspected ones were temporary structures or simply marked-out, appropriate ground. More will be found: that at Beth-Shean was discovered in 1981. They may have derived ultimately from the traditional practice of using fora, with their circumscribing porticos and galleries, for gladiatorial shows.[49] In time, separate facilities were
107 provided by, in effect, joining two theatres, minus their stage buildings, face to face. Oval plans were usually assembled from segments of circles. Some were round or nearly so (Dorchester; Lucus Feroniae; Amiens; Pergamon), a few were of irregular, unusual shapes (Cherchell; Ulpia Traiana; the later one at Carnuntum), and now and again a theatre was converted into an amphitheatre by substituting a more or less oval arena for
108 the original orchestra and stage (Augst; Cyrene; Dodona). There were hybrid arena-theatres deliberately so built (Drevant; Grand; Paris; Sanxay). Some were let into conveniently sloping terrain (Trier; Cagliari) or made of banked-up earth (Dorchester); wooden ones existed (Chester; on Trajan's Column; Antioch in Pisidia).

107. Merida, amphitheatre; probably begun in 8 B.C.

108. Amphitheatres. Above, El Djem (perhaps early third century); below, Cyrene, the theatre-amphitheatre from the air, a Greek theatre transformed

The first permanent one, built in Pompeii immediately after 80 B.C., is set partly below surrounding ground level and thus has only one story of external arches. Most examples, however, were freestanding, their arenas at ground level or nearly so (El Djem; Arles; Pola). The largest, the Flavian amphitheatre, is 188 by 156 m. overall and 48.5 m. high (exclusive of the 250 or so timber masts, connected by webs of ropes, that rose vertically from the masonry structure and from which a vast adjustable awning was suspended); the building covers 2.3 hectares (about 5.7 acres) and could seat perhaps 50,000. A small structure could measure about 65 by 50 m. (Caerwent), a medium-sized one 110 by 65 m. (Beth-Shean). Ample internal systems of ramps, stairs, and encircling corridors and walkways insured efficient traffic flow. Screen-like exteriors of tiered, continuous arcades tended partially to diminish the sense of mass by making the huge structures visually penetrable.

Basilicas. A catchall of the history of architecture, the word *basilica* is used here to refer to a public hall, a tribunal and place of public business, almost always bordering on the forum or agora.[50] Of rectangular plan, it normally was timber-roofed. Examples range in length from modest (Madauros, 14.6 m.) to sizable (Cyrene, 85 m.; London, 130 m.), to one of the largest buildings in the empire (the Ulpia, Rome, 169 m., with a 22 m. nave span). In the east, narrow, elongated versions were built (Corinth had three, all told; Ephesus). A basilica might have a rectangular tribune, set within the building or projecting from it, a single apse, or two apses (one at each end); some had no such axial recesses. Interior colonnades were common in the larger examples (Pompeii) but were not found in all (Trier); the major entrance might be on either the transverse or the

109. Trier, the basilica; early fourth century

longitudinal axis. At least one late example was vaulted (Maxentius and Constantine, Rome).

Bath buildings. The major success story among Roman building types, baths are found in a very wide variety of sizes, plans, and degree of formal complexity. They are often mentioned by Roman writers. Because of their hydraulic and thermal installations, small surviving portions will often suffice for identification. Roman architects let their imaginations run freely in bath design, producing many highly original compositions. Like fountains, baths were never far to seek. Timgad had at least fourteen, Athens at least twenty. By the end of the fourth century, Rome had eleven huge, symmetrically planned imperial baths and more than eight hundred lesser establishments. The essentials were dressing rooms, an ample water supply, furnaces and boilers, and at least three tubs, plunges, or pools—cold, tepid, and hot. Latrines were almost always included. The larger the building the more elaborate the offerings, ranging from sweat rooms, tanning areas, and ball courts, to libraries, lecture halls, running tracks, gardens, and spacious peristyles. The largest had lofty, groin-vaulted central halls lit by clearstory windows. Decorated with sculpture, marbles, and mosaics, major baths were as representative of the political and social order of the empire as fora or triumphal arches. With their large swimming pools and many other facilities, these were grand, multifunctional social centers, in some senses analogues of urban life; all were meeting places central to the life of their cities and towns. Almost every example, and hundreds are known, some in considerable detail (Trier; Pompeii; the Hadrianic and Hunting Baths   36 at Lepcis Magna; the Forum Baths at Ostia), is partially or wholly vaulted, its various rooms usually rising to different heights. The perimeter walls of large rectilinear ones tend to break out here and there in symmetrical projections; middle-sized and small baths are frequently asymmetrical in plan, with irregular, partly curving peripheries enclosing diverse room shapes.

Baths are difficult to classify, but with regard to degrees of size, variety, and prominence in the urban fabric, they fall roughly into groups:

> the small, street-corner variety, its facilities minimal (four to six rooms) and its architecture undistinguished to the point of anonymity (Ostia; Rome; Timgad)
> the bath associated with a specific organization or building complex, usually moderately elaborate, with five to ten rooms (the Baths of the Seven Sages at Ostia; of Placcus at Gerasa; the Hunting Baths at Lepcis Magna)   110

110. Lepcis Magna, Hunting Baths; mid-third century

the building of considerable size, with ten or twenty rooms, that flaunts its asymmetries and irregularities, eschewing almost all formal connection with the rationally organized imperial type large or small (Amiens; Thenae; Khamissa; the South Baths at Timgad; those of Faustina at Miletus; north of the Athens Olympieion)

23, 179

the lesser (yet in their own way quite large, often with twenty rooms or more) version of the imperial type: symmetrical, with duplicate facilities set out in parallel on either side of the main axis in many different plan formations (Djemila; Cherchell; Odessos; Gerasa; the North Baths at Timgad; the two at Lambaesis), and

1, 23

the imperial type proper, on the model of the Baths of Trajan, Caracalla, and so on, in Rome, huge symmetrical complexes with forty or more rooms plus courtyards, all set within or fronted by vast walled precincts (Trier; Ephesus; Sardis).

170

111. Rome, Circus of Maxentius, air view; early fourth century

Circuses. Nearly a hundred are known or suspected to have existed, but only about fifteen have survived in recognizable condition; two or three are fairly well preserved (Lepcis Magna; the Circus of Maxentius by the Via Appia). There was a cluster of them   111 in southeastern Gaul but only three or four further north; in the east, Roman-style structures prevailed in high and later imperial times. The essential elements were a long, hairpin-shaped track divided for about two-thirds of its length by a low median wall (the euripus or spina), usually set at a slight angle to the track's centerline; a gently curved line of starting gates at the open end of the hairpin; and banks of seats all round except where the gates were.

No doubt some racetracks, like some amphitheatres, were simply suitable ground appropriately marked out, with temporary seating if any. Grand versions had ceremonial archways set in the curved end and boxes for officials; the whole building might be aligned at an angle of about 45° to the path of the sun.[51] Provincial circuses could be small (Gerasa, 250 m. long), but a proper one measured 400 to 500 m. (Salonika;   35 Sirmium; Caesarea Maritima; Milan). Rome had the largest, the Circus Maximus, at 600 m. Until the tetrarchy, circuses were almost always built outside city limits, and armatures were extended to include them. The exteriors of freestanding examples were usually, but once again not always, arcaded. Racing was and remained immensely popular. The Circus Maximus, in its earliest form, dates to the fourth century B.C. or even earlier; that at Constantinople was in use at least until the tenth century.   19

Cisterns. Cisterns are important because of their ubiquity and bulk and the use sometimes of the level roofs of the largest ones as urban terraces (Ptolemais in Cyrenaica; Constantinople; Termessos). The enclosed versions, almost universally vaulted and often let partially or wholly into the ground, range from single chambers to large, hardy structures composed of many interconnecting volumes or cells (Carthage) or parallel aisles defined by arcades (Albano). High ground, naturally, was often sought (Tiddis; Dougga; Hierapolis). Many baths had their own cisterns (Hippo Regius; the Baths of Neptune at Ostia; the imperial structures of Rome). There were also uncovered cisterns (Thuburbo Maius), some of them vast reservoirs (Bosra; Constantinople).

Concert halls. Containing curved banks of seats facing a stage, but small in comparison to theatres and unlike them usually roofed over, these might be rectangular in plan (Pompeii; Cretopolis; Termessos; Agrippa's in the Athenian agora). They were for recitations and rehearsals as well as concerts. That built in Athens by Herodes Atticus was very large; though roofed, it resembled a theatre. There may have been a tendency to place concert halls close to urban centers, beside fora (Vienne; Lyon? Corinth; Aphrodisias; Nicopolis ad Istrum).

Cryptoporticos. Sometimes connective, functioning as covered passageways, cryptoporticos are vaulted corridors. Cool and shaded, they are occasionally found alongside streets, sunken below pavement level (Bosra), but much more often they lined platforms   112 or terraces erected to support major buildings and functioned as ambulatories (Arles; Aeminium; Aosta; Smyrna). The street type is lit by smallish, raking windows set in the haunch of the vault along one side; the other, the same way or by larger, lower openings

112. Bosra, cryptoportico

113. Dougga, Cyclops Baths, latrine

(Reims). There are unlit, tunnel-like examples (Tipasa; under the Roman Forum), some of which are largely non-functional voids resulting from construction methods used to lessen masonry volumes.

Latrines. Latrines were enclosed but public multiple facilities, sometimes with a dozen or more individual positions. Located at points along the armature, they are often found at the edges of fora and at the outer corner or corners of major baths. Water flowed, in many continuously, through channels under the perforated seating. Well-preserved examples are common (Merida; Vaison-la-Romaine; Dougga; Sardis).

113

Libraries. Some libraries were part of the larger structures or building complexes, such as baths (the imperial ones in Rome) or fora (Philippi; beside the Column of Trajan and in the Forum Pacis in Rome). Some were separate buildings (Timgad; Ephesus; Hadrian's Library in Athens). Whether rectilinear in plan or exedra-shaped, the chief interior requirement was a series of elevated rectangular niches in the walls into which wooden scroll-cases were fitted. Dry facilities were essential; sometimes libraries can be identified by their double-wall construction whose intermediate air space or narrow corridors helped protect the enclosed library structure proper from excessive humidity (Nysa). Perhaps some buildings thought in modern times to have been built for other purposes were libraries (the so-called Saalbau or Temple of Diana at Nîmes).[52]

42

Markets. Permanent market structures were the norm. In the west and south, forum-side locations were favored originally, but with prosperity other locations became attractive. Files of shops (*tabernae*) or stalls were essential, and in the commonest market type were set along the sides of rectangular unroofed courtyards. As so often in Roman towns, activity took place both in a regularized open space and in its sheltered periphery. Round buildings were set in many such courtyards (Pozzuoli; Pompeii; Aquincum; Hippo Regius; Lepcis Magna; the forum market at Djemila; compare Alba Fucens). At Timgad, in the market within the grid, the stalls were set radially around two exedra-

114
55

114. Hippo Regius, market; first century, later altered

shaped courtyards placed side by side. The ground floor of the House of the Lararium at Ostia is taken up by a dozen or so shops set around a rectilinear interior courtyard. Basilicas or basilica-like plans were also used (the dry-goods market at Djemila and the Market of Sertius at Timgad both had large terminal apses). The Markets of Trajan at 26 Rome contained a two-storied, covered street of shops; what was perhaps an uncovered one can be seen at Ostia (Is. II, Reg. 1, unexcavated). Numerous stately colonnaded market plazas were found further east (Dura Europos; Petra; Palmyra; the Agora of 16, 63 Caesar and Augustus at Athens), some of which were renovated, Romanized agoras (Miletus; Ephesus).

Religious buildings. The traditional Roman temple, with a high podium and with steps leading up to a portico at one end only, stood in every western town. Derived 125, 128 partly from the front-porch (prostyle) temple popular in Hellenistic times, it was built frequently in the east as well, where the larger examples were often set in broad precincts colonnaded on three or four sides (the Temple of Artemis at Gerasa; that of Trajan at 127 Pergamon); similar arrangements are found also in the west (Pompeii; the Temple of Venus and Rome in Rome). Western cities required capitolia, temples to the Capitoline triad of Jupiter, Juno, and Minerva, sometimes but not always with three internal chambers. Once in a while capitolia were composed of three separate structures set close together (Baelo; Sbeitla), but though they varied greatly in size and detail, it seems they 115 were always one-ended, with porch and steps facing a plaza, usually the forum.

The design of temples dedicated to the universal deities and the imperial cult was on the whole conservative in the European provinces (Evora; Vienne), less so in North 116, 128 Africa (the capitolium at Lambaesis; the Temple of Mercury at Dougga), and in the east sometimes very inventive, where interiors in particular were elaborated (Niha; the "small" temple at Baalbek). There were as many varieties of cult buildings and sanctu- 117 aries, east and west, as there were deities, mystery cults, and local shrines requiring

115. Sbeitla, forum and three-temple Capitolium; probably mid-second century

116. Vienne, Temple of Augustus and Livia; early first century

monuments or gathering places and liturgical spaces. Some were of the traditional temple-form, for example those to Fortune, Victory, or imperial persons or families. Others, such as Mithraic lodges, might be freestanding (London), underground or partly so (Ostia; Rome), or man-made caves (Tiddis). Buildings for the worship of eastern divinities proliferated, including, especially in the third century, Christian shrines and meeting places, but with some exceptions they were not armature structures; the exceptions were often temples to quasi-official deities such as Serapis (Ephesus; Pergamon), and synagogues (Ostia; Sardis; Caesarea Maritima). Because religious life, both private and official, was so varied, the spectrum of religious building types was extremely broad, equaling or perhaps surpassing bath buildings in formal variety. But for armature studies the single-ended podium temple, with or without colonnades continuing around the building, counts most.

Senate houses. Normally a fairly plain, wide hall of rectangular plan opening onto the forum, with city offices nearby, the senate house or curia was the elders' meeting place

118

117. (LEFT) Baalbek, small temple, interior detail; mid-third century

118. (ABOVE) Tigzirt, cult building

130 both in Rome and in the provinces. Vitruvius says it should be a dignified building with a coffered (that is, wooden) ceiling.[53] Several were curved in plan (Augst; Corinth); apses were common (Pompeii; Sabratha). On the whole it was a stubbornly conservative type, confined almost entirely to the west, small except at Rome. It may however have existed in some eastern towns, such as Augustus' Pisidian foundations, where Italian colonists and their descendants clung to western ways.

Shops. Architecturally undistinguished, shops were fundamental urban units, the commonest of all public building types. They lined thoroughfares and many lesser
37 streets, sometimes uninterruptedly block by block, and many plazas as well. Most were
57 single volumes of rectangular plan, 4 or 5 m. wide and 5 to 10 m. deep, open wide to the pavement or sidewalk. Deeper ones might have a second room behind; many, of whatever size, had wooden stairs leading to a low mezzanine. About 800 can be seen at
44, 203 Ostia, which is about one-half excavated; if the population was say 40,000, that would work out on the evidence at hand to one shop for about every twenty-five to thirty inhabitants.[54]

Rome may have had a comparable ratio, given the large number of units recorded on
119 the existing fragments of the Marble Plan. At the Markets of Trajan, over a hundred can still be seen intact; others, still in use, are preserved on the Via dei Cerchi. Archaeological evidence across the provinces records a high proportion of street frontage taken up by shops, so these ratios were probably not exceptional. Italian shops were usually
120 vaulted. Elsewhere, wooden roofs were more usual; stone ones are known (Musti; Umm al-Jamal; beside the agora at Cyrene). Shops bordered nearly every forum, agora, and market, and fronted many atrium and peristyle houses, as well as insulas (multistoried tenements and apartment houses).

119. Rome, Severan Marble Plan, fragment   120. Musti, shops

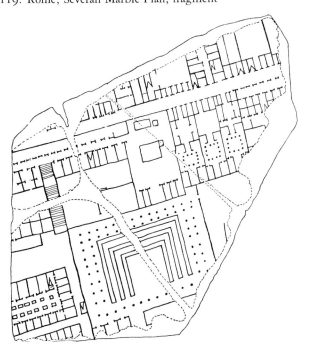

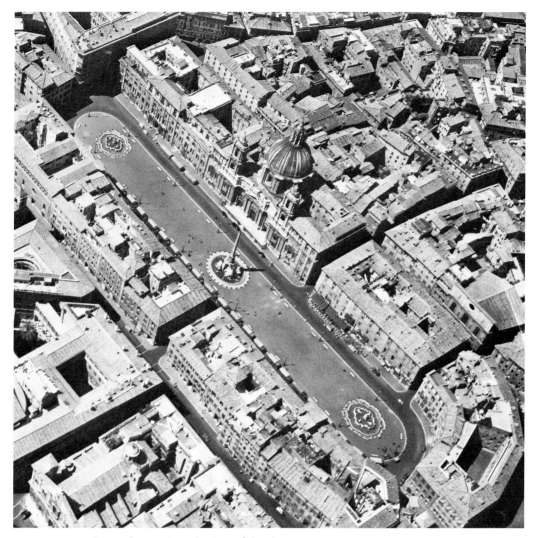

121. Rome, Stadium of Domitian, air view of the site; ca. 90

Stadiums. Not a Roman building but Greek, for foot races, a stadium was a structure of hairpin-shaped plan with a track 170 to 220 m. long bordered by banks of seats. Although both Caesar and Augustus built temporary ones in Rome, and Domitian a 121 permanent building, others are rare in the west (Vienne?). Forty-odd are known, many of them built in the imperial age; well-preserved examples survive at Perge and at Aphrodisias (where both ends are closed by curved rows of seats, a common arrangement). Seating was carried either on vaulted arcades (Rome; Aspendus) or sometimes, as with other huge structures requiring immense lengths of it, on the slopes of suitable natural declivities (Sillyon).

Storehouses. Almost any kind of dry, enclosed space could be used for storage, but Roman storehouses and granaries built specifically as such (*horrea*) can often be identified by their forms when inscriptions are lacking. The common denominator was the repetition of plain storerooms usually of identical shape, all opening the same way one after another in a row, or in double rows back to back, or in rows around courtyards. Normally vaulted, the storerooms proper resemble shops—or the units of chambered cisterns, except for the lack of hydraulic passages and waterproof cement (Constanţa;

Patara). They might be squarish, oblong, or very deep in proportion to their width; these last were common in North Africa and Asia Minor. The courtyard type is common (Carnuntum; Corbridge; Ostia; the evidence of the Marble Plan of Rome); both this and the row type might be two stories high, even three (Amastris; the Horrea Epigathiana at Ostia). Military sites and strongholds are particularly rich in granaries, their floors raised above the ground to protect the grain and allow the air to circulate; some of these were of wood (Richborough; Fishbourne; Rödgen). Large ports preserve much relevant evidence (Portus; Lepcis Magna; the eleven major horrea of Ostia). These buildings were little adorned, though decorative detail was sometimes applied (Ostia; Myra).

Theatres. In the Roman form of the classical theatre, the seating and the flat space (the orchestra) it enclosed were semicircular in plan. The chord of the semicircle marked the forward edge of the stage, behind which there were one or more tiers of columns;

122

202, 44

122. Trier, storehouses, model; early fourth century

123. Khamissa, theatre; late second century?

immediately behind that was the solid stage-wall proper, often articulated with niches and broad, curved recesses, to which the tiers of columns largely conformed (complete walls at Orange and Aspendus). Scores of theatres are known, many have been studied. At first they were placed inside city walls (expansion brought extramural siting), freestanding, their exteriors arcaded (Minturnae; Ostia; Bosra), or against hillsides (Lyon; Verona; Fiesole; Dougga; Amman). Some were cut partly from natural rock (Petra; Apollonia in Cyrenaica). Greek and Hellenistic theatres, whose banks of seats usually extended more than halfway around circular orchestras, continued in use though often altered, their simpler stage buildings replaced by elaborate Roman constructions (Buthrotum; Taormina; Miletus). The Theatre of Marcellus in Rome was 120 m. wide and about 32 high; it may have seated 11,000 people. That at Ephesus could accommodate about 24,000.[55] At Sabratha the theatre was 92 m. wide, at Bosra 88, at Philippopolis about 43, and at Apamea 139. Like amphitheatres, theatres were fitted internally with elaborate ramp and stair systems, the larger structures with wide horizontal walkways between tiers of seats. Good acoustical properties were sought, and spacious, sheltering peristyles, refuges in inclement weather, might be provided behind the lofty stage buildings (Orange; Pompeii; Lepcis Magna).[56] The scenic qualities of the stage architecture have stimulated modern reconstruction (Merida; Dougga; Sabratha; Gerasa).

124, 165
123
124

In descriptions of building types one by one, the sense of their urban context, of being tied firmly together by armatures, is lost. When a single type is defined independently of the others, an autonomy is suggested for it that in fact did not exist, and only a rough sense, if any, of its relative quantity or popularity emerges. But if the list is rearranged according to function, style, or number, instructive juxtapositions and contrasts appear. First, broad functional categories.

administrative buildings: basilica, senate house
commercial: market, shop, storehouse
cultural: concert hall, library, theatre; sometimes the bath; now and then the amphitheatre
hydraulic/hygienic: bath, cistern, latrine
recreational: amphitheatre, bath, circus, stadium; and sometimes the theatre
religious: capitolium, other temple, cult building

Of the seventeen types, ten were open to all, and of these ten, seven were recreational and cultural buildings. There were twice as many recreational as administrative types. Bath buildings were always multifunctional, one or two other kinds sometimes. Much of the typology, then, was of fully public buildings built for secular, largely non-commercial purposes. These relationships are self-evident, unlike the relationships between the buildings and architectural form.

Several stylistic modes were used. The more traditional and conservative ranged from archaizing designs (the Roman market gate in Athens) to those with Greco-Hellenistic

187

124. Merida, two views of the theatre stage building; begun
late first century B.C., later rebuilt

125. Tebessa, temple, model; second century?

forms attached to purposively Roman frames (the Maison Carrée at Nîmes). The more 125 innovatory modes, evolved under the empire, were the vaulted style, with orders and curving volumes combined (the Pantheon; all large baths), and a plain, or austere, manner, vaulted or not, with few if any traditional classical design elements (the Hunting Baths at Lepcis Magna; the Curia in Rome).[57] The archaizing mode was rare. 110, 130 The others were seen on every hand, as the following schematic tabulation suggests. The columns are roughly chronological, the earliest at the left, but the divisions are by no means absolute.

Traditional (orders, no vaults)	*Vaulted* (vaults and orders)	*Austere* (no orders, vaults or not)
	amphitheatre	amphitheatre
basilica	basilica	basilica
	bath	bath
	circus	
		cistern
concert hall	concert hall	
		cryptoportico
	latrine	latrine
library	library	
market	market	market
religious buildings (all three types)	temple not a capitolium, cult building	cult building
senate house		senate house
		shop
	stadium	
storehouse	storehouse	storehouse
	theatre	

No doubt there were such things as shops with orders, and certainly there were recreational structures made of wood. The purpose of the table is not to be all-inclusive, or to label Roman stylistic modes precisely, but to provide a serviceable basis for discussing relationships between typology and broadly defined architectural modes.

Certain patterns are suggested by rearranging the table to show how stylistic modes relate to function.

	Traditional	*Vaulted*	*Austere*
Administrative buildings			
basilica	x	x	x
senate house	x		x
Commercial			
market	x	x	x
shop			x
storehouse	x	x	x
Cultural			
concert hall	x	x	
library	x	x	
theatre		x	
(bath)		x	x
Hydraulic/hygienic			
bath		x	x
cistern			x
latrine		x	x
Recreational			
amphitheatre		x	x
bath		x	x
circus		x	
stadium		x	
(theatre)		x	
Religious			
capitolium	x		
temple not a capitolium	x	x	
cult building	x	x	x

Almost half the typology was restricted to single modes, but the diversity of the balance could make identification by function difficult. Religious and administrative buildings, the chief structures of authority, were stylistically the most traditional. Cultural, commerical (the most varied), and recreational works were less so. Hygienic/hydraulic structures, partly for functional reasons, were externally the least traditional, the least 82 "classical" in the sense the word has today; along with aqueduct bridges they were the modern works of the Roman world. Together with those intended for general public use—cultural, commercial, and recreational buildings—they fall chiefly into the two specifically imperial columns and reflect that response to human needs characteristic of much design under the empire. As the imperial synthesis took root and matured, buildings became proportionately less historical, from the Roman point of view, and more varied and apposite. The capitolium stands alone, unchanging. Other types appear either in more than one column or as members of stylistic groups. This widespread formal variety, cutting across functional and chronological boundaries and regional ones as well, is a definitive characteristic of imperial architecture.

As to quantities, some figures can be garnered from the North African provinces. Of a group of 408 public buildings (two types of passage structures are included for comparison) known from archaeology, texts, and inscriptions, the typological breakdown is:

temples excluding capitolia	79	(20% of the total)
baths	74	(18)
theatres	57	(14)
amphitheatres	41	(10)
arches	29	(7)
capitolia	25	(6)
cult buildings excluding Mithraea	23	(6)
major fountains	22	(5)
basilicas	17	(4)
markets	17	(4)
circuses	9	(2)
senate houses	8	(2)
Mithraea	7	(2)

These data are incomplete and misleading in any absolute sense. Among other deforming factors they reflect survival rates—major temple podia outlast senate houses, for example—and to some degree archaeological difficulties or selectivity; and evidence from texts and inscriptions is bound to be random. But enough is known about North African sites to give these figures some validity. There were about 680 established municipal entities spread from the Atlantic shore to the Egyptian border, "the vast majority little country towns with quite small territories," just hamlets.[58] Because of the care with which the North African ground has been examined, it is unlikely that vestiges of unknown towns, of substantial places with major public buildings, remain to be found (there are one or two places, their names preserved in topographically uninformative texts or orphaned inscriptions, whose sites have been identified only recently: Hadrianople in Cyrenaica, for example, known as a prominent center in later imperial times). It is fairly certain, then, that nearly every North African site having a broad spectrum of the public building typology is known. There are forty to fifty of these, about six or seven percent of the total number of entities.

This suggests that the numbers listed for permanent theatres and amphitheatres, and perhaps for circuses as well, are reasonably complete, given the resistance of such massive works to complete dilapidation by man or nature. A degree of corroboration is provided by a tabulation of known North African construction costs wherein the temple, arch, and theatre are cited, in that order, more frequently than other building types.[59] The figures for capitolia, baths, arches, and cult buildings, however, seem shy (capitolia—which can sometimes be difficult to identify without inscriptions—because of close imperial ties to Rome; baths, because if Timgad had a half-dozen or so substantial ones, then most large towns, less fully explored, probably had several; and arches and cult buildings for reasons already mentioned). For the other kinds of buildings, it is difficult to make judgments, in view of incomplete exploration and excavation at most of the forty-odd sites.

Religious and recreational buildings are the most common, together making up almost two-thirds of the total; if theatres are included, nearly four-fifths of the total is accounted for. These primitive calculations rest partly, and precariously, on the urge to inscribe public buildings with dedicatory and honorific phrases. Yet the proportionate relationships ring fairly true, and the first third of the list—perhaps the first half—is useful. The proportion of three religious buildings to two public baths, one theatre, and one amphitheatre, for a large town, is probably not inaccurate, given the respectable size of the sample. Extending this crude model of typological factors suggests that statistically every other major place had a public market building and a scenic fountain. All provincial and regional centers seem to have had amphitheatres, and some smaller places had theatres.

North Africa was plentifully supplied with the functional and symbolic apparatus of imperial town life. Innovative architecture (the recreational buildings) was as common as traditional (religious structures), a clear reflection of the mixture of past and present Rome cultivated. It may be useful to inquire about the ways these public buildings were interrelated within their towns, about how they were dispersed to form, with the architecture of connection and passage, the symbolic core and functional patterns of urbanism in the imperial age.

DISTRIBUTION

A broad architectural homogeneity was assured for the cities and towns by the appearance in all regions (always excepting much of Egypt) of numerous Roman buildings: arches, prostyle podium temples, scenic fountains, baths and more baths, Roman theatres, hydraulic works and, it is beginning to appear, perhaps even amphitheatres. Distribution through the provinces was uneven, but not so uneven as to leave significant areas untouched. The spread of Roman forms was not halted at any internal stylistic frontiers, and by Antonine times there were few islands of architectural nostalgia or uninfected tradition left, east or west. Regionalism existed, but it is easy to overestimate, particularly when a single area or province is under examination.

Greek forms had of course spread far and wide, but this did not result in their architectural ascendancy in Roman times or in making towns look Greek. Pervasive as Greek influence was, it failed in the final analysis to dominate the urban scene: Roman public buildings won out. Their functions and design helped insure this, factors to which Greek patterns and details were subordinated. Although such patterns and details were nearly ubiquitous, essential to the broad formal constancy that pervades so much classical architecture, they were made to serve Roman purposes, just as the colonnade, the stoa, and the temple front were. In the pan-empire melting pot, many individual Greek forms held their own, but they never quite took the conqueror captive. Nor did Greek building types. The palestra, for example, was adapted to western bath design, while the Roman bath building proper, probably first fully defined in south central Italy, soon appeared in all the provinces. A few older cities or quarters—Priene, the acropolis of Pergamon—preserved much of their pre-Roman aura, but most brought themselves up-to-date or were modernized through gifts. Newer towns were never in doubt; the world had changed.

Adoption of the typology furthered architectural Romanization across the empire. This was the more effective because of the way public buildings were distributed within the cities and towns. Although certain building types—capitolia, basilicas, senate houses—are often found beside the forum and sometimes beside the agora, the typology overall is almost invariably widely dispersed. There are no discernible schematic principles in this, no standard, repeated patterns of the kind produced by city planning based on an accepted theory widely applied. The distributive characteristics of the typology are, first, almost no forceful concentrations, in the sense of a multipurpose Near Eastern citadel surrounded by a sea of houses and shops, or a Norman keep in a Saxon town; and second, a corollary of the first, public buildings are spread broadly throughout each community in apparently random fashion (often the result of that gradual expansion and change over the years mentioned above). Frontier towns excepted, there were few fortresses; Jerusalem's Antonia, perhaps the best known today, was the work of Herod the Great. The norm was a fairly peaceful and fairly prosperous place, garrisonless, with one or more public buildings of Roman design in nearly every district or quarter.

Because the construction of so many large public buildings was enduringly solid, insuring high survival rates, the principle of distribution is readily verifiable. Whatever the degree of excavation, the locations of major public buildings are the things likely to be most obvious about a site, as the city plans illustrated here suggest. Even wholly or largely unexcavated sites record dispersal if major ruins can be seen. The conclusion seems inescapable that public buildings—save those by the forum or agora—were as widely distributed as passage architecture. Compact civic centers, encompassing all basic public functions, were apparently rare in the high and late empire; places like Augst may have been exceptions. Some newly made towns, such as the original tract at Djemila, began with a more or less self-contained center or core, but their typological composition was soon altered by expansion and additions. Dispersal is a primary fact of imperial urbanism.

Long-established cities were invaded in strength. At Pergamon, for example, over a distance of about two km. south-southwest of the acropolis, there are remains of the vast second-century shrine centered on the "Red Court," an amphitheatre, a Roman theatre, a monumental arch, and the largely imperial Asklepieion with its ceremonial avenue of approach, as well as the unexcavated site of a circus of Roman dimensions—all in addition to the Temple of Trajan on the acropolis. At Ephesus three or four times as

200

many major Roman buildings are known, and there again they are spread through the entire city. Similar evidence is seen at many other sites of both Roman and pre-Roman origin about which less is known: Paris, for example, or Thuburbo Maius, or Gortyn. Merida is typical of this large group because although important domestic buildings and art have been recovered there, the public structures—the theatre and amphitheatre, the shell of a monumental arch, bridges, lofty aqueduct arcades, a circus, vestiges of temples and, outside the city, large reservoirs—are the dominant remains. Scarcely a house is now visible at Lepcis Magna or at Gerasa, but at both sites the typology is well defined and widely spread out. There are few places where both domestic and public architecture can been seen in quantity, as at Pompeii, Ostia, or Timgad. But excavated or not, evidence is lacking at these and other sites of planned, city-wide interrelationships among public buildings. There are major axes and vistas, and connections between buildings and their precincts, forecourts, or approaches, but no stock alignments of widely distributed monuments. Casual accumulation and expansion precluded them.

Spread about, unavoidable, always recognizably Roman, these robust objects were instruments of architectural colonization, symbols of the claims and ways of Rome. Bound together by the architecture of connection and passage, they were anchor points of the loose and unschematic frames forming the cores of imperial cities and towns, the cores of mind and memory, of dominant images and functional associations. One or two buildings alone would not do because it was the sum of an interdependent typology that counted, that produced townwide effects. With plazas these buildings were urban nodes, like fountains, never far to seek. And like monumental arches they spoke unambiguously of the ultimate fact of life under the empire, the binding authority of Rome—something a town without them might misprize. Such a town would lack the coherence, the loose yet palpable unity that a dispersed typology insured. Connective architecture led to these public buildings; they determined one's bearings, and bearings bring a plan alive.

Dispersal was as Roman as the buildings themselves. The main tendencies hindsight can uncover are wide distribution and an impulse to create an effect as important overall as the functional services provided; in this sense public buildings are comparable to connective and passage architecture. Taken together, these buildings were essential to a distinctive architectural creation, the specifically Roman town. In a distant sense, Rome itself was the model, with its widely distributed public facilities. Although the fora with their halls and colonnades were kept together there, nothing else was. Baths, for example, were everywhere, immense ones in most regions and scores of smaller ones as well. There was no single religious quarter in spite of the reverence paid to the hallowed Capitoline, nor was there one for entertainment. There seem to have been few large tracts of residential buildings without a sign of a major public one; the same was true in the provinces. Public and private structures were not set in territorial opposition to each other but were mixed together. Districts with no commercial facilities were apparently all but unknown.

As a result, imperial cities and towns seem to have lacked architecturally undifferentiated quarters of any size, quarters without a large public building, a rallying point whose formal and functional image could be effortlessly and naturally retained in the mind. This had been true earlier, as Priene for example makes clear, but under the empire the typology was of its time. Because of these things, districts that might be thought déclassé because they lacked any modern landmark or major popular facility were rare. A kind of general level of regional equality was achieved, an evolution furthered by a decline in interest in the acropolis, in the need to search for sites with dominating, defensible high ground on which to build the chief symbolic monument of the city. Interest in official civic religious observances also waned, no matter how much lip service might be paid to them, a process hastened not only by the growth of unofficial and private cults but also by a determined preoccupation with town life.

These observations about the typology are borne out in the discussions above about Djemila, Timgad, and Severan Lepcis Magna. At Ostia, the most imperial of towns,   44 dispersion ruled even inside the orthogonal scheme of the central core. Its storehouses are found in nearly every quarter, not just alongside the Tiber, and its religious and thermal buildings are also widely scattered. For Athens, by 1968, twenty-four Roman baths could be listed, spread across the city. At Cyrene Roman typology proliferated from one gate to another, and a major bath building was set down in Apollo's sanctuary itself. These distributive characteristics are found in every province; all known sites large enough to have public buildings are witness to them. Roman imperial towns had districts or quarters—all towns do—but because of the presence of distinctively Roman civic buildings held together and interrelated by the devices of the armature, they were partners in architecturally coherent wholes.

VISIBILITY

Monumentality was a Roman specialty, apparently a passion. Large-scale buildings rising high above their surroundings were commonplace, and the frequency of their appearance in small places is striking. Facilities for large crowds presuppose great bulk, but other monumental structures, with less functional justification for their size, were begotten by official policy or public spirit, or, in lesser towns particularly, by pride and vainglory.

The Temple of Claudius at Colchester records policy. It was a fixture of the new colony of the year 50 (the first in Britain) and was rebuilt after its destruction in Queen Boudicca's siege and sack of 61, events inspired in part by the temple's existence (the date of its dedication to Claudius is debated but not its imperial purpose and content). Its precinct covered 2.4 hectares, somewhat more than a twentieth of the total area of the walled town. The temple platform or podium measured 24.4 by 32 m. and was 3.35 m. high, about twice the height of a person. The order was approximately 9 m. high, and although nothing is left of the superstructure, the combined height of the entablature and pediment would have been in the neighborhood of 5 m., giving an overall facade height of about 17.5 m., that of a five-story dwelling today. (A useful if rough rule of thumb is that the facade of an official temple of more or less traditional form will be about twice as high, ground level to peak, as the height of its order.) Because of the temple's height in relationship to its surroundings, together with a theatre mentioned by Tacitus it would have dominated the town (there may also have been an amphitheatre, but if so it was probably outside the walls).[60]

A sense of typological scale is suggested by contrasting the approximate heights of the orders of a number of temples.

	4.6 m.	Si', Temple of Ba'alshamin (4 vertical units)
	6.3	Cori, Doric temple (4)
	6.3	Athens, circular temple of Rome and Augustus (9)
	7.9	Bath, Temple of Sulis Minerva (4)
7	8.4	Djemila, Severan temple (4)
115	8.4	Sbeitla, middle Capitolium temple (4)
	8.5	Thuburbo Maius, Capitolium (6)
	9.0	Nîmes, Maison Carrée (6)
	9.0	Colchester, Temple of Claudius (6? 8?)
116	9.7	Vienne, Temple of Augustus and Livia (6)
	11.0	Rome, Temple of Saturn (6)
	12.5	Rome, Temple of Castor and Pollux (8)
127	13.1	Gerasa, Temple of Artemis (6)
	14.0	Rome, Pantheon porch (8)
27	14.0	Timgad, Capitolium (6)
	15.2	Rome, Temple of Vespasian (6)
	18.2	Baalbek, Temple of Zeus (10)
	21.3	Cyzicus, Temple of Hadrian, if Cyriacus of Ancona's observations of 1431 are correct (8)

Though considerably smaller than the well-known giants on the list, the Colchester temple was nevertheless of respectable size—monumental, in comparison to its setting. With its 32 m. ridge-line making it twice as long as it was tall, its scale enhanced by the comparatively low precinct walls (this seems certain by analogy), it would have been "the eye-catching focus" of the colony.[61] Close up, the imperial nature of the ensemble was signaled by revetting part or all of the precinct entrance works, probably after 61, with "colored marbles imported from many distant parts of the empire," an early example, in a new and distant province, of the familiar Roman symbolic deployment of empire-wide resources in major public buildings. That part of these works were arcuated is further proof of the swift progress of new architectural thinking across the provinces.

In spite of being on the periphery of things, the Colchester temple was typical of its kind. Though an urban temple might be sited on a slope or hilltop, the great majority were built on flat or flattish ground (three-quarters of those listed above). In order to insure high visibility, to gain sufficient bulk and commanding silhouettes, height was secured by building terraces, podia, and steep pediments; slender orders could help. In a world of horizontal forms, of block-long entablatures and lengthy files of verticals of equal size, these measures produced effective contrasts in scale. One of the commonest sights in the cities and towns is the artificial terrace that supported a public building. If that building was a temple, it was elevated in turn on a podium, a kind of artificial mound of prismatic shape from which the familiar columns rose. These devices were used for other building types as well, and were so common that it is not unreasonable to suggest that a major Roman objective was to lift public buildings well above street level in order to increase their visibility and thus their symbolic effectiveness.

Of course making a terrace meant making level ground, but leveling alone would not produce one. A terrace must be elevated, its platform a level stretch set well above an   126 area or vista whose existence was part of the terrace's definition. Terrace-building, a   7 prime Roman occupation, invited the incorporated construction of cryptoporticos, simultaneously lessening the amount of fill required and providing useful space. These versatile, adaptable corridors, in a sense internalized stoas, were typical results of Roman architectural thinking: begin with an axis, and then carry out along that axis the logical extension of a simple concept, in this case the arch. Roman builders and architects were not much at home with huge, solid volumes. Vaults 6 m. in span supported the Colchester temple platform, and though the resulting hollows, filled in with earth, were not cryptoporticos, the kind of thinking about design and structure

126. Musti, terrace of the temples

that produced them was similar. Stairs, terraces, vaults, cryptoporticos, and podia are all evidence of preoccupation with elevation, and elevation, not confined to temples by any means, was a primary instrument of visibility.[62]

Three successive levels, then, underpinned the colonnades and enclosed volumes of many monumental public buildings: the earth; a terrace or other level, paved surface; and a podium. The podium, a superposed terrace conforming to a building's plan—a kind of continuous pedestal—is almost as important to Roman architecture as the column or the vault, and though an inextricable part of subsequent monumental 116, 125, 128 classicism, it has been neglected by architectural writers. Podia define relationships between ground level and their superposed buildings, which if mishandled can weaken otherwise satisfactory designs. The traditional arms projecting forward from central facades help give buildings directional axes, fix them firmly in relation to their surroundings, and emphasize entranceways. Lacking vertical elements, podia with their resolute horizontality are effective foils to the rising verticals they support. Lacking openings, podia signal the wholeness, the integrity, of their buildings, which are held together by their continuous, broad bands. And their impenetrable solidity, together with their height, mark buildings as distinctly different and distinctly separate from their surroundings, which, as a result, they tend to dominate. Because terraces and podia raised the pavements of many civic monuments well above the level of busy streets and shops, the monuments were elevated, so to speak, to another, less familiar realm. The splendor of the Parthenon's setting is universally admitted, but if it is envisioned as embedded say in Trier, or Sabratha, its need for exalting elevation, for a more visible presence, is instantly felt; the building requires spatial independence and full exposure in the round. In crowded urban contexts, elevation was essential.

Making a building large in contrast to its neighboring structures and clearing a space around it was not enough. Columns and walls, rising from ground level where ordinary life took place, would tend to deny a monument's special qualities. The intervention of the podium solves these problems. Its spreading base mouldings marry the building to the ground, conveying a sense of solid footing and permanent existence. Its cornice flares out, emphasizing its role as a powerful supporting block. The resulting lines of shadows, separated by the massive but unfeatured wall between, twice describe the building's plan. And the fitted quality of the podium—its neat, tight definition of the building's circumference—prevents it from being demandingly obtrusive. Its height was equally important. If one could see up over a podium, see the paving from which the meaningful building proper rose, the sense of the monument's separateness, of its limited accessibility, would be diminished. Thus podia almost always rise well above human height, as the following table of largely approximate measurements suggests.

1.4 m.	Alexandria, temple at Ras-el-Souda
1.9	Pola, Temple of Rome and Augustus
2.0	Side, circular building in the agora
2.8	Nîmes, Maison Carrée
2.8	Split, Temple of Jupiter

2.9 m.	Evora, Temple of Diana	128
3.0	Pompeii, Temple of Jupiter	
3.0	Narbonne, Capitolium	
3.15	Vienne, Temple of Augustus and Livia	116
3.3	Baalbek, Temple of Venus	156, 157
3.35	Colchester, Temple of Claudius	
3.55	Rome, Temple of Mars Ultor	
3.6	Djemila, Severan temple	7
3.75	Orange, hemicycle temple	
4.1	Ostia, Capitolium	
4.3	Rome, Temple of Antoninus and Faustina	
4.32	Gerasa, Temple of Artemis	127
4.6	Thuburbo Maius, Capitolium	
5.1	Baalbek, Temple of Bacchus	
6.6	Baalbek, Temple of Zeus	
6.7	Timgad, Capitolium	27
7.0	Baalbek, sanctuary propylon	
7.0	Rome, Temple of Castor and Pollux	

The encircling temple podium was interrupted only for stairs placed, as Vitruvius says, at the front.[63] It is easy to pass by this remark without comment because the arrangement is so familiar. But the obvious is crucial: the urban temple plan was unambiguously asymmetrical, the porch facade being by far the most significant one. Only there were stairs found, their position emphasized and fixed by wide, projecting podium arms alongside. Together with the pediment apex and the central intercolumniation of the porch, the podium and steps were rigorously symmetrical around the longitudinal axis of the building. Released from the constraint placed upon it at the rear of the building by the continuous and unbroken travel of the podium wall, the axis was   127 free to interlock with the space beyond, to extend its authority out across the altar and forecourt and help join them with the temple building proper. This axial continuity was aided by the half-open, half-closed porch, which by mediating between the open court and the enclosed cella made the transition between public and sacred spaces seem less abrupt.

The cella, seen or not, was the climax of the whole ensemble. Elevated on its podium, sheltered by its peaked roof, it rode above the common level below, its entrance accessible only by way of a tightly defined path that overcame the obstacle of the podium. The resulting combination of elevation, visibility, and axial authority was repeated across the Roman world, a response to the need for highly visible religious buildings within dense urban surroundings. Without a high podium, the power and effectiveness of this familiar composition was drained away and the temple's visibility and claims to rank much diminished.

Within this construct of interlocking elements, podium arms performed yet another function. Reaching forward from the building but clearly an integral part of it, bound to it by continuous surfaces and mouldings, they assist in uniting the secular and the

127. Gerasa, Temple of Artemis; mid-second century

128. Evora, temple "of Diana"; ca. 200

divine. Out beside the lowest stair they stand at the edge of the habitable world. Back a
bit they become the supports of the side columns of the porch, and, further on, of the
cella walls or its peristyle columns. Because they reach forward like the forelegs of a
recumbent sphinx or lion, they define the place the building surveys, what space or area
it illuminates.

Thus temples suggest poised energy, like stationary locomotives on their tracks: a
podium, its projecting arms, and the robust mouldings combine to give a temple a
directional stance, a suggestion of forward thrust, an immediacy. The scoop-like front
both receives and projects. At the root of these effects lies the lucid formal definition of
the long, identical, parallel sides and the contrast between them and the shorter ones,
which are distinctly different. A temple without podium arms is more self-contained
and less directionally composed (no wonder Greek temples, far less urban in character,
have been found to be anchored in space by means of references to distant natural
features). Podium arms help join sacred architecture with open spaces for worship and
assembly; classicizing monuments can hardly do without them. The force of this
connection, of the visual and axial functions of the arms, is suggested by the disengaged
condition of temples that have lost them, for example those in Rome to Mars Ultor, to   129
"Fortuna Virilis," or to Antoninus and Faustina, or the Antonine temple at Sabratha.

129. Rome, Temple of Mars Ultor, detail; dedicated in 2 B.C.

Stairs restored in modern times without podium arms appear temporary and incomplete, and the temples proper are somewhat more tentative and withdrawn than when their podia are preserved. When the projecting blocks, their uppermost surfaces smooth and free of any superstructure, seamlessly connected with the rest of the podium block, have disappeared, much of the power of Roman temple to dominate the open space below vanishes.

Some have seen in this an analogue of Roman political policy and even of Roman oppression, observations that seem merited at least to the degree that a desire to order and organize underlay so much of what the Romans did. Furthermore, the evidence for these arrangements of form and space reaches well back into the Republican past, and might be thought to record a national characteristic or inclination. The notion that monumental buildings house collective memories, that they represent a kind of architectural anamnesis, may be supported by these forms and their history. Whatever the truth of these matters, so intriguing but so difficult—perhaps impossible—to prove, the significance of the Roman podium-plaza relationship for the history of architecture is that it was applied so widely and so effectively.

Vertical accents abounded. Statues and rising architectural sculpture along cornice lines and at roof peaks and corners proliferated. Pediments were usually proportionately higher than those of Greek buildings; the Pantheon is the best-known example, but there are many others. The one- and two-story heights of most town buildings insured the prominence not only of prismatically-shaped temple superstructures but also of the multiple surfaces of baths' roofs and the tiered arcades of theatres, amphitheatres, and circuses. If formal distinctions among functions were sometimes blurred, monumentality and visibility were not abandoned. In high and late antiquity, for example,
130 major senate houses could look rather like decolumniated temples (the Curia in Rome). Arcades were applied ever more widely (Dougga, the Licinian Baths; Split, the Porta Aurea; Aachen, the baths; Trier, the basilica). But the following approximate overall heights of several building types record the continuing desire for monumentality.

	18 m.	Lambaesis, large baths
86	19.2	St.-Rémy, mausoleum
	26.9	Alexandria, Diocletian's column
170, 171	27	Rome, Baths of Diocletian
109	31	Trier, the basilica
	32	Trier, Porta Nigra tower
	32	Salonika, Galerius' Mausoleum
	34	Rome, Baths of Caracalla
	34.8	La Coruña, Trajanic lighthouse
	35	Rome, Basilica of Maxentius and Constantine
	37.4	Baalbek, Temple of Zeus
137	40.2	Petra, the Deir
	44	Rome, the Pantheon

130. Rome, Curia; ca. 285

Thus citizens and deities, magistrates and soldiers, all were provided with tall, highly visible structures. The gods and goddesses became citified, having abandoned raw nature forever. Sacred springs and holy high places with their sanctuaries diminished in importance as town life flourished. The exhilarating hill-climb became largely a thing of the past, with only the temple stairs as a reminder. By the end of the second century the building of traditional prostyle podium temples had come almost to a halt, though the hundreds already in existence, some very old and often repaired, continued to be served for generations.[64] So as long as Roman authority existed, towns continued to look much as they had. Dougga is a case in point. Naturally hilly, provided with fine building sites, it was furnished with tall monuments. A capitolium, large bath buildings, two theatres, a circus, and temples to Mercury, Minerva, Tellus, Pluto, Fortune, Augustan Piety, Concordia, Frugifer, Liber Pater, Saturn, and Caelestis were scattered through the town, whose "narrow, winding streets edged with massive blocks of buildings (presented) a tiered architectural arrangement, with the most striking monuments rising from it at the most favored points."[65]

To pursue the subject further, to point to podia or stairs inside temples, as at Niha (Temple A) or Baalbek (the Temple of Bacchus), to discuss other devices of elevation such as pedestals and piers, would reveal the same principles, and the elements themselves can be studied here in the illustrations. In addition, classical and classicizing buildings of all periods abound with examples of their application and translation. Copied from ancient buildings since the early fifteenth century, investigated and described by antiquarians, taught in the academies, and illustrated in scores of handbooks over some four centuries' time, these later versions are often useful in studying and testing qualities of imperial design such as visibility and elevation.

Without a high degree of visibility, public buildings would not have been able to play a successful part in the creation of the Roman urban order. If the ground surfaces of the essentials of an armature are envisioned for a moment as already leveled and graded, but without any walls or columns or piers standing on them, the pavements, platforms, and terraced surfaces will appear joined in a primary network. Shallowly channeled conduits (thoroughfares), widening here and there (plazas), would be seen leading to level platforms prepared for public buildings and their precincts. These streets and plazas and platforms would form a continuous urban pavement, the essential underlying circulatory system of the town. The leveled platforms or terraces, set into hillsides or raised from the flat, would carry the chief objectives, both referential and functional, of public life. In contrast, infilling construction would be low, with fairly level rooflines and without rising, distinguishing silhouettes. Lacking the platforms and their tall civic structures, thoroughfares would have had few intramural goals; with them, the town's visual and functional frame was completed, and its architectural symbolism widely and prominently displayed.

Secure construction was the rule. Frontier posts might have to settle for less, but in most towns well-built public buildings were found whose solid fabric suggested security, strength, and permanence. Surely this contributed to a sense of being in civilized places, places clearly differentiated from those of the supposed or actual barbarians beyond the pale, who (if they were not nomads) lived in primitive shelters and lacked all public amenities.

Another aspect of this urban framework was the effect of the typology overall. Its presence was as important as its functions: that it was *there* counted greatly in making and defining a Roman town, important though temples, baths, and theatres were in their own right. Since there was rarely a district other than the neighborhood of the forum or agora in which a number of public buildings were grouped closely together, except in some of the largest cities, there were fewer topographically drawn tensions between the governed and the authority placed over them than in towns dominated by citadels or castles; considerable walking was required in order to take in all the public buildings. Roman towns were legible, with well-marked paths, largely visible objectives, and quarters loosely centered on big public buildings. Main streets always led to these buildings, to major gates, or to both.

VI

CLASSICISM FULFILLED

ROMAN INTERVENTION in the historical evolution of Greek forms changed classical architecture profoundly. Though properly Greek elements were used lavishly in Hellenistic architecture, the spare clarity of the earlier buildings was abandoned in the creation of a more intricate and often scenic architecture in the Near East. This was the epitome of sophistication for many architects of the later Republic and early empire, who both imitated it and expanded upon it. From the perspective of Greek architecture of the fifth and fourth centuries B.C., the Romans created a hybrid classicism in grafting Greek and Hellenistic motifs onto Italian cores. This architecture, its surface patterns predominantly Hellenistic, was in turn gradually integrated with the arched and vaulted structures resulting from Roman investigations of novel spatial enclosures. Largely because of this chain of transformations and interactions, mature architecture of the imperial age was stylistically complex, of greater formal range than anything seen before.

This condensed summary of the origins and diversity of imperial design suggests both the difficulty of composing a comprehensive stylistic definition of it and the multiple roots of its imagery. But in spite of its heterogeneity, the buildings themselves are clearly Roman, members all of a broad if highly diversified whole. If one of the necessary qualities of a major style is unambiguous differentiation from other styles, then there was a distinctively Roman architecture in imperial times. With few possible exceptions, Roman buildings cannot be mistaken for Greek ones, any more than Renaissance or later classicizing buildings embodying Romanizing elevations and details can be confused with their ancient sources. Why are these things so? What is the essence of imperial architecture that assures its ready visual identification? At the root of the matter lies the composite nature of the imperial system itself, the matrix for creative conjunctions of varied artistic forces.

TOMBS

In Roman society as in others, tombs reflect the full spectrum of architectural taste and fashion. Pride discards restraint, and fine monuments are investments in family prestige. Privately built, Roman tombs were public displays, often inventive in design and always intended to attract attention. The hope of having a splendid, eye-catching monument is nicely sent up by Petronius when he has Trimalchio give detailed instructions to his friend Habinnas about building him one that would do him justice.

> Put up round the feet of my statue carvings of my little dog, some wreaths, bottles of perfume, and all the fights of the [gladiator] Petraites . . . I want the monument to be a hundred feet wide and two hundred deep, for I would like to have different kinds of fruit trees and plenty of vines growing around my ashes . . . I am appointing one of [my] freedmen to be caretaker of the tomb, to prevent people from damaging it. I beg you to put ships in full sail (on it) . . . and me sitting in official robes on my official seat, wearing five gold rings and distributing coins out of a sack . . . And make me a dining room with couches, if you can manage it, and show all the townspeople enjoying themselves. On my right hand put a statue of Fortunata with a dove in her hand and leading her pet dog; and my dear little boy . . . and big wine jars . . . and a broken urn with a boy weeping over it; and a sundial in the middle so that anyone looking at the time will read my name whether he likes it or not. And again, please think carefully whether this inscription seems quite appropriate to you: "Here lies Gaius Pomponius Trimalchio, freedman of Maecenas. He was made an official of the imperial cult, in absentia . . . Pious, courageous, true, he came from nothing but left thirty millions. He never listened to a philosopher. Goodbye, Trimalchio, and you also, passerby".[66]

What Trimalchio orders is a substantial garden-tomb complex, overrun with statuary and planting, covering nearly 2000 sq. m., where tableaux of his life as he wished it to be remembered could be seen.[67] It was to be a distinctly public place, like all Roman monumental tombs; this and stylistic diversity make them particularly relevant to the study of form and design in urban architecture. Large numbers survive in cemeteries and beside major roads leading up to city gates. Many of these tombs are substantially complete, and examples are found in almost all regions.

Like baths, tombs vary greatly in plan and elevation in spite of their common function. They show no stylistic coherence. No attempt was made to identify them by means of formal similarity, though homogeneous groups do appear, as for example at Palmyra, or at Isola Sacra; functional identification was usually left to location and context and to funerary symbols and inscriptions. This apparent contradiction between use and style was common in Roman architecture. Patrons and builders often felt free to use whatever architectural features and motifs they wished, irrespective of the purposes of their buildings.

The resulting intersections of design and function must be taken into account in the search for an understanding of Roman style. Tombs make a good starting point. They record a full appreciation and understanding of the flexibility, the ready adaptability, of classical design elements—orders, mouldings, pediments, niches, arches, vaults, podia, and so on—and provide detailed evidence of the rich variety of possible combinations of them. Roman monumental cemeteries looked somewhat like Victorian ones in Britain and America, or like those of Genoa or Catania.[68] Syntheses of Greek, Hellenistic, and Roman ideas, together with the intrusion of exotic, non-classical forms, appear in both periods. The following discussion may serve as a working guide to formal categories. In it the word *tomb* is used loosely, for the actual coffins or urns were often placed below the visible monuments, or nearby, and some memorials or cenotaphs lacked coffins or urns altogether.

From a visual standpoint, tombs can be divided into two basic categories, scenic (externalized and highly articulated) and unitary (geometric and comparatively unarticulated). In the first, what counts is an unabashed display of architecture and sculpture; tombs of this kind often derive from temples, four-square structures, the stage buildings of theatres, and other urban types. Monuments of the second kind are each composed of a primary shape clearly defined, a single volume or solid mass such as a cylinder or a prismatic, boxlike form, also familiar in urban contexts. The wide variety of types and the many possible combinations of motifs resist orderly, detailed classification, though several broad schemes have been suggested.[69] The one that follows emphasizes architectural effects and silhouettes—that is, the imagery of forms—and though it cannot absorb every Roman tomb, it includes the major divisions of the genre. Its chief purpose is to suggest the extensive range of Roman funerary design.

I.   Scenic displays
    A.   With one principal facade
        1.   Aediculas, loges
        2.   Elaborately patterned walls
        3.   Prostyle structures
        4.   Exedra forms
    B.   Intended to be seen from any side
        1.   Staged, articulated towers
        2.   Four-square monuments
        3.   Tholoi
II.   Unitary forms
    A.   Strongly verticalized
        1.   Orders standing free
        2.   Plain towers
        3.   Pyramids
        4.   Obelisks
    B.   Volumetric, with horizontal emphasis
        1.   Cylinders and rotundas
        2.   Single chambers
        3.   Massive, rectilinear blocks

High bases or platforms often supported pyramids or tholoi, altars or sarcophagi.
86   Aediculas are also almost always so elevated. The monument of the Julii at St.-Rémy is
typical of a class with one motif piled atop another (I.B. 1.). There is at least one example
131 of a *tombeau parlant,* that of the baker Eurysaces just outside the Porta Maggiore in
Rome, studded with simulacra of the kneading-tubs of his trade. The ashes of his wife
Atistia may have been placed in a marble bread-basket, an example of allusive practice
seen elsewhere in other guises, for example a ship-shaped tomb at Utica or the wine-
barrel tombstones found in Portugal.[70] No single fashion prevailed, though there were
regional preferences, some quite pronounced. Taken overall, tombs record greater
formal variety than any other class of Roman building.

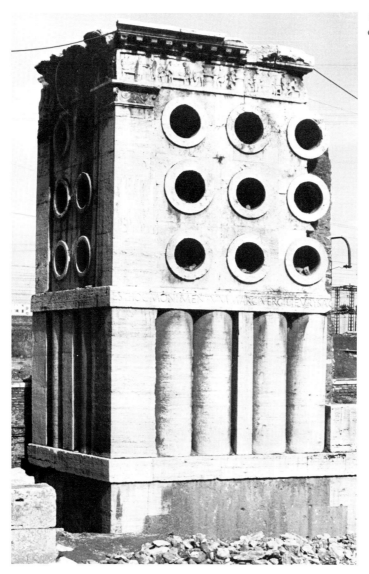

131. Rome, Tomb of Eurysaces;
ca. 30 B.C.

Symmetry rules Roman funerary design, and nowhere is it more apparent than in *facade tombs* (I.A.). Through its agency, attention is focused on the central feature—an image of the deceased, or an axial link between the spectator and the center of the main structure, such as the frontal steps of a temple form or an exedra's centered curve. Display is emphasized, of sculpture or architectural space or both. Facing one way only, these tombs are designed to attract, even demand, attention from passers-by. An *aedicular tomb* with its sculpture is a small, fixed theatre of the dead, embowered by a miniature proscenium (Rome, three along the northeast side of the Via Appia, past the Raccordo Anulare, between the seventh and ninth milestones; Pompeii, tomb of P. Vesonius by the Porta Nuceria). When the niches are deep and protected by roofs supported partly on columns, they resemble the traditional roadside shrines of Christian times (Pompeii, west tomb. no. 9 by the Porta Nuceria; Sarsina, the twin tombs of the Murcii; Šempeter, those of C. Spectatius Priscianus and the Enii). The *loge tomb* is much the same except that the niche-chamber or stage is larger and is screened by columns, usually four, forming a porch (Ammaedera; Cologne, the tomb of L. Poblicius; Sarsina, that of Aefionius Rufus; compare that of M. Octavius at Pompeii, by the Porta Nuceria; Termessos, the tomb of Mamastis). Both types embody a major Roman architectural trait, one-sidedness, that bonds them to the open space in front, however small. Both exploit not only the primacy of a single or principal facade but integrate it with the space-forming and space-fixing qualities of the open niche or chamber and its symmetrical enframement. This potent three-dimensional configuration subtracts visual interest and formal presence from its surroundings and concentrates them in one, centered cavity. A cardinal motif of Roman and of much subsequent classicizing architecture, this configuration appears in low relief on many Roman gravestones.

A *wall tomb* is one with a principal facade of three or five units or bays in a row, all of the same height. These bays may or may not be of equal width but are arranged symmetrically, and one or more may contain a niche; divisions between them are marked by pilasters. The multiplicity of parts and emphasis on horizontality diffuses somewhat the focal power of the symmetry. Stepped bases are common. If there is a podium, it will not be nearly so high proportionately as those supporting aediculas or loggias. The result is an articulated wall wider than it is tall, carrying sculpture (normally in relief, more rarely freestanding) and inscriptions, usually placed low enough to be read easily. The wall may be curved (Athens, the monument of Philopappos; or straight (Sadaba, that of the Atilii), and may mask a sizable but comparatively plain structure behind. The bays themselves, in addition to the pilasters and any niches, may be set in planes forward and back alternately. The origins and architectural context of this type are to be sought in a conflation of the traditional wall carrying funerary sculpture and symbols, so familiar both in Rome (along the Via Appia) and in the provinces, with what might be called the palatine wall, the forward-and-back, pavilioned structures seen in the grand salons of many imperial buildings, from the Aula Regia of Domitian's palace in Rome to the marble halls of imperial baths.[71] In the tombs, however, freestanding orders are rarely used, and no matter how richly and

132. Athens, monument of Philopappos; 116

133. Rome, "tomb of Annia Regilla", model; ca. 16o

deeply worked the wall may be, it remains a solid wall. In this sense, wall-tombs are related to the long sides of architectural sarcophagi.

Prostyle tombs have facades composed of freestanding columns placed in front of accessible chambers, constructed or rock-cut. Some are versions of the podium temple, in their original condition complete with frontal steps (Ghirza, in the north cemetery;   133 above Wadi Latrun; Rome, S. Urbano; Iasus, the Roman mausoleum; Elaeussa; there is an example of the first century B.C. at Agrigento, called the Oratorio di Falidario). It is probable that some structures now called chamber or "house" tombs (category II.B.) were originally prostyle buildings but have lost their stairs and porches. Stepless types were also built (Fabara, the tomb of L. Aemilius Lupus; Ruweiha). An elaborately decorated temple-tomb, raised on a high podium gained by the usual flight of steps, is   90 depicted on a relief from the Haterii monument now in the Vatican Museum. It records the high point of a tradition that continued for another three centuries, as the simple temple-tomb of Lazarus, seen in Christian art, shows. The design principles of the civic podium temple apply to most of these buildings.

A case in point is the rock-cut structure at Petra known as the Khasneh or treasury. Its   134 use and date have not been established; it may or may not have been a tomb. But given its proportions, detailing, sophisticated composition, and its clear artistic distance from the other rock-cut facades of Petra, it probably dates from the Roman period (after 106), when classical influences were strengthened there.[72] Well preserved (and well known), it is a major example of one of the chief strains in imperial architecture overall: near-baroque scenic compositions based on a reordering of traditional forms.

For the present, only the Khasneh's main characteristics need attention. Divided into two stories, it is 39.6 m. high to the top of the centered urn. In the lower story, a temple front stands somewhat forward, its pediment set against an attic. Above that is a blind tholos standing largely free and flanked by halves of a temple front. Above these in turn   135 rise truncated, unfinished forms—apparently huge obelisks, which, had they been completed, would from the classical point of view have unbalanced the composition and given it a barbaric cast. Within this immense work of sculpted architecture the parts are successfully harmonized in a balanced whole, the result of well thought-out planning (the presumed obelisks aside; perhaps that is why they were never finished?). Details such as the handling of the moulding at the base of the central tholos relief, which retreats confidently behind the columns in the manner of Borromini, make this clear. The upper and lower stories are ingeniously balanced. Neither overpowers the other, partly because of the way the lower temple front is repeated, riven in half, at the sides of the upper story. This is the work of a gifted architect who, while creating a complex design, regulated the relationships of its parts precisely. The overall effect is one of stability and repose in spite of complexity and inversion (the pediment systems above and below). The other large rock-cut tombs of Petra appear heavy-handed in comparison.

Though not the same shape, nor as large, several tombs with facades of freestanding columns were responses to the same urge toward a scenic, even dramatic unity composed

134. Petra, the Khasneh; probably
second century

135. Petra, the Khasneh, detail

of many parts (Pozzuoli, the tomb with a concave lower story surmounted by a polygonal tholos; compare S. Maria Capua Vetere, the tomb known as La Conocchia, where 136 the cylindrical order-like forms are not quite free of the main body of the building). There are numerous paintings in a similar mode (Pompeii, in the Corinthian oecus of the House of the Labyrinth, or the scene of Apollo with Hesperos and Phosphoros in the 181 House of Apollo; Herculaneum, the rotunda painting in Insula V; Boscoreale, in the cubiculum of the Villa).

Exedra tombs have semicircular or U-shaped recesses at ground level that open directly 103, 143 onto central paths or roads. An ancient form, with sacral associations, the exedra was common in Republican times (Rome, the Tomb of the General in the Conservatori Museum; Delos, the Agora of the Italians). Numerous examples of both Republican and imperial date are seen at Pompeii in the tomb areas outside the major gates. At Ostia, beyond the Porta Marina, there is a monument with two exedras flanking a wide 204 rectangular recess; all three had benches. As with civic exedras, those marking tombs created spaces for relaxation off the lines of traffic, in the hope that the deceased's public-spiritedness would be remembered. The type does not include tombs having benchless curving facades (those in Pozzuoli and Athens just mentioned; Petra, the central ground-level bay of the Deir), or open, semicircular niches vaulted over, such as the one 137 found about 60 m. outside the Porta Ercolano at Pompeii. Architecturally, the radiality of exedras counts most because it suggests focused groups of people of the kind exedras accommodated when used as meeting places for philosophers and other worthies.

Of the class of scenic, articulated *tombs intended to be seen from any side* (I.B.), towers were the most common; they were built in many regions. With the exception of the lighthouse, the tower is not usually regarded as a significant element of Roman architecture, though in fact it was. There were military towers in abundance (beside the gateways of cities and towns; along frontier defense lines; rising from army buildings, as at Umm al-Jemal), and towers were once normal features of towns and villas (Pompeii, water towers; painted and mosaic scenes of town and villa life). *Tower tombs* seem either to have been built in groups, spaced quite well apart (Dura Europos; Palmyra) or alone, away from cemeteries in more or less isolated positions (Maktar; the so-called Tower of 138, 142 the Scipios near Tarragona). The proportionate height required to make a building a tower is debatable, but in general the ratio of base width to overall height should be at least 1:3. And to be a proper member of this class, all four sides of the tower must display the same architectural configuration, save perhaps for a real or false door at the base of one side.

Tower tombs are divided into stages or stories—usually three, sometimes two or four—by entablatures or cornices; no continuous features connect base and summit (compare lighthouses, as at La Coruña and in mosaics and on coins). In most examples the stages are somewhat narrowed, one above the other (Dougga), though some have slightly sloping walls (Hermel). There is much dramatic variety in the silhouettes of the top stories. There are pyramids of normal triangular outline (Maktar), stepped versions 142 (Diocaesarea), and even S-curve shapes (Igel). There are cones convex (St.-Rémy) and 86

136. S. Maria Capua Vetere, La Conocchia; second half of the second century

137. Petra, the Deir; possibly early second century

concave (Jerusalem, the so-called Tomb of Absalom). Slender spires are found at Ghirza, 139, 140
Gsar Umm al-Ahmed, and other Tripolitanian wadi towns. (These are often called
obelisk tombs, but their tall spires rose nearly to points, and lacked the mansard-like
change of slope of the pyramidons necessary to true obelisks.) Many were finished off
with distinctive finials in the fashion of the Lysikrates monument in Athens. At the
bottom of a tower, the square first stage—often framed by corner pilasters—functioned
as a high podium, rising from circumscribing flights of three to five steps. By these
means, distinctive outlines and pronounced architectural character were obtained, in
strong contrast to plain, flat-roofed tower tombs (category II.A.). Most scenic tower
tombs are solid (Igel; Dougga; Dura Europos), but a few were pierced through (St.-
Rémy; Nettuno).

136   As in the case of prostyle tombs, a proto-baroque strain existed, exemplified by La
          Conocchia, a tower tomb that stands, somewhat restored, just east of S. Maria Capua
          Vetere. Well known, studied and drawn by Ligorio and Piranesi, among others, it may
          have been the inspiration for Borromini's tower for S. Andrea delle Fratte in Rome. Like
134   the Khasneh at Petra, its counterpart in stylistic mood and direction if not in form, it is
          not firmly dated, though it may have been built in the later part of the second century.
          The first of its three stages is unexceptional, but the mediating second stage is dis-
          tinctive if not unique. By exploiting the diagonals inherent in the square base below,
          the designer created a swinging structure of four vanes that point away from the implied
          orthogonal axes of both the base and the centered features between them.[73] These vanes
          terminate in cylinders barely attached to the main body of the work, which is an
          aediculated block set well back from the wall planes of the podium below. Toward the
          top of this composition, in the zone of its pediments, parallel stringcourses (now partly
          lost) reach out and loop around the cylinders, seeming to fix and stabilize them at the
135   top. This is related to the way the tholos cornice is handled at the Khasneh and
          reminiscent of the embracing bands that tie the engaged columns of the entranceway of
157   the Temple of Venus at Baalbek to the adjacent doorframe. Immediately below these
          cornices, in the recessed zone of each aedicula, three shallow niches—the flanking ones
          narrow and arcuated, the central one rectangular—are shouldered closely together, the
          side ones toed in by virtue of the curves of the vanes. In each of these niches is a blind
          circular window. Above the middle stage, on a plain, round podium, sits a solid tholos,
          with arcuated, recessed panels set into its columniated wall.

          The design is brilliantly successful. First, although the building is entirely blind, it
reads as if it were not: the three dozen niches and circular recesses graven on its surface
give it, by means of their shadows, the lineaments of a windowed structure. Second, the
plain podium keeps the design from being overly exuberant, and the bold, bollard-like
cylinders appear to rise from the podium to anchor the middle zone and keep it from
rotating on the podium surface. Third, the only lines that are drawn, so to speak, on the
building's surface are string cornices. All of the normal, traditional elaborations were
suppressed, giving to what is a somewhat massive structure a certain lightness and
vitality. To appreciate the significance of this, imagine the forms of the building
outlined by elaborate stone borders. Finally, the curving surfaces of the middle stage
retreat toward that of the cylinder above nearly to the planes of tangency, locking the
middle-zone aediculas and the verticals of the tholos together in rational vertical relationships, harmonizing the juxtaposition of the two disparate, counter-curving zones.
As at Petra, the designer managed to create a powerfully unified building out of diverse
forms and design elements without sacrificing any of the dramatic originality he sought.
Even if the tomb was once stuccoed, painted, and decorated with relief sculpture, its
essentially baroque character, its tight and complete unity, would have been as apparent
as it is today.

          The architectural character of civic *four-square structures* applies only in part to tombs
of this class because they are almost always elevated on podia. Many are of the quad-

138. (LEFT) Tarragona, near, the tomb "of the Scipios"; first century?

139. (BELOW LEFT) Jerusalem, tomb "of Absalom"; first century B.C.?

140. (BELOW) Wadi Messueggi, spire tomb; probably fourth century

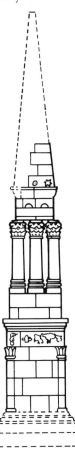

141. Aquileia, tomb of the Curii; mid-first century

rifrons kind, with the roof, usually vaulted, carried on piers or columns. The type with piers was popular in the east (Brad; Alif) but was also built in the west (the second stage at St.-Rémy). An example in Commagene has a pyramidal roof of concave silhouette (Assar; compare the tomb of the Curii at Aquileia, with three columns only, set on a round base and topped by a three-cornered pyramid with concave sides). A plain pyramidal roof is found on a quadrifrons at Djuwaniyeh, where there is also a variant on this type, a tomb of oblong plan with dissimilar long sides, the principal one with a broad gabled arch, the other with an extra, centered pier. At Ephesus the Memmius monument, with deep niches on three of its four sides, hints at an emerging quadrifrons.

The type with column supports seems to have been more rare (the restored Bierbach canopy tomb, now in the Speyer historical museum, approximates this form; that from Ghirza, now in the Castello in Tripoli, also arcuated but lacking its uppermost feature, has a sturdy central ashlar pier, seen in other Tripolitanian tombs, that may originally have supported a spire). The quite unclassical domical baldacchino tomb seen on one of the Haterii reliefs in the Vatican is also of this type. At least one columned example with horizontal lintels is known (Dana north), where the roof is a flattened, stepped pyramid; this structure is schematically like one of the individual four-column systems of the restored Palmyra tetrakionion. At Pompeii, outside the Porta Nuceria, there is a tomb on the model of a tetrakionion. A high, square podium supports four corner pedestals, from each of which rises a pier with engaged columns at its corners. This is as original a design as that of La Conocchia, where the four tall cylinders of the middle zone hint at the tetrakionion concept. There is a somewhat similar composition at Ariccia, the "Tomba degli Orazi e Curiazi," where four cones rise from the podium corners and a conical feature from the center. This too is related to La Conocchia in that both have quincunx plans (based on X-shaped axes placed diagonally within a rectangular outline).

The *tholos* (technically the monopteros, a ring of columns), perhaps because of its relative fragility, is not often preserved. Besides those atop the tower tombs of St.-Rémy and Nettuno, and the blind forms of the Khasneh and Capua Vetere, there are examples at Pompeii (the tomb of the Istacidii, just outside the Porta Ercolano, had eight columns and a conical roof, topped by a pinecone, all placed on a high podium block) and at Aquileia (a restored six-column structure with a slightly concave conical roof and a pinecone finial, also all on a massive base). The Tropeum of Augustus at La Turbie was a grandiose version of this kind of structure: first an immense podium, then a masonry cylinder encircled by twenty-four freestanding columns, then a low drum and a stepped cone supporting an over-life-sized statue of Augustus, the whole 49 m. high. The lost "Tour d'Horloge" of Aix-en-Provence may have had two circular stories rising from the usual high cubical base, the lower with engaged columns, the upper with columns standing free around a comparatively slender masonry cylinder. And there were polygonal forms too (Pola; Split).

Far simpler in design than scenic tombs, those of unitary form (group II) require less comment. *Strongly verticalized tombs* frequently rise well above their surroundings, clear-   142

142. Dougga, tower tomb; said to be second century B.C.

ly signaling the location of hallowed ground (II.A.). The volumetric, relatively horizontal ones, with lower silhouettes, can be of monumental size. Of the category of vertical
structures, the forms of the first two divisions are traditional (orders standing free;
plain, unarticulated towers). The second two (pyramids, obelisks) are from Egypt,
products both of Roman fascination with things Egyptian and of Egypt's influence on
the southeastern region of the empire. All four types are instantly readable. Little
sculpture was applied, and architectural detailing is scarce on the whole. There is scant
evidence of that fascination with scenic design so evident in the tombs just discussed, so
there are very few openings or recesses of consequence. Any flamboyancy or theatricality
is achieved by height or size, not by complex composition.

Monumental and memorial *freestanding columns,* common in antiquity, were frequently used. Single shafts had been numerous in the cemeteries of Greek cities, as for
example at Athens, and the paired honorific columns of Delphi have already been
mentioned.[74] These practices were continued in Roman times, for example at Mainz
(the Jupiter Column), Brindisi (the twin columns marking the arrival of the Via Appia
at the sea), Edessa, Damascus, Rome, Constantinople (the several imperial columns),
Alexandria (Diocletian's Column ["Pompey's Pillar"]), and Jerusalem (Hadrian's column, shown on the Madaba mosaic map, its stump now visible). Freestanding columns
appear in Roman paintings of sacred landscapes. Tombs marked by single columns are
found east and west (Kfer Rum; Rome, the Column of Trajan; Pompeii, among others
143   the tomb of Aesquillia Pollia outside the Porta di Nola, with an Ionic column rising

143. Pompeii, exedra tomb with column

from the center of the curve of an exedra and carrying an amphora-urn). Twin columns standing on oblong podia are found in the east (Sermeda; Benabil; Qatara, the tomb of Aemillius Regillus, with a vaulted crypt entrance whose extrados rises above podium level between the column bases; compare Sitt-er-Rum, the tomb of Isodotus, where piers were substituted for columns).

Unarticulated tower tombs, their internal stories indicated externally, if at all, by simple mouldings, are found chiefly at Palmyra (of the 150-odd tombs known there, many fall within this category). There is another in the environs of Qanawat; compare the sober tower tombs of Hatra. At Palmyra some of the major examples have elaborately architecturalized interiors (that of Elahbel, for example, whose exterior is unstaged and almost entirely free of decorative features). It may be that some of the dilapidated hulks found in the west—beside the Via Appia, for example—were plain towers. *Pyramids* are harder for time to disguise, and a considerable number have survived. They range from quite small (Pompeii, inside a walled enclosure beyond the Porta Ercolano, at the base of the narrow triangular piazza where the street to the Villa of the Mysteries branches off) to the monumental (Rome, the famous tomb of C. Cestius; Lepcis Magna, the Gsar Sciaddad). There are numerous examples in Syria of pyramids set on podia (Bara [three]; Hass; Dana south; Taltita), including an octagonal one (Qalat Kalota); there is another octagonal example, very high for its base width, at Quarto di Marano in Campania. In Africa, pyramid-building continued until the fourth century (Meroë).

Obelisks were popular; forty-two are known to have been transported from Egypt to Rome in imperial times. Augustus placed an obelisk on each side of the entrance to his mausoleum in the Campus Martius. At Petra the Obelisk Tomb has four carved in high relief on its facade, and two others stand free on the Attuf hights just south of the city proper. In the cemetery outside the Caesarea Gate at Tipasa are several moderately sized 144 stones shaped like pyramidons, and the remains of what was probably an obelisk shaft, cut to the same scale. An obelisk may perhaps have stood beside the Canopus at Hadrian's Villa as the chief feature of a monument to Antinoüs.[75]

The last group (II.B.) is of *tombs of cylindrical or prismatic outline,* with some exceptions wider (or longer) than they are high. Augustus' mausoleum sparked the popularity of the *cylindrical form;* Hadrian's Pantheon, of the imperial rotunda. Chamber tombs, standing free or in rows, are versions of the basic volumetric unit or room common to most architecture; massive blocks are podia become monuments, or versions of public altars.

The cylinder faced with masonry, a mortuary form of great antiquity, is common in the west (Rome, the tomb of Caecilia Metella; near Tiddis, the tomb of Lollius). 145 Internal chambers are normal, reached directly by straight corridors (S. Maria Capua Vetere, "Le carceri"), or in more roundabout fashion by curving segmental or annular ones (Gaeta, tomb of L. Munatius Plancus; the mausoleum of Augustus has both kinds). But these structures are not hollow, for their encircling walls (usually little adorned) do not define corresponding spaces within. Instead they are a species of circular podium, partly or largely filled with masonry or earth. Some are huge (Augustus' tomb, 87 m. in

144. Tipasa, west cemetery

145. Tiddis, near, Tomb of Lollius; mid-second century

146. Antalya, tomb; first century

diameter; Hadrian's, 64; Vize, the largest tumulus, 55), few are small (Lollius' tomb, 10.2 m.; Pulborough in Sussex, 18.3; Plancus, 29.5). Low cones of piled-up earth rose from the encircling walls of larger monuments, and the exteriors were sometimes sheathed in masonry rising to a centered pedestal carrying sculpture (Augustus; Gaeta, Plancus' tomb; compare the war memorial at Adamklissi). Elevation of cylinders on podium blocks was common (Pozzuoli, two tombs at S. Vito; Marano di Napoli; Antalya; compare the discussion of tholoi, above). There were polygonal versions also 146 (Neumagen; Cyrrhus).

Tombs in the form of *domed cylinders,* with or without temple-front porches, are prominent in the literature of Roman architecture. Several were built as imperial mausolea (Rome, those of Romulus beside the Via Appia and of Helena on the Via Labicana; perhaps the "Tor de' Schiavi" on the Via Labicana; Split, Diocletian's tomb; Salonika, Galerius' tomb). Some seem not to have had projecting entrance features (Alife; Marano di Napoli). In rotunda tombs, as in the Pantheon, only the walls and vaults were solid, so the interiors were unobstructed, unitary spaces. The curving interior walls were recessed with niches, and sometimes columns were deployed before them. At Cassino a cross-plan example has a domed crossing (the tomb of "Ummidia Quadratilla").

Chamber tombs are of square or oblong plan and usually enclose a single space, though they are sometimes subdivided internally or raised to two stories. Very common, mostly of modest size, they look like trim, gable-roofed houses (though their vaults might be left uncovered). In Rome and its environs they are made of brick and concrete; elsewhere 147 they are normally of stone. The more sophisticated of the latter are much like the smaller prostyle tombs, but lack porches (Hierapolis; Elaeussa; Apamea; compare the shrine by 161 the Alcantara bridge). These often have corner pilasters, full cornices, and pedimental mouldings. Most have traditional, moulded doorways, but archways taking up whole facades are known (Elaeussa). Scores of brick-faced examples have survived in the area of Rome (Isola Sacra; Ostia; under S. Peter's and S. Sebastiano).

As with imperial domed rotundas, their chief architectural interest often lies in their interiors, for some are highly articulated and brightly colored. In the first tomb of the Caetennii, for example, found under S. Peter's, the walls are composed in a fashion 148 reminiscent of the Khasneh and La Conocchia. On the north, a niched aedicula is centered under a larger, enframing niche, which is flanked by subordinate rectilinear niches surmounted by half-pediments, the whole embellished with stucco colonnettes. The side walls were designed in a comparable manner. The floor was black and white, the walls purple, greenish blue, white, and Pompeian red. Similar if somewhat less exuberant interiors are found at Isola Sacra (tombs 19, 57, 87, and 93, for example). In the eastern cemetery at Ostia there are roofless tombs lacking any decor, whose walls 193 were similarly configured.

The final class of tombs has as its primary feature *massive, usually solid masonry blocks,* rectilinear in form, which may or may not support another element—a sarcophagus or other funerary image. Stepped at the bottom and edged around the top with mouldings,

147. Rome, tomb by the Via Ostiense; probably late second century

148. Rome, under S. Peter's, tomb of the Caetennii, axonometric partial view of the interior, seen from below; mid-second century.

0   1   2   3   4 m.

these blocks are essentially freestanding podia. Some are shaped like altars, and many blocky tombs recall them in a general way as well; biers and catafalques may also have influenced this choice of form. There are numerous examples beside the tomb streets of Pompeii and Rome, and many provincial ones also (Aquileia; Sepino; Reggio Calabria; Taliata).

For the sake of completeness, mention should be made of podium blocks supporting compositions that cannot easily be fitted into the schema used here, such as the handsome, unusual variants found in cemeteries of Tripolitanian wadi towns (Ghirza, square podia carrying triple arcades around all four sides, with a square central pier, perhaps a support for a spire, inside). At Gsar Doga, northeast of Tarhuna, a U-shaped podium of rectilinear plan, two stories high, once carried a doubled Corinthian colonnade of thirty-six columns, the whole rather like a compressed, narrow version of the Great Altar at Pergamon.

The inclusion here of several examples from the Tripolitanian hinterland is not simply eccentric, for there the classical architecture of cities and towns was concentrated in cemeteries. This is good evidence, from the edge of civilization, for the pervasiveness of the desire to build elaborate funerary monuments and for the high rank they held in the typology of Roman architecture; it follows that these examples help validate the use of tombs in studying formal variety in imperial buildings. At the outpost on the Wadi Ghirza (by direct line about 180 km. south of Lepcis Magna), sophisticated architecture served only the dead. The place was founded in the second half of the third century, one of a straggling row of southern defensive positions roughly defining the frontier in the region. The occupants, by Constantine's time *limitanei,* or resident border troops, had to support themselves in an inhospitable setting. They lived with their families in a small village (about twelve hectares) of stone-built, fortified buildings of unrelieved plainness; thirty-five are known, four of them courtyard structures about 25 m. on a side. When the rains cooperated, about 250 hectares could be cultivated, the water caught and temporarily held by a system of barrages; there were of course also cisterns. Very few if any of the amenities routinely found in the coastal cities to the north were available.

87, 140

Yet in spite of this marginal existence the inhabitants managed to put up at least eight prominent architectural tombs of various kinds out among the ordinary graves. Like the houses, these major projects were carried out without the benefit of some of the specialized labor and other resources real towns could provide. Fine tombs, however, were prized, and the examples of Ghirza and other southern Tripolitanian sites are fine by any standard. Their significance in the broad scheme of things is that columns, arcades, and temple forms were not seen in the wadi settlements themselves but in their outlying cemeteries, the only places favored with urban architecture. These village cemeteries were the local equivalents of those for example at Pompeii or Hierapolis, where so much of the formal spectrum of imperial architecture was displayed. Even at Ostia, whose buildings were the most overtly functional of any town, tomb interiors in the cemeteries by the Porta Romana and at Isola Sacra mirrored the style of public monuments elsewhere.

DIVERSITY

Tombs record best the variety of architectural form under the empire, when the number of viable combinations of classical building elements reached its zenith, never to be seen again. Understandably enough, they are sometimes called fantasy buildings, but their very exuberance makes them relevant to discussions of mature Greco-Roman classicism because taken together they come close to describing its formal limits. In addition, there are more complete or nearly complete examples of tombs than of any other kind of building except shops. Polarities of originality and tradition are fully represented, as well as the Roman habit of using different stylistic modes for structures of the same function. Most important, tombs make up cities of the dead in a literal sense, reflecting and recapitulating urban building types and most stylistic modes of imperial architecture. These familiar intramural forms gave monumental cemeteries a quality of stilled urbanism, where sculpture replaced people and the buildings recalled surroundings the dead had relinquished.

Diversity in tomb design was not regional, for most types were widespread. Arcades, both blind and open, appeared in Spain, Germany, Italy, Libya, Greece, and Syria; towers, single chambers, and round monuments were pandemic; pyramids and especially pyramidally-roofed structures were quite common (solid blocks of square plan invite pyramidal roofs); and so on. As with tombs, so with a large portion of architecture generally: baths and passage structures were the next most diverse in appearance. Such extensive variety inhibits stylistic definition—so much so that variety itself appears to have been a major characteristic of imperial design. But since the buildings are unmistakably Roman, they must have common features, and these will be discussed shortly. For now the freedom of design seen in cities and towns needs emphasis. It was a freedom fashioned from the vigorous—almost relentless—pursuit of new combinations of familiar elements. Many architects and builders were willing to abandon tradition and attempt new and untried combinations and compositions. Some of the tombs just described are cases in point. Familiarity today with many of these innovations, gained from their recollection in later architecture, makes it easy to forget that they first appeared during the last phase of classical architecture, so highly creative.

If buildings from this period are contrasted with pre-Augustan ones, on the one hand, or Early Christian ones on the other, the abundant richness of their formal diversity is immediately apparent. The complexity of Roman design is greater than in preceeding or succeeding styles. It is often held that the origins of this are found mainly in Hellenistic architecture, but not enough is known yet of the principles of that architecture to make the argument entirely persuasive; thorough study of the character of Hellenistic design is one of the primary desiderata of the history of Western architecture. Whatever the reasons, diversity ruled, and as a result no single governing principle for the management and creation of form stands out. Imperial architecture in this sense has no equivalent of the lucid, sculptural Doric or Ionic systems, no omnipresent identifying shape such as the pointed, repeatedly moulded arch of the Gothic style.

Thus diversity of form lies at the heart of imperial architecture. A tentative definition can be attempted, one that begs the question to a certain extent but helps mark out its boundaries: the architecture of the empire is that phase of classicism in which the elements of Greco-Roman design are used in the greatest number of combinations. The standard handbook examples of this architecture—the Maison Carrée, Arch of Titus, Colosseum, Pantheon, Basilica Ulpia, Palace at Split, Baths of Caracalla, and so on—do not represent the subject adequately. It is no surprise that the structure and materials of major buildings are often dealt with at length, for they are reassuring quantities in buildings whose stylistic character is so problematic and diversity so great. The evidence shows that by the end of the first century some individual elements of design had either lost whatever meanings they may once have possessed or else had transferred them to buildings of quite different character from those where they had originated.

Thereafter, combinations of elements took over, some all at once, some long in gestation. This is clearly seen in tombs, where traditional building parts were assembled in novel compositions. The orders were deployed in ways that would have seemed irrational to Vitruvian architects, sacred symbols such as the fastigium descended to everyday use, and families of mouldings fine or coarse ran along the surfaces of nearly every building. More than that, these changes took place with ever-decreasing relevance to function, so that the most ordinary, even banal, secular buildings included familiar themes from the past, those from temples in particular. This was a crucial development in the history of classical architecture. While it was happening, another kind of archi- 56, 110 tecture, quite plain and little decorated—the austere mode—came to prominence. Old and new, plain and scenic, came to stand side by side.

Tombs and paintings of architecture aside, Pompeii records the coming of these events, of the expanded architectural imagery of the high imperial age. Between the earthquake of 62 and the disaster of August 79 the new forms appeared in strength in places where domestic buildings and many civic structures had previously been given over nearly entirely to traditional design. After the earthquake, novel buildings ap- peared, and some older ones were revised along progressive lines. The building of 149 Eumachia, facing the northeast side of the forum, is a case in point. Its forum facade was articulated with small rectilinear niches alternating with large segmental recesses. The colonnaded interior peristyle, wrapped on its long sides within two sets of parallel walls and at its far end by three sets, terminated in a large exedra. This had three radially placed niches arranged symmetrically and centered on a statue representing the Concor- dia Augusta; it was screened by two columns and framed by spur walls projecting slightly toward the columns, all set along the exedra's chord.

Just to the southeast, past the Temple of Vespasian, is the building known as the civic 150 lararium (some say a library). Here an oblong court, open to the forum colonnade and to the sky, and measuring 18.2 by 19.9 m., is expanded left and right by deep rectangular recesses half as wide as the court is deep. The court is flanked along each side by three niches, the responding pair furthest back being doubly recessed. At its far end is a wide apse, like that at the building of Eumachia slightly masked by short spur walls set along its chord; it is anchored by a wide, powerfully framed rectilinear recess.

Other evidence of the new mood is found at the Temple of Isis, especially in the

149. Pompeii, building of Eumachia, facade; early first century

150. Pompeii, lararium, plan; after the earthquake of 62

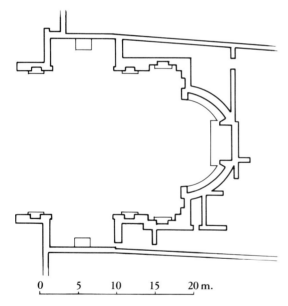

0   5   10   15   20 m.

151. Pompeii, Sanctuary of Isis, Purgatorium, detail; between 62 and 79

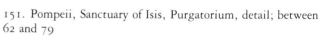

arcuated pediment of the Purgatorium; at the unfinished Central Baths, with their 151
wide-windowed interior facade with its engaged columns, all of brick-faced concrete;
and in numerous other structures such as mosaic fountain niches, open and blind
arcades, paneled walls, and the stage building of the large theatre. None of these forms
would be particularly remarkable at Lepcis Magna, Ephesus, or Side. But at Pompeii,
given the date of its destruction and the subsequent development of imperial architecture, formal variety is solid evidence for the popularity of new ideas. Not only that, but
these are buildings located securely in the west, where, it has often been assumed, the
kind of architectural thinking they represent was less at home than in the east. And at
numerous points in Pompeii, as in Herculaneum, it is clear that the planar, brick-faced
domestic architecture seen at Ostia and Rome was beginning to be substituted for the
traditional atrium house. Even these comfortable Campanian towns were being transformed.

Common Features

In this evolution of increasingly diverse compositions the familiar classical elements
of design persisted. Linking the new with the old, they were potent contributors to the
broad stylistic coherence of imperial architecture. The number of their combinations is
beyond counting, but a brief discussion of some common features can suggest how
classicism was fulfilled. As always in Roman architecture, deviations and unclassifiable
examples—sports in the biologist's sense—appear now and then. Even without them,
the variety of forms is so great that the notion of "correct" or "normal" ones should
probably be avoided, except sometimes for those of specific regions or schools or from
particular periods. Had "correct" forms continued in use with little change for two or
three centuries, creativity would have languished. It is risky to evaluate the design of
little-known buildings because few if any adequate criteria for judgment exist. Non-
subjective assessments usually evolve from comparisons of well-studied monuments,
and there are not many of those.

The most common feature of classical design, the column, began as a treetrunk or as a
structural pier made round. Much refined and given great prominence by the Greeks, it
was long employed mainly on important buildings, set out soberly in pairs or in evenly
spaced rows. Very slowly it came to be used with greater freedom, and by the fourth
century B.C. it had been given many tasks, artistic as well as functional. Non-structural
versions appeared in relief as parts of walls, pilasters (flat, sometimes paneled), and 132, 160
engaged columns. The pilaster was used to harmonize the narrow ends of spur walls with
columns aligned with them, and to divide expanses of wall into rhythmic patterns.
Increasingly it was put behind columns standing before a wall, shadowing and echoing 133
them by forming responding pairs. Engaged orders set at regular intervals recalled the
rhythms of freestanding colonnades.

Hellenistic architects favored slimmer column shafts, experimented with new uses
for the orders in complex and dramatic compositions, and tampered extensively with the

canons of proportion and form predominant in the fifth and fourth centuries B.C. And though some conservative Roman architects and patrons looked back to that distant period—a habit that continued off and on well into the empire—the Hellenistic interest in new solutions and variations was enthusiastically continued by others who were also stimulated by Italic tradition and by the introduction of novel building materials. In later Republican times, the orders commenced a new life in architecture, one that came to maturity under the empire.

In a profound sense, all classically formed columns are the same: rounded and lofty, subtly modeled, self-contained, and independent. Powerful in both fact and appearance, they are the essence of verticality, their stance against gravity echoing the posture of the upright human frame. As reminders of Greece and Rome, and indeed of Western civilization itself, they possess unrivaled symbolic authority. But even so, Roman usage differed greatly from Greek. Variants appeared on the Doric system (whose traditional forms were all but abandoned), and a composite order, its capital combining Ionic and Corinthian forms, came into fairly common use toward the end of the first century. Important as these evolutions were, both in antiquity and to later eyes, they were not as significant to the fulfillment of classicism as the *way* the orders were put to use. Well before Augustus' time the signs of change were clear, as can be seen in the reversed half-tholoi of Terrace IV of the Sanctuary of Fortune at Palestrina, where half-circles of columns were used to screen solid exedra walls rather than to embrace centered structures; or the facades of the Tabularium and related buildings, with their arched openings framed by entablatures and engaged columns. The Arch of Augustus in the

77 Republican Forum has already been mentioned, with its large and small orders side by side, all on pedestal-like bases perhaps derived from podia. After that a true revolution took place at the very heart of the classical tradition in the design and deployment of the orders. No doubt it had some roots in Hellenistic practice, but in its full expression it was as purely an imperial phenomenon as the creation of vaulted monumental interiors.

152, 191 Great freedom in handling individual elements revealed the flexibility inherent in an architectural system easily thought static and intractable. Together with the spread of the orders through almost the entire building typology, this freedom gave the new classicism its distinctive character. The use of the orders as decorative, non-structural design features greatly increased, ranging from miniature pilasters and colonnettes (Rome, the wall behind the pool in the fountain court of the Domus Transitoria) to huge pilasters and engaged columns (Palmyra, the cella wall of the Temple of Bel). Mixed orders appear, as on the arch at Aosta (Corinthian and Doric). Structural and decorative

172 orders of different sizes existed side by side (the Pantheon interior; Athens, Arch of
96 Hadrian), and there appeared what in effect were two-story orders (Lambaesis, the
95 groma; Palmyra, pilasters of the temenos wall of the Temple of Bel; a votive shrine at
158 Alzey, near Mainz). Local variations on classical capitals, some highly original, some Hellenistic, were numerous, especially at sites near the frontier (Trier, in the episcopal museum; Tiddis; Gigthis; Aquincum). Though these might be indebted to regional influences, they were part of a larger, free development of the classical column-and-capital tradition.

152. Ephesus, Prytaneion, double column; third century

153. Sardis, bath-gymnasium complex, marble court, detail; 211

Shafts might be fluted or not, the lack sometimes because of the material; granite, for example, was unsuitable. Spiral flutes were popular, small scale ones on tombstones or inside mausolea (Tilurium; Narona territory; Tomb I under St. Peter's; compare Trajan's Column), and larger at major buildings (Sabratha, the theatre stage building; Timgad, the library; Sardis, the marble court of the bath-gymnasium; compare the spiral shaft in the chapel of the Pietà at St. Peter's). Even pilaster forms in decorative wall inlay might be so treated (Herculaneum, House of Orestes; compare a silver lanx from Corbridge). Floral, vegetal, and viniferous orders, like those seen in Campanian wall paintings, also appeared (Andetrium; Tripoli, quadrifrons of Marcus Aurelius; Rome, the arches of Titus and of the Silversmiths and one of the Haterii reliefs). Shafts, bases, and capitals were made of stone, brick, or concrete faced with brick; stucco, sometimes fluted, would be applied to columnar brickwork. Many different-tinted granites and white and colored marbles were used, as well as porphyry and local stone. Bases and capitals for the more exotic materials were often made of whitish marble. Finally, the use of the pedestal, a kind of individuated or abbreviated podium, became common, both freestanding (Athens, the facade of Hadrian's Library; Lepcis Magna, the street along the east flank of the Severan basilica) and attached (Baalbek, interior of the Temple of Bacchus; numerous honorific and triumphal arches).

Grand temple complexes, stoas, colonnaded streets, and porticos were not the only prolific displays of the orders. Theatre stage buildings, their end walls included, used large numbers of columns (Sabratha, 108; Bosra, 96), as did scenic fountains and re-

53 lated buildings (Rome, the Septizodium, perhaps 162; Lepcis Magna, the Severan nymphaeum, at least 28; Miletus, the great nymphaeum, 74 columns and 36 pilasters).[76] These figures suggest the length to which architects would go in using the orders; in the examples cited, most were broadly non-structural. Often the purpose was

102 to create aediculas for statuary (Olympia, nymphaeum of Herodes Atticus, perhaps 48 columns). Another way to gain a sense of the orders' proliferation is to envision the

7–10 number of columns visible from, say, the center of the Severan plaza at Djemila (at least 61); in the terraces and main building of the Temple of Zeus (perhaps 170) or of Artemis

153 (205) at Gerasa; or from the marble court at Sardis (excluding the external portico on the east [134]), or the propylon and courtyards of the Temple of Zeus at Baalbek (126). Smaller places might lack grand buildings, but not columns, as the reused drums and shafts found in many Byzantine and later religious buildings and defensive works suggest (Kos and Paroikia, the fortifications; Cordova, the Great Mosque; Madauros, the fort).

Indispensable parts of the orders, mouldings are identified by their profiles. These can be rectilinear (the fillets, projecting or recessed), concave (cavetto; scotia), convex (torus; bead), or some combination of these (congé—plane and concave together; the cymas, with coupled concave and convex forms). All require adjacent surfaces, flat or moulded. Traditionally each order has its own selection of mouldings layered in particular sequences to form cornices, entablatures, and column bases (save the Greek Doric). Some are carved and patterned with repeating geometric or stylized natural forms. There are archaeological and comparative studies of mouldings useful for their chronologies of formal evolution, but for artistic functions and effects Beaux-Arts treatises and handbooks are more informative. Since a classical design without mouldings is incomplete, and since mouldings give a building so much of its character, it follows that they are major constituents of classical architecture. In Roman times, Hellenistic precedent was often followed, but just as often mouldings were used in innovative ways.

Mouldings are the most versatile of classical architectural elements. As a designer's pencil, traveling along the paper's surface, evokes in lines the building forms envisioned, so mouldings define by linear shadows and surface modulations the overall shape and primary volumes of the finished structure. Almost no podium, pedestal, gable, entablature, plaque, or doorway is without them. They are also put to many other uses, as the description above of non-traditional tombs suggests. With the change and diversification of classical architecture, mouldings were adapted and given new roles. But whether used traditionally or not, their primary function was to educe and emphasize architectural shape. Narrow, small-scale in section, mouldings gain power over larger forms by being placed on or close to their edges. Used repetitively, as in layers

97, 159 across the surface of an elaborate entablature, their combined effect is greater than the sum of their individual shadow-lines and intricate carving. What they lack in scale they

gain in length, for they are the only building-long, continuous elements found in a classical composition—in an entablature, for example, or at the base or cap of a podium. Discontinuous uses are common, but when mouldings run on, frameworks of continuity bring localized areas and volumes into harmony with the building overall.

Mouldings outline, frame, divide, join, and enrich; the illustrations here give examples of these functions. Contrast is all, the contrast of light and shade. Its effectiveness is shown by the transformation a plain wall undergoes when lines of moulding are placed along its crest: anonymity gives way to greater interest and improved definition. If mouldings are used to edge a good-sized volume, its shape is firmly outlined and given   93, 127, 169 greater presence; the volumetric character of a boxy shape is brought out strongly. Framing, as of plaques and windows, is self-evident; so is the division of walls into more complex and interesting surfaces, or of stories one from another. Joining takes place when a moulding, without any break, leaves one surface or feature and travels round a contiguous one and then returns to continue its original assignment. In such cases mouldings act as packaging agents, suggesting that it is they that hold several features together in a proper relationship. They often look as if they were doing something to bind, tie, or connect different parts of a design when in fact they are not much more than the equivalents of graven lines.

Subtle, powerful, and delicate all at the same time, mouldings are easy to misuse. They can enrich blank surfaces up to a point, but there are no rules for their application; every eye and every age will view the matter differently. If an entablature, for example, is given two dozen mouldings (forty-odd profile changes), like those of the Arch of   97 Titus, the proportions and the amount and character of the carved ornament must be nicely calculated for the effect to be successful. Paradoxically, the detail, if correctly handled, does not stand out particularly. Casual inspection registers only the general effect.

Greek precision in cutting mouldings continued where the tradition was still alive, as in western Asia Minor and some of the larger Syrian sites, and where experts were available or could be summoned to work on major, often imperial projects. But where this expertise did not exist, and where suitable materials were neither available locally nor imported, mouldings were usually simplified and less sharply cut. Those on official buildings might recall Greek forms, but there was a general tendency to treat them with less reverence. And in the west at least there was an Italo-Etruscan tradition of bold, simple forms, partly the result of having to use coarse-grained stones, that probably contributed to this tendency. The small-scale details and quirks of egg and dart or bead and reel, or the veining and undercutting of acanthus and other leaves, besides being   153, 158 time-consuming to make, could not be sharply cut in the rougher stones. But the chief reason for the change was the general direction of Roman architecture, which used classicism through an expanded building typology distinctly non-Greek in its diversity of forms and motifs. This resulted in a partial domestication or disestablishment of the achievements of the Greeks, which was a significant aspect of Roman work and a distinctly urban one. If Greek work is one's gauge of success and beauty, Roman work can appear somewhat gross and debased, as has been said. But whatever subjective judgments are invoked, the nature of Roman architecture remains, its qualities well expressed by new forms and tasks given to mouldings.

The functions and effectiveness of mouldings were not lost because of these changes, but were extended ever further into the diverse whole of Roman architecture. The use of brick for architectural details as well as for columns and capitals is an example. Common in and near Rome, moulded terra-cotta forms there came to carry much of the message of classicism. The same is true of the stuccoed membering of domestic and public buildings at Pompeii and Herculaneum. Sometimes the traditional cornice, made up of layers of mouldings, was replaced by a simple broad band of rectangular section, in effect an oversized fillet, as at the Tomb of Eurysaces just by the Porta Maggiore in Rome, the Porta Maggiore itself, and the great northeast wall of the Forum of Augustus.[77] Almost every building, and in many cases every constituent part of a building, was outlined by mouldings, the wrapping or packaging systems of classical design brought to their logical stylistic conclusion—outlining, emphasizing, and underlining quintessential parts. This was not only a basic fact of Roman urbanism; it was also a stimulus to design, as in the looping, rising and falling cornices of late antique and early Christian Syria, or the mighty belt cornices of the Hagia Sophia's interior, which curve in and out as they embrace the interior void, helping to define its form and confirm its very substance.

Nearly all significant planes and volumes, then, were outlined by mouldings, which played a leading role in formulating architectural imagery and defining essential shapes. A pediment, for example, is manifested more by its enframing raking and horizontal cornices than by the triangular surface enclosed. The pediment's image and meaning are easily evoked by simple raking lines of tiles, with hints of a horizontal base-line, as at the Insula of the Painted Vaults at Ostia, where echoes of traditional stone enframements suffice. This is a revealing example of the inherent power of even the very simplest

154. Ostia, Insula of the Painted Vaults, doorway, detail; ca. 120

mouldings to intimate a more substantial architectural presence. Mouldings not only emphasize pedimental form, but also seem firmly to contain the tensions between vertical and horizontal forces within it. And the mitered joint where raking cornices   115, 160 meet forms the apex from which the centered, invisible plumbline of temple-front imagery is suspended. As the Romans pursued implications of such Greek creations as these and sought the further architectural possibilities inherent in them, they substantially expanded the boundaries of classical architecture and changed it permanently.

Earth-related features—steps, stairs, podia, platforms, terraces—have been discussed already. Curves and curvature remain. They are found throughout much of the typology, not just in baths and fountains, rotundas and palaces. Curved plans or elevations, or both, were common, as the survey above of tombs showed: eight out of the fourteen basic types display them. Tombs suggest also that curving roof silhouettes may have occurred in other types, and their presence in paintings seems to bear this out. Few deviations from curves of circular derivation can be found other than in approximately elliptical plans (Rome, the fountains of the Domus Flavia and the vivarium on the Palatine; Gorsium, the forum nymphaea; amphitheatres) and now and then in a roughly catenary section or elevation (Ghirza, the aedicular spire tomb; Philae, Arch of Diocletian; perhaps Baia, the so-called Temple of Diana). Curves joining others traveling in the opposite direction, in the manner of a cyma moulding, are found not only in mosaics (Ostia, pavement of the hall of the Augustales) but in buildings as well (Baia, the   155 vestibule of the so-called Temple of Venus; Constantine, the monument of L. Iulius Martial[is] at the museum; compare Tivoli, Hadrian's Villa, the nymphaeum of the   210 Piazza d'Oro). Exedras, apses, and curving niches were commonplace.

Curves had been used sparsely by the Greeks except in theatres and round temples, mostly only in plan. But in imperial architecture they flourished, contributing to its independent stylistic character. Vaults and arches account for part but by no means all of

155. Ostia, Augustales' building, mosaic, detail; ca. 150

156, 157 this, as funerary monuments make clear. By giving curved form to many elements and spaces that before had been straight or rectilinear, the Romans staked out much new territory, enlarging the definition of classical architecture. Signs of this appeared in Hellenistic times, but its potential was realized only later. The Temple of Venus at Baalbek is a striking example of the Roman-style classicism of curves. Although individual parts can be found in earlier buildings, the way they are put together at Baalbek is original. The basic form of the cella with its external ring of columns echoes the Greek tholos, but the combination of porch, cylinder, and dome is Roman, as are the high podium and the effective cascade of steps. The rhythmic scalloping of the podium and entablature is vertically congruent, as logical in its way as traditional trabeation. The play among these concavities, those of the cella's exterior niches, and the convex form of cella wall is the product of a willingness to investigate possibilities inherent in giving design elements new plan forms while largely retaining their original sections; an original building was created out of immediately recognizable parts. The temple may be thought atypical, but it summarizes in an integrated way this major impulse of imperial architecture.

156. Baalbek, Temple of Venus, plan; probably mid-third century

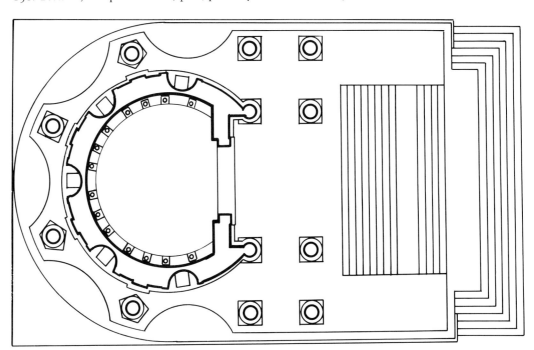

57. Baalbek, Temple of Venus. Above, model; below, side view and detail of door frame

It is not easy to say why the use of curving forms increased so. With theatres and the like the explanation is simple: more towns and greater prosperity. Arches and their effects have already been discussed, and the qualities of vaulting are explored else-where.[78] An interest in variety, a natural disinclination to repeat the past, the expansion of the building typology, and the mixed sources of imperial architecture must all be reckoned with. And it may be that the embracing, harboring qualities provided or implied by receding forms or volumes of curved plan were also significant. The idea of protective shelter is projected by the seamlessness and continued flexure of inward-curving structures, whatever their scale or function. This is as true of a statue niche as it is of a monumental exedra, for with its intimations of focused embrace, concavity is a powerfully suggestive presence. In fixing spaces in a fashion clearly differentiating them from their surroundings, it shapes them firmly into localized quantities each with a kind of palpable immediacy. In urban contexts these qualities were welcome, particularly when forming refuges from the directional pull and agitated motion of the streets. But whatever their size or purpose, curving forms enlivened cities and towns with effects and volumes in sharp contrast to those of older, trabeated buildings.

URBAN SOURCES

As the boundaries of formal variety were pushed back by urban needs and fashions hitherto unknown, classicism was fulfilled. Even in small towns the scale of expansion and change was proportionately great, and enlarging and reconstructing older places was at least as important as founding new ones. Peace, pride, and a prosperity sufficient steadily to underwrite major building projects combined to put architecture increasingly into local hands. Interwoven with these forces were a desire to reflect contemporary fashions seen in large cities, a willingness to experiment with the classical system, and an ability to see in it fresh possibilities. All this was carried along by the strength of an evolving, advancing urbanism that swept much of the past away.

Towns building in outdated modes would have been thought retarded. Pure regionality was smothered by Roman buildings, localisms submerged in a sea of up-to-date forms. Variety was in charge, anticipating the hope of modern writers for differentiation of form and imagery within their cities and towns. In this sense, imperial towns were truly alike, different though they were in plan, measurement, or personality; the overarching imperial system influenced almost all aspects of life and art. It is often said that most towns were little Romes, because they had baths, arches, and the like. The speed with which the new architectural ideas spread through the empire and took firm root insured this, and not to have these new buildings was not to belong. To say that towns often rushed to conform would be no overstatement.

The old, received architecture was either abandoned or, as in the case of the traditional official temple, held in stasis. Cities and towns remained recognizably Roman not only because of the presence of buildings of chiefly Roman origin but also because the new architecture retained features of design common to all classical work. Although the

Doric stoa disappeared, orders, mouldings, pediments, and the like, all of Greek origin, continued to be used. These broadly linked almost all imperial buildings in a diverse but always recognizable classicism, and, thus the imagery and framework of the original classical idea were sufficiently preserved. Diversity and variety rarely carried design beyond these boundaries of classicism, so that although innovations were quickly seen nearly everywhere, the past was not abandoned.

Of greater significance both for the study of classicism and the story of Western architecture in general, was the change in classical architecture from an art relatively monumental and separate, made up largely of buildings for gods and abstract concepts perhaps out of the reach and experience of most people, to a more ordinary and commonplace one. Fulfilled classicism had a less august and awesome content than earlier classicism. It was a popular architecture, available and accessible to more people than before, both as a mechanism of town life and in its appropriation of many of the old images associated with gods, rulers, and other matters. These potent forms remained but now had to coexist with their commonplace counterparts, and inevitably something of the force of the former devolved, in a diluted and domesticated condition, upon the latter. This was another proper revolution in architecture. It produced a quotidian classicism, a fulfillment both in popular and in social terms, in contrast to the ancient classicism where so many of its roots are found. The Greek stoa had of course been popular and essential, but it was one of a small number of Greek building types, all less important, in the Greek architectural scheme of things, than the temple.

That many were proud of their new town architecture is recorded in texts and inscriptions, some no doubt self-serving; yet in the aggregate this evidence is impressive. That many buildings were provided by the government—local or imperial— does not mean approval and taste were always imposed from above. Many structures were gifts of wealthy citizens (maintenance endowments are known), buildings whose appearance and location would have been unlikely to give offence. Ordinary people took what they got, but what they got was usable and could be seen as contributing to their collective pride in and allegiance to their town. Whatever their sources, town buildings were intended largely to satisfy practical needs and local pride, spiritual needs, too, but the old gods took something of a back seat. One's very tomb might imitate, in miniature monumentality, a grand religious or secular structure, a practice typical of the wide and general association of public, official architecture with that for private purposes.

Thus imperial architecture became to a great degree one of everyday life, its basic principles of design used in both monumental and humble buildings. People and public buildings were brought closer together, not least by the architecture of connection and passage. Classicism took on some characteristics of a street-level commodity. At most sites this is hard to see because time has tended to preserve mainly the hulks of huge monuments and covered or destroyed the rest. As a result classicism has for long been thought of in terms of these monuments; it could not have been otherwise. Renaissance architects and writers knew little of this popular, everyday classicism and almost nothing of Roman urbanism except what they could read in Vitruvius. Their impressions still tend to form the basis of many of our conceptions. But at the least it is possible now to suggest that there was no "correct" Roman classicism in the imperial age. The true common denominators of the times were first, classical images and classical trim, still recognizable however modified, and second, the presence of specifically imperial instruments of urbanism. Combined, they made a town Roman.

Invention flourished. No compunction was felt about using different motifs and themes—arcades, aediculated walls, rotundas, and so on—for buildings of the same function. As a result, distinctions based on style became blurred, and this broadening and loosening of what was thought appropriate for a given purpose was itself a force for change. Of course the Romans did not view their architecture as classical in our sense of the word. The ancient literature seems to suggest that they may have thought of it simply as town architecture, as the vehicle of daily life and the obvious primary symbol of their civilization. Even if these suppositions are misconceived, the fact remains that the towns and imperial architecture were one. Little from beyond the frontiers penetrated this stylistically coherent whole, and in that sense classicism was fulfilled under almost hermetic conditions. Town buildings were related to each other and to those of other towns across the empire, and the centerpiece of the whole was an apposite imagery resonating in architecture even yet.

VII

EMPIRE IMAGERY:
CARDINAL THEMES

SCORNFULLY REJECTING fashionable conceits in contemporary painting, Vitruvius denounced representations of buildings piled one atop another:

> For example, at Tralles, Apaturius of Alabanda skilfully designed the scenae of the little theatre . . . representing in it columns and statues, centaurs supporting architraves, domed buildings, angled projecting pediments . . . then on top of it all he made an episcenium on which were painted rotundas, temple fronts, half-pediments, and all the different kinds of roof forms. The effect . . . was pleasing to all . . . [but] Lycimnius the mathematician came forward and said that "the Alabandines . . . lack a sense of propriety . . . Which of you can have houses or columns or extended gables on top of his tiled roof? Such things are erected on supporting structures, not over tiled roofs."[79]

He adds that Lycimnius made his point, for Apaturius altered his work "so that it conformed with reality." Blind pragmatism or not, this kind of conservative attitude is often associated with Augustan state architecture. According to this view innovation was unwelcome, for the old ways were best.[80] Support for this is found in some of the buildings, particularly in carefully worked orders and mouldings of Hellenistic pattern, and in planning and proportions; a cool propriety does inform many Augustan structures, and in them, as in much official sculpture, a deliberate attempt was made to associate the regime with Greek traditions and culture.

But the architecture Apaturius depicted was partly formed by a more liberal force, one also operative in Augustan architecture. At odds on many points with tradition, it fostered new orchestrations of traditional elements, combinations that lay outside the limits of Vitruvian decorum, together with painters' "frauds" and such achievements as the Sanctuary of Fortune at Palestrina or the gallery of the Tabularium, which Vitruvius passes over in silence.[81] Apaturius' structures, condemned as unbuildable, seem to have been formally suspect as well. Possibly their profusion offended. Since Vitruvius emphasizes their formal variety and complexity, it may be that he found them too showy, too richly articulated, for his taste. One can get the impression that he disapproved of such things as temple fronts used for scenic and symbolic purposes, of pediments split and angled, and he may have thought domed rotundas overemphasized and out of place. He did however approve of the artistic effect, the result of the kind of professional draftsmanship and shading he admired.

Vitruvian disapproval of the new fashion came too late and made little headway. The essentially Hellenistic architectural forms Apaturius painted had already been taken up and explored in Rome and other western centers while traditional design continued to flourish. When the one was married to the other, the basis for an architectural imagery of empire emerged. This was not solely an Augustan process, but combinations of design elements and primary forms that we read as imperial came strongly to the fore in Augustan times. Architectural symbols without which no city or town could properly claim to be Roman were first given broad currency and apposite symbolic content while the imperial synthesis was being constructed.

Two main shifts in formal compositional principles occurred. First, the degree of complexity of design increased greatly, and architecture moved away from what can be called a Vitruvian spareness to enriched, more fully articulated designs. Second, this redeployment and multiplication of classical design elements, based in part on Hellenistic innovations, was welded to archetypal Roman forms, resulting in the architectural manner recorded in way stations and tombs. The relatively simple became relatively sophisticated, as when the functional cores of monumental arches—the mechanisms of entrance and exit, of submission, and of the profound differentiation between space on one side and on the other—were civilized and made less stark. Scenic architecture was used to shift arches' primitive imagery toward one of contemporary significance in an age when, in theory at least, Greece and Rome were not just joined but allied. These combinations of curves and straight lines speak of both east and west, while the tensions their propinquity generates give Roman honorific arches much of their expressive power.

By the time of Augustus' death in 14 the imagery of empire was well begun: the forms that populated the cities and towns and gave them their imperial identification stemmed largely from innovations and emphases sponsored in his time. They include design elements such as the ressaut, pedestal, and attic—the attic the setting for the stately imperial lettering that first became common then. Equally important was the emphasis given to tripartite designs (the Parthian arch in the Roman Forum; the arch at Orange), to arcades embellished with orders, and to exedras, apses, and niches (as at the Forum of Augustus). Colored building stones largely unfamiliar in the west became popular in public buildings, for example also at the Forum of Augustus, the Temple of Apollo on the Palatine (dedicated in 28 B.C.; Numidian yellowish marble) and the Basilica Aemilia (rebuilt after 14 B.C.), a process facilitated by the imperial system, which made the products of quarries in Africa, Greece, Egypt, and Asia Minor widely available.

Thus elements of architecture we identify in later buildings as essential to empire symbolism came to prominence in Augustan times, when their imperial intent was strongly declared. Greek and Roman forms were combined prominently in creative ways. The results caught on, one suspects, largely because they had Augustus' approval or that of his lieutenants. In any event, architecture was set along a new path, one now familiar because of centuries of repetition and reinterpretation but in its day fresh and commanding. Because it contained traditional elements it suggested roots—real or putative—and continuity, qualities similar to those found in approved contemporary literature, with its Roman reworking and refashioning of Greek concepts. Both arts reflected political and social reality by showing that although traditional ways were by no means dead, a new age had arrived. One of the most significant things about the period is that state architecture, closely imitated in private monuments, followed much the same evolutionary course and hewed to much the same purpose as government and approved literature and art.

This shift in architectural direction records the seismic nature of Augustus' work. The rate of change of Hellenistic architecture toward more scenic and highly articulated design rapidly accelerated, while the practical arches and vaults the Romans had long used gained in architectural prestige. By 14 the new ideas had spread through much of the building typology. Even the hallowed civic temple had been invaded, as the cella of the Temple of Mars Ultor, with its apse and articulated wall, shows; and if the details of Agrippa's Baths in Rome (25–ca. 15 B.C.) were known, the beginnings of the most successful Roman building type would be better understood. That Hellenistic architecture in Roman times would in any event have taken some of these new directions seems likely; that it did so very rapidly and, from the point of view of imperial iconography, so successfully, must be ascribed mainly to the compelling ascendancy of the first emperor.

The architectural message of the new age quickly established itself outside Italy. In the east, elements and configurations prominent in the new Augustan mode were already well established. In the west its scenic qualities stood out strongly against a background of orthogonal colonial planning and an often somewhat austere public architecture. The transalpine arches already mentioned are cases in point, as is the well-preserved tower tomb at St.-Rémy (probably 5/10). Many other structures qualify, such as the renovated tholos of the Athenian agora, the Memmius monument at Ephesus, and the elaborate market at Lepcis Magna. Recently revealed remains of the extensive building programs of Herod the Great (37–4 B.C.) do also; in both planning and construction these buildings "seem to have leaned heavily upon contemporary Roman experience."[82] The planning at Herodion foreshadows architectural thinking of a kind that flourished in Hadrianic times, and the palace at Jericho contained, among other imperial characteristics, a round bathing-room of Campanian type with the same plan and presumably a similar elevation as the Augustan bath structure at Baiae known as the Temple of Mercury. Common Hellenistic roots or not, such widely separated parallels are examples of a Roman architectural imperialism characterized above all by a distinctive formal imagery.

As always happens when the architectural profession is strong and open to innova-

86

tion, there were those eager to respond in non-traditional ways to contemporary needs. Such architects seem not to have been restricted by regional or ethnic boundaries. The practices of the Greek masons and sculptors who shaped the orders and decor of the Forum of Augustus were probably balanced to a degree by the masters of Roman-style concrete and vaulting who worked for Herod. During the late Republic, Hellenistic designers emerged who put their books aside and struck out boldly on their own. This regional and stylistic give-and-take, which helps explain monuments such as that at Palestrina, was intensified after Augustus took control of the classical world. Part of the stylistic genealogy of leading first- and second-century architects can be traced to Augustan design, as can most of their specifically imperial themes.

The chief feature that all Augustan empire imagery has in common is a high recognition factor. This is by no means always a matter of size, though that is common enough. It also springs from the underlying simplicity of essential forms and contemporary familiarity with the patterns of their embellishment. Simplicity of forms is a key to understanding Roman architecture: the fundamental form—a prismatic block, a grand arch, an unobstructed vaulted space—is kept clearly in view no matter what decor is applied to it. Such decor is at the service of the designer's first conception, the major form, its surfaces and outline. But the ornament then applied is of immediately identifiable derivation, for almost without exception each part has a long ancestry and thus, from the point of view of imagery, is familiar and meaningful. If the engaged and attached elements are removed from a Roman imperial building, the stubborn Roman geometry remains; this is immediately apparent today in Rome, for example at the
56   Domus Augustana on the Palatine or the Basilica of Maxentius and Constantine, where modern clearing has revealed an essential structural geometry shorn of its fitted marbles. If Augustan buildings are envisioned without their orders and applied details, much the same result appears: an architecture of Euclidean spareness, of a kind of unfettered clarity, one found also in numerous Augustan utilitarian works such as bridges and aqueducts. So empire imagery in these buildings was effected by the dual mechanisms of a clear, strong, stable geometry and of an overlay of traditional classicism that civilized forms and made them relevant and recognizable in every province.

These designs cannot be mistaken for Greek ones. When in imperial times architec-
187 tural archaism was practiced deliberately, as at the Roman market in Athens or parts of
61   the forum and basilica at Cyrene, the ancient touch had been lost, intentionally or not.
168 In the entrenched centers of later Greek architecture—the grand Hellenistic cities of the east—the process begun in Augustan times took root to a surprising degree. The imagery of empire appeared nearly everywhere, and largely because of this, cities and towns were stamped as Roman. Imperial architecture, many-faceted and difficult to sort out, has common factors of form and intent first given prominence in Augustus' time. Princes and magnates took their cues from Rome, lesser personages followed suit, and very soon the new usage was firmly established.
80   The Rimini arch (see chapter IV) summarizes Augustan empire imagery. Its combination of Greek and Roman elements and evocation of the potent form of the temple

fastigium speak forcefully of the new Augustan age. Its message of Roman authority, inherent in the archway and its massive frame, is tempered by architectural reminders of Greek tradition and culture, which, though interpreted in a Roman fashion, relieve the structure's ancient Latin gravity with slender, sophisticated forms. The arch represents the advent of a distinctly Roman branch of classicism, an addition to the mainstream of ancient architecture and the source of a sequence of artistic and symbolic events that has not yet run its course.

COLUMN DISPLAYS

Of cardinal themes not buildings, two stand out. The first consists of gatherings of columns not primarily structural and built largely for their artistic and symbolic effect; the second, of elaborately worked walls, all plainness abandoned. The primary characteristics of both are symmetry (however complex), a pronounced iteration of parts, and a ready adaptability to buildings of different functions. Neither is by itself a building type, for both are compositional motifs adaptable to exterior and interior architecture, and are suited as well for independent use, in the manner of a Spanish reredos. Both are highly scenic formations with much pictorial play of light and shade. Although they usually incorporated temple fronts and aediculas, they were based on principles of design unhampered by traditional formulas. Walls and orders alike were looked at afresh and given new roles. The result was a strongly defined modality or version of classicism, the last before the Renaissance.

Columns. Before discussing column displays, some basic qualities of the orders should be examined. All columns share these, and they are at least as significant in classical architecture as the identifying forms of the traditional orders. Knowledge of proportions, fluting, capitals, appropriate auxiliary elements, and the formulary spacing of the orders, though important and necessary, needs to be supplemented by that of columns used as elements of design—why they were placed where they were, how they related to adjacent features, and how their shape (particularly their roundness) encouraged architectural creativity and shifted classical imagery. The familiar suites of the orders, arranged on plates showing several columns, with each order perched precariously on an isolated pedestal and carrying an orphaned length of entablature, disregard their inherent flexibility as design elements. You must, these exhibits caution, be as punctilious about proportion and detail as Vitruvius ordains. This attitude, this belief in a Vitruvian ideal, arose in the Renaissance, when ancient texts were scripture and for architecture there was only one. Thus the Renaissance tradition largely ignores the most fundamental change the classical use of the orders ever underwent. In fulfilled Roman classicism, so often at variance with Vitruvian principles, the orders were viewed quite undogmatically and were freely set about: the results resemble neither Vitruvius' putative norms nor the work of his Renaissance interpreters. The architecture of imperial content is often more in sympathy with mannerist and baroque design than with Roman republican, Renaissance, or neoclassical architecture, partly because the architects of the empire seized on the fresh possibilities they saw both in columns themselves and in the manner of their deployment.

Thus the columnar aspects of imperial imagery rest on two shifts away from traditional usage. The first was that the orders were no longer confined largely to positions located at regular intervals along undeviating straight or circular plan-lines; the second, that they were used as often for artistic as for structural purposes. Columns were freed from many restrictions. Both Hellenistic and Roman architects saw how versatile they were, that they did not have to be limited to rational patterns dictated by structural necessities. In their best, spare work, the Greeks had used columns as indispensable supports, however carefully shaped and proportioned. But some post-Periclean architects began exploring the decorative, non-structural design potential of the orders, and by mid-Hellenistic times the display of columns as a significant architectural theme was well on its way to becoming accepted practice. What would have seemed irrational usage to most architects of the fifth century B.C. increased rapidly, culminating in the scenic compositions found, for example, in the passage and tomb architecture of the empire.

Decreasing the column's load—sometimes removing it entirely except for a length of entablature—greatly expanded opportunities for its use and meant that orders in the round could be deployed as liberally as pilasters. These increased opportunities for positioning were facilitated by the fact that column shafts have no horizontal axes. Taken by themselves, it cannot be said which way they face. In traditional buildings they were given direction by being placed in files whose alignments were underscored by continuous baselines, entablatures, and often parallel or concentric walls as well. Once columns were removed from this controlled environment, their inherent axial neutrality encouraged experiment.

The principle behind the change can be explained by envisioning a tholos with sturdy piers of square plan instead of columns. In such a design, relationships between the verticals and the base and entablature rings become awkward and unsatisfactory because each pier has two unambiguous horizontal axes and a different dimension along its diagonals than across its faces. Thus, as the viewer moves, thicknesses change, sharp corners obtrude, and flat planes and shadows, unsympathetic to the concept of the building overall, stand out. Replace the piers with columns and these awkwardnesses vanish because of the roundness of the shafts. So because it does not face in any particular direction, the column is remarkably adaptable with respect to position. It can go in a corner, along a curving plan either concave or convex, or in a colonnade moving forward and back (as in a theatre stage building). It is well suited to the exedra form because it reflects and reinforces the radial travel of the wall behind without setting up any contrary axial directives of its own. In short, the column shaft, unlike the rectilinear pier, makes no jarring individual assertion about its orientation; if it could be rotated about its vertical axis its relationships to adjacent features would not change. Thus, in spite of its structural origins, it is a widely compatible, multipurpose architectural member.

158. Capitals. Left, Herculaneum, from
the House of the Stags (before 79); right,
Sbeitla, from the Capitolium, center
temple, probably mid-second century

Capitals. Capitals did not particularly affect this. The Doric order, round all the way up to the bottom of its abacus, was as adaptable as the other orders, but it was not slender enough for Hellenistic taste, so both the original form and its watered-down Roman successors became somewhat unfashionable (there are exceptions, as at La Turbie and the Baths of Diocletian). The Ionic order, the volute faces of its capital usually parallel, was less adaptable, though it was used fairly frequently in straightforward, usually non-scenic Roman compositions. The Corinthian and composite orders, on the other hand, having capitals with diagonally set volutes, were well fitted to the new manner, which helps explain their popularity; at Gerasa, for example, Corinthian work replaced Ionic in several public structures after about the middle of the first century. Corinthian and composite volutes are diagonally placed only with respect to their relationships with contiguous orthogonal solids—pedestals, podia, entablatures—not with their shafts, which have no direction. But because a Corinthian or composite capital has directional implications, it suggests that the shaft below does also, reducing the shaft's theoretical potential for rotation and partially disciplining its architectonic aimlessness. These orders also facilitate negotiating corners by accenting and extending, through diametrically aligned pairs of volutes and angled abacuses, the diagonals inherent in the corners themselves.

158

Pilasters. Other aspects of the orders contributed to column-display imagery. The pilaster, unlike the freestanding column, is owned by the wall of which it is a part. Because of its shallow projection it is brought into play only slightly by the effects of parallax. Its contributions to architectural composition are the shadows it creates and its usefulness in patterning and dividing wall surfaces. Used along walls that have no columnar screens in front of them, pilasters sketch in the spacing and rhythms of colonnades, largely by means of the shadow lines thrown by their vertical edges and their laterally spread footings and capitals. In column displays, where they often back up freestanding orders, pilasters help increase the impression of directionality. They are sometimes paneled vertically (Athens, Philopappos' monument) or horizontally (Petra,

159. Ressauts. Left, Rome, Forum of Nerva (ca. 96);
right, Rome, Arch of Constantine (315)

the 'Qasr el-Bint' temple); rusticated examples also exist (Rome, the Claudianum; Verona, the amphitheatre).

Pedestals and Ressauts. Pedestals also imply directionality, but more aggressively than pilasters because of their greater projection and bulk. Their natural partners are ressauts, also major devices of imperial imagery. Placed between the two, a column is held out somewhat from the wall behind it, the ressaut bridging the space defined by the two vertical solids; the column is kept in place rather as a dowel is held between the jaws of a 159 cabinetmaker's clamp. This construction appeared throughout the empire. The ressaut, essentially a fairly short stretch of entablature turned 90° from the plane of the wall or entablature from which it projects, is a kind of shortened lintel; structurally, it is often a corbel, cantilevered out from the wall behind. It was a distinctly non-traditional form, its right-angled position out of step with past classical practice. Columns with ressauts 41 were infrequently used alone, appearing usually in pairs or extended files. In late antiquity the pedestal sometimes became a console as the whole assembly was moved up onto the wall (Rome, niches in the rebuilt [tetrarchal] cellas of the Temple of Venus and Rome; Split, the exterior embellishment of the Porta Aurea; Cillium, the honorific arch, where, exceptionally, the verticals are square piers). Ressauts above engaged 58 columns are common (Ancona, the Arch of Trajan). The idea may have been given currency when the entablatures of the short sides of honorific arches were brought forward slightly over engaged corner columns, as at the Arch of Augustus at Aosta, or when paired engaged columns, with attic pedestals above, suggested a corresponding 91 projection of the intervening entablature, as at the Arch of the Sergi at Pola. No doubt there were also Hellenistic sources.

Variety. As the illustrations make clear, the proportions and detailing of the orders varied greatly. They were freely interpreted; the presumed Vitruvian canon was often

ignored, perhaps unknown. The Split peristyle order is very slender, and the shaft alone   163
of a standing Corinthian column of the so-called Kalybé at Bosra is about fourteen
diameters high; by comparison, the overall height of the Pantheon porch order is about
9-1/2 diameters (diameters are taken at the base of the shaft, above any flare). At the
other end of the scale were the squat forms found on tombs at such sites as Sarsina and
Cologne. Rustication of columns, both freestanding (Porto, the portico of Claudius) and
engaged (Sbeitla, the rear wall of the center temple of the forum) was not uncommon; in   160
this connection, the prevalence of rusticated walls should be mentioned (Alcantara, the   161
temple-like building; Rome, the back of the great wall of Augustus' Forum, the south
wall of the Forum Pacis by the Basilica of Maxentius and Constantine; Bu Ngem, the
south gate; Perge, the exterior of the theatre stage-wall).

Although more or less standard Corinthian capitals flourished, many changes were
rung on them; in one popular interpretation, details are omitted and unveined leaves
and other elements are represented by smooth, almost abstract representations of their

160. Sbeitla, Capitolium, rear of
middle temple; probably mid-second
century

161. Alcantara, shrine; early second
century

shapes. At Gigthis, eight distinctively different kinds of Ionic capitals were found, all robust idiosyncratic creations when compared with classical Athenian work, for example that on the Temple of Athena Nike or the porches of the Erechtheion. Throughout imperial architecture one searches for norms largely in vain.

Frontispiece   *Double Entasis*. Further evidence of changing Roman attitudes toward the orders is the spread of what can be called double entasis, a gradual swelling of the column shaft, as it rises, to a height approximately one third of the way up, and then diminishing, on up to the capital, in more or less the usual way. In normal entasis, though the shaft is sometimes said to bulge, the curve swells only with respect to the sides of the slightly inclined, conical form that would exist if base and capital (the latter somewhat smaller in diameter) were connected by a regular, straight-sided figure. In other words, traditional entasis did not widen the shaft horizontally beyond the theoretical cylindrical envelope that could be erected upon its bottom circle. In this normal kind of column, the diameter decreases continually, though very slowly and at a changing rate, as the shaft rises. This produces a barely visible, subtle, sculptured taper, said to correct
127, 162   optical distortions caused by straight-sided, cylindrical shafts. But in double entasis, successive diameters taken up the columns first increase, spreading the shaft slightly outside the theoretical cylinder just spoken of, and then decrease as in normal entasis, though at a faster rate. The resulting curve is more obvious than that of normal entasis.

162. Gerasa, Temple of Artemis, columns; mid-second century

Columns with double entasis (always unfluted) are significant because they produce quite different effects from those of the elegantly shaped orders of the fifth and fourth centuries B.C. and their progeny. Double entasis stresses the roundness and fullness of columns. Their bulging silhouettes suggest the strength required to support heavy loads, while increasing their anthropomorphic affinities (Bu Ngem, cold room of the baths). The individuality of these columns, when set in rows, is greater than that of the traditional kind, and the spatial gaps between them, if not destabilized to a degree by their concave boundaries, are made more agitated. The overall effect is of heightened drama, partly because the inherent rigidity of the underlying orthogonal patterns of post-and-lintel construction is eroded (Dougga, Temple of Caelestis; Gerasa, Temple of   127 Artemis). Double entasis is further evidence of the strong tendency in imperial architecture to make classicism more informal and scenic.

The Corinthian and Composite Orders. In all these developments and changes the Corinthian order and its ornate stepchild, the composite, more than held their own.   158 That the diagonal setting of the volutes probably contributed to this has already been suggested, but there were other reasons. The upward and outward direction of its leaves and volutes allows a Corinthian capital to mask somewhat the direct way the column receives its superposed load: the point where the load is concentrated is less clearly marked, less exposed, and therefore less emphasized than with a Doric or Ionic capital. This illusion is partly created by the undercut detailing and the resulting thicket of light and shade, which dematerialize the solid working core behind. This profusion of natural shapes makes a stone building appear more supple; in this sense, Corinthian forms are related to double entasis.

Furthermore, Doric and Ionic capitals, with their horizontal emphases, are visually less suited to arched and vaulted architecture than are Corinthian ones. The Corinthian capital's rising, spreading curves both prefigure the arcuate forms above and mediate sculpturally between them and the verticals below, making the crucial shift from one kind of equilibrium to an entirely different one more fluid and less discontinuous than it would otherwise be. This harmony of curving, turning forms, aided by the plate-like thinness of the Corinthian abacus, which allows the bell proper to rise almost to the plane where the order and its load meet, is particularly effective when no entablature block is interposed (Lepcis Magna, the Severan forum arcade; Split, the peristyle). In   163 dealing with this relationship, Brunelleschi interposed entablature blocks whose uppermost mouldings extend well out into the spaces spanned by the arches above, thus creating over his Corinthian capitals another spreading, transitional zone (S. Spirito).

And the dense weave of the Corinthian order's natural forms suggests fertility and fecundity in the manner of the vines and other images of nature found, for example, on the Ara Pacis Augustae. Leafy Corinthianesque chiaroscuro also appeared on such ancillary elements as consoles (Rome, the Curia interior, the tetrarchal niches of the Temple of Venus and Rome), on scrolled modillions and brackets (Rome, the Temple of Venus Genetrix; Split, the Temple of Jupiter), and around the bottom drums of column   164 shafts (Gerasa, the Hadrianic arch; Apamea, the north forum; Lepcis Magna, the second

163. Split, peristyle arcade, detail; 300–305

164. Split, temple of Jupiter, doorway scroll-console; 300–305

story of the Severan nymphaeum; Ptolemais in Cyrenaica, the Palazzo delle Colonne; compare the shafts in the Corinth and Delphi museums). These details are signs of empire, like the traditional Corinthian colonnade, which, with its slender shafts rising from bases of layered stone discs to wreathed capitals above, epitomized the grand formal manner of the age.

The Gerasa Stage Building. Parsing a typical example, the facade of the stage building of the Gerasa south theatre, illustrates how column displays, equally imperial in content, were different from orthostyle colonnades. Constellations of predominantly Cor-   165
inthian decorative orders were closely set about and combined with the features just described to create richly patterned effects. Though only the partly reconstructed first story stands at Gerasa, it is very informative; this choice, however, does not imply that all examples of the column-display motif are *scaenarum frontes.* Some aspects of the restoration are cavalier, but photographs made in 1927, shortly after the area was cleared, show that all of its important features are original.

Built in the Roman manner, the theatre was a compact, unified whole. The original stage building, two stories high, was efficiently joined to the auditorium by tall,   166
boxlike *versurae* or corner structures containing transverse passageways at stage level; beside and below them are similar ones at orchestra level. These dispositions repeat an almost canonical Roman design solution that can also be seen, for example, at Aspendus, Orange, and, restored, at Sabratha (Greek auditoria, on the other hand, traversed somewhat more than semicircles in plan and were not fused with their stage buildings).[83] The deep Gerasa stage, about 6 m. by 35 and supported on vaults, was rhythmically decorated along its low forward wall with niches, pilasters, and abbreviated podium-like projections aligned with major features of the stage wall behind.

Although the Gerasa wall was screened by monolithic Corinthian columns, they were not at all arranged like those in traditional orthostyle alignments. Four groups of six each stood on high podia separated by the three traditional doors for the actors. Each of the flanking corner structures was faced with an additional pair, making twenty-eight large columns in all for each story. Centered behind each of the four major groups of the first story was a niche flanked by smaller columns set tight to the solid backing wall and carrying a scrolled pediment; the three doorways were similarly framed except that engaged piers were used. This story thus had a total of forty-two columns and piers, which if they were placed in a straight line across the stage would largely conceal the lower portion of the masonry wall, there being only about 0.8 m. available for each one; normal spacing would extend them over two or three times that distance. This hypothetical repositioning points up the multiplication of units and their concentration in such displays. That the columns are actually spaced fairly well apart is of course explained by the nature of the plan upon which they are set.[84] There are no pilasters.

At stage level the plan is determined by the positions of the three doors and the four projecting podia that carry the six-column groups. All the podia are outlined top and bottom by robust mouldings and are deeply cut into by centered rectangular recesses reaching back almost to the elevated lesser podia of the enframed back-wall niches. The

165. (TOP) Gerasa, south theatre, stage; late first century and after

166. (LEFT) Gerasa, south theatre, stage building, raking view

167. (ABOVE) Gerasa, south theatre, stage building, detail

flanks of the two central podia curve back on both sides to abut the doorway piers; those of the two outer ones are curved on the door sides only, for their far extremities continue straight to the corner walls, meeting them at right angles. These curves do not continue behind the doorway enframements, where the back wall is flat (the wall has its own considerable fluctuations of form, however, as will be seen). Presumably these plan-lines were repeated in the stage-wide entablature whose forward traverses were supported by the six-column groups. There were also other plan positions, or depths, front to rear—the face-planes of the niches and doorways, the surfaces of the masonry wall projections against which the niche and doorway enframements are placed, and the line of furthest penetration into that wall of the niche surfaces. It is sometimes said that these column displays undulate in plan, but technically they do not; truly sinuous lines, with smoothly reversing curves, are rare in Roman planning (Baia, "Temple of Venus" vestibule; La Conocchia). Here as elsewhere, curves are played off against straight, flat elements, and the junctions between the two are clearly corners. At Gerasa, columns are set on these corners, but not alongside the travel of the curves proper as they are for example at the theatres of Palmyra, Miletus, or Dougga.

There were complexities of elevation as well as of plan. Three levels predominated: those of the stage floor, the upper level of the podia, and the entablature (a section can be seen in the photograph). In addition there is an intermediate zone containing the 165 pediments of the doorway and niche enframements. The former are lower than the latter, which were located just below the level of the capitals of the large forward columns. So while a clearly defined story rose from the stage floor to the entablature, its horizontality was challenged by pronounced differences in level between the doorway thresholds and the adjacent high podia, and by the alternating heights of the door enframements and their pediments. These contrasts were accentuated by orders of different heights and proportions that rose from various levels. The columns were made of stones of at least two different colors (at Sabratha, the columns of the theatre stage were made of white, green, dark gray, and mottled violet stones). Chromatic design had a long history.

This multiplication of units and assembly of diverse formations was held together and given its compositional integrity by the power of symmetry. When several dissimilar, repeating forms are arranged symmetrically, and overall patterns become complex, success depends largely upon locating the iterated features properly with respect to each other and to the whole. These distinctive formations or groups in turn create the basic rhythms of the whole. While using the four forward columns of each six-column group as the dominant features of his rhythm, the Gerasa architect provided accents that gave his design its particular character. None of these was unique, though each was used ingeniously. For example, each set of four columns was divided, like its podium, into pairs, setting up a subordinate rhythm within the major compositional groups; the beat, or meter, of vertical spacing across the stage was thus subtly varied by a secondary spatial chord or stress. Paired couples of orders such as these were common, evidence of the shift from structural to more purely artistic uses (columnar and other tombs men-

191, 92   tioned previously; Ephesus, Baths of Scholastikia; Reims, Porte de Mars; Madauros, entranceway to the large baths).

      Ressauts seem to have been used at Gerasa only above the solitary face columns of the versurae where, at entablature level, they intimated formal continuities with the stage-wall. The rear columns of the six-column pavilions were handled most unclassically.

167   Deeply recessed in rounded vertical channels formed in the stage-wall, their shafts were overlapped by the acute angles of the door-enframement pediments. Each channel, tight to its shaft, is eccentric rather than cylindrical in shape, a semi-teardrop form rather like the profile of half an egg. This may have resulted from being set at an angle where the wall breaks forward, or from the need for space when installing the shaft. This arrangement—reminiscent of Michelangelo's recessed order in the vestibule of the Laurentian Library, or of unfinished facade columns at S. Nicolò in Catania—is related to that of

133   certain house entranceways at Ostia and along the flanks of the "tomb of Annia Regilla" northeast of the Via Appia just outside Rome. There polygonal shafts, though parts of walls, appear to be sunken into half-round channels. The capitals are shorn of their rear volutes and leaves in order to fit into the channels, and something similar must have been done to accommodate the freestanding order at Gerasa.[85] By such means, among others, the composition was given variety and an intricate play of light and shade; some concentration would have been required of viewers to isolate individual parts. The overall impression was what mattered, the sweep of a detailed pattern formed by elements large and small placed forward and back.

      Pavilions. At Gerasa, as in many column displays, the large pavilions dominate the design. These are the columned, porch-like constructions that project further out from the back wall than any of the other trabeated elements, airy space-cages enchained laterally across the stage. Pavilions may or may not have pediments, unlike the smaller, more highly focused aediculas, which, because they derive from temple-fronts, always do. Pavilions are more spacious than aediculas, which function as tabernacles or shrines, have niches, and do not project nearly so much. At Gerasa the pavilions enclose and guard aediculas, whose putative religious content is emphasized by the trough-like axial approaches suggesting the frontal address of the traditional Roman temple. Spatially, pavilions are almost as significant laterally as they are frontally, a quality that helps give many column displays their fluid coherence.

      Sometimes the pavilions of a column display's upper story were placed over the open

168   spaces between the pavilions below (Ephesus, Library of Celsus; Miletus, the great nymphaeum—where on the second-story wings there were pavilions that turned in and faced each other across the large basin below). But however they were positioned or oriented, their entablatures, in any given story, were usually aligned at the same level. The idea of the pavilion probably stemmed to some degree from the temple front, but perhaps it owed more to the forward facing, projecting ends of stoas that went back at least to the later part of the fifth century B.C. (Athens, the Stoa of Zeus in the Agora).[86] Use of pavilions burgeoned as the orders were unshackled, and by imperial times they were extremely popular, not only in stage buildings but in many other structures, such as fountains, imperial salons, and bath halls.

168. Ephesus, lower Embolos, looking west to the Library of Celsus

The stage buildings of the Palmyra and Orange theatres for example, had single, centered pavilions breaking up through their first-story entablature lines, as well as columns set along their forward-and-back plan-lines in the usual way. At Lepcis Magna, Dougga, and Merida, pavilions were centered in all three major recesses, but they rose only to the common entablature level. At Bulla Regia and Amman, these recess-centered features began their forward projection as spur walls, like the axial feature of the so-called civic lararium at Pompeii. All such arrangements were variations on the same theme, the stage wall with rectilinear or curving recesses or both. Something like half of the Roman stage buildings well enough preserved to give evidence had one or more major curved recesses (Herculaneum, one; Khamissa and Saguntum, three); these might flank a central rectilinear feature (Priene; Rome, the Theatre of Pompey). All had columns, and most had pavilions, niches, and aediculas. In many of the other examples the stage-walls are straight in plan but embellished with repeated aediculas or pavilions (Stobi; Philippopolis; Magnesia; Taormina; Sagalassos). At Aspendus there were sixteen of each arranged in two stories, plus a central feature composed of two pavilions below and a temple-front motif above of the kind seen at the Khasneh at Petra, but without the blind tholos. On the basis of what evidence there is, it seems likely that the vertical proportions recommended by Vitruvius for stage buildings were observed in a general way in imperial times.[87]

124

150

123

135

Stage-Walls and Streets. The theatre stage-wall, in its original Greek form an independent building of simple design, represented a palace facade, the central door for royalty, the flanking ones for guests. When the Romans connected it with the auditorium, they altered the spatial relationships between actors and audience, bringing them closer together, with an increased sense of being united within a circumscribing structure. At the same time the meaning of the scene architecture was altered. In closing off the lateral extremities of the stage with high walls pierced by arches, two more entrances were added, one from the forum and one from abroad, at right angles to the back wall.[88] Thus the stage became an elongated trough of space of a clearly marked length, open along one side only (toward the spectators), its far wall masked by plaited architectural forms. Although the traditional, functional palace divisions survived in this new arrangement, together with some of the impact of their imagery, the stage was now shaped like a length of street open on its near, auditorium side. The audience watched the performance take place in front of a stylized representation of a most familiar sight, the thoroughfare. So the Roman stage building was not meant so much to represent an imaginary place as a recognizable urban locale, one composed of facsimiles of religious and secular buildings, full-sized or nearly so, compacted together.

165

As along any thoroughfare, columns and the other motifs of classicism—pediments, niches, podia, and so on—were repeated again and again. In the more sober stage designs, with flat back walls faced with iterated, identical pavilions, a greater restraint prevailed, the product perhaps of images of streets in planners' ideal towns. In more complex designs, the allusion to close-knit city buildings was stronger, in spite of the effects of symmetry, because of varied heights and scale. So Roman scene structures were essentially all-purpose streets, the more elaborate ones representing goals lesser towns might aspire to. All could have responded to the early Latin playwrights' customary stage directions—"on a street," and "in front of the house of so-and-so"—though such plays were no longer seen, taste in entertainment having changed.

That stage buildings were street images is further suggested by their plan shapes. Long and fairly narrow, marked off by arches, stages were abbreviated models of thoroughfares leading from city gates to forum entrances, stylized transcripts of high streets in the towns where the theatres stood. As in those streets, aediculas stood ready as if to receive offerings, and the pavilions, casting shadows against walls in the manner of columned entranceways and porches, induced illusions of streetside depths. (Theatres oriented to give the audience the maximum amount of shade—Gerasa, for example, stands 9° west of north—also gave architects maximum illumination of their work). As in a town, statues of divinities and worthies presided over the proceedings from elevated niches. Most seats were sufficiently elevated to allow the audience to look down onto the stage, where people were perceived along a street repeating the most common, familiar kind of public experience. This reproduction of everyday visual impressions against a backdrop of usually full-scale connective architecture, with its scores of columns, may help explain the Roman theatre's persistent popularity, whatever the nature or quality of the performances. Typically, the Roman stage building was an elaboration of a Greek tradition, the early palace facade. The royal connotations of triple entranceways and multistoried fronts were preserved as the palace came to be fused with the Roman avenue, which in time became at least equally important iconographically in stage-building design. The result was a stylized urbanism strongly reflecting, in the condensed way of stage scenery, the town's public architectural reality.

Other Kinds of Column Displays. Non-theatre column displays also proliferated. The connections among these versions of the motif are problematic, their interrelated evolutionary threads a complex skein. One common source seems to have been a desire or need for elaborate, decorative civic imagery; what evolved was an architectural parallel to the formal gestures and groups found in so much official sculpture, for each expressed common purpose and experience in a forcefully concentrated way. By the second century, the theme of a nimiety of columns compacted in elaborate symmetrical compositions was used for several purposes: stage buildings, major nymphaea, grand halls, and non-functional colonnades. In these, street imagery might or might not be ascendant, but the generative devices of stage design—symmetry, advancing and retreating forms, and concentrations of the orders and other classical features—were always present.

The stage-like facades of the Library of Celsus at Ephesus and the huge pavilioned nymphaeum at Miletus have already been mentioned. Both had pavilions staggered horizontally so that those above spanned open spaces between those below. At Miletus   169

169. Miletus, South Market gate (in Berlin); ca. 160

also there was a dramatic gateway, now in Berlin but once adjacent to the nymphaeum, leading to the south market. It is a two-story structure with three arched passageways and four pavilions. From the end pavilions, broader than the center two with which they are aligned, narrower pavilions project, making double re-entrant angles at the corners of the whole. Centered in the upper story is a temple-front feature of the broken-pediment kind seen at the Aspendus theatre and suggested at the Khasneh at Petra. At Side, and probably also at Aspendus, stage architecture was also used for large civic nymphaea.

In Rome the Septizodium, placed below the south side of the Palatine in the time of Septimius Severus, was also derived from theatre architecture. With three segmental exedras flanked by projecting rectangular pavilions, it was, although a nymphaeum, an almost literal transcription of a common stage-building type (Sabratha; Lepcis Magna; Bulla Regia; Corinth). At least 162 columns were ranged across three stories. It has been said that its architectural function was to screen the buildings behind. But since it was placed at right angles to the Via Appia coming up from the southeast and at pretty much the same level, its architectural function was more probably that of an imperial sign or billboard, a statement in three-dimensional form of pride both in the imperial capital and in the fealty of so many imperial cities.

20   At Side the nymphaeum was placed just outside the main city gate at a slight angle to the line of the walls, an equally commanding position, particularly as the city's two main colonnaded thoroughfares converged at an acute angle upon a plaza just inside the gate, arrangements that suggest a deliberate continuity of the imperial imagery of passage. At Aspendus the immediate contextual setting of what was certainly a stage-like building, but which may or may not have been a nymphaeum, is more problematic. Since it was placed orthogonally between the basilica and the market hall, which were parallel, it must have been a major structure in the matrix of the city's overall architectural imagery. Other monuments, and numerous coins showing elaborate, multicolumned nymphaea, suggest that this was a common kind of symbolism (Rome, the so-called Trofei di Mario; coins of Ptolemais in Syria, Pella, and Neocaesarea). Such structures were all apparently related.

170   At Diocletian's Baths in Rome, exterior scenic walls reached their apogee. On the northeast side of the main building, facing a capacious open-air swimming pool, is a wall about 100 m. long and 32 high (including the once pavilioned buttress towers; S. Peter's facade is 115 m. by 44 overall). Three rectilinear recesses alternated with two semicircular ones, an uncommon scheme in theatre stage design, though something like it was built in Roman times at Priene. The surfaces of the five recesses were in part arranged in three stories of aediculas, those of the four projecting, massive piers in two stories (the ends of the wall were marked by lesser piers whose inner surfaces were aligned with the sides of the pool enclosure). Above the roofline of the wall, pavilions were placed in front of the rising piers, whose weight was necessary to help counter-

171 balance the thrusts of the vaults below and behind them. Most of the wall's marblework has disappeared. There were perhaps seventy-two aediculas in all, some unpedimented,

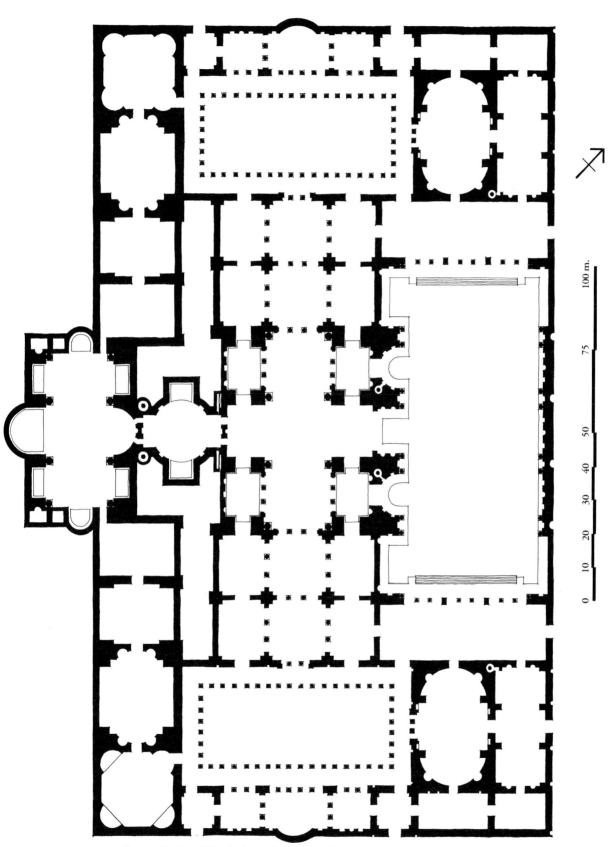

170. Rome, Baths of Diocletian, plan; ca. 298–305

171. Rome, Baths of
Diocletian, scenic exterior wall

plus single columns and many windows; some if not all of the aedicular pediments were tall for their width, like that of the Pantheon porch. Because of the great importance in imperial architecture of the decorative use of the column, it is worth giving—one last time—an indication of the number used: 168 at the least. Again a theatrical urban image was created, a grandly recessed wall repeatedly withdrawing in major and minor rhythms from the pool, which had become stage and auditorium both (compare Trier, S. Barbara baths).

Most of the foregoing examples, whatever the details of their plans, were laterally spread-out systems backed by walls. A related kind of column display, one almost
105   entirely contained in a good-sized exedra, was also much used. Gerasa has a good example, a thoroughfare nymphaeum of semicircular plan with short, straight lateral extensions or wings set on the chord of the curve. It had at least eighteen niches, and columns of different sizes, and its forward part, a kind of pavilion, projected somewhat beyond the line of the thoroughfare colonnade; the half-cylindrical recess was once vaulted over by a semidome. The result was a textbook essay in the Roman way of combining the orders with spaces of curved boundaries. Unroofed versions of columned
101, 53 exedras existed, for example at Tipasa and Lepcis Magna. At Olympia the nymphaeum
102   of Herodes Atticus—also unroofed—had as its main feature a semicircular pool about

16 m. in diameter. This was backed by a congruent, curving wall of thirteen continuously coupled aediculas and niches, all containing statues. Two more aediculas stood on the chord of the exedra, and below there was another pool, long and narrow, flanked by graceful tholoi with conical roofs.

Of interiors with pavilioned column displays, that of the Aula Regia in Domitian's palace in Rome may have been the most influential; similar architecture was used subsequently in the east to evoke imperial associations and as a setting for imperial cult ceremonies.[89] Each of the side walls of the Palatine hall consisted of four projecting spurs flanking three re-entrant features with centered podia or pedestals. The middle recesses were rectangular, the others concave. The shorter wall toward the palace peristyle was cut by two wide doorways with a broad, shallow apse between them, also flanked by projecting spurs; it had no centered feature. At the other side of the hall rectilinear recesses, of the same kind as on the long walls, stood on either side of the main entrance from the outside. By analogy, all the spurs can be said to have carried columns and the podia or pedestals statues; surely this arrangement continued up through another story or two. That the entire design was pavilioned there can be no doubt, though most of the details are lost. The general appearance would have been that of stage-building architecture set continuously around the interior.

Whether the Aula Regia had any direct connection with the pavilioned halls and courts of Asia Minor is moot (Ephesus, Harbor and Vedius Baths; Side, southeast agora hall; Sardis, marble court of the Roman bath). These are found in major baths and other 153 civic buildings and were used for imperial cult ceremonies. Since imperial associations inhered in the Aula Regia design, the possibility of its influence on later constructions abroad intended to have palatine associations cannot be ruled out. Column displays in general were certainly suffused with imperial content. This was not only a matter of signaling dominion or authority. Across the empire, column displays conveyed an architectural message of common membership in an urban society under the care of Rome, the steward of received classical culture. The realities might be less pleasant, but about those the columns were silent.

Non-Functional Colonnades. A related but different kind of display was the non-functional colonnade. In this, columns and walls were so close together that no walkway space existed. The columns were lined up in the traditional way, evenly spaced, usually on pedestals, but instead of being connected by an entablature running parallel to the wall were connected to it by ressauts (Athens, Hadrian's Library; Lepcis Magna, along 42 the external flank of the Severan basilica). The first monumental expression of this type 41 seems to have been the entranceway to the Temple of Peace ("Forum of Vespasian") in Rome from the Forum Transitorium ("of Nerva"). The freestanding pedestaled columns 159 of honorific arches might have been contributory sources (perhaps the Parthian Arch of Augustus in the Roman Forum). 77

At the Forum Transitorium six columns, rising from bases, not pedestals, were joined to the Vespasianic northwest wall by ressauts carrying spur walls up through the attic range in the manner of an honorific arch, with sculpture in the re-entrants so formed. The west facade of Hadrian's Library displayed a similar theme. Fourteen unfluted columns, set in two files on either side of a projecting entrance porch, were placed on freestanding bases; their ressauts presumably carried statuary. The shafts are of green cipollino, the balance of white marble, the workmanship neo-Attic of high quality. The Lepcis example, originally of twenty-seven columns, borders a narrow street or alley furnished with archways at both ends. Again the unfluted shafts are of cipollino, and the bases, capitals, and ressauts of white marble, but the pedestals are made of the tawny local limestone. As at Athens, the pedestals stand barely free of the wall; in both places the distance between the orders and the wall is hardly equal to the diameter of the shafts (wide spacing, as at the Antalya arch, was rare). But at Lepcis the ressauts were considerably taller than at Athens. Behind the zone of their architrave blocks (which, unlike those of the friezes and cornices did not reach back to the wall), the cornice of the basilica wall ran along at right angles to the projections, tight up under the frieze blocks. This is a chromatic, dovetailed architecture that condenses space by altering radically the usage of the past. The effect resembles that of a compressed stoa, its sheltering space excised—unusable, but wholly familiar in form and rhythm. Yet these colonnades do not shrink from the open space before them, for they engage it with their projecting, probing ressauts.

Much ingenuity was exercised in designing column displays. At Lambaesis a small temple to Asclepius was flanked by curving, colonaded wings that swept out and forward to end in half-tholoi turned toward each other, the whole bow-like in plan, with the temple at midposition on the bow. At the harbor end of the Ephesus Arkadiané there was a multiple-pavilioned gateway, and beside one of the quays an airy, two-storied columnar cage of three sides, all concave in plan. Other open, elaborate Ephesian structures stood at the south end of the Marble Street and at the west entrance to the agora. At Miletus, at one end of the stadium, stood a remarkable late antique construction: two parallel rows each of eight pedestaled columns, their lengths of common entablature changing direction in a complex rhythm longitudinally and transversely, carried an arcaded, roofed superstructure.

All examples of the theme, which was applied to different kinds of public buildings, show the column in full bloom, unrestricted and unreticent; combined with vaulted interior space, column displays formed the essential stuff of empire imagery. In these displays the relationship of the orders to the wall was changed greatly. What had been a clear spatial joining of two structural systems built in parallel, one solid, the other only intermittently so, as in the colonnade of a temple or stoa, was obscured: the two systems were brought close together, often both moved forward and back repeatedly, and the restraints imposed by structural necessities inherent in fully-roofed, space-enclosing buildings were largely removed. The principle of display, of extending iterating patterns along a lengthy course, became a significant act in the making of architecture. These cardinal themes were not minor, wayward developments with no future. As always with the Roman orders, variety of scale flourished (the miniature columned wall

172. Athens, Hadrian's Arch; probably 131

of the Domus Transitoria nymphaeum on the Palatine; the mixed scales of the Arch of   172
Hadrian in Athens). Columns, axially neutral, were closely attached to their walls either
by common entablatures or by ressauts (Split, mausoleum interior). As a result, what
might seem to be openness was really not. Column displays are an architecture of
implication, of spatial promises unrealized.

If it were not for the persistence of the orders through the long history of Greek and
Roman architecture, many Roman buildings would seem to have little classical content.
From a traditional point of view, architecture in imperial times lost its bearings; from
the Roman, it found new ones. In this innovative branch of classicism, columns formed
much of the design, carrying so to speak the melody, which was set against the continuo
of the wall. And columns, in their profusion, spoke of urbanism. A town could not be
imagined without them, and there could hardly be too many.

ELABORATED WALLS

Unlike the wall of a column display, screened by freestanding orders and thus of
secondary visual importance, the elaborated wall was intended to be seen. No large-scale
elements were placed between it and the viewer. Its surface was carved and constructed

in patterns and rhythms similar to those of column displays but set in planes forward and back, all integral with the wall fabric. It was a structural solid finished with architectural forms in relief—orders, mouldings, and often pediments, arch-forms, or shallow niches as well (Rome, the Markets of Trajan, upper story of the hemicycle). The wall might be pierced by rectangular or arched openings; if repeated, these reduced its lower portion to a range of piers but did not compromise its fluid surface continuity (the exteriors of theatres and amphitheatres; Maktar, the southeast baths). Usually there were no freestanding elements, but if there were they were either small in scale (aedicula colonnettes, for example) or were placed in openings along the plane of the wall, to be negotiated like any colonnaded entranceway (Baalbek, the flanks of the great court of the Temple of Zeus). Elaborated walls were used in nearly the entire building typology.

The effect of an elaborated wall was that of a column display in relief, with the orders drawn or pressed back into the wall, a relief architecture lacking silhouetted forms and thus heavily dependent on shadows for its impact. Sometimes the wall was empaneled, in the manner of Vignola's surfaces, as if by cutting back from the major surface another was found behind it (Rome, Villa di Papa Giulio, hemicycle facade, S. Andrea in Via Flaminia, interior; Pompeii, the Temple of Vespasian, the building of Eumachia). There were blind arcades similarly wrought (Pompeii, the water castle near the Porta di Vesuvio; compare the exterior of the Trier basilica), and alternating triangular and segmental pediments were common. Engaged columns—more properly wall-orders, since they are structurally unrelated to proper columns—were ubiquitous. The ways of assembling the constituent elements were similar to those used in column displays and, like them, ranged from comparatively simple to quite complex.

The central baths at Pompeii had plain, half-round wall-orders spaced at regular intervals, made from the same terra-cotta as the wall surface. At the Porta Maggiore in Rome, large aediculas were used as facings for the perforated piers, their wall-orders almost detached. The entire curving facade of Philopappos' monument in Athens was an elaborated wall of corniced zones, paneled pilasters, and niches, richly embellished with sculpture. Three blind, garlanded arches were framed by slightly projecting aediculas on the Atalian monument at Sadaba; the spaces between them, slightly sunken, were also arched (compare S. Maria Capua Vetere, the tomb called Le Carceri). The piers of the sober upper arcade of the Porte Saint-André at Autun were decorated with pilasters, and its ends were brought forward somewhat in boxy, two-arch units resembling sturdy defensive pavilions. One of the most scenic and complex examples is seen at the three-storied Porta dei Borsari in Verona, a work of the late first century. Its ground-level archways are simply framed by wall-orders, entablatures, and pediments. But the second story has repeated enframements (arches flanked by pilasters carrying segmental pediments, in turn surrounded by standard two-column aedicular forms, all largely in relief); located between these is an unpedimented enframement sheltering two small relief aediculas. On the third story there were further embellishments, including an early example of enframed units placed over the spaces between units below.

Sophisticated uses of the theme are summarized at Baalbek. The scenic interior walls

173. Baalbek, Temple of Zeus, great court, detail of flank; second century

of the Temple of Bacchus are divided into tall bays by projecting spurs faced as huge
Corinthian wall-orders carrying an enriched, ressauted entablature of an unusually 117
decorative nature. There are arches between piers in the lower zone and aediculas in the
upper; the columns and sculpture of the latter are lost. The interior of the Temple of
Venus is an elaborated curved wall, and the exterior of the cella combines the same with 156, 157
elements of a column display.

Along the flanks of the neighboring courtyard of the Temple of Zeus, behind 173
traditional orthostyle colonnades now dilapidated, are the most imposing examples of
Roman elaborated walls surviving. With their large re-entrant rectangular and curved
volumes (often called chapels), which are screened by columns, these compositions are
closely related to the side walls of the Templum Pacis and Hadrian's Athenian Library, 42

though in both the latter cases the re-entrant volumes are rectangular. Almost continuously articulated, the Baalbek walls move forward and back like those of an extended
stage building, but without any wall-high columns of their own out in front. The
composition is like that of the curving, recessed first story of the Pantheon's interior
wall, and the faces of the strips of wall between the recesses, with their two stories of
aediculas (the lower deeply niched) flanked by giant pilasters, are somewhat reminiscent
of Michelangelo's exterior wall system at S. Peter's. Every detail of scenic classicism can
be found—stone of different textures and colors, varied pediment shapes (some are
sharply cut back to the wall surface at both base and crown), differing scales, pilaster
capitals crowned by shallow entablature projections that spread as they rise, and so on.
And in the corners of the rectangular spaces there are features that may be unique—
independent projections made of mouldings outlining fish-mouth shapes, placed at the
level of the upper aedicula-pediment cornices. Perhaps they were meant to be read as
134, 135   angled pediments of the kind seen at much larger scale on the Khasneh at Petra; if they
were softer in form they would be Guarini-like.

In contrast to a column display, an elaborated solid wall was congealed architecture, a
species of solid space. On it familiar forms were seen, but their spatial three-dimensionality was missing. The advance and retreat of column display elements was preserved,
though much flattened out, so the effects of parallax were all but erased. Yet the two
themes were closely related. In their different ways they showed the same things—
stylized, rhythmical parades of everyday forms. In this sense, the sinuous returning wall
136   of the diagonally-planned middle zone of La Conocchia was the cousin in imagery of the
four-square kiosk at Naga, northeast of Khartoum, half a world away.

It is difficult to say where these themes originated, or how they evolved and spread.
They became fashionable, and probably essential, imperial images, but why? They were
ultimately based on the possibilities inherent in simple architectural elements, the wall
and the column—the basic continuous and discontinuous supports, the spatially embracing and the spatially embraced. Roman architects do not seem to have been able to
resist exploring their design potentialities. The urge to deal with them in new conceptual ways culminated in the major examples, but the process by which that stage was
reached was probably a slow one. In time the new ideas were clearly accepted everywhere, however modest the execution may have been in some regions. That they were
not rejected is obvious but important; that they succeeded partly because they were used
in court architecture may help explain the matter, though little else can be said about
the subject with assurance.

Architecture was shifting rapidly even while some traditional ways retained their
hold. The Roman elevation of the arch and vault to respectable and indeed sometimes
pre-eminent employment is prime evidence for this. Perhaps success was due in part to
the nature of cities, where in prosperous times improvement, pride, competition with
other cities, and the need for approval often leads to construction in the latest mode; if
Siena builds in a new way, Florence must do the same, and better. In addition, it is
significant that no new basic elements were introduced; each one had a respectable
pedigree. What changed was the use of ancient forms and the novel relationships among

them that resulted. Through these changes the new and apposite symbolic effects were achieved. Had different basic elements been introduced, the results would not have been classical but of another style entirely. What probably counted most was familiarity, the recapitulation in these themes of the urban architectural environment.

PERISTYLES

Peristyles and temple-forms were the most common Greco-Roman architectural themes. Spatially sequestered from the construction surrounding them, peristyles were walled, level enclosures primarily of Hellenistic origin. Open to the sky, usually rectangular in plan, they were lined with colonnaded or arcaded porticoes. A Roman neighborhood seen from the air would have appeared to be pitted with these prismatic wells of space let into its tightly built-up fabric. Part of the lingua franca of Mediterranean architecture, peristyles were simple courtyards given manners, made *signorile*. They ranged in size from those in fairly humble dwellings, with only three or four columns on a side, to spacious civic clearings laden with statuary. Usually all four of the roofed porticos were the same height, though in the Rhodian version (not limited to the island) three sides were the same, the fourth higher. Because they were simple in concept, peristyles were unusually adaptable, almost as much so as the orders themselves, and were put to use in many different kinds of buildings—houses, palaces, markets, military structures, storehouses, theatre annexes, baths, and so on.

A peristyle is essentially an unroofed interior, a place to remove to from other places.   174, 60, 14
It answers appropriately to the characterization of Roman architecture as the first to emphasize interior space. The open court proper measures out nature like a *templum* (the augurs' ancient squared ground set aside for taking auspices), echoing the frame of that hallowed, marked-off place. The regular repetition of verticals around the sides intimates the existence of successive identical spatial units, but these vanish in the continuous axial corridors of space behind the colonnades; this quasi-divided continuity is a kind of ambiguous relationship common in classical architecture. The peristyle's doubled perimeter of wall and columns is also typically classical, one structure finite and impenetrable save at the entranceways, the other its conforming but perforated reprise.

As armatures with their thoroughfares underwrote a town's physical continuity, peristyles provided it with a strong measure of symbolic coherence. Repeated over and over in public and private settings, always in the same basic configuration irrespective of size or of the function of the building it served, the peristyle was as common a kind of architectural backdrop as the street. Though scattered about, peristyles nevertheless formed a chain of kindred urban images not long out of view—surely it would have been somewhat unusual not to have entered several every day. Many were eddies or pools of relatively quiet and undisturbed space off the hectic shores of the streets, trafficless islands in the commotion of everyday life. And each open, colonnaded court conveyed much the same effect as all the others, one of an ordered, discrete enclosure not without dignity and fit for whatever purpose its context required.

The peristyle house was found in all regions, from Conimbriga to Dura Europos, from   16, 119

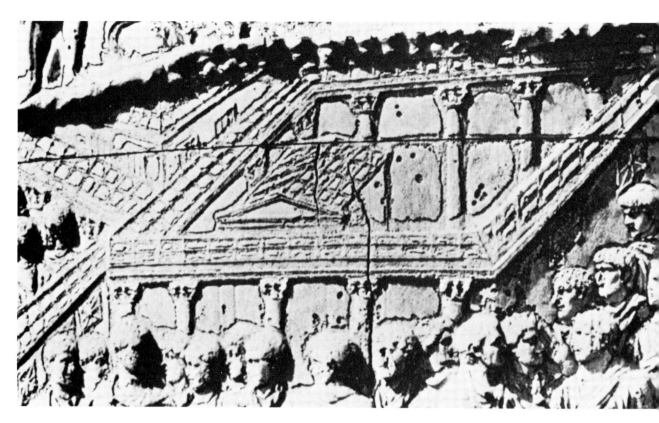

174. Peristyles. Above, Rome, Trajan's Column; below, Thuburbo Maius, peristyle of the Petronii (225)

St.-Rémy to Delos. It was taken by the Romans to the west (Italica; Ampurias) and north (Caerwent; Cologne), as well as to the edge of the desert (Timgad; Sbeitla). In the Hellenistic east, it was endemic (Ptolemais in Cyrenaica; Antioch in Syria; Palmyra). In the provinces it was built for centuries, but on the evidence of the surviving fragments of the Severan marble plan of Rome, few existed in the capital after the early empire, probably largely because of land values; at Ostia it all but disappeared as the city was rebuilt in the first and second centuries. Palaces always had peristyles (Rome, the Domus Flavia and Domus Augustana; Apollonia in Cyrenaica; Salonika; Constantinople; Dura Europos). They were common in army headquarters and lesser military establishments (Valkenberg; Bu Ngem; Vindonissa, the magazine) and in markets (Pozzuoli; Djemila; Gigthis; Lepcis Magna). The pierced and arcaded courtyards of apartment houses and various commercial buildings, lacking columns, were not, strictly speaking, peristyles but offshoots of the basic idea (Ostia, House of the Muses, Horrea 175 Epigathiana); however, some storehouses did have colonnaded courtyards (Rome, Hor-

175. Ostia, Insula of the Muses, courtyard; ca. 130

rea Lolliana, recorded on the marble plan; Ostia, Horrea of Hortensius). Sheltering peristyles often abutted theatres (Merida; Rome, Theatre of Marcellus; Corinth). Though rectangular plans predominated, there were other shapes: semicircles (Athens, 130 m. northwest of the Olympieion; Corinth, by the Lechaion road; Timgad, by the south baths), stadium-like (Vetera), and trapeziums (Vaison-la-Romaine, House of the Silver Bust; Lepcis Magna, by the theatre). Some temples were placed within peristyle enclosures (Rome, Temple of the Sun; Sabratha, Temple of Serapis; Palmyra, Temple of Bel).

The peristyle was a primary, omnipresent image of the era. It was imperial because although it was taken over and used again and again by the Romans, it was Greco-Hellenistic in origin, standing for Mediterranean rather than specifically Roman culture, and suggested the increasing fusion of the two. In expressing this polycultural basis of empire it paralleled the double implication inherent in the Greco-Roman style of so much official and private sculpture. Unlike the monumental freestanding arch, the peristyle did not directly imply dominion, but because of its ubiquity—in both number and function—it strongly reinforced the architectural affinity of the cities and towns.

BATHS

In describing his villa below Ostia, the younger Pliny explains that if he arrives there unannounced or stays only briefly and does not wish to have his own bath furnaces fired up, there is "a village, just beyond the neighboring villa . . . [with] three baths for hire, a great convenience."[90] Three baths, however humble, in a very small place (Vicus Augustanus) is in proportion with the more than eight hundred Rome eventually accumulated, or the dozen or two found in provincial towns of middling size. These numbers point up strongly the Roman need and passion for the baths. Of Greek origin, the idea seems to have been elaborated in Campania, the first huge municipal versions appearing in Rome during the early empire. Today baths are the celebrities of imperial architecture. Excavators can hardly avoid them, and for a long time they have been prime subjects for restoration drawings. The basic book on the subject is now nearly sixty years old and still valuable, but in need of a modernized successor. More recently several baths have been studied in detail, as has bath technology. The present purpose is not to review these materials but to discuss the architectural syntax of bath buildings and to comment on their role as vehicles of empire imagery.

It is tempting to think of them as secular temples, so close were they to the central core of daily life and habit. That they were intended to be pleasant and attractive is clear from statements in contemporary texts.[91] Their universal popularity gave architects

176, 177   exceptional opportunities, of which they took full advantage; no other building type displays such varied configurations of plan and elevation. There was a normal sequence for using cold, tepid, and hot rooms with their plunges or pools, and although it apparently was not always followed, these three essential features and the plan relationships and connecting spaces (if any) among them formed the starting points of all bath design. The only other absolutes were heating and hydraulic installations, service facilities, and a dressing room. Southern exposure for the hot rooms and furnaces was desirable. Latrines were quite standard as were sweat rooms; exercise grounds, modeled on the Greek palestra and usually peristylar, were normally included where adequate space existed. Elaborate baths also contained halls for strolling and conversation, tanning rooms, ball courts, and other amenities; within the compounds of the vast imperial baths there might be concert halls, libraries, and gardens as well. Examples of figural art abounded, partly of imperial content and allusion in the largest baths, popular and sometimes local in intent in the smaller ones. A museum-like atmosphere in the largest cannot be ruled out.[92] Whenever possible, colored marbles were used both for architectural elements, particularly pavements and wall facings, and mosaics.

Baths were widely distributed through the towns. At Ostia, about one-half excavated, seventeen have turned up between a point just inside the Porta Romana at the east end of the city to two just outside the walls beside the Porta Marina at the west, where construction extended to the sea. Of these, two were large municipal structures with spacious exercise grounds (the Forum Baths and those of Neptune, each with main blocks about 70 m. long). At Pompeii, exclusive of bathing suites found in grand houses, four are known, spaced fairly well apart; again the site is not completely excavated. Athens' minimum of twenty and Timgad's fourteen were all randomly

176. Tivoli, Hadrian's Villa, Small Baths, plan; 120s

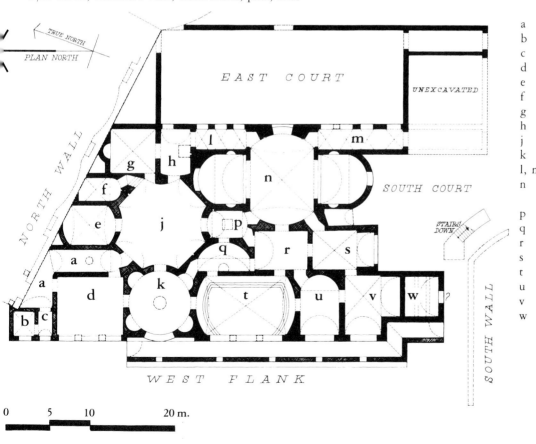

a	entranceway
b	latrine
c	vestibule
d	dressing room
e	nymphaeum
f	service room
g	shrine?
h	passageway
j	atrium
k	sun room
l, m	corridors
n	room with two cold pools
p	massage room?
q	sweat room?
r	hot room
s	hot plunge
t	tepid pool
u	hot plunge
v	hot plunge
w	boiler room

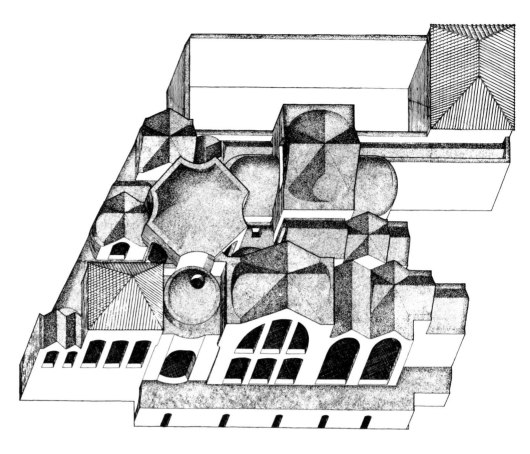

177. Tivoli, Hadrian's Villa, Small Baths. Above, restoration; below, restoration cutaway view

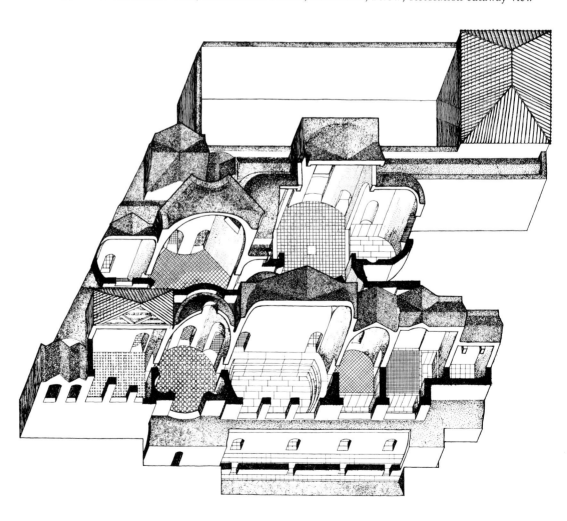

distributed in the topographical sense. Few neighborhoods lacked bath buildings. *Balnea,* smaller, privately owned establishments, did not have the duplicate facilities and large central halls of the much grander municipal or imperial *thermae* (in the ancient sources these terms overlap somewhat in meaning, but they are usually separated in modern discussions). Smaller baths, which might be mean and poorly lit, yet fitted with marbles and mosaic, frequently abutted other buildings and usually lacked exercise grounds. Municipal and imperial baths normally stood free, and sometimes their main blocks of bathing facilities and halls were centered within extended walled compounds (Rome, Baths of Trajan). The size reached by large baths of the kind found at Trier, Rome, and Ephesus is suggested by the near equality of the Baths of Caracalla in Rome with the entire area of Timgad in 100, or by the 300 m. length of the Antonine Baths at Carthage.

Two contrasting but broadly conceived groups of plan types stand out, roughly corresponding to the distinction between balnea and thermae. In the first group, mostly made up of smaller buildings, plans are asymmetrical (Anemurium), sometimes flagrantly so (Athens, just north of the Olympieion). These rarely exceed 40 m. along their major dimensions; many are quite small. In the other group, chiefly of larger buildings, symmetry around centerlines rules. There are of course exceptions: small symmetrical buildings (Rottweil, bath 3; Lepcis Magna, Hunting Baths) or large municipal baths 110 either asymmetrically organized (Miletus, Baths of Faustina) or warped in plan to fit existing surveyors' lines or topographical peculiarities (Dougga, Baths of Licinius). For architectural analysis these two contrasting groups are revealing. The fact that baths could be either forcefully irregular in plan or rigorously symmetrical set them apart from most other building types, and the presence in them of rooms not only of varied shapes but of unequal heights makes the separation complete: baths were distinctly different— in form, function, spatial organization, and effect, from the rest of the typology. The necessary inclusion of varied functions invited experiment, and Roman city-dwellers welcomed the resulting novelty and innovation.

Except for the largest thermae, which perhaps evolved from Agrippa's baths in the Campus Martius by way of the Baths of Titus and of Trajan, no single, widely admired building seems to have served as a model. The architects' inspiration came largely from the need both to deploy and to interconnect varied functional areas of differing plan shapes and heights. It took some ingenuity to fit these into blocks with overall symmetrical plans. But once the novelty of the exterior exposure of bulging and curving interior forms had abated, expression on the outside of what was inside flourished (Brad; Bosra, the south baths; and many of the balnea just cited). Modeling spaces in response to specific bathing needs and traditions could not easily be accomplished using such standard motifs as plain spatial boxes. The use of partly or wholly circular bathing rooms had been established in Greek times (Gela; Gortys; Eretria; Cyrene) and was continued, probably partly because circles promote the social proximity fundamental to the ancient concept of bathing. While a circle gives maximum floor area for a given length of wall, it is an awkward form to fit into an orthogonal plan; this however was of little moment

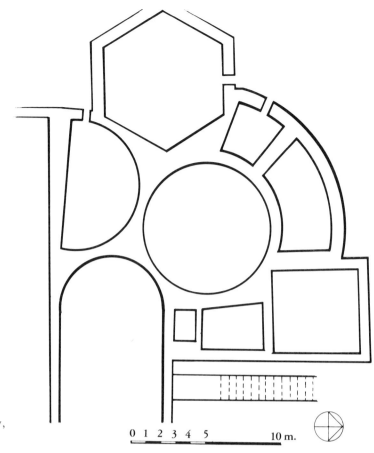

178. Athens, bath; third century: Above, plan; below, remains

0 1 2 3 4 5   10 m.

to Roman designers and builders, who sometimes let circular forms stand nearly free and other times paid the price and either used large amounts of masonry fill between their straight and curved surfaces or left dead spaces there—both techniques were used at the agora baths at Side. There are cases of circular forms partially embraced by concentric but abbreviated corridors or chambers (near S.-Père-sous-Vézelay, the Fontaines Salées; Athens, baths at the corner of Robertou Galli and Karyatidon Streets). As popular as the   178 circle in bath plans were its polygonal kin, hexagons (Belalis Maior, Forum baths; Sabratha, baths of Region VII; Lepcis Magna, unfinished "imperial" baths) and octagons (Sala; Olympia, east baths; Antioch, Bath C; compare Carthage, Antonine Baths, where two hexagons were tightly fitted between three octagons, with two more octagons nearby).

The intrusion of these non-rectangular plan shapes, almost irrational forms in contrast to those of traditional multiroom planning, gave baths much architectonic energy. Apses large and small, often containing plunges or tubs, did the same (fourteen at Trier in the imperial baths). Sometimes apses appear in pairs or doubled pairs facing each other across a central rectangular chamber or hall (Rottweil; Champlieu; Sardis, Baths CG; Hierapolis), and they often extended circular or polygonal volumes on the diagonals (Herculaneum, Forum Baths; Conimbriga; Jericho, in Herod's palace). Apsidal forms very often projected from the bodies of bath buildings, in staggered rows along the southern boundaries of some (Ostia, Forum Baths; Perge, bath by the south gate; compare the bath on fragment no. 33 of the marble plan of Rome). Juxtaposing such varied shapes created wall solids and leftover voids of unusual forms. Sometimes they necessitated the provision of oblique passageways, mostly quite short. Straight passageways were fairly common (Djemila, large baths; Lepcis Magna, Hadrianic baths); dog-leg plans also appeared (Badenweiler; Rome, Agrippa's Baths). Service areas and corridors had also to be provided, no small part of a large bath's plan.

These perhaps tedious details are necessary to an understanding of bath complexities. Two examples of plans, both of moderately-sized buildings with tightly organized configurations, suggest the maze-like qualities of the patterns upon which three-dimensional volumes, usually vaulted over, might be erected. The building at Thenae,   179

179. Thenae, baths, plan; second or third century
   a entrance
   b latrine
   c cold plunges
   d warm rooms?
   e hot plunges

0   10   20   30 m.

perhaps of Severan date, was the work of an independent soul for whom the well-established intricacies of bath-planning do not seem to have been enough. For him, circles (five) and semicircles (six) were irresistible. His plan, about 30 m. across, is based on diagonals crossing at its center. From a generously proportioned apsidal vestibule one gained, by a circuitous route, the main chamber, a circular, domed room in the center of the building. On three of its four diagonals cold plunges were set, recessed from the circle's edge; on the fourth was the tepidarium, which led to hot plunges beyond. Between these four diagonal extensions nestled round rooms, smaller than the central one, of which the southernmost (the sweating room) was extended to the south.

Tight to most of this wheeling central composition was a variety of differently-shaped rooms—an outward-facing apsidal chamber, large oblong salons with apsidal ends, the hot room and its annexes, a latrine, and the furnaces. Most inter-volumetric solids were cut through by short, narrow passageways of various shapes and reduced by niches large and small. In this fashion at least twelve major rooms, only two of the same size (two of the smaller round rooms), were compacted together so efficiently that no traditional connective corridors or passageways were needed. This was a plan not only of striking ingenuity but also of great economy of design. To gain light, the interior rooms would have had to rise above their neighbors. Though it is impossible to know just what the completed building looked like, pyramidal compositions come to mind, and the embedded X-plan, or quincunx, of cylindrical, domed forms suggests a silhouette vividly changing as the effects of parallax came into play.

178   The second example is a partial plan of the baths at the corner of Robertou Galli and Karyatidon streets in Athens. Here the solids, as they spun out to lap around the varied rooms set about the central circle, formed a pinwheel-like pattern. Hexagonal angles and apsidal wall-curves pushed in close to the circle and to each other, creating thin stretches of wall. As at Thenae, the stouter sections of the fluidly modeled structure would have strengthened the building by functioning as thickened piers. Since some threshold positions are unknown, it cannot be said whether one could step directly from the circular room into the bathing rooms or had largely to circumnavigate the circle from room to room. But again the planning is ingenious and economical: the bather would have been conscious of changing volumetric shapes while going from room to room, but not of the intervening solids' true shapes. By analogy, as at Thenae, an oculus in the central chamber is likely. And here the perimeter of the building, along this portion at least, is more certain, and it is revealing: nothing was done to hide the design's lucid Euclidean anatomy, for the exterior wall was the slave of the interior spaces.

Designing baths consisted largely of putting many rooms close together. In the large symmetrically planned ones, volumetric frictions were lessened by avoiding non-rectangular room plans, but the compositional aims remained much the same: relationships between rooms were made as close as possible, so that wasted space caused by corridors or passageways of any length was minimized. Thus baths consisted of clearly differentiated internal spaces directly joined, one experienced immediately upon leaving the other because no marked or memorable enclosures intervened; without a formal architectural introduction, the next view was revealed quite abruptly. In the biggest buildings this effect was necessarily diluted here and there, for example by internal peristyle courts, but even at large scale, strongly marked differences in the plans and heights of the various chambers were maintained. This compaction brought not only increased efficiency (less structure, less heat loss) but, together with varied heights, something much more important: novel architectural experiences, wholly interior environments of serial, changing volumetric enclosures uninterrupted by corridors.

Baths of more than a few rooms rising to fairly uniform rooflines (Herculaneum, Suburban Baths) would have been rare because of lighting needs and the differing proportional heights required by varied room shapes. Sometimes the resulting irregular silhouettes were partially masked by parapet walls, but enough vaults and walls stand to suggest that rooflines were usually visible, and that window placement, as one would expect, was carefully thought out (Baia; Rome, Caracalla's and Diocletian's Baths; Trier; Olympia, east baths; Hierapolis in Phrygia; Philippopolis; Tivoli, Hadrian's Villa, private but well-preserved structures).

Middle- and large-sized baths were riddled with windows (Trier, imperial baths, probably 67 windows 3 to 4 m. wide, around the second floor of the main block alone); many had oculuses and raking light shafts as well.[93] Except for the southern rooms, for which both heat and light were naturally sought, only smaller openings were usually found at ground level, though some huge baths were exceptions (Caracalla, along the northeast side). Groin vaults, springing from pier-like forms, were particularly effective, making it possible to bring light into central halls from high up and all sides, while also illuminating decorated vault surfaces directly. Windows were often placed higher and lower according to the shapes and needs of the volumes they served, making irregular elevation patterns that together with rising and falling rooflines declared the interiors' spatial complexities.

Entablatures and cornices were not eliminated, for they continued to be used to edge roofs and line room interiors. But their essential characteristic, the continuous, level capping of vertical elements, was a less dominant feature of design in baths than in trabeated buildings because inside spaces continued to rise above the entablatures' zones, and because these buildings were not unitary shapes that could be continuously and neatly edged and bound in the traditional way. Since baths were not based on the iteration of an architectonic unit or formal concept, the whole apparatus of traditional classicism was fractured; signs of this, such as ressauts and non-structural columns, were noted above.

The nature of the bath building offered few opportunities to make use of those continuities and repetitions lying at the heart of Greek design. As a result, except for the column displays already discussed, Greek design was used piecemeal—column screens under archways, supporting only a length of entablature; huge orders apparently but not in fact footing converging groin-vault forms; strips of entablature or cornice marking junctions of major forms or the principal zones of a wall design; and so on. The many curving forms in both plan and elevation competed with the orders for attention, lessened their authority, and robbed them of their former dominance. Considering how varied in form and relative scale these buildings were, the use in them of classical design elements is surprisingly successful. The orders and their mouldings, also variously scaled in order to fit the major forms, largely set close to walls and crowded into corners, did not look out of place. But they were no longer primary elements: in buildings supremely functional, they were decorative and symbolic.

The wall also changed, and not just in degree of elaboration. Its two sides were often different in plan, and in sophisticated buildings the same was largely true of elevations also. Walls were not the undisputed determinants of interior volumetric shapes that they were in trabeated buildings, because of the pre-emptive role in bath design of curving and polygonal space boundaries. Though their structural role of course remained, the walls of a vaulted room stood tangent to rising, inward-spreading curves, part in theory at least of a seamless, continuous envelope rising from the floor at one side of the room to curve up and across to the responding, duplicate system on the other.[94] This was clearly different in form and effect from planar walls supporting a flat, wooden-framed ceiling to enclose a spatially unequivocal box-shaped volume. In a bath building a wall might look as much sculpted as built (in the sense of a straightforward ashlar structure).

Experimentation went on to the end (Lepcis Magna, unfinished "imperial" baths; 207 Piazza Armerina villa, octagonal bathing suite).[95] The momentum of spatial innovation continued unbroken into Early Christian and Byzantine architecture, where in non-basilican buildings the influence of bath design is often seen. The particular qualities of baths make typological studies, often based on degrees of similarity to or deviation from a supposed norm, not very useful. Cases of close resemblance exist, but there does not seem to have been any direct duplication. Near-standardization did occur in other building types when simple units could be effectively repeated—for example storehouse rooms, cistern chambers, and shops (over eight hundred found at Ostia, all much the same). In conservative buildings such as official temples there was in general a community of formal principle if not of dimensions and detail. But this was not true of complicated structures such as baths or stage buildings. These are the buildings, together with other vehicles of imperial imagery such as honorific arches and four-way structures, where typically Roman combinations of old and new elements were most successful: trabeation with vaults, orders with arches (near-Renaissance sensitivity of 198 design in pilastered arcades at the baths of Dougga and Maktar), and standard, workaday features, including technological ones, embedded in neoteric innovative structures of many parts. It is ironical that some Renaissance and Beaux-Arts architects regarded the bath building as a model of antiquarian perfection when it contained what in its own day were such unclassical traits.

That the bath was a vital theme of Roman urbanism, central to everyday existence, is certain. It was thought indispensable. As design was little affected by regional preferences, and the larger baths were derived from those in Rome, imperial content seems beyond doubt. Furthermore, baths reflected their urban context. Passing slowly through the varied chambers of a large municipal bath, pursuing its lengthy route in stretches measured out by the plunges, tubs, and pools, one negotiated a compacted, reductive analogue of the town itself (compare Ausonius, quoted in chapter II). For baths too had public halls, latrines, fountains, archways, and exedras, and sometimes peristyles as well, all set at different intervals along ritual armatures. In lesser baths such paths were traced out in abbreviated form. In this sense, baths were like abridged towns, with some of the chief sights of outdoor life provided indoors in sometimes sensational and luxurious form: town models free of the less desirable realities found outside. They were extremely popular, and the largest, with many amenities, provided splendid settings for leisure within nearly everyone's reach. Rising from ample, level concrete platforms honeycombed with cavities for heating and hydraulic installations, the bulky volumes and vaulted chambers of civic baths matched and perhaps surpassed official temples as symbols of *romanitas*.

Other symbolic qualities inhered in bath buildings. In every town they brought people together, standing in a social sense for the unity of regions and cultures the Romans encouraged or enforced. Bath design was innovative and sophisticated, in tune with the latest ideas, in step with municipal self-regard and ambition. Roman technology supplied ample quantities of water for hygienic facilities in settings conducive to social intercourse. People east and west avidly welcomed all this. Historically resonant sculpture, in the form of innumerable copies and some originals by old masters, grafted culture onto the bathing experience. Baths early on became badges of imperial status, of membership in the broader Roman community, and these figural tokens of long-lived continuities were set about in them, unread perhaps, like uncut books, but highly visible nonetheless. Above all, bath buildings are landmarks in the history of architecture, and not only because of their attraction for Renaissance and subsequent masters. They were the first ubiquitous public amenities in Western architecture set in consequential buildings not solely devoted to entertainment. Their like was not seen again, the eastern empire aside, until modern times.

The cardinal themes of this empire imagery focused on the scenic unification of spaces and elevations. Highly mnemonic because they alluded to familiar compositions of the past—colonnades, temple fronts, recessed volumes, and the like—they recapitulated these older images in inventively articulated designs. Reflecting urban themes and images in condensed yet complex form, individual elements were placed closer together than before, creating textured patterns with sharp juxtapositions of light and dark of the kind important in late antique art. At the same time, simple, rational spacing of design elements gave way to more involved rhythms, some with suggestions of visual counterpoint; the contrast between new themes and plain, traditional structures became more pronounced. Verticality challenged or superseded horizontality: stories were multiplied and vaults rose higher, changing the urban skyline. Every town built in the new way if possible; cities rushed to do so. Strolling down the Embolos at Ephesus, for example, 168

104 from the civic buildings above to the huge agora below and then along the Arkadiané
 31 boulevard to the harbor, the architecture of imperial imagery would have been seen
     again and again just as in Rome—in fountains, temples, baths, memorials, a library,
     archways, peristyles, and column displays. In these buildings one would often have
     detected a strain that partially prefigured seventeenth-century architecture in Italy.

VIII

EMPIRE IMAGERY: BAROQUE MODES

AN INCLINATION to baroque design, as in numerous tombs and column displays, extended architectural composition into territory that today may seem hardly classical at all. This is not a new topic. Seventeenth-century masters in Rome knew of this tendency from ancient structures surviving in the city and its environs; the possibility of direct connections between the two periods has been suggested. Piranesi, in spite of his prejudices one of the most acute observers ever of imperial architecture, saw the tendency clearly for what it was.[96] Modern writers often emphasize eastern examples— Baalbek and Petra having cast their spell—though in fact baroque modes (to identify the whole complex phenomenon by one convenient phrase) were common in the west; again, regionalism was not particularly significant.

Though close affinities exist up to a point, the confident fluidity of seventeenth-century design is usually missing in the ancient buildings, where something of the classical independence and individuality of each element persisted. While iconographical differences are unbridgeable, rhetorical intent remains constant. Of Roman seventeenth-century architects it has been said that in this respect they "aimed at creating buildings which would be immediately striking and would appeal to an unsophisticated as well as to an educated audience," that this appeal "was to be to the emotions as much as to the intellect," the architects aiming "at arousing astonishment, at giving the impression of grandeur, at imposing their effects immediately, even abruptly, on the spectator," objectives indistinguishable from those of antiquity.[97] In addition to this sympathy of imagery, formal and compositional similarities exist: unity, focus, and the kind of surface variation often spoken of as movement. These are not so much matters of detail, of cornices and capitals—subservient features in baroque design—as of complex symmetries, unitary volumes, and carefully calculated, effective marriages of major elements with smaller, subordinate ones.

Each example has many parts and is highly inflected, but in it a single major feature,

180. Side, building M, detail; perhaps second century

dominating the composition from the center, is flanked or embraced by choruses of lesser elements confirming its supremacy. Unlike traditional classical architecture, this is a climactic art in which the effect of a centered pre-eminent feature is magnified by a 148 complex equipoise of satellite forms enframing it. In the first tomb of the Caetennii (under S. Peter's), for example, the central arch and its sheltered aedicula, played up to by symmetrical flanking elements, dominate the proto-baroque north wall; the same 182 principles governs Bernini's Cornaro Chapel in S. Maria della Vittoria, where the entire elaborate design is in the service of the centered figural tableau within its ornate tabernacle. In buildings with unified volumes, the main space or mass is bounded by subordinate ones inseparably joined with it to enhance its dramatic effect, as in Rome in the Horti Sallustiani round salon or the Domus Aurea octagon, or in S. Andrea al Quirinale; baroque walls often border these primary forms.

PREFIGURATION

If examples from the two periods are contrasted and compared, similarities and differences surface and the character of baroque modes begins to emerge. Although direct links between some ancient and later buildings may exist, the present objective is not to show what might have influenced whom, but in what way the earlier work may have prefigured the later (irrespective of what was then known about antiquity), and the degree to which ancient buildings can properly be called baroque. The complexity of imperial architecture with its several substyles suggests this referential use of a culturally disparate style in order to isolate, for the moment, and identify one key Roman strain. And though it may be an exaggeration to say that a real if shadowy Italian continuum was at work, it is significant that Counter-Reformation architecture arose in Rome at a time when Renaissance-Vitruvian formulas were in eclipse, and the ruins were observed from a less restrictive point of view than before. Examining the evidence for imperial architecture without Vitruvian preconceptions is always useful.

In spite of major differences, there are telling formal and compositional likenesses between imperial and baroque architecture. Incipiently baroque qualities were widespread in Roman art. These are readily perceived in elevation, as in the central portion of the architectural painting that gives the House of Apollo in Pompeii its name. Of 181 Neronian date, it shows the god adjudicating a dispute between the morning and evening stars, Phosphoros and Hesperos. Such settings are said to derive directly from theatre architecture, but there are differences, here at least. The three traditional doors have become windows, and the elevated podia carrying the architecture and the figures' thrones are inaccessible from stage level, since there are no stairs. The elaborate, spindly architecture is symmetrically arranged in a familiar triad of forms, and the centered half-tholos (its completion intimated by a circular entablature above the god's head) is flanked by projecting columnar elements, apparently splayed outward in plan, with ressauts and narrow podium arms of their own. The rectilinear pavilions enframing the stellar figures display spatial ambiguities of the kind often found in Roman architectural painting—unclear relationships between foreground and background and between figures and their architectual frames. These are readily revealed if sketch plans are attempted.

But the artist's objective is clear: an impression of an elaborated setting for three figures of equal size, in which the most important is given prominence by location and setting, and the lesser ones marked by subordinated, less elaborate architecture and inward-turning poses. The result is both static and dynamic. The figures are frozen in time and space, displayed as if under glass in a museum, their conventionalized gestures notwithstanding. But the architecture itself breathes space and light, moving back and forth at all levels in a trinity of delicate cages whose attenuated forms and insubstantial entablatures are wrapped in tendrils and rinceaux. This is an architecture of illusion at which actual stage architecture, with its solid realities, only hints. In the painting, only the upper wall surface and the advancing and retreating podium seem substantial. The

181. Pompeii, House of Apollo, Apollo and the
morning and evening stars; wall painting from the end
of Nero's reign

182. Rome, S. Maria della Vittoria, Cornaro Chapel,
central composition; 1640s

empaneled podium, painted both with miniature scenes and with representations of sculptured reliefs, appears solid; without it the figures, weighty and roundly modeled though stiffly posed, might easily fall into the cellar and bring down the whole airy, tentative structure.

In contrast, the main section of Bernini's Cornaro Chapel is architectonic and sub-   182
stantial. Yet here also illusion reigns, though three-dimensional and far more effectively wrought. Again there is a dominant design triad, but without figures in the flanking subordinate rectangles. Again there is an illuminated tholos (oval in plan) and splayed-out orders beside the central scene. And again the tholos podium is convex and the crowning entablature decorated with a rinceau. As in the painting there are figures turned inward, the members of the Cornaro family kneeling in their loges, though they are brought forward into actual space in a very theatrical way. The Chapel is infinitely superior artistically to the painting, but the two are closely related in composition. Bernini's creation is an undoubted masterpiece, of which the Pompeiian painting, in limning the chapel's underlying organization, is a ghostly, adventitious precursor.

Specifically architectural relationships can be perceived by comparing for example the plan of Carlo Rainaldi's stately church of S. Maria in Campitelli in Rome (1663–1667)   183
with imperial buildings. In plan the church appears to have an oblong nave, but because along its central transverse axis it is opened up left and right into broad, deep chapels whose arched openings rise above an otherwise continuous entablature line (one that runs back in and around these chapels), it verges on a cross-shaped volume. Smaller chapels stand beside these larger ones, so that triads of large but compositionally secondary volumes draw space directly off the central vessel toward the sides, where it is firmly held by repeatedly angled, enveloping walls. This transversal emphasis is furthered by the extension of the main chapels into receding altar bays, making the cross axis between them about 7 m. greater than the length of the nave.

This design has been compared to that of Magenta's S. Salvatore in Bologna, begun some sixty years earlier, in 1605.[98] Although the juxtaposition is apt in the sense that the Bologna church also has wide transverse chapels with archways reaching above the nave entablature line, the plan remains essentially basilican, with Gesù-like, if larger, axial passageways running between the chapels that resemble secluded aisles. Another comparison, perhaps more relevant for its plan, is Giacomo della Porta's S. Maria ai Monti in Rome, begun in 1580, where the transverse recesses are not interconnected, and the middle ones function as entranceways from outside the church. In all these churches, however, the naves are joined as at Rainaldi's building with domed volumes separating them from spacious apses beyond. What differentiates the nave of S. Maria in Campitelli from the others is the harmonic play between the central nave volume and the triadic side elements, which are scaled first larger and then smaller in plan and height and therefore in volume, and which if they were any larger would come close to usurping the longitudinal spatial authority of the nave.

At the end of this ingeniously balanced rectilinear web of spatial energy, the nave narrows sharply where a truncated passageway leads to a domed chamber of implied

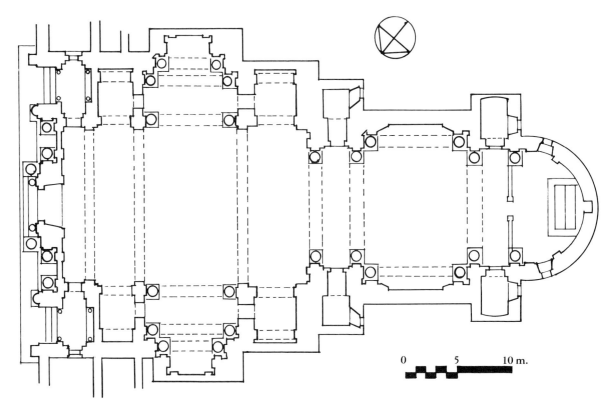

183. Rome, S. Maria in Campitelli, plan; 1663

184. Djemila, building opposite the great baths; second or third century

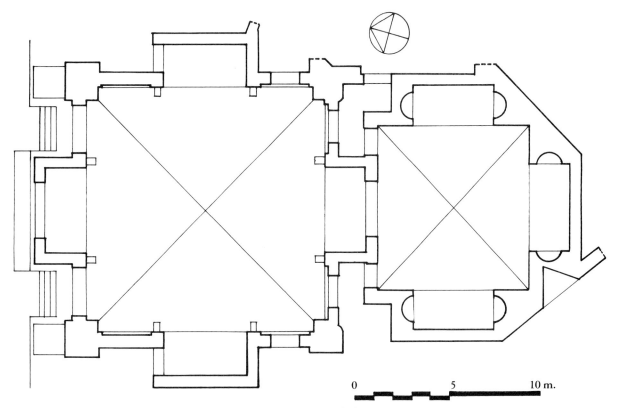

185. Tivoli, Hadrian's Villa, the "Greek Library", plan; probably early 120s

cross-shape plan (the Bologna and Rome churches also narrow this way, though only slightly). At S. Maria in Campitelli this passageway is pierced at ground level by narrow transverse corridors or vestibules reminiscent of similar features just behind the building's facade at the commencement of the nave. Beyond the domed chamber is another facing pair of small chapels beside the apse arch. Here there are no files of columns along the nave as there are in Bologna, nor are there any in the other Roman churches cited. In Rainaldi's church, however, monumental Corinthian columns are placed at strategic points to emphasize the main configurations of the plan. They line the interiors of the central transverse chapels, stand in pairs both at the sides of the truncated passageway and the chapels flanking the apse, and near the corners formed by the shallow arms of the cross from which the pendentives and their dome rise—twelve columns in all on each side of the church.

The design is a study in harmonics whose tonic is the main axis (about 50 m. long). Chords are repeatedly struck by subordinated spaces of different sizes and shapes paired symmetrically along the progress of this central line. The building's enclosing wall narrows progressively overall from entrance to apse, but in measured steps of expansion and contraction that come to a halt at the narrowest, furthest part of the building. The result is a series of right-angled sequences unifying rather than unsettling the building's configuration, which is superlatively scenic. From the entranceway, ranges of coulisses are seen left and right. Without column files, volumes predominate. Triads thrive, and various shapes are played off against each other with great success. As in most baroque churches, the whole repertory of ancient architecture is used: monumental and lesser orders, barrel vaults, a dome and a half-dome, niches, aediculas, and so on, all unified in a design whose final purpose is to focus attention on a venerated icon centered in the apse wall.

Because this way of planning and juxtaposing volumes lies at the heart of full baroque design, S. Maria in Campitelli has been described in some detail. More sophisticated and complex than any ancient example, it demonstrates fully the intricacy of baroque unity. Each part of the design contributes to the strength of the overriding controlling concept, a relationship that must be discernible in ancient buildings if they are to be classed as proto-baroque. There are some that do this in a Rainaldian if generalized way. The so-called civic lararium at Pompeii suggests this unity compactly but sketchily. Re-entrant spaces and niches of differing sizes face each other across a central void, at the far end of which is an apse, in itself proportionately broad but considerably narrower than the space before it; there seem not to have been any freestanding columns. At Djemila, opposite the entrance to the great south baths, there is a building whose ample oblong vestibule gave onto a wider, squarish main salon by way of an opening narrower than either. The main space terminated in a broad apse, slightly masked, like the one at Pompeii, by short projections of its face-wall along the chord. Though cleared, the building is dilapidated, but apparently the vestibule had niches left and right, and each successive space—vestibule, main room, and apse—was raised a full step higher than the preceding one.

There is another ancient building, closer in concept to Rainaldi's, the so-called Greek Library at Hadrian's Tivoli villa.[99] Although it was a complicated structure more than one story tall, whose original appearance is uncertain, its ground plan is clear. The long axis could not be traversed throughout the building, which had to be negotiated by way of paired entrances and passageways flanking large arched openings or windows set in the center of the facade and in the opposite recess and giving onto the secondary square space (an arrangement reminiscent of the tablinum/andron juxtaposition found in some Pompeiian houses). But the planning principles were similar to Rainaldi's: a primary, square volume (about 13 m. on a side) was expanded by spacious transverse recesses, once vaulted over but not up to the height of the central vault; symmetrical recesses were also located along the main axis. Beside all four of these, footings for columns stand in the main space, close to the walls. The second space is also square (about 8.6 m. on a side), and was also once vaulted, with three very nearly identical rectilinear niches, each with small curved niches facing their re-entrant spaces on either side. The axis view, framed by two large windows, may by analogy be thought to have focused on a statue placed in the farthest recess.

The neighboring "Latin Library" was somewhat similarly planned but could be entered on its axis directly through a half-tholos open across its chord to the library's first main space. That had transverse recesses, and beyond it were internal side passages flanking a large axially-placed window. Then came the second space, slightly oblong in plan and larger than the first, without niches but with a broad semicircular apse with a raised platform and statue base. Both designs strongly emphasized proto-baroque fea-

150

184

185

tures: unified composition made up of hierarchically joined volumes, scenic focus on a final, climactic element, and spaces that enlarged and diminished symmetrically in a fashion supportive of the controlling axis. Like Rainaldi's building they were exercises in carpentering space, in fitting volumes of various sizes together to obtain particular effects without inducing confusion or disorder. The result was a baroque order, primitive from a seventeenth-century point of view perhaps, but a baroque order nonetheless. Both libraries show what could be done with the pedestrian square if the architect was willing to think in terms of complementary focused volumes. There is one more connection between Rainaldi's church and the "Greek Library": high, narrow vaulted spaces—blind structural corridors—ran transversely over the three axial recesses of the villa structure, and at S. Maria Rainaldi placed a similar, vaulted buttressing space, curved in elevation, over the truncated passageway between the main nave and the domed space beyond.[100]

In the literature of baroque architecture, three ancient buildings in particular are seen as possible stylistic precursors: the Conocchia, the Khasneh, and the Temple of Venus at Baalbek (described above). The Conocchia, nearly seamlessly unified, its diagonal   136 projections reinforcing the unseen vertical centerline of the whole, has been invoked in connection with the facade of Borromini's S. Agnese in Agone and his superstructure for S. Andrea delle Fratte. The drum of S. Andrea has been singled out for comparison, but except for the diagonal extensions, the suggested relationship with the Conocchia is not particularly convincing—the curves are reversed and the smooth transitions from the Conocchia core to the projections and back to the core are abandoned.[101]

But the church's tower is another matter. Below the uppermost circle of cherub-   186 herms, the tholos and its supporting story closely follow, intentionally or not, the formal organization of the Conocchia. In the lower story, the curves have been transcribed as straight lines, but the blind aediculas are retained (for Borromini's diagonally-set columns, compare Ligorio's Conocchia drawing); in the upper, the blind tholos has been partially opened up. But in spite of these changes the compositional principles remain the same: a block, whose vertical centerline is powerfully fixed by an implied internal intersection of vertical planes set on the diagonals, is surmounted by a cylinder evoking the same centralizing effect by contrasting formal means. Borromini continued the vertical energy of the design through another story, gaining height for a coda of culminating symbols, a vertical bouquet of scrolls holding a spiky crown and a cross. Figuratively speaking, he threaded blocks and spools on a vertical rod set in the angle between the main body of the church and its apse. Each zone, in the manner of staged towers, is narrower than the one below, and two of these, though attenuated in contrast with ancient work, reflect its spirit.

The two-story facade of four columns each, with A-B-A spacing (that for example of the temple-front motif of S. Peter's) and crowned by a pediment, goes back at least to the second century B.C. (Pergamon, the two-story gateway to the Athena sanctuary, Doric below and Ionic above, re-erected in the Pergamon Museum in East Berlin; compare Athens, the Roman Market gate, and Claudian coinage of Nicaea   187

186. Rome, S. Andrea delle Fratte, tower; early 1660s. Left, the tower; below, lowest tower stage, detail

gateways).[102] In various versions such facades became almost commonplaces of imperial architecture, with their emphasis on central features or carriageways (Athens, Hadrian's Arch, upper story; compare Bernini's S. Bibiana facade, or Hardouin Mansart's Dôme des Invalides facade, second story). To display in the center of an arched or divided upper story an important feature—statuary or a tholos—was a natural development, and in this sense the Petra Khasneh was not exceptional. Its extraordinary setting, in a town at the edge of classical civilization, beside open ground at the end of a narrow, winding canyon, and its sophisticated monumentality and good state of preservation, justify its fame. Though its differently spaced bays, unequal story heights, and powerful play of light and shade can suggest baroque principles to our eyes, it is in fact a logical product of the evolution of classical architecture.

172

134

In a general sense, the Khasneh points toward the formal framework of baroque design, but it remains essentially classical because its individual elements are not absorbed into the overall effect. The integration of subordinate features, the interweaving of verticals and horizontals, is from a seventeenth-century point of view incomplete. Indivisible parts such as the areas enframed by orders, entablatures, and cornices are sharply defined and have too much independence for the flowing continuities of prop-

187. Athens, Roman Market, gate; late first century B.C.

erly baroque architecture. What is significant in the present context is that the Khasneh does have several incipiently baroque features, among them a projecting ground-story temple front (again, like S. Peter's), a continuous but stepped-back entablature below an attic, ressauts, and a triad of prismatic and cylindrical forms in the second story; in addition, relief sculpture enlivened the stone panels enframed by the orders, vaguely foreshadowing the similar treatment of baroque church facades in Rome.

137   The immense Petra facade-tomb known as the Deir is approximately as high (40.2 m.) as the Khasneh. Wider than it is tall, with no freestanding orders, it lacks the confident balance of the Khasneh design. But it too incorporates baroque elements. The spacing of the first-story bays, including those of the central concavity, runs A-B-C-D-C-B-A, and the terminal orders of both stories are pilasters (shadowed on their inner sides by slivers of engaged columns); this use of pilasters instead of rounded shafts at the ends of a facade distinctly prefigures later practice, when it was common to reduce the projections and increase the setbacks as the facade expanded left and right from its centerline. The extremities of the upper story are formed by what are in effect spur walls

168   (compare the upper story of the Ephesus library), their topmost zones in harmony with the ressauts over one pair of orders below. Here the statuary was placed in niches (two with pediments, three without) in a seventeenth-century manner. The centered curve of the ground story is played off against the opposite curve of the half-blind tholos above (compare the similar relationship seen at a tomb on the Via Celle outside Pozzuoli).

Also at Petra, the Bab el-Siq triclinium facade has half-pediments; the Corinthian tomb has two sets of them. In the tomb, one set is centered atop an abbreviated or chopped-off intermediate story set above a first story of uniform horizontal spacing except for the entranceway; a third story with a tholos is flanked by bays with half-pediments in the manner of the Khasneh and the Deir. None of the individual features makes these designs baroque. But the Khasneh comes within striking distance, and that is due in part to its high degree of classical sophistication—the others, which have their own splendor, often use quasi-classical motifs in quite non-classical ways. As has often been said, the Khasneh's closest known relatives in Roman times are certain paintings in Campania, that of the tholos flanked by columns carrying half-pediments in the House of the Labyrinth in Pompeii, for example, or, more distant, the scene of Iphigenia in Tauris in the House of Pinarius Cerialis (also at Pompeii).

156, 157   Nor is the Venus temple at Baalbek, unlike Petra's facades fully volumetric, truly baroque. Many would agree that it is extraordinary, in its own way at once complete and satisfying, but its parts are clearly articulated, and its neatly self-contained unity is the result of an elaborated geometry, not a unified interweaving of elements clearly subordinated to the effect of the whole. The cella's external order makes this clear. Although four columns are set out around the curve of the wall, and their podium and entablature are scalloped in plan, the shafts stand well away from the wall. They are spaced evenly (the distance increases slightly toward the facade, though this is all but indistinguishable on the ground). In this sense the wall-to-order relationship is not much different from that at the mausoleum at Split. A fresco in a house in Insula V, Herculaneum, shows a similar arrangement.[103]

It is the iterated horizontal curves and their play against the countercurve of the cella wall that catch the imagination, particularly as Borromini's lanterns at S. Carlo alle Quattro Fontane and S. Ivo have scalloped horizontal members. But in Rome the orders do not stand free (just tangent to the main body at S. Carlo, engaged and about three-quarters round at S. Ivo), and, more important, the wall sections between them are concave. It is true that at Baalbek there are five curved niches set between the column shafts, but they are small in contrast to the cylindrical surface area of the wall they

188

188. Rome, S. Carlo alle Quattro Fontane, lantern; early 1640s

inhabit. Furthermore, though at S. Ivo both podium and entablature are scalloped, only the entablature is at S. Carlo. Perhaps Borromini invented this feature anew or got it from G. B. Montano's (fanciful?) drawing of a temple near Tivoli, published in 1624; or just possibly he saw it on some Roman ruin now gone.[104] Whatever the connections with antiquity, if any, there remain certain remarkable similarities of detail, for exam-
135   ple the statue-base moulding toward the bottom of the Khasneh tholos, which seems to travel round behind the order and then reappear on the other side, almost exactly as Borromini's shoulder-high moulding does on the S. Carlo lantern (compare La Conoc-
136   chia, the tholos moulding; and the Vienna Karlskirche, facade mouldings behind the helical columns). As at the Deir, the tholos order is only about half as high as the tholos itself, which, like the one of the S. Andrea tower, has an unusually tall entablature and is also partially opened up.

Imperial buildings having plans composed of interconnected circular curves approached the flowing quality of walls enclosing centralized baroque spaces and the resulting sense of an indissoluble interdependence of parts (patterns also seen in paint-
155   ings and pavements: Ostia, Insula delle Ierodule and the Augustales' building). The curves do not overlap but join in reversing sequences to form quatrefoils (Baia, so-called Temple of Venus, vestibule; Hadrian's Villa, Piazza d'Oro main nymphaeum, Ac-

189. Ostia, Insula of the Painted Vaults (ca. 120), Severan painting

cademia; compare the three-shaft monument in the Constantine museum[105]). These plans prefigured those of undulating baroque centralized spaces such as that of the vestibule of Borromini's S. Maria delle Sette Dolori; it is significant that buildings at Hadrian's Villa were studied by architects from at least the middle of the sixteenth century onward.

Centralized spaces roofed by vaults composed of converging gores or panels are still partly or wholly preserved in several ancient buildings, for example at the Villa (the Piazza d'Oro vestibule, the octagonal salon of the Small Baths, the half-dome of the Serapeum), beside the Pantheon-like so-called Temple of Mercury at Baia, the round salon at the Horti Sallustiani and that in the Park of the Gordians in Rome (compare the Palatine Maxentian baths), in several ruins near Viterbo, and in the "House" of Diana at Bulla Regia.[106] Surface decoration was often similarly arranged. In the Insula of the   189 Painted Vaults at Ostia, an overhead painting is centered on an octagonal medallion from which eight panels expand radially to a circular border, each ending in a semicircular lunette (compare Isola Sacra, tomb no. 42). Looking up, the effect is roughly similar to that of a ribbed baroque dome with its crowning lantern opening, as at S. Ivo   190 or S. Andrea al Quirinale, representative evidence of interest in imperial times in powerfully unified volumetric composition and climactic focus.

190. Rome, S. Ivo, interior; begun 1643

Baroque details played major supporting roles in mature imperial design. Some have been discussed already, but an expanded list will suggest how many familiar seventeenth-century features existed in imperial times.

96   Orders rising through two stories (Lambaesis, groma interior; cf. Pantheon, interior first story)

191   Orders set close together (Ptolemais in Cyrenaica, Palazzo delle Colonne, small-
140   scale scenic parapet over the north side of the large peristyle; cf. Wadi Mesueggi, tomb)

Orders immured or nearly so (Rome, "Basilica of Neptune"; Ostia, Domus del Pozzo facade)

Orders of mixed heights (Baalbek, small temple, interior)

127, 162   Orders with double entasis (Split, the peristyle)

191. Ephesus, Baths of Scholastikia, columns; originally second century, rebuilt ca. 400

These are not aberrations or entirely new creations but essentially the products, like the Khasneh at Petra, of traditional classicism's gradual transformation. That in and near Rome they caught the attention of baroque masters seems indisputable from the evidence of buildings and texts. References to ancient remains in sympathy with seventeenth-century objectives are fairly common. Borromini refers to Hadrian's Villa, for example, and in a manuscript by Orfeo Boselli the reaction of Borromini and others to a newly-found capital in Rome is recorded: they "were struck . . . to see with what beautiful novelty and variety the ancients treated architecture," in other words, by the freedom, in contrast to Renaissance-Vitruvian ideals, of its conception and carving.[107]

Unity

Baroque design depends upon complex compositional unity. In all examples the elements are arranged around a central feature or axis in such a way as to converge upon it, to concentrate attention there. Centerlines and central features are as old as architecture itself, but their dramatic reinforcement by means of a confluence of supporting subordinate features was brought forward by Roman designers seeking to dramatize and quicken architecture. Successive theatre stage-wall reconstructions demonstrate this.

At Pompeii the first stage-wall was straight, with three openings and no freestanding columns. In its next version, five plain pavilions, each with four freestanding columns, were erected in front of the straight wall, the central pavilion about a third wider than the others. After the earthquake of 62, an entirely new two-story structure was put up. This had a curving central recess, almost a third as wide as the stage overall, flanked by two shallower, slightly narrower, rectangular recesses.[108] Freestanding columns marked the forward-and-back play of the wall, which was emphasized by an array of niches. These changes record an essential feature of proto-baroque development: strong emphasis on a large central feature through the use of subordinate motifs deployed symmetrically right and left to give it a prominence and ascendancy it would not have standing alone. By keeping the columns close to the wall, the powerful underlying design framework was protected from any spatial dilution that trabeated, roofed architecture would have introduced. This, and the depth and shape of the central recess, created the desired effect—the dominance of a sheltering presence, its importance proclaimed by duplicate, corroborating flanks of satellite forms.

To center a major structure in a symmetrical court or temenos, or a statue in an aedicula, had long been Roman practice. The unity of proto-baroque design evolved in part from this, but the means used to emphasize it did not. The self-evident tectonic character of traditional work gradually decreased, as for example when columns became increasingly non-structural and moved close to walls to form scenic rather than functional constructions. Such changes helped create a descriptive architecture nearer in artistic effect to architects' drawings made of lines and shading than to bulky temples or basilicas with their structural clarity. The new modes were not those of plain walls and framed roofs, of powerful beams and posts angled together, but of walls elaborated and modeled and spaces vaulted over—vaulted partly because tangential, flowing transitions from vertical supports to curving ceilings helped unify interior spaces. In every example, unity was sought by arranging design elements in a reciprocating, balanced fashion so as to concentrate attention on a cardinal feature such as a niche, apse, tholos, temple front, or dome.

The simplest and most common form of this arrangement was that with a central feature wider (and usually taller) than smaller ones at either side, as in an honorific arch
181   with three openings, the Apollo painting discussed above, or temple fronts with A-B-A spacing (Si', south temple; Pompeii, tomb of M. Octavius by the Porta Nocera). This theme, an invention momentous for the history of architecture whenever it took place, found some favor with the Greeks from early times onward (Delphi treasuries). Hellenistic builders liked it. With the Romans it became something of a habit, liberally
187   applied through the building typology (Pantheon, apse and flanking elements; Athens,
115   Roman market gate; compare Sbeitla, the sizes of the three forum temples; the aisle-
60   nave-aisle basilica transverse section, as at Smyrna, Cyrene, or Augst; or the underground basilica by the Porta Maggiore in Rome). The version with an arched centerpiece and oblong panels set vertically beside it was widespread. With the addition of columns and a full complement of bases and mouldings, and sometimes an enframing temple

front, a major imperial image was created, one linking many different buildings across the empire and an ancestor of the three-unit Serliana (the "Palladian motif"), still in use.

This A-B-A system also thrived in interior architecture (Rome, the Domus Aurea, chambers in the west wing under Trajan's Baths; innumerable tombs such as the Sedia del Diavolo in Rome). Curving surfaces added to the incipiently baroque flavor of some, as in a chamber tomb just outside the Porta Romana at Ostia. Along its two-story south wall the rectilinear re-entrants of the immediate side features are replaced at the center by a shallow convex surface below a comparatively deep concave one; a shelf shaped in plan like a three-quarter moon marks the transition.[109] Only the upper zone had orders, which were engaged colonnettes made of terra-cotta like the rest of the structure. To the far left and right, the lower wall is slightly concave, and the effect resembles the facades of Pietro da Cortona's SS. Luca e Martina and Borromini's S. Carlo, with their sculptured, energized surfaces.

In order to give weight to the centered elements, frequently cavities, of A-B-A compositions, systems of enframement, often quite elaborate, were supplied around them. They were akin to those used on honorific arches, and their purpose was to underscore the presence of controlling (if usually invisible) centerlines, locking compositions firmly onto their dominant features. Often two or more frames—normally of arches, mouldings, orders, and pediments—were placed around each other in diminishing sizes, all sharing the same centerline as the central form. None was as elaborate as

192

193

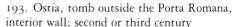

192. Rome, tomb called the Sedia del Diavolo, model; mid-second century

193. Ostia, tomb outside the Porta Romana, interior wall; second or third century

194, 195   for example the upper story of Maderno's S. Susanna facade, with its overall temple front, projecting central rectilinear bay, lesser temple front with a segmental pediment, and arched enclosure, all encasing successively the sculptured plaque with its martyr's crown; but the principle was the same.

148   The north wall of the first Caetennii tomb can stand for nearly all such Roman systems. Four enframements embraced the central niche: the lunette curve formed by the wall and vault juncture, the large arch, the temple-front aedicula, and the moulded outline of the final niche with its shell-decorated vault. The larger niche containing the aedicula was almost rhetorical, functioning as a kind of architectural gesture presenting the aedicula to the viewer and saying, in effect, that it is the treasured heart of the wall. The aedicula is revealed as in a temple split open, its halves moved off to the sides. The rhythm overall is B-A-B-A-B, but the A-B-A relationship of the central section stands out forcefully because of the height and width of the main, umbrella-like arch. Enframement and excurrent lateral subordination, essential baroque principles, insure unity. The central aedicula niche, though small, controls the whole design, and from it other parts expanded as the panels of an open fan from its handle's end. The perimeter of the composition, where expansion ceased against bulwarks of stout mouldings, described a protective, sheltering building whose precise symmetry implied stability and permanence.

As pointed out in chapter VI, these effects were sharpened and strengthened by moulding and banding the conspicuous edges where discrete surfaces met (with stone or

194. Rome, S. Susanna, facade, upper story, detail; ca. 1600

195. Gerasa, Temple of Artemis propylon, detail; mid-second century

sometimes terra-cotta, in the larger buildings; terra-cotta, stucco, or just paint in the smaller). This ancient usage is epidemic in imperial architecture. Irreducible geometric entities (as well as whole buildings) were often heavily outlined, their basic shapes reinforced the way boards nailed along the edges of a heavy wooden shipping crate accentuate its boxy bulk (compare Rome, Tomb of Eurysaces). These raised, running 131 elements and their shadows insured that individual parts were given full definition and were not overpowered by the deeply shadowed recesses and crevices typical of such architecture. Wandering, traveling mouldings, doggedly following each change of direction and binding multiform compositions together by girdling them round, contributed strongly to unity of design and effect. Certain bundles of mouldings might be very elaborate (Ephesus, Temple of Serapis cornice fragments; Rome, Arch of Titus, 97, 133 "Tomb of Annia Regilla"), but in near-baroque constructions, traditional detailing was less important than the effects produced by raised enframements, whatever their profiles or patterns.

Of symmetrical enframements, two- and four-column temple fronts are at once the most common and the most heavily charged with meaning. A doorway or a window enframed with mouldings is much altered by the addition of a pediment; if pilasters or flanking columns, engaged or freestanding, are added, the sense of the importance of the opening thus surrounded is increased. In the history of Western architecture it is remarkable how powerful this temple-front image is, for after all it is only a shallow, gable-end portion of a simple, practical roof structure supported by columns or columnar forms. But its capacity to lend both dignity and heightened meaning to many different elements and building types—doorways, niches, shrines and tabernacles of all kinds, palaces, cult buildings, tombs, honorific arches, and so on—is central to the formal nature of Roman classical design. Because it can be used at any scale builders can manage, the temple front can be grandly monumental or familiarly domestic. Its flexibility has few rivals, and its imagery is almost universally recognized. Probably this is due less to its prestige as a temple symbol than to its description of the built enclosure, the archetypal sheltering, protected place construed, unlike the primitive hut, in sophisticated architectural form. Symmetrical and stable, the temple front intimates entrance as well as shelter; it is multipurpose both functionally and symbolically and may be the strongest architectural image yet produced in the west.

These qualities made the temple front an effective agent of unity. In addition, they helped bring architecture and its viewers into a closer relationship than would otherwise have been the case because they suggested if they did not actually offer the possibility of entrance. A temple front alters the character of a simple wall, breaking up the adamant separation plain masonry construction makes between the space before it and that beyond by suggesting the existence of spatial extensions and depths that a real temple porch gives onto. So embryonic baroque walls or facades, with their temple fronts, are to a degree disguised to look like something else—constructions theoretically penetrable, evocations in stone of places experienced and familiar, marked by devices suggesting the possibility of movement from one place to another. They are truly scenic, as has often been said, because they are scenes; they are closely related to theatre stage-walls. Compressed and unified as they are, ordered and logical in their hierarchies, they even so bring their walls alive by modulating the space in front and strongly intimating the existence of more behind. Paradoxically, though they are usually solid, they convey the suggestion of spatial connection between front and back, and this is due as much as anything to their temple fronts.

When a temple front enframed a niche, especially a concave one finished with an arched vault, a powerful effect of place, of a location of special significance, was
196 produced (Herculaneum, in the House of Carbonized Furniture; Isola Sacra, several tombs, for example numbers 87, 90, and 94). The niche compounded the temple front's implications of shelter, and its recessed, sanctuary-like space, sunken into the structural wall, was crowned by the spreading, sheltering, sacred form of the fastigium and surrounded and cradled by the hallowed temple-outline. The result was one of the most powerful and persistent themes in Roman architecture. Even if there was nothing in the niche, guardianship was implied, guardianship of a place set back from the wall plane and therefore special. The whole compound device spoke of protective presentation. It

196. Herculaneum, House of the Carbonised Furniture, garden niche; ca. 50/60

was not a hiding place but a distinctive cupboard without doors, an honored abode that might be reached into (but not casually), and as it could not be fully entered it kept its space and contents apart and thus in theory inviolate. For these reasons the temple-fronted niche was an exceptionally strong presence and often the centerpiece of nascent baroque designs. Through both form and association it implied focus and unity, and it demanded to be centered on its wall.

Variations on this theme were common: temple fronts enframed by larger ones (Petra, tomb of Sextus Florentinus, with a half-story like the Corinthian tomb but containing a large segmental pediment, resulting in a triple enframement; compare temple-forms within temples, as at Niha, temple A, and Baalbek, the small temple); temple fronts with segmental pediments (Isola Sacra, tombs, for example numbers 41 and 87; cf. number 57); and both actual temples and other buildings with four-column facades whose entablatures arched up between the two central columns. Free interpretation thrived, begetting many combinations of niches, temple fronts, and pediments. Arcuated entablatures, of Mesopotamian origin, infused temple fronts with something of the sheltering geometry inherent in the rounded niche. Because these infringed upon the fastigium's explicit triangular shape, lessening its authority, the center of attention moved downward somewhat to the space between the two central columns. It seems unlikely that this development was related in Roman times to practical needs arising from a lack of suitable stone for spanning central intercolumniations; though this explanation is sometimes advanced, surviving early examples hardly bear it out, being small-scale and more or less embedded in the wall structure behind (Orange, the arch; 76 Pompeii, Isis sanctuary, purgatorium).[110] Larger, more fully integrated examples are 151 probably partly attributable to increased freedom in the use of classical design elements, energized in this case by the pervasive influence of arched niches (Termessos, temple; Baalbek, Temple of Venus; Split, palace face of the peristyle court). But whatever its 157 sponsors, the arcuated pediment is good evidence for increased use, in imperial architecture generally and its baroque modes in particular, of curving elements and surfaces.

Radial implications of curved forms have already been discussed. These qualities, essential to baroque purposes, thrived in this architecture of unity. The Greek tholos, meant to be seen from all sides, as at Delphi, Epidauros, or Athens (Lysikrates' monument), was taken over by the Romans (Tivoli, Temple of Vesta) and in due time adapted to their needs and artistic inclinations. In the monumental form of the tholos a porch was added, anchoring it directionally in the Roman urban context (Rome, Largo Argentina, Temple B; the Pantheon and its progeny; compare Athens, the Augustan version of the agora tholos). As a compositional element in painting, both its vertical axis and its infinity of horizontal ones served the purposes of larger compositions (Boscoreale, the cubiculum in the Metropolitan Museum of Art; Carthage, schola tholos mosaic). In scenic architecture the tholos became a fairly common centralizing motif. Centripetal and centrifugal radiality was reduced by a good half when the tholos was set against a wall, a contraction suiting needs for focus and compositional unity. There the tholos functioned like a niched aedicula except for this wider angle of exposure and

136 attraction; sometimes the angle was given diagonal definition by radial extensions of the
181 kind noted at the Conocchia tomb and the House of Apollo painting (as also at the
182 Cornaro chapel). Finials, often large and elaborate, continued the upward energy of
vertical axes. And half-tholoi are also relevant because of the way they could be used to
eliminate exterior wall angles (Tivoli, Hadrian's Villa, the "Latin Library" and Accademia; Ostia, forum baths; compare Pompeii, painting in the House of M. Lucretius
Fronto of a villa with wings terminating in two-story half-tholoi; Capri, Villa Jovis,
semicircular east salon; compare Rome, S. Maria della Pace, S. Andrea al Quirinale).

With the advent of sophisticated vaulting techniques, the cylindrical tholos cella, its
encircling peristyle usually abandoned, became the familiar Roman rotunda. As the
number of interior niches at ground level increased, so did the potential for approximating a baroque interior composed of a dominant central volume served by smaller satellite
ones radially set out and open to it (Tivoli, Tempio della Tosse; Ostia, Round Temple;
200 Rome, Minerva Medica; Pergamon, Asklepieion, multilobed rotunda). One significant
result of using circles and cylinders was to reduce the amount of dead space rectangular
rooms contain; orthogonal corners are rarely congenial to baroque space. Whole temple
cellas became broad apses (Side, Temple P; Hössn Suleiman; compare Rahle, and
Dougga, Temple of Caelestis, temenos). Oval plans, other than for amphitheatres and
plazas, scarcely flourished, but they were used (Aachen, bath chamber; Ostia, Forum
Baths; Rome, Domus Flavia fountains; compare the marble plan of Rome, fragment 43,
the Balneum Caesaris, and the vivaria on the Palatine and at Horace's Sabine farm near
Licenza, the latter with niches on its "diagonals"). Rooms in baths often approximated
170 oval shapes (Rome, Baths of Diocletian; Tivoli, Hadrian's Villa, Heliocaminus). At the
207 Piazza Armerina villa there is a truncated oval courtyard, and the Minori villa has an
oblong room with a shallow oval dome. Trefoils and quatrefoils could be seen (Piazza
Armerina villa; Dougga, Trifolium house; compare Rome, Diocletian's Baths, cal-
idarium). Hexagons and other regular polygonal figures were popular (Bulla Regia,
House of the Fish; Aquincum, palace; Conimbriga, baths; Ad Maiores, villa; Baalbek,
hexagonal court). In short, centralized forms flourished, as did decorative curving forms
in general (pools and gardens at Fishbourne, Volubilis, Italica; round fountains at
Djemila and at Rome—the Meta Sudans; near Augst, the Septizonium).[111]

These are the chief elements and compositional themes making up Roman baroque
modes. Making up is an accurate phrase, for this architecture was more clearly an
assembly of singular parts than much seventeenth-century work was, with its almost
continuously modeled surfaces throughout entire buildings or rooms. Yet in spite of
this considerable artistic difference, some Roman designers thought in terms of unified,
focused patterns and spaces, and in their best work de-emphasized the sense of individuality each building unit had traditionally expressed. They also managed to compose
underlying frames of unified parts without abandoning the formal imagery and identity
of classicism. Apparently they were better at this with facades and internal walls, on the
one hand, and centralized interior spaces, on the other, than with whole buildings. But
in any event the evidence strongly suggests that the existence of baroque strains was not

an accident or aberration, but the result of the pursuit by some architects of an authentic stylistic goal.

SIGNIFICANCE

To characterize proto-baroque designs as fantasy architecture, as some have done, suggests a preference for the less intricate buildings of earlier classicism and a disposition to see as marginal an architecture of substantial purpose and meaning. In Greco-Roman antiquity classical design evolved almost continuously, and baroque strains constitute one facet of a many-sided history. Though taste or fashion may from time to time favor one Roman period or modality more than others, classical meaning inheres in them all because the instantly recognizable vocabulary of parts remains constant. Thus the baroque modes, far from being marginal, contributed significantly to the distinctive texture of Roman urbanism and the shape of empire imagery as well.

One key to this imagery is the compelling stress placed on a single view or axis in proto-baroque architecture. For the Greek temple builder, the difference in length between ends and sides had long been sufficient to establish his building's orientation. Because the temple was closely integrated with the surrounding landscape and was meant to be fully revealed from any quarter, neither end was made architecturally dominant. Of course single-facade buildings were built in Greek and Hellenistic times, but far less often than in the Roman cities and towns, where facadism ruled. So in directing attention in a concentrated fashion to one side or one overriding compositional feature of a wall or building, these baroque forerunners were simply extensions of a well-established, customary Roman theme. And as the buildings were collocations of classical features, and thus examples of the lists, tables, and catalogues the Romans liked, for example the labeled collection of Nilotic exotica in the Palestrina mosaic, ties with the broader classical tradition were obvious. The elements' roles changed, but not their basic character. This is further evidence of the flexibility of classical design, whose orders in Roman buildings express membership in a larger artistic community.

Another characteristically Roman trait may have been expressed in the hierarchical arrangements resulting from firm reciprocal associations between cardinal features and lesser ones in their service. This was an architecture of gradation, of what was more important and what was less so, the kind of statement inherent in the organization of the administration, the army, the legal system, and society itself. At the same time it is balanced, so that in it the pyramid of the social fabric—any social fabric—may have been suggested and, more important, the paramountcy of a belief, deity, memory, or political construct as well. That such readings were consciously made in Roman times is not contemplated here, but certain resemblances between socio-political forms and architectural ones may not have been entirely fortuitous. In this respect it is significant that the baroque strain was the most hierarchically organized kind of classical architecture. It was one of implications, as all architectures are, and as it appeared at a time when order was thought to depend chiefly on a fixed, cohesive hierarchy of authority, it may be worth considering the possibility that there was some connection between the two, as there was between the social order and, for example, graded programmatic painting, sculpture, and mosaic, or cult and religious ceremonies.

The wide typological spread of near-baroque formations is not in doubt. Largely unrelated to function, they embellished temples, other cult buildings, tombs, baths, palaces, villas, houses, some basilicas and markets, and most kinds of passage architecture. The formations' many parts packed tightly together into a schematic crowdedness reflected the density of urban construction. Like so many Roman structures, they made strong statements about the fixity of their locations. Thus they were working parts of the mechanisms of nodal points, of the referential systems of interrelated places underlying city imagery and memorability. They were modern, not old-fashioned. Though found in the emperor's palaces and the villas of the rich, anyone might construct them, for, unlike the imperial arch or civic basilica, they were common property and could be just as effective at small scale as at large.

This architecture may reflect in some general and practical way the growing interest in arithmetical approaches to the properties of numbers (as opposed to the geometric analysis of the classical Greek masters) so brilliantly represented by Diophantus of Alexandria (dates uncertain but after 150 B.C.).[112] He was not the first to treat equations algebraically (he shows how to solve simple and quadratic ones), but he moved the science of notation and the efficiency of problem-solving forward greatly. His *Arithmetica,* still in circulation in the fifth century, could suggest to an informed architect that proportions, column-spacing, and the like might be thought of in other than the traditional numerical and geometric ways—even if the apparatus of equation solutions held no interest for him. The architecture of the geometry-oriented past, though still very much alive, was perhaps supplemented to some degree by work dependent upon arithmetic advances, work in which unclassical lateral intervals and other proto-baroque tendencies are found. Conscientious imperial architects, products presumably of Vitruvius' celebrated ample curriculum, would have mastered elementary plane and solid geometry as a matter of course. In a time of change, would they not have known of new tools? The matter needs study.

And a time of change it was. The Pantheon marks the watershed between old and new. It is at once static and incipiently baroque: the great sphere of its generation holds its spacious form fixed and immutable, but around the base of the interior it is agitated by the cylindrical wall moving powerfully forward and back. The apsidally anchored elements rise and fall in a double scale, all so to speak in preparation for things to come. Its chromatic precocity, intersecting curves, and structural niceties are all high-empire features. Roman architecture at this point was rather like architecture in Rome in the last decades of the sixteenth century—on the verge of great things. In antiquity no resolution came; too much else was happening, and we are left with the exploratory beginnings of what could have become a mature style. Searching the remains turns up much evidence of incipiently baroque solutions: a perspective staircase (Minori, the villa), multiple, toed-in niches embraced by apses (Palmyra, tomb of Yahai, south wall, re-erected in the Damascus Museum), an approximation of the underlying forms of Pietro da Cortona's facade of S. Maria in Via Lata (Rome, Via Latina, tomb of the Valerii). But taken overall they do not add up to an independent baroque presence.

IX

FORM AND MEANING

IT IS DIFFICULT to come to grips with the essence of imperial architecture. Examples abound, but so does formal variety. There are almost no documents, no project or competition drawings of the kind that enrich and support the study of Renaissance and later architecture. No minutes of professional or academic meetings and no substantial contemporary opinion or criticism exist. Inscriptions give information about donors and dates, and ancient writers often refer to particular buildings, but these sources do not include critical or analytical material. There are works on mensuration, surveying, and water supply, but neither they nor those of Vitruvius' anemic successors—Faventius and Palladius, for example—speak of the art of architecture, of the significance of its forms.

Vitruvius, judging by the attention paid him since the fifteenth century, ought to be a help, but as he wrote early in Augustus' reign he had seen very few imperial buildings. He was a conservative for whom the best architecture was found in the past, where the models to be emulated were enshrined, and this, together with his strong practical bent, prevents him from being a guide to imperial architecture in more than a limited way. Clearly he disliked modern ideas (as already noted, he never mentions those incorporated in the Tabularium or the great sanctuaries at Terracina, Palestrina, or Tivoli).[113] Because no other substantial text by an ancient author survives, his precisian's formulas are usually tried out by scholars on buildings put up after his time. They sometimes fit: certain traditional procedures persisted for a long time, and there are constants in pre-industrial construction that Vitruvius, a hands-on, pragmatic man who had acquired some historical knowledge, knew well. But Vitruvius is no interpreter or critic of architecture in our sense, nor should we expect him to be, for his book, a manual of historical examples and the architect's curriculum as well as a practical guide, was written for makers of buildings and of simple machines, not for architectural historians or critics. And he was out of date, a condition often admirable and useful, but one that makes him only tangentially relevant here. One must turn to the buildings, most of them fragmentary, and make of them what one can.

ROMAN CLASSICISM

Classical architecture in its long history has passed through seismic political upheavals and profound social and technological change without losing its identifying characteristics and coming to an end. Historical reasons for this are documented for certain periods, such as the fifteenth-century revival of antiquity in Italy or the early adoption of ancient models in the United States, but classicism's apparent immortality surely cannot be due to them alone. There will also be inherent reasons, stemming for example from the humane implications of its forms, or the deep-rooted power of its imagery, or the flexibility and adaptability of its constituent elements and compositional themes. Urban imperial architecture, which placed the last full flowering of ancient classicism directly in the path of subsequent Mediterranean and Western architectural events, seems to contain useful evidence for this. Representing not the first great shift in classicism (which had taken place in the Greek east in Hellenistic times), but the second, it was evolved in part from experience accumulated over half a millennium. But as in all post-Greek phases of classicism, the original elements, freshly observed and newly deployed, were combined with features previously unknown.

Imperial architecture evolved more or less continuously from Augustus' time onward. No single early building displayed its chief features the way the chevet of S. Denis or the Ospedale degli Innocenti exhibit fundamentals of their styles. Nor are there any classic moments of the kind embodied in Chartres, Maisons, or the Barcelona Pavilion. And because it was an evolving architecture based partly on traditional concepts, imperial architecture was also a cumulative one, ultimately defined in the fourth century, in the sense that only then could its consummation be seen in the cities and towns. Thereafter, its momentum was largely deflected to Christian purposes, and a new style arose. Whether Roman architecture reached completion or not is probably impossible to say; in important ways, architects were as creative in the fourth century as in the first. In any event, imperial architecture can profitably be considered a process with mature cities and towns its culmination, inclusive exhibits of its development.

To use the evidence from a single period or reign, to interrupt the natural course of things in order to assess style and content (understandable in light of the need to make sense of so much diverse material), would be counterproductive: the nature of an evolving process is not revealed by stopping it. Roman classicism was on a particular course toward some unknown state. It may be better to include the entire experience in attempting to define its essential qualities. If change is accepted as being as significant as style or presumed norms, and varying rates of change in different building types and regions as equally significant, the evidence immediately becomes more tractable: it does not have to be fitted into superimposed categories, and its very diversity becomes a norm. It may be profitable to abandon for the moment the usual labels (Flavian, for example, or Late Antique) and search for fundamental characteristics and meaning in the flux of change. To these proposed principles of change and cumulative definition, context should be added. The buildings need to be seen not as isolated archaeological or typological examples, but as essential, interdependent parts of urban configurations, members of civic families rather than of functional or stylistic groups. The buildings are evidence of an evolutionary process whose consolidated effects in urban settings comprise Roman classicism.

Imperial architecture makes up a division of classicism taken overall, a part of the perennial, ubiquitous style identified primarily by interdependent columns and entablatures that arose in the seventh century B.C. Clearly distinguishable because of its non-Greek usages and additions, imperial architecture nevertheless belongs to the large, loosely connected classical family whose root signs have survived until today. Stone-built, in fact or by implication, as when stucco was drafted to look like masonry, free of frivolity or irrelevancies that would erode or destroy its balanced order, it never deformed essential Greek elements beyond recognition and thus helped to insure their continued artistic life. But at the same time Roman architects added their own compelling formal and symbolic themes, and in so doing altered classicism irrevocably. It was their creative synthesis of old and new that became later classicism's chief source, a wellspring of prodigious post-medieval modes.

The bedrock essentials of imperial architecture are few: the vocabulary of classicism, the shaping of interior space, the urban content and context of its buildings. Individual design elements stood out less forcefully than in Greek work, being intended to serve the whole building, to be taken in more or less altogether by the eye. Though for the Greeks the overall effect was also paramount, the sculptural and tectonic qualities of single columns and other features were nevertheless conspicuous. Because of greater subordination of parts to the whole, these qualities were less evident in Roman buildings; imprecise execution of classical forms may sometimes have been due to this deemphasis, which helped knit forms together across a wall or around a building in an un-Greek way (Pompeii, Temple of Isis; Baalbek, small temple interior). In this sense, Roman work is more painterly than Greek. The preference for unfluted shafts and pilaster faces, and the frequent use of engaged orders, ressauts, pedestals, and the like—all throwing broad, blocky shadows, not iterated parallel lines—is evidence of this. Across their facades and within and around their interiors, Roman buildings other than traditional temples show a formal continuity different from the Greek, the result of diminishing the sense of the individual presence of single parts and emphasizing assemblies of them. Sometimes this was handled subtly, sometimes not, but either way it marked a major departure from Greek practice.

Wall and column were brought closer together; in baroque modes design elements were placed nearer to each other than before in an attempt to gain greater fluidity of form. Specifically Roman uses of the column have already been discussed, but the freedom gained by relieving it of major structural responsibilities should be emphasized. It was a rare building that showed no trace of the orders inside or out; even such austerely plain buildings as many of Ostia's commercial ones had entranceway pilasters or engaged columns done in the Roman manner. So while past tradition and imagery were continued chiefly through the orders, their revised forms, and more particularly

151, 117

the positions and roles assigned to them, were Roman. These elementary shapes, so freighted with meaning, more than anything else made Roman architecture classical. With the addition of arches and vaults, the formal repertory of classicism was complete.

The message of the ancient column and its derivative shapes spread to nearly every street and building. However diluted the form or crude the execution, the message remained; the merest outline was almost as effective in this respect as a freestanding monumental example. Both spoke of the strength and condition of upstandingness, of supporting weight, of the significant distance between what is above and what is below. Through these forms the measure of a building was taken and its primary stylistic genealogy defined. Today the orders are so familiar that it can be difficult to see that their very existence is startling; that architects and sculptors saw at the beginning that they were the essence of architecture, as opposed to building; that the differences among them are profound; and that their origins and meaning are connected to primal forces. In antiquity they stood for Architecture, and when the Romans made them common property, the art of building was put on another path. In this way more than any other, the cities and towns were related one to another stylistically and were made visually and symbolically coherent. And that was the object and result of Roman classicism.

Roman formal order was the controlling architectonic underpinning of Roman buildings. After the use of classical elements it was the most important feature of imperial classicism.[114] It was based on the need to make buildings relevant to both function and context; they had to fit with their surroundings and serve as vehicles of particular activities as well. Because they had to fit, they were almost never idiosyncratic or expressionistic in design. They never stepped beyond the boundaries of acceptable appearance, turning up out of place. Like all classicism, the Roman kind was free of willfulness, of disparate, unrelated forms juxtaposed. Bath buildings, built in so many sizes and plan forms, demonstrate this. They are bound together as a group by function, circulation planning, technology, and Roman spatial formulas. However complex their plans, they are orderly, rational buildings, arranged according to paths established by bathing customs. Asymmetries, if any, have logical explanations, even though baths were designed from the inside out more and more as time passed.

Partly this Roman order arose from a powerfully developed sense of the importance, and the necessity, of strongly stated boundaries, as recorded by the pomerium, the templum, and ritual and ceremonial paths. In mature architecture, this evolved into systems of orderly control, not only of axes and vistas, but of the definition of a building overall. This definition was in large part the product of a keen sense of boundary functions in Heidegger's terms, who speaks of the boundary as "not that at which something stops but . . . that from which something begins its presencing."[115] A concept of possessive location, of the clear and indisputable definition of place, was crucial to the nature of Roman architectural order. Order was realized by defining and relating structural and spatial relationships exactly, by holding them together firmly in rationally conceived frames. Together with the Roman use of the design elements, this order explains why Roman buildings look the way they do and not like those of other styles. It was also a principal reason for Roman historical influence, as attractive to post-1400 architects as Vitruvian prescriptions and ratios. The self-contained, rational and orderly quality of classicizing buildings from then on descends from it.

Though certainty is of course impossible, it appears that architecture was not regarded as a high art, allied with sculpture as an artistic activity. It seems often to have been something to get on with by making use of whatever was needed from among the various design elements and the repertory of vaulted units. There are few if any masterpieces in the modern sense of the word, though fine buildings as well as strikingly original ones appear; the evidence ranges from the commonplace and banal to monuments of considerable beauty and refinement. By Greek standards it is in great part an impure architecture, one of combinations and recombinations, and thus without any readily identifiable center or goal against which given examples can be evaluated and judged. Perfection was rarely if ever sought, and theory was apparently all but unknown. Tastefulness was common and, as always, dull, conditions typical in neoclassical architecture but found less often in Renaissance and baroque buildings.[116] Much Roman classicism had a lowercase grandeur, a parochial monumentality. That was fitting, for in an often repressive world it was to a considerable degree a people's architecture. But whatever its artistic quality, it kept its ordered relevance, the order of the cities and towns reinforced by functionally suitable design. And always it displayed the tectonic emblems of Rome.

In being commonplace, in chiefly serving diurnal, familiar purposes, it carried the seeds of success: it could be interpreted in faraway places easily and its essence reproduced without striving for Art. It was practical, workable, and available, not reserved for high purposes alone. Eastern cities adopted it enthusiastically. Exotic Palmyra, for example, though it had buildings partly of Near Eastern derivation, had many Roman-style features: its armature, much of its typology and imagery, and its architecture of connection and passage were largely imperial. That the impetus for some of these features came in part originally from the Greek-speaking east is no bar to calling them Roman, because it was for specifically Roman purposes that the imperial style evolved. A leading authority, for whom distinct regionalism was a primary feature of Roman architecture, said of Ephesus that it was

16, 17

104, 168

> probably the most influential single architectural centre in the Greek-speaking world [in imperial times]. The overall impression conveyed is one of a vigorous continuity of local development, a development within which the language of traditional classicism was continuously being reinterpreted to meet the requirements of contemporary taste.[117]

The last phrase defines well the Greek-derived side of Roman classicism. But by excluding the numerous Roman buildings and urban features of Ephesus, and by not pointing out that contemporary taste belonged less to those who originally developed the language of traditional classicism than to a later, much different period, the distinctively Roman presence so conspicuous at Ephesus is devalued. The key word is *requirements,* which were determined to a large degree by the needs and expectations of

urban patrons of some architectural sophistication. Their standards were those of imperial times, not of a past long gone.

URBAN CONTENT

Ostia was directly under the thumb of the capital, 30 km. away. Its commercial
buildings and three- and four-story multiple dwellings followed the brick-faced concrete mode of post-fire architecture in Rome. But its transformation, particularly in
Hadrian's time, through extensive rebuilding and addition, is the best documented of   197
any site we have. Though Hadrianic activity at Ostia may have been exceptional in
amount, it indicates the strong tendency in imperial times not only to add passage
buildings to cities and towns but to undertake major revisions throughout. At Ostia
new baths, markets, apartment houses, a Capitolium, private religious structures, and
municipal buildings, among others, were put up; not all of this was government work.
As the plan shows, at least a fifth of the town was made over in twenty years. Subsequently, among other changes and additions, the theatre was rebuilt, a Pantheon-like
temple was erected, and twin arches were placed over the main thoroughfare where it
passed close beside the theatre's curving exterior. Still later, luxury houses were set into
the existing fabric.

Other sites also record abundantly the strength of an urbanism never static that can be
readily measured by comparing the size and civic appointments of new colonial foundations, or of foreign places just before their acquisition, with conditions a century or two
later. A near mania for putting up new buildings, recognized by ancient and modern
writers alike, gripped both potentates and municipal authorities. Columns, pediments,
and arches spread through the cities and towns unhindered by past rules for their use.
This was greatly different from Egyptian or Greek times, and not only with regard to
appearances. Several thousand self-governing municipal entities, many connected by
permanent roads and served by well-fitted ports, made up the greater Roman world;
except in Egypt, most were freely accessible. Fed by ideas and fashions moving unimpeded through this system, a demand for more and more buildings was sustained for
several centuries.

The distinctive, identifying character of this architecture arose largely in response to
the need that arose in cities and towns for collective identity. It is a definable body of
work largely because particular urban needs determined its forms and imagery, an
architecture more of content than of style, derived more from daily reality than from
artistic ideals. The core signs, the messages of this, were not esoteric but clear to see,
conveyed directly by elevations and plans and by contextual relationships among buildings. No building stood alone, not only because of the simple fact of urban density, but
also because of formal and symbolic connections with other buildings and their common
purpose of framing and accommodating town life. This was an architecture of context
and of community, the community both of the individual town and of all the towns
together. Urbanism and architecture changed and matured in mutual interdependence.

This process was much aided by the adaptability of Roman design elements, which

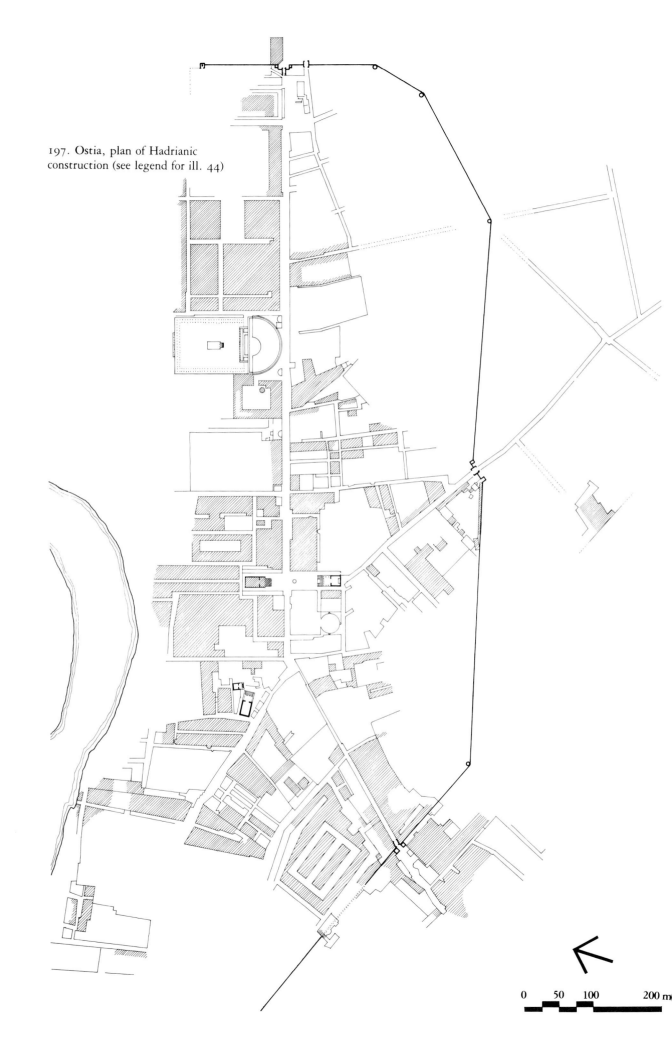

197. Ostia, plan of Hadrianic
construction (see legend for ill. 44)

0   50   100   200 m

made it easy for lesser buildings to echo huge ones. Examples of this are the scale sequence niche / exedra / hemicycle, or the fact that the orders were used in any size from small, decorative pilasters to the largest columns builders could manage. Arches and vaults ranged through many sizes. A common repertory of defining and articulating   198, 177 forms was available across the typology; a distant, rising monument was often in formal harmony with much of the beholder's immediate, smaller-scaled surroundings. When new needs pushed architects toward new solutions, as when public bathing became a community-wide preoccupation, the new type, whatever its spatial and technical innovations, was clothed in familiar forms. Communal visual relationships were as important as functional expression. Theatre and amphitheatre exteriors were related to tiered aqueducts, theatre stage-buildings to elaborate thoroughfare nymphaea, and temple fronts to innumerable secular buildings.

Architects and builders responded successfully to functional needs. At the same time, they created a popular architecture, one of availability and assembly, much of it the

198. Maktar, baths, arcade; third century

everyday property of all. Their deep concern for the concept of place, of fixed and well-marked centers, is shown by numerous formal devices and hundreds of buildings. They dealt effectively with the need for architectural communality, for contextual interdependence among the varied buildings making up a town. And they set their buildings firmly in the Greco-Mediterranean tradition, giving them that sense of continuity—classicism's chief message—that nearly all Roman architecture conveys, however novel it may be in other ways. Through pragmatism combined with talent and a willingness to experiment, new building types and solutions were brought forth. By meeting contemporary urban needs while creating forceful symbolic themes, these architects fashioned the visual definition of Roman urbanism. They may not have planned it that way, but it came about because they worked along the same formal lines.

Armatures and connective architecture gave towns their underlying, organizational patterns, articulated by passage structures; widely distributed and often highly visible public buildings met collective needs. The dialogues among these features, the relationships and connections established by form and imagery, by location and directional focus, embody the intrinsic meaning of Roman architecture, whose ultimate product was less style or typology than the visible town. In order to achieve this, a strong effect of a united whole free of any suggestion of egregious fragmentation, of unresolved diversity, was required. Various devices held the towns together and provided the coherence among different structures essential to their identity. Street colonnades and arcades are obvious examples. Intermittent or continuous, partly masking, at ground level, variations of shape and size in the structures behind, they furthered the impression of interconnection between different areas, between one major building and the next; the seventy-odd colonnades of fifth-century Constantinople (they suggest the scale of the

19 largest Roman urban undertaking ever) record the last grand response to this essential requirement. And consistency of building material was common, for local quarries often supplied every need, though in central Italy and some other localities brick was also used, sometimes in vast quantities as facing for structural cores of concrete. Few things unify all the buildings in sight as forcefully as the use throughout of a single material of consistent character, particularly if their stylistic nature is broadly similar (Sabratha; Carnuntum; Bosra; compare Sousse, Mdina, or inner Dubrovnik today).

Lesser devices tell the same story. The plans of smaller structures were frequently adjusted to insure the unbroken integrity of continuous, major connective elements. Irregularly shaped blocks of shops and offices, such as the wedge-like ones along the

44 front of the forum market at Pompeii and the northwest enclosures of the Small Market and the Garden Houses at Ostia, suppressed or lessened the effects of wayward plan relationships. Though in practical terms these were obvious rational adjustments, they were also part of the larger need for clear continuity in the urban pattern. In hiding inconvenient salient angles they brought unaligned features into apparent harmony

57 (Lepcis Magna, alongside and inside the Severan Forum; compare Rome, Marble Plan, fragments 11, 20, 28). They also fitted otherwise non-conforming buildings to their

16 armatures (Palmyra, Senate House, northeast wall and rooms; compare Gerasa, shops

around the tetrakionion). Until late antiquity, the strong need for uninterrupted link-   35
age of major places and buildings suppressed most awkward armature intrusions, and
the towns' connective mechanisms were kept free and clear.

Urban content, derived from contextual relationships among public buildings and
from the architecture of connection and passage, is illustrated in a compact but typical
way by Dougga's tightly knit civic quarter. Its communications lines lay along those of   65
the natural groundfall, north–northeast to south–southwest, and traversed one or both   199
of two flagged plazas (the larger, western one was the forum). These are on different
levels, connected by a flight of steps aligned with the west side of the (restored)
Capitolium. The area overall measures about 90 m. east–west and about 55 m. along
the Capitolium's north–south axis (the sections of wall built mostly of reused materials
are remains of a Byzantine fort). Erected chiefly in the second half of the second century,
the buildings and plazas, all of different sizes and shapes, were arranged in loosely
orthogonal relationships, though their collective periphery is irregular. Along the south
side, three long stairways, two descending from the market building and one from the
southwest corner of the forum, joined the area with the densely built-up hillside below.
Such adjustments to inclined terrain were common and can be seen in many hillside   69
towns and building complexes (Tiddis; Khamissa; Termessus; Rome, Markets of   45, 205
Trajan).

From the point where the road from Dougga's theatre approaches the first, upper
plaza (that of the wind rose), to the far end of the forum, ten major structures lined the
path. One or two have not been identified, but at least five were religious buildings—
one or perhaps two dedicated to Mercury, the god of trade. A large market hall or court
had some two dozen shops and offices ranged alongside and behind it. Immediately to
the west was another large building with an apse, set directly across from the Capitolium, its interior the same length as the temple's podium platform but somewhat
wider; flanking it was a narrow portico or hall with columns set in line very close to its
side walls. Colonnades ringed three sides of each plaza. Only the roof heights of the
Capitolium and the facade exedras of the adjoining Temple of Mercury are known, but
the plan shapes and spans of the other buildings strongly imply varied heights and
silhouettes. In all there were six major exedras and apses, not including those of the
Capitolium and Temple of Mercury cellas. Local limestone was used throughout, but
the possibility of revetments of stucco or imported stone cannot be ruled out.

Perhaps the most striking feature of the ensemble is its inward-looking, self-contained quality. This is only partly due to the terrain (which because of its fall to the south
limited access from below), for the known entrances, at the northeast, are narrow even
though the approaching street slopes downward there only slightly, and generous
entrances would have been easy to build. All buildings face the longer, east–west axis,
the principal unifying element. From it was generated a kind of broad, colonnaded but
truncated thoroughfare nearly closed at both ends. Across it, pairs of buildings faced
each other, first the market and the temple of Mercury, joining commerce, then the
apsidal building responding axially to the Capitolium, surely joining Roman tradition

199. Dougga, forum area, views

with symbols of some aspect of Roman hegemony. Beyond, the narrow portico related in a similar but less emphatic fashion with a structure of unknown purpose across the way. Then the westering forum spread out to occupy fully a third of the whole area, its periphery unfeatured except for what may have been a shrine to Saturn at its further end.

Thus a considerable degree of formal complexity was accommodated in a quite orderly way through the operation of the main axis, the echoing pairings, and the level expanses of the two plazas, as well as by iterated columns and the use throughout of the same kind of building stone. Both curved and rectilinear recesses occurred within nearly every building, one or two sizable vaults were built, and a tripartite composition of non-traditional form was used for the Mercury temple. There were no real side streets, so the wholeness, the immediacy and directness of the place was not leached away, but was preserved in spite of the variety of building shapes and sizes. In plan it looks something like a large bath building with exercise ground attached, or the core of a luxury villa (see the appendix). If it were stretched out and its buildings interpolated among major streets, it would resemble schematically many other towns. Dougga's is the essence of a   65
Roman urban center, a paradigmatic expression of the principles of urban context, for Roman architecture is defined as much by the way buildings are joined in meaningful functional and symbolic ways as by any other. It is worth repeating that the chief characteristics of imperial architecture were contextual suitability and the imagery of urbanism; as at Dougga, the whole counted more than the sum of its parts, and style, in the traditional sense, was only a means to that end. One might ask what a Capitolium would be without a plaza, or an honorific arch without a thoroughfare—or either without a town.

These contextual imperatives dominated all large building complexes, all places frequented by throngs of people—major sanctuaries and ports, for example, as well as towns. The Pergamon Asklepieion, in its final form largely Hadrianic, is a case in point.   200
Lying 2 km. southeast of the Hellenistic acropolis, extending over perhaps two hectares (five acres), it was composed of urban building types and infused with forms of imperial content. The monumental approach mentioned earlier brought one to a spacious vestibule, some 30 m. square; beyond lay a vast open court containing various facilities. The far end of this court, certainly the long north side, and presumably the southern one as well (where there was a cryptoportico), were lined with colonnades. Along the near,   201
vestibule side stood a library and a Pantheon-like temple of Asklepios. At the southeast corner was a multilobed rotunda, and, more or less diagonally across the court, a theatre. All these buildings turned inward on the court, making the periphery of the sanctuary quite irregular (from the far western end, a colonnaded file of rooms extended).

Although the buildings were lined up beside the courtyard, their positions there were not controlled by its major axes, which were not exploited, being marked, if at all, only by minor accents. The two largest structures, curved in shape, faced each other slantwise across the court. The vestibule and library, though of different dimensions, were similarly shaped, and both contrasted sharply with the two rotundas. Yet the vestibule and the temple were related to each other through the provision of similar porches; at

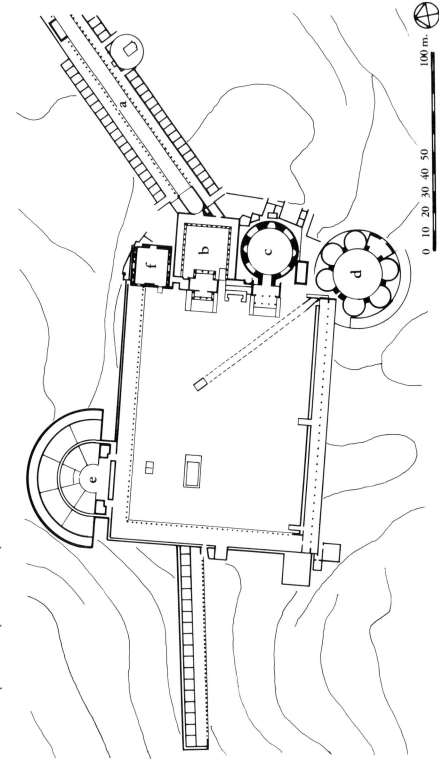

200. Pergamon, Asklepieion, plan
a thoroughfare   d rotunda
b vestibule   e theatre
c Temple of Asklepios   f library

100 m.

0 10 20 30 40 50

ground level, at least, they were treated as equals. The courtyard corners, in the planning sense, were avoided: the library was not aligned with the north colonnade; the multilobed rotunda, though placed close in on the courtyard diagonal, sat there uneasily; and the theatre, though sited far enough away from the northwest corner to match the edge of its stage building with the west courtyard colonnade, was not put far enough east to align the building with the courtyard's west wall. Overall, there was little symmetry and much variety. Though further excavation and study will bring new readings, the visual interconnections among the buildings, and their quite assertive independence of the orthogonal courtyard plan, seem assured. These things were due to the essentially urban derivation of the place, whose net effect was that of the center of a large town, its huge plaza sparsely lined by monumental buildings related to each other in the Roman way.

201. Pergamon, Asklepieion, partial view from the theatre, looking southeast

Ports were also fitted out with urban architecture. Moles and jetties were given colonnades (Mothone; Pozzuoli; Sabratha; Ptolemais in Syria) or arcades (Side), as archaeological, numismatic, and pictorial evidence shows. Harbor-side structures were not limited to warehouses and offices, for colonnades were erected there also (Aegina; Kenchreai; Vienne). Large temples might provide secondary landfalls as well as suggest the presence beyond of urban amenities (Lepcis Magna; Caesarea Maritima, Temple of Rome and Augustus). Honorific arches stood on both moles and shore (Pagai; Pozzuoli). Judging from coins, ports were lavishly furnished with statuary, often of monumental size and sometimes placed atop freestanding columns (compare Brindisi, terminus columns of the Appian Way). Elaborate thoroughfares might lead directly from the quays into the town (Soli-Pompeiopolis; Lepcis Magna). Each port of consequence had a lighthouse, a signal tower, and harbormaster's quarters, and perhaps a shrine or temple to Portunus as well. A reception area for notables was provided at Portus (the Claudian portico); others can be assumed, for example at Caesarea Maritima, so much used, as Josephus makes clear, by Roman generals and governors.[118] Port buildings, like those of central Dougga and the Pergamon Asklepieion, also faced inward; sailors safe in their roadsteads would have been almost surrounded by city-like buildings. Architects and engineers paid much attention to port-building (even giving artificial islands a natural appearance): to build a large port meant creating a specialized suburb with enough features of complete towns to give it an acceptably urban aspect (Aquileia).[119]

202. Lepcis Magna, Severan port, reconstruction; largely third century

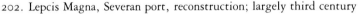

Specifically Roman uses of architecture for urban purposes gained footholds in the provinces early on. By Augustus' death the framework for this had been well laid, particularly in northern Italy, Spain, and southern Gaul; south central Anatolia may have been penetrated as well. Veterans' colonies, particularly in Africa, imperial gifts to numerous cities and towns around the Mediterranean, and locally sponsored pro-Roman projects speeded the process. In the east, client rulers helped, none more than Herod the Great, relics of whose immense building programs extend from Nicopolis in Epirus and Pergamon to Masada. Some two dozen cities and towns bore his stamp; at least three of them were largely his creations (Sebaste—formerly Samaria; Caesarea Maritima, also rebuilt and enlarged; Herodion). His architects sometimes followed local preferences but they could be strikingly original, as at Herodion. In much of this work, Roman ways were not far to seek. Italian building techniques (concrete, brickwork, and *opus reticulatum*, a wall facing of small, squared stones set in diagonal patterns) appear. More important, purely Roman buildings were erected—a villa, baths, an apsed basilica or audience hall, an amphitheatre, and a Roman-style theatre.

Much remains to be learned about this architecture, but it seems certain that it reflected western practice more fully than anything previously seen in the east. There was for example a cavalry veterans' town, Gaba, "reminiscent of a Roman *colonia*."[120] But it was probably at Caesarea that Roman ideas were most on display. In his description, Josephus details the construction and appointments of its harbor, with its massive mole 60 m. wide, and says the city was built entirely of white stone. He mentions the Temple of Augustus and Rome, placed on a bluff facing the harbor, as well as palaces, the theatre, and the amphitheatre, and refers to other public places. He adds that the equidistant streets came right to the harbor's edge, where there were houses.[121] At the site a large, level terrace or temenos can be seen, supported on vaults in the Roman manner; there is a similar one at Sebaste for the Temple of Augustus. A Roman-style circus has been identified and studied, and the port is being explored. Though the information is sparse, western forms and content in Herod's work at Caesarea are not in doubt. If the evidence is coupled with the imperial references in the names he gave to the two cities (Augustus had given him both), it is possible to infer that Roman ways stood out in these foundations, whatever Hellenistic or eastern features they may have possessed. And this happened early on.

Subsequently, when cities and towns expanded, as Djemila and Timgad did, architecture's strongly stated involvement in city life and imagery persisted. Incomplete without armature extensions and the apparatus of connection and passage, newly built-up areas also required plazas, porticos, and baths, and not just for practical reasons. With these they were proper urban creations, able to hold their own with the established city centers to which they were thus so closely linked.

What happened at Ostia, as it expanded south and southwest to the sea past the Porta Marina, is instructive (compare Ephesus, lower Embolos). In Republican times tombs had been built outside the walls in the usual way. When baths were added, one set, the Maritime Baths, was placed upon the line of the old Republican wall and presumably

203
104

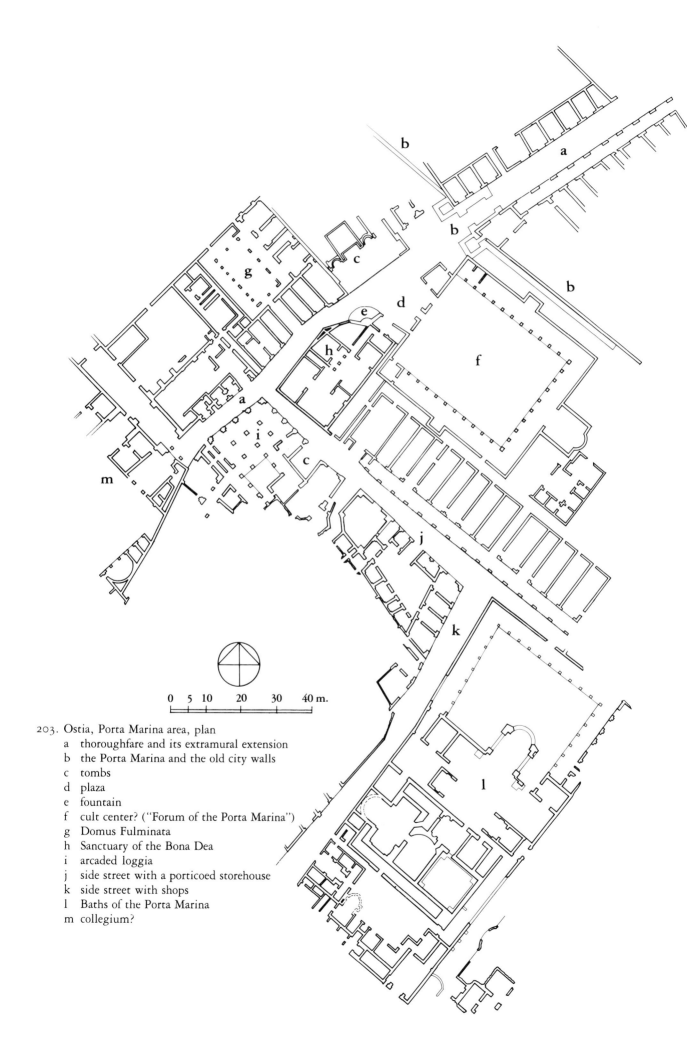

203. Ostia, Porta Marina area, plan

   a thoroughfare and its extramural extension
   b the Porta Marina and the old city walls
   c tombs
   d plaza
   e fountain
   f cult center? ("Forum of the Porta Marina")
   g Domus Fulminata
   h Sanctuary of the Bona Dea
   i arcaded loggia
   j side street with a porticoed storehouse
   k side street with shops
   l Baths of the Porta Marina
   m collegium?

served the Garden Houses just to the northeast. Another, the Baths of the Porta Marina, 44
one of the three or four largest known at Ostia, was built further south, close to the
shore. Not far outside the Porta Marina, a public, streetside fountain stood next to a
small plaza beside the northeast–southwest thoroughfare's extramural extension.
Across the street rose a monumental tomb faced with exedras. Beside the plaza was a 204
spacious, enclosed courtyard colonnaded on three sides, with an apsidal hall at the end of
its main axis. This is called the Forum of the Porta Marina, but its function is unknown;
perhaps it was a cult center. Outside, just to the south, was a multichambered sanctuary
of the Bona Dea; across the main street stood shops, taverns, and an elaborate first-
century house, the Domus Fulminata, flanked on its seaward side by large commercial
structures. Opposite them a handsome arcaded loggia stood at the corner of a side street
leading past a long porticoed warehouse, another tomb, and more shops, to the Porta
Marina baths. Finally, where the thoroughfare came to an end close to the sea, are the
battered remains of a large building complex set behind colonnades facing the water,
perhaps the seat of a *collegium*. Just beyond is the modern road to Fiumicino, lying
approximately along the line of the ancient shore.

Though the list of building types and urban features within this limited area is

204. Ostia, exedras of a tomb just outside the Porta Marina; late first century B.C.

already long, further excavation between the modern road and the city wall would probably yield additions. Excluding the Maritime Baths, the inventory reads:

gateway	warehouse
thoroughfare	other commercial structures
side street	baths of the Porta Marina
small plaza	house
fountain	sanctuary
loggia	tombs
exedras (in front	cult center (?)
of the monumental tomb)	*collegium* lodge (?)
portico	(rooms, apartments, above the shops
taverns	and elsewhere?)
shops	

This was not a quarter identified by a common factor such as a single commercial activity or housing for those of a particular trade or social class, but an abbreviated, localized extramural armature encompassing most urban activities. A cat's cradle of functional connections crisscrossed this tightly built-up, hemmed-in strip of city ground: lodging, laboring, conducting business, warehousing, shopping, strolling, idling, meeting, worshiping, eating, and drinking—as well as other, unidentified communal activities—were all accommodated. Since each function was served by its own Roman building form, a varied and richly articulated ambience resulted. This multifaceted, direct architectural involvement with all phases of daily life, far more complex and specialized than in earlier times, was typical of the cities and towns, which were so largely defined by the strength of their buildings' urban content.

    To interpret classical architecture as a language with grammatical rules is useful as far as it goes, but too Vitruvian, too academic (in the architectural sense of the word) to apply to all of it. When for example Summerson discusses architecture as a language and says so felicitously that the orders "conduct the building, with sense and ceremony and often with great elegance, into the mind of the beholder," he strikes the right note for his purpose, which is to explain the familiar forms seen all about.[122] But there is more to it than that. Mature Roman classicism, governed less by circumscribing rules than most other classical modes, was livelier and more flexible than the linguistic analogy allows. Examining Roman meaning and contextual setting suggests that correctly wrought orders and other design elements were not sovereign features, because this classicism arose in a relatively pragmatic age from practical and political needs, not from a pursuit of beauty or propriety seen as inhering in rules or in an aesthetic canon. To some degree the traditional temple was an exception, but gradually it too succumbed. Another analogy, that of narrative, may be more useful. This is not to imply that people regarded their towns as narrative vehicles, but to suggest that the definition of Roman architecture may be sharpened by exploring its narrative aspects.

205, 45

A physically complete but wholly empty town is useless, a cipher; only people can fulfill it, bring it and its buildings to life. Once people come, and go about their affairs, the buildings begin to function, and architecture and humankind enter into the repeated collaboration that makes a town what it is. These obvious facts underlie the frequent use of the word theatre in discussions of towns and town life: there is a stage, and there are players. But there is also the regular round of activity involving numerous buildings, which, if not a plot in the playwright's sense, is a form of simple narrative. The reason for going to a given building is clear to the person undertaking it, who has another reason for then going to a different one. These meanings and movements, collected serially, comprise the purposive and topographical narrative of one's day in a town. The architectural membering of Roman towns insured that these narrative journeys proceeded, with few longueurs, from one clearly marked point to another—from the market to the forum to the law court, for example, or from the baths to the theatre, from a city gate and its plaza out to the circus, and so on. Many shops and familiar stations of passage stood along the way. These sequences, the well-worn channels of daily existence and the foundation of Roman urban coherence, were set out at comprehensible pedestrian scale in all but the very largest places.

206

As a prose narrative is forwarded by the flow of words, so urban narrative evolves from movement. Because the town had goals, places with things people wanted, and because those goals were fixed, people had to supply movement. As they moved, the town's

205. Rome, Markets of Trajan, detail of facades; ca. 100–112

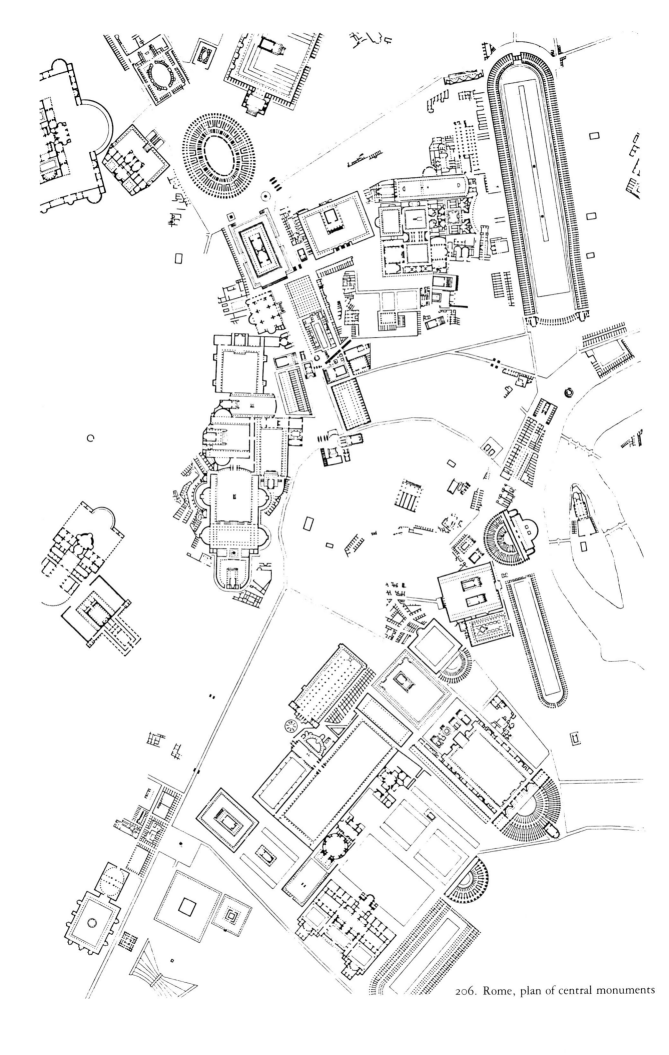

206. Rome, plan of central monuments

multiple narratives came to life. Their meaning was repeatedly evoked by a form of kinetogenesis, a bringing into being through motion. Le Corbusier, speaking of Arab North African architecture, says that it "gives us an invaluable lesson. It is appreciated while walking, and it is only thus, in moving around, that the observer sees the architectural dispositions deploy."[123] Walking around energizes architecture so it can play its part in the mobile observer's narrative experience. In this sense Roman towns were richer than their predecessors. They could tell a longer, more detailed story, because they offered more varied formal and symbolic features. And since those experiences were of a specifically Roman kind—the podiated temple, the place-fixing arch, and the other themes of empire woven from ancient forms—the cumulative effect of traversing a town was to have experienced the full effect of a dozen or two pointedly Roman images. They could not be avoided, and as they all proclaimed essentially the same message, they were not in conflict. This can be seen as clearly along the switchback hillside streets of Tiddis as beside the Ephesian Embolos or Gerasa's north–south   104, 168, 35 thoroughfare.

The message, the subject of the narrative, was about membership, about communality—human membership in the community, and the community's in the larger whole. It was not a statement about unity but about an essential quality upon which unity depended. A simple and partial notion, though perhaps a useful one, narrative helps explain the towns' visual coherence: buildings had to fit into it, be directly involved in ordinary town life and fashioned to serve it. The bounds of tolerance were wide, but foreign forms, symbols of foreign ways, could not be allowed to dominate Roman town centers or armatures. In architecture, as in so much else, the Romans overcame; their buildings quickly arose in distant places that knew Rome's power and its agents. Because of that power and of Rome's often rapacious and ruthless ways, it is surprising that its architecture was so rarely one of oppression, that it was so open and sometimes, in important ways, sensitive to human needs. The repeated provision of places for pausing and resting, shaded perhaps, where one might feel comfortable in the sense of the Spanish *querencia,* hardly suggests tyranny. In minor arcades and small exedras, on the benches of markets, fountains, and tombs, in corners and recesses outdoors and in, one might simply by standing or sitting claim for a few moments participatory ownership of a bit of public space.

Such features suggest that imperial architecture was a popular architecture. It worked; otherwise it would not have survived. The unexpected readiness of some cities and towns with proud non-Roman pasts to cooperate enthusiastically with Rome—as opposed to sullen acquiescence to its presence—may have been due in part to desirable features of the Roman urban system. Largely because of Hellenistic traditions, its buildings were solidly made. People in Roman times were good at such things, at excavating huge areas and moving immense stones (one scholar suggests that Trajan's Column may have originally stood elsewhere and been moved to its present position, showing great and probably merited confidence in the corps of engineers[124]). This solid work suggested reliable continuity; considered in that light, the attraction of workable,

Roman-style towns is easy to appreciate. Strewn with streetside references to human scale, they were less oppressive and forbidding than some of their predecessors. Files of plain unfluted limestone columns were in this sense more effective than fancy, fluted marble ones, being less artistic, more down-to-earth, and more expressive of a simple tectonic strength intimating reliability and permanence. Multiple openings and passages provided the choice and opportunity essential to a sense of urban possibilities, and the profusion of niches and columns obscured the positive statements about exclusion made by solid, unfeatured walls. Roman towns were not without humane content.

Comparing Roman work with Greek exposes differences and similarities effectively if the types of buildings compared correspond sufficiently—theatres, for example. Often the pared-down, scrupulously precise Doric temple of the fifth century B.C. is the standard offered or implied, but it is only minimally useful, being so far removed—six or seven centuries—from Roman ways and purposes (its romanticized modern status, tenaciously established long ago, is being questioned[125]). If, however, Greek standards are posited, original Roman building types have to be left out, and innovative uses of the orders, crucial to understanding imperial architecture, are almost certain to be ignored as Vitruvius is quoted yet again. Our general concept of Roman architecture seems to be somewhat askew, partly because of the long-lived but natural ascendancy of the capital's own monuments and partly because of the pejorative content of the word provincial, which implies that what is found outside Rome will probably be inferior. In fact, some 163 of the best work is preserved in the provinces—the peristyle at Split, for example, or the 82, 115 Spanish bridges and aqueducts, or the Sbeitla forum, with its triad of temples so effectively composed. But the gravest problem lies in the common assumption, based partly on the seductive fact of chronological sequence, that Roman work is derived from Greek, and that therefore it can be effectively evaluated by comparing the two. The difficulty is that at best the assumption is probably less than half right, as these pages are in part intended to suggest. So if Roman architecture is to be evaluated by contrast and comparison, the question arises, with what?

Probably the answer is that there is nothing appropriate. Because it encompassed much of the Mediterranean world for several centuries, the Ottoman empire comes to mind, but its architecture put down few roots outside the homeland. Across the Maghrib, up through the coastal Near East, and in the Balkans, Ottoman works are fairly rare.[126] Major Western styles incorporated classical design, mostly descended from Rome but interpreted in limited, un-Roman ways, which prevents them also from being useful. One must return to antiquity and to the traditional phrase "Greece and Rome." Almost one word in our minds, the phrase's implications for architectural history should be minimized when appraising Roman work, not because it was better or worse than Greek, but because it was different. The distinction needs emphasis, particularly as "classical" has now become an even more inclusive and loose word than in the past. When the concept of architectural classicism in general surfaces today, the broad Western tradition is invoked, not rules or norms, not Greek or Roman architecture specifically. So there does not seem to be any satisfactory standard against which imperial architecture overall can profitably be measured. That in part explains the organization and objectives of this book, which through a city-oriented viewpoint attempts to describe some of the subject's essentials. Needless to say, the method is partly experimental and some conclusions tentative.

Statements about Roman repetition and sameness are belied by the evidence. Copies, save of arches, are very rare, and no Western historical style is formally more diversified (the range of building types was probably surpassed only in the nineteenth century). This architecture is so varied that it appears to be unresolved, to lack the central core or governing intent necessary to traditional concepts of style. Both planning and form range so widely that there seem to be no buildings embodying paradigmatic formal principles against which a given example can be compared in order to locate its evolutionary position or place it on a scale of values. Formally, it is held together by an extended, loose classicism of traditional origins, of the kind often judged inferior. Normative analysis is inadequate; customary art-historical method founders on so wide a differentiation of form. Imperial architecture is too inclusive, diverse, and irregular to fit into a neatly defined category; when that is attempted, many buildings must be left out.

There are Roman buildings of quality and renown, but none contains all major features. The immense world-bowl of the Pantheon is for many the paramount symbol of imperial architecture, not only because of its unique size and effects but also partly because of its accessibility and state of preservation. But it is not wholly representative, and it too is somewhat incomplete and unresolved. The apse is all but overpowered by the vast space in front of it, and the awkward junction of the porch and rotunda is notorious; like so much major Roman architecture, the Pantheon is experimental. It contains a wide spectrum of workmanship and finish. When expensive imperial monuments laden with marble work were put up the best sculptors and carvers were employed, ranking specialists carrying on in a very old craft; their work in the best stone is often given preference in restricted modern value systems.

Only a small proportion of Roman architecture belongs in this category. Does it follow that the rest was inferior? If not, then standards are needed, and if they are sought, it becomes apparent that the less painstaking, less canonical work, often in limestone, terra-cotta, or concrete, is by contrast far less classical (in the usual sense of the word), sometimes almost anticlassical. No Guarini or Hawksmoor created more varied forms than are found in this work. And in much new wall and vault work, concrete—a commonplace, amorphous builders' material—was piled up against formwork or rough boards. After it cured it could quickly be brought into line with the architect's specifications by using cement coating, then finished by stucco workers, painters, marble workers, or mosaicists. One can hear the shop stewards and proud old artisans bemoaning the loss of proper ways to such slapdash methods of putting up buildings, and worse, of finishing them. Entablatures, routinely cut to somewhat rough standards, were efficiently winched and levered into position like so much three-dimensional stencil work. Though this sort of thing can offend purists, it may lie close to the heart of Roman architecture, much of which was a vernacular classicism, classicism with a common touch, intended for ordinary life in the towns. Had it all been of carefully cut marble, majestic and formal, it might not have served or persisted.

The paradoxical simultaneous presence of the commonplace and the grand, of what might be called popular and high classicism, is another reason that Vitruvius can be misleading. Naturally he put his best foot forward, writing about what to him were proper, time-proven standards, displaying his hard-won learning. Most builders and stone carvers probably knew little or nothing about such things; of those who did, one suspects few cared. It is difficult to carry on a grand tradition in prosperous, changing times. Perhaps the work by ordinary talent could be called Roman urban classicism, work whose decor was based on antecedents discernibly Greek but much altered and in a sense domesticated, work with few pretensions to lofty grandeur or fine art. Somewhere behind the symbolic and cosmetic overcoat of classical forms there is a ruling principle in both popular and official architecture.

Much of it was service architecture, not patrician, as in those later styles that speak of power, rulers, the church, and wealth. Most major Roman buildings were for everyone, and the elusive core principle may lie there. Control of towns had passed from priests and tyrants to municipal officials. They might be corrupt or incompetent, and the central government might intervene at any moment with crushing force, but local authority decided most local matters. Town fathers and prosperous donors were not often told from afar what buildings they would have, but chose for themselves, and surely the effect of this on architecture was considerable. What was built was what was wanted: buildings of a familiar kind, broadly in line with appearances elsewhere, that would serve the town well.

Empire buildings were town buildings, closely involved with each other. Each was an essential functioning part of a pattern of urban activities carried out in a particular way at a particular time. In that sense architecture and the towns were one. In being Roman, a building conformed to this by assisting in the flow and purpose of daily activity, and especially by bringing those activities together in a meaningful, town-making fashion. Each part was firmly tied to the others, creating the basis of the coherence and rough homogeneity of Roman urbanism everywhere. In the far west and north, and along the Rhine-Danube frontier, buildings other than in provincial capitals and a few other major centers were usually modest, with the inescapable imperial imagery subdued, but neither quantity nor quality is the issue. In addition to the forum with its temple and basilica, a simple arch over the main street, a decent, up-to-date bath building, and a theatre, perhaps of wood and built to double as a small amphitheatre, would do. Such towns may have been poor relations architecturally, but schematically and symbolically they were in close touch with grander places.

The possibility that urban cohesion and imperial imagery were as strong or stronger, as architectural and urban forces, than town planning or the building typology has been argued above. Within the limits of ability and financial resources, the towns strove to strengthen that cohesion and imagery. Inferiority in these matters could hardly be tolerated, so up went the second arch, another bath, the new stage building for the theatre. In this way each town gained and held its architectural citizenship. The dogged vitality that assured success is recorded in these solid, effective instruments of urbanism. Combined with the creation of Roman classicism both informal and monumental, this was part of a major architectural advance, an architecture for a new and ecumenical, workable kind of town.

Looking at separate plans of great cities certainly will not tell you about the form and order of the world.—Polybius

There are now as many cities as there once were houses.—Tertullian, *De anima*

You are very near the Pont du Gard before you see it. . . . Over the valley, from side to side, and ever so high in the air, stretch the three tiers of the tremendous bridge. . . . The hugeness, the solidity, the unexpectedness, the monumental rectitude of the whole thing leave you nothing to say. . . . The preservation . . . is extraordinary; nothing has crumbled or collapsed; every feature remains, and the huge blocks of stone . . . pile themselves, without mortar or cement, as evenly as the day they were laid together. All this to carry the water of a couple of springs to a little provincial city!—Henry James, *A Little Tour of France*

APPENDIX

THE PIAZZA ARMERINA VILLA

207, 210

207–209 Towns and luxury villas had much in common. If the dispersed building typology and sprawling plans of the villas are examined from this point of view, they become easier to understand, and the possibility emerges that they were derived from urban configurations and imagery. The famous complex near Piazza Armerina, with its apparently disjointed and irrational plan, is a useful starting point.[127] It can be shown to have had many urban affinities, and from these one might profitably work back to its predecessors. Built probably about 315–325, it is in my opinion a summary of Roman urban principles in villa form. I do not propose that it was consciously planned as a private town (though it may have been), but its plans and dispositions are to me best explained as the results of adapting imperial town-making to private purposes on an ample scale. The mosaics are almost entirely left out of this discussion, which might be furthered by including them, but I am not convinced that is necessary and believe advances can be made by analyzing the plan and architecture alone.

Our knowledge of the site is limited. More excavation and study are needed; for example, the peripheral area is largely unexplored. Some sense of the plan of the earlier, underlying building, probably a villa (second century?), if it could be obtained, would probably be useful. Still, what we do have is very informative, as the few studies of the villa's architecture suggest.[128] In capitalizing on this material, the observation, so often encountered, that the plan is distinctly odd, can safely be discounted. The plan is not orthogonal, and it has its idiosyncracies, but it is not much different in principle from the plans of some other great villas, and it is closely related to the kinds of urban patterns described in the preceding chapter.

Terraces roughly corresponding in shape to the major building groups or clusters (centered on b, f, i, m, and s, on the plan) measure out the gradual east–west fall of the ground. The long axes of the baths (e, f, g) and the basilica (m), as well as the north–south axis of the large, curved peristyle (s), all if extended inward converge approximately on the center of the somewhat asymmetrical main peristyle (i). Furthermore, the centerpoints of the outlying clusters, as well as the entrance-court fountain (b), are nearly equidistant from the center of the main peristyle: they all lie on or quite close to the circumference of a circle 41.5 m. (140 Roman feet) in diameter, whose center is the point where the peristyle's diagonals intersect. Intentionally or not, the villa plan as we have it was organized around a generalized radial composition of strongly focal character. In the plan overall, orthogonality is rejected in favor of an orbital scheme

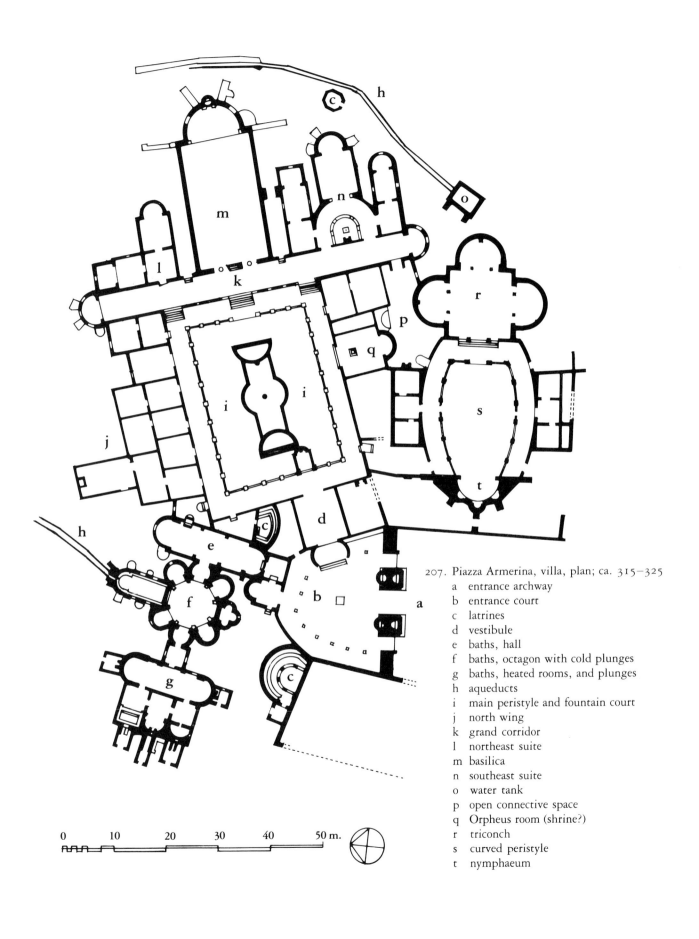

207. Piazza Armerina, villa, plan; ca. 315–325

a entrance archway
b entrance court
c latrines
d vestibule
e baths, hall
f baths, octagon with cold plunges
g baths, heated rooms, and plunges
h aqueducts
i main peristyle and fountain court
j north wing
k grand corridor
l northeast suite
m basilica
n southeast suite
o water tank
p open connective space
q Orpheus room (shrine?)
r triconch
s curved peristyle
t nymphaeum

0   10   20   30   40   50 m.

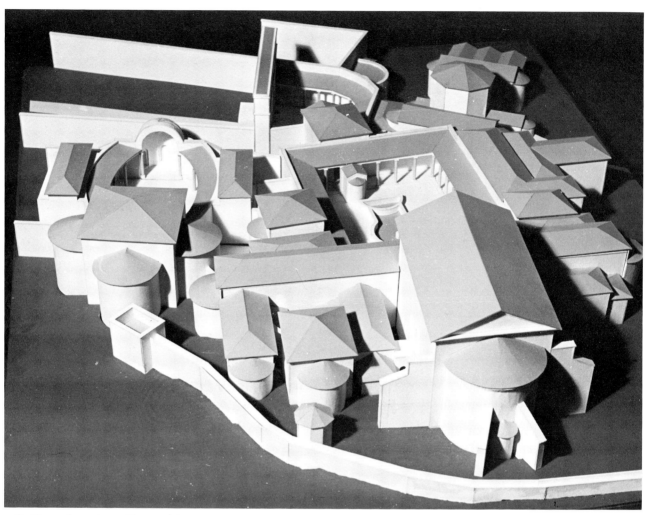

208. Piazza Armerina, villa, model

209. Piazza Armerina, villa, model

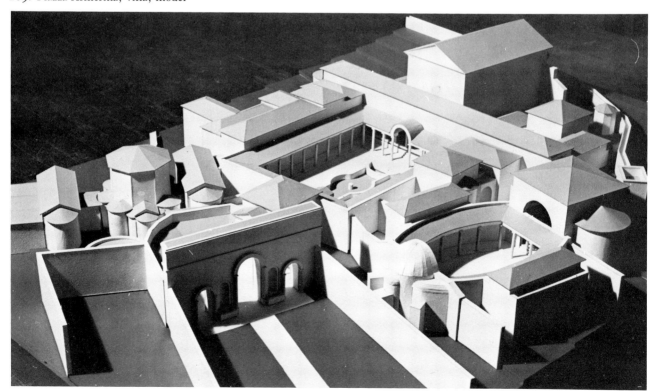

anchoring the peripheral clusters directly to the central feature. But the plans of the clusters themselves, save the entrance court (b), are orthogonally framed.

There are other significant plan alignments. For example, the north–south centerline of the arched entranceway (a), if extended, passes through the center of the baths' octagon (f); the projected north–south axis of the triconch (r) crosses the central peristyle's east side close to its midpoint; and the common axis of the triconch and the curved peristyle (r–s–t) is parallel to the east-west axis of the entranceway (a). That some of these relationships are only approximate will not surprise students of later imperial architecture. Oblique relationships occur at the villa at a number of points, as where the not-quite-parallel north–south walls of the northern tiers of rooms (j) meet the north boundary of the central peristyle (i), or all along the east flank (l–m–n), where a dozen parallel walls are set obliquely to the great corridor (k; one wall so set brings the others in train). There is some evidence of designing, albeit offhandedly, with a five- or ten-foot module: the basilica (m) is 50 by 100 Roman feet, approximately; the corridor (k), exclusive of its apsidal ends, is 200 feet long; and the curved peristyle with its nymphaeum (s–t) is 100 feet in length. Although neither these measurements nor the plan's axial relationships can be calculated precisely from the published materials, enough can be read from them and from sightings made before the present protective structures were erected to suggest that the popular view of the villa as a place assembled more or less at random from a variety of room shapes is very likely misdirected.

Before going further, the question of the North African connection should be mentioned briefly. Given the forceful arguments demonstrating African sources for the villa's mosaics, it is easy to think of its architecture as similarly inspired. There are features of the villa that stand out in North African architecture, for example the triconch. But thus far no villa has been found there resembling the Piazza Armerina one. The plan most frequently invoked in this connection, that of a villa or mansion near Portus Magnus, does not seem to me to be particularly relevant.[129] It is orthogonal overall, essentially the record of a traditional, if fairly elaborate, peristyle mansion composed of rectilinear formations. What is put forward as its most telling correspondence to the Piazza Armerina plan, an axial sequence of a peristyle, a fairly long, transverse corridor, and a large, oblong room, fails to convince because the peristyle and corridor are so widely separated; the Portus Magnus oblong room, moreover, was a triclinium, opened up at its far end.[130] Though there were probably North African sources for some elements found at Piazza Armerina, the sources for its overall plan and architectural character should, I suggest, be sought elsewhere, in the common properties of Roman towns and in earlier luxury villas.

Arriving at the villa, visitors passed through the three-arched entranceway. Of monumental size, it was fitted with large wooden doors and had pairs of fountains on each face. The core of the villa's circulation system or armature began with the irregularly shaped entrance courtyard (b), continued through a vestibule at a slightly higher level (d) to the four walkways of the main peristyle, and concluded, on higher ground, with the grand corridor (k), reached by three steep flights of steps. Both the central peristyle's north walkway and the corridor were analogous to streets. From the walkway, six regularly spaced entrances gave onto shop-like units (j), and an exit led to the baths; from the corridor, ten openings and stairs connected with adjoining spaces.

Some of these openings led to secondary paths or corridors such as the alleyways flanking the basilica (m) or the wide corridor connecting the central peristyle with the curved one (s). Others gave access to smaller connective spaces, for example those joining the easternmost room of the baths (e) with the entrance court (b) and, to the northeast, with the central peristyle. Between the corridor (k) and the curved peristyle (s), there was another connective space, unroofed, its convoluted border determined by the surrounding exterior shapes (p).

The three spacious courtyards, each of which had one or more fountains, brought light and air to the villa's interior while separating continuously built-up areas, in the manner of the broad, open spaces of city plazas. The court inside the main entrance was related to the triple archway as the vantage courts of fortified cities were related to their massive gates (Rome, the Porta Maggiore; compare Jerusalem, the Neapolis [Damascus] Gate and its plaza-court). Its asymmetrical, canted plan is similar to that of the courtyard of the Temple of Baalat at Thuburbo Maius; and the arena-like, truncated oval form of the southern peristyle at Piazza Armerina had parallels in certain of the curving civic plazas discussed in Chapter III, above (Palmyra; Constantinople). Also within the villa were smaller, semicircular courtyards, one in the elaborate suite (n) opening off the great corridor, and another in the westernmost latrine (c).

Passage architecture was represented at the villa not only by the entrance archway and structural arches (between t and the outer court wall just to the west, and between m and n), and by curved benches placed between the entrance court and the vestibule (d), but also by at least twelve fountains (all found in the southern half of the complex). Some fountains were set within their architectural spaces (b, i, and q); others were placed against walls or piers (a, n, and at the west side of p); and one was a large-scale, elaborate nymphaeum (t). All in all, much of the urban building typology is found at the villa, either in fact, or implied by plan or by mosaic subject matter, or both:

    aqueducts (2)
    arches (3)
    basilica
    baths
    circus (e, mosaic and shape; a children's circus mosaic in southernmost room of n)
    exedras (the benches before d)
    fountains (12)
    latrines (3)
    peristyle courts (3 large, 2 small)
    shops (j)
    shrines (just east of d, and possibly q and at the west end of b)
    water tank (o)

Reasonably analogous examples can be found elsewhere for all of these—for the baths, for example, at Antioch in Syria (Baths C), and at Bulla Regia (the baths northwest of the theatre). The great corridor seems to have had some of the qualities of an urban cryptoportico, and the triconch form, by the fourth century, was found fairly often in both public and private buildings. [131]

That spatial and directional articulation within the villa paralleled what was found in towns can be seen by tracing possible routes on the plan. In going west from the great corridor to the curved peristyle by way of an unroofed length of leftover space (p), one would have found it enlivened and defined by the devices of passage. Upon stepping out of the corridor, the broad niche on the north side of the passage would have been seen only from an acute angle, but after a few steps it and its contents—presumably statuary—would have been fully revealed. Straight ahead one would have seen a small, niched fountain set against the western wall. To the left was the entrance to the peristyle, marked by a step-high, projecting platform whose leading edge was curved and whose parallel sides were defined by small spur walls with columns set out at their ends (not shown on the plan). Thus flowing water, a counterpoint of rounded projections and recessions, and probably statuary, were added to this otherwise lifeless trough of eccentrically shaped space in order to accentuate its passage functions and give it some of the architectural cachet of more significant villa locations. In other words, a minor area was animated and given character by using familiar methods of urban articulation (the street behind the Basilica of Maxentius and Constantine in Rome, though grander, 56 was treated somewhat similarly).

Architectural motifs and imagery at the villa were much the same as those of the cities and towns toward the end of the empire, as is probably self-evident. At least 110 column positions are known, and columns would once have embellished the scenic nymphaeum (t). The orders were used frequently at entranceways and openings, in both forward and wall-plane positions. They were also placed at definitive design points in two of the bath chambers (e and f). There were at least three elaborated walls (a, f, and t), and several spatial groups qualify as incipiently baroque (f, n, and r–s–t). Many niches and two dozen apses appear, almost all of the latter on the outer periphery of the complex. Major curves exist also in the main peristyle's fountain pool, whose terminal semicircles are slightly and cleverly rotated toward the non-parallel lines of columns they face. Only about half of the villa's known sixty-six rooms and courtyards are essentially rectangular.

These features, composed in this plan pattern, suggest a reductive urbanism. The result resembles a domesticated town without streets, wherein the traditional architecture of dwellings is secondary to that of rather grand structures clearly of a public nature. The Piazza Armerina villa is a splendid if ostentatious complex that reaches toward a town-like inclusiveness of functions and forms. Paradoxically, in view of its inward-looking quality, so often remarked upon, it is quite spread out for a dwelling (it covers almost a hectare, a twelfth as much as Timgad's grid). In being a city-like residence, it 23 illustrates nicely Alberti's thoughts about the nature of a building's chief parts:

"If a city, according to the opinion of the philosophers, is no more than a great house, and, on the other hand, a house is a little city, why may it not be said that the (parts) of that house are so many little houses, such as the courtyard, the hall, the portico, and the like?"[132]

Relating villas to the city goes back at least as far as the younger Pliny. He, with his good eye for a view, knew what they resembled: at the end of his letter to Gallus about the Laurentine villa, he speaks of the appearance of the neighboring shore and says that "it gains much from the pleasing variety of the villas . . . [which] from the sea or the shore look like numerous cities."[133] Other ancient writers emphasize their villas' amenities and complexity, and villas were frequently represented by painters and mosaicists.[134] Fields of ruins within easy reach of Rome have fueled the imagination of architects and scholars since the early Renaissance and have spawned a considerable literature, extended now by knowledge of many other sites in Italy and beyond; villas have always had a strong appeal.

The architectural nature of the grandest ones has usually been explained by the influence of earlier villas and by the contours of given sites, and the plans have been called loose, restless, and inorganic. These derivations and descriptions, often pertinent, may be incomplete. In trying to augment them, to broaden the basis of villa studies, it may be useful to ask what, in imperial architecture, luxury villas most resemble. Since they all contain clearly defined single buildings and groups of buildings, and in every example these are distributed across armature-like plans and made accessible by connective architecture, the answer is that they most resemble towns or city quarters. This is reinforced by the common presence in the grand villas of the same kinds of thematic recapitulation found in Roman urbanism. At Piazza Armerina, for example, it can be seen in that repetition in the southeast suite (n) of the composition of the entire eastern range of spaces (l, m, n). The reductive essence of this Albertian resonance can sometimes be found in villa baths, whose plans and internal relationships, like those of their urban counterparts, reflected the configurations of the extended precincts they served.

170
210–212

176, 177

In other words, just as the Baths of Diocletian are a species of specialized town with respect to size, varied functions, and planning, the forms of lesser baths may recapitulate those of their surroundings. Hadrian's Tivoli villa records this doubled reciprocity. Its typology—theatre, baths, nymphaea, a stadium-shaped fountain-garden, terrace-plazas, tabernae, and so on—is urban, as are its passage devices, symmetrically planned groups of spaces, peristyles, and the like. Inside this vast archipelago, near the center of its familiar plan (incomplete, for more structures exist north and south, and much is unknown), the Small Baths repeat, within their own walls, the organizational scheme of the villa itself. The Baths thus declare their formal, as opposed to their obvious functional and locational, connection with the villa. At the same time they are a typological part of the villa's recapitulation of urban effects, landscape views and manipulation notwithstanding.[135]

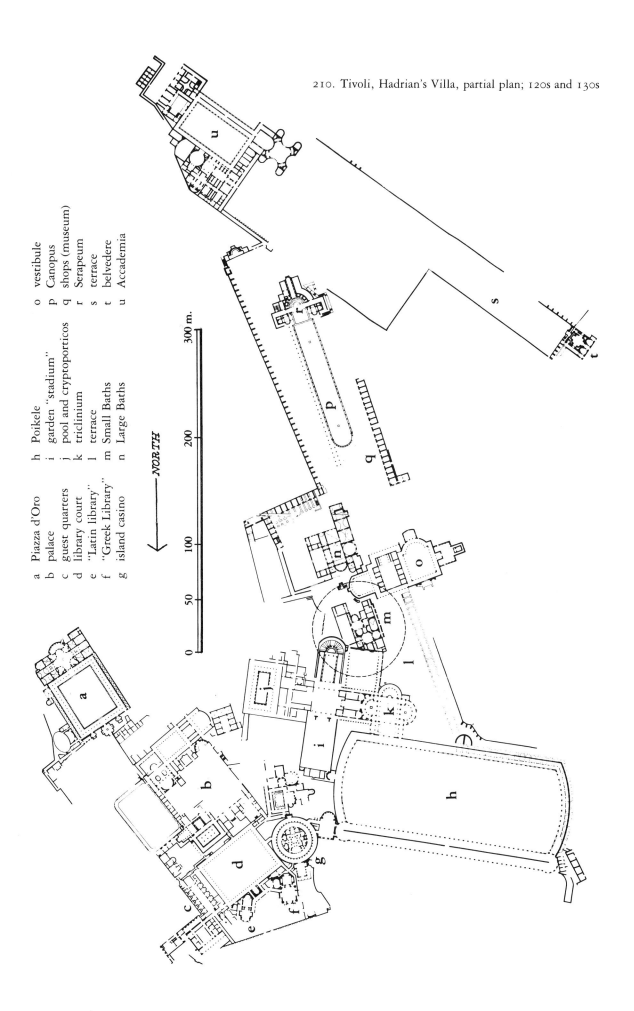

210. Tivoli, Hadrian's Villa, partial plan; 120s and 130s

a Piazza d'Oro
b palace
c guest quarters
d library court
e "Latin library"
f "Greek Library"
g island casino
h Poikele
i garden "stadium"
j pool and cryptoporticos
k triclinium
l terrace
m Small Baths
n Large Baths
o vestibule
p Canopus
q shops (museum)
r Serapeum
s terrace
t belvedere
u Accademia

← NORTH

0   50   100   200   300 m.

211, 212. Tivoli, Hadrian's Villa, model

Both Hadrian's villa and the Small Baths have local areas of symmetrical planning. Neither has a single central axis throughout, but both have secondary, more or less localized axes that can be followed for certain distances but which then meet others obliquely. Before the Small Baths were built, the villa's axes were loosely related to the eccentrically placed circular Island Casino (g). In the Baths plan, these dispositions are reflected—conceptually, not literally—in the location of room k and its position common to the axes d–k–t–u, k–j, k–q–p–n, and k–d–a. Other similarities exist. Room t, in this interpretation, represents the huge plaza, or Poikele, to the northwest (h; both have the same plan shape and contain pools of similar outline, and the proportions of these shapes are much the same). The areas of near symmetry in the Baths (around rooms n and j, for example), reflect villa groups similarly balanced, such as that of the Piazza d'Oro (a).

The Small Baths sprang from the same kind of architectural thinking that produced the villa itself. Intentionally or not, they mirrored the villa, and the villa, whatever else it may have been, was composed of urban building types spread about the landscape and connected by terraces, cryptoporticos, and walkways. That the design of some of these buildings was highly original, even exotic, does not alter this urban correlation. Finally, if Hadrian's villa were compacted and simplified, the resulting plan would be much like that of the Piazza Armerina villa. In all three examples—the two luxury villas and the Small Baths—the apparent randomness of the plans may in the last analysis have been chiefly the result of the pervasive influence of imperial architecture's solidly urban basis, which also powerfully affected orthogonally planned grand villas such as Montmaurin 213 and Sette Bassi.

213. Rome, Villa of Sette Bassi, model; mid-second century

ABBREVIATIONS

AB	*Art Bulletin*
AJA	*American Journal of Archaeology*
BC	*Bulletino della commissione archeologica communale di Roma*
BollCentro	*Bolletino del centro di studi per la storia dell'architettura*
Coarelli	F. Coarelli, *Guida archeologica di Roma* (Verona, 1975)
EAA	*Enciclopedia dell'arte antica*
JDAI	*Jahrbuch des Deutschen archaeologischen Instituts*
JRS	*Journal of Roman Studies*
JSAH	*Journal of the Society of Architectural Historians*
A. & M. Levi	A. and M. Levi, *Itineraria picta. Contributo allo studio della Tabula Peutingeriana* (Rome, 1967)
MacDonald	W. L. MacDonald, *The Architecture of the Roman Empire*, I: *An Introductory Study* (rev. ed. New Haven, 1982)
MEFRA	*Mélanges de l'école française de Rome, Antiquité*
Meiggs	R. Meiggs, *Roman Ostia*² (Oxford, 1973)
Nash	E. Nash, *Pictorial Dictionary of Ancient Rome* (2 vols., rev. ed. London, 1968)
PBSR	*Papers of the British School at Rome*
PECS	*Princeton Encyclopedia of Classical Sites* (Princeton, 1976)
Price and Trell	M. J. Price and B. L. Trell, *Coins and their Cities. Architecture on the Ancient Coins of Greece, Rome, and Palestine* (London, 1977)
Quaderni	*Quaderni dell'istituto di storia dell'architettura*
RE	*Realencyclopädie der classischen Altertumswissenschaft*
RM	*Mitteilungen des Deutschen archaeologischen Instituts, Römische Abteilung*
Toynbee	J. M. C. Toynbee, *Death and Burial in the Roman World* (London, 1971)
Ward-Perkins	J. B. Ward-Perkins, *Roman Imperial Architecture* (Harmondsworth, 1981)

NOTES

1. T. Cornell and J. Matthews, *Atlas of the Roman World* (London, 1982).

2. Vitruvius 1.4.9.

3. But see P.-A. Février, "Notes sur le développement urbain en Afrique du Nord. Les exemples comparés de Djémila et de Sétif," *Cahiers archéologiques* 14 (1964), 10–11.

4. J. H. Oliver, *The Ruling Power. A Study of the Roman Empire in . . . the Roman Oration of Aelius Aristides* (Philadelphia, 1953; = *Transactions of the American Philosophical Society,* 43, no. 4), p. 906, par. 97; cf. Aristides' description of Pergamon in *Orations* 23.13–14.

5. *Fontes iuris anteiustiniani,* ed. S. Riccobono (Florence, 1968), I, 462.

6. *The Order of Noble Cities* 8; see R. Krautheimer, *Three Christian Capitals* (Berkeley, 1983), pp. 70–71.

7. Cf. for example Strabo 5.3.8; Pliny, *Natural History* 36.101–115; Aelius Aristides (n. 4, above), par. 94; Libanius, *Oration* 11; and encomia of other cities such as those by Ausonius and Menander. Proper cities possessed a certain building typology: M. Frederiksen, "Changes in the Patterns of Settlement," *Hellenismus in Mittelitalien* 2 (Göttingen, 1976; = *Abhandlungen der Akademie der Wissenschaften in Göttingen* 97), p. 341; G. A. Mansuelli, *Architettura e città* (Bologna, 1970), chaps. 5 and 6.

8. For references, as for many other topics discussed in the text, see the bibliography; relevant illustrations appear in A. & M. Levi, where Tavv. XIV, XV, LXXI, LXXIII, and LXXVIII are particularly pertinent, and in Price and Trell, for example Figs. 25, 56, 159, and 190.

9. See for example the drawings of Column scenes in Coarelli, nos. 45, 59, 64, 75, and 92, on pp. 122–125. The best illustrations are in *La colonna traiana. Rilievi fotografici . . .* (Rome, 1942), and F. B. Florescu, *Die Trajanssäule—Grundfragen und Tafeln* (Bucharest, 1969). Cf. I. A. Richmond, *Trajan's Army on Trajan's Column* (London, 1982; an augmented reprint of *PBSR* 13 [1935], 1–40).

10. For roads and paths on the Column, see G. M. Koeppel, "A Military *Itinerarium* on the Column of Trajan," *RM* 87 (1980), 301–306.

11. A. & M. Levi, Tavv. VI–IX; cf. O. A. Dilke, *The Roman Land Surveyors* (Newton Abbot, 1971), pp. 110, 153, 171, 172, etc.

12. A. & M. Levi, pp. 151–159 and 210.

13. Coarelli, drawing 59 on p. 123; cf. the mosaic from the House of Isguntus at Hippo Regius, showing buildings presumably of Hippo "which together add up to a picture of a town," K. M. D. Dunbabin, *The Mosaics of Roman North Africa. Studies in Iconography and Patronage* (Oxford, 1978), p. 128. Coin views are of course labeled.

14. Monotony: among others, H. Plommer, *Ancient and Classical Architecture* (New York, 1956), pp. 314–315; L. Mumford, *The City in History* (New York, 1961), p. 208; and M. Hammond, *The City in the Ancient World* (Cambridge, Mass., 1972), p. 225; cf. F. Castagnoli, *Orthogonal Town Planning in Antiquity* (Cambridge, Mass., 1971), p. 125.

15. Ward-Perkins, p. 32; cf. MacDonald, p. 192.

16. M. D. Vernon, *The Psychology of Perception* (Harmondsworth, 1966), pp. 120–122; cf. T. Schumacher, "Buildings and Streets. . . ," in S. Anderson, ed., *On Streets* (Cambridge, Mass., 1978), pp. 138–139.

17. W. F. Jashemski, *The Gardens of Pompeii, Herculaneum, and the Villas Destroyed by Vesuvius* (Port Washington, N.Y., 1979), p. 13.

18. See for example H. I. Bell, "Antinoöpolis: A Hadrianic Foundation in Egypt," *JRS* 30 (1940), 136; R. Chevallier, *Roman Roads* (London, 1976), pp. 66–74; C. Foss, *Ephesus after Antiquity: A Late Antique Byzantine and Turkish City* (Cambridge, 1979), p. 65. Cf. R. MacMullen, *Roman Social Relations, 50 B.C. to A.D. 284* (New Haven, 1974), pp. 66–70 and Appendix A; and P. M. Fraser, *Ptolemaic Alexandria,* I (Oxford, 1972), pp. 35–36.

19. K. Lehmann-Hartleben, "Städtebau," *RE* IIIA (1929), 2105–2110; J. B. Ward-Perkins, *Cities of Ancient Greece and Italy* (New York, 1974), p. 32;

J. Lassus, "Quelques remarques sur les rues à por-
tiques," in *Palmyre. Bilan et perspectives* (Strasbourg, 1976), pp. 175–189; Ward-Perkins, p.
393 and p. 482, n. 23; G. M. A. Hanfmann,
Sardis from Prehistoric to Roman Times (Cambridge,
Mass., 1983), p. 142; cf. Vitruvius 5.9.3.

20. G. Downey, *A History of Antioch in Syria* (Princeton, 1961), pp. 173–175; J. Lassus, *Antioch-on-
the-Orontes* 5 (Princeton, 1972); Ward-Perkins, p.
313.

21. Lehmann-Hartleben (n. 19, above), 2109–2110;
Ward-Perkins, pp. 286–287.

22. Vitruvius 5.1.2; cf. *EAA* 3, p. 724 ("rarely
followed").

23. M. Lyttelton, *Baroque Architecture in Classical Antiquity* (London, 1974), pp. 227–228. Bosra had
both an oval plaza and a circular one.

24. J. B. Ward Perkins, "Severan Art and Architecture at Lepcis Magna," *JRS* 38 (1948), 59–80; cf.
Libyan Studies 15 (1984), 81–92.

25. A. Segal, "Roman Cities in the Province of Arabia," *JSAH* 40 (1981), 108–121, suggests locations for immense fora at these sites, based on
aerial photography.

26. Classrooms: *Scriptores Historiae Augustae,* "Severus
Alexander," 44.4.

27. Tacitus, *Annals* 15.38–43; Suetonius, *Nero* 16.1.

28. J. S. Ackerman, *The Architecture of Michelangelo*
(Harmondsworth, 1971), p. 141.

29. Cf. MacDonald, pp. 43–44.

30. Pliny, *Natural History* 34.27.

31. M. Pallottino in *EAA* 1 (1958), 595–598; C. D.
Curtis, "Roman Monumental Arches," *American
School of Classical Studies in Rome, Supplemental Papers* 2 (1908), 26–83; cf. *RE* VIIA (1939), 373–
464.

32. Price and Trell, entries under "Gate," p. 292.

33. P. Zanker, *Il foro romano* (Rome, 1972), pp. 15–
17 and Figs. 20–24; Nash 1, pp. 92–101; cf.
Ward-Perkins, p. 236.

34. D. S. Corlàita, "La situazione urbanistica degli
archi onorari nella prima età imperiale," in G. A.
Mansuelli, ed., *Studi sull'arco onorario romano*
(Rome, 1979), pp. 29–72.

35. In *RE* VIIA (1939) Abb. 1–24 under "Triumphbogen".

36. R. Martin, *L'urbanisme dans la Grèce antique*²,
(Paris, 1974), pp. 177–181; Corlàita (n. 34,
above), pp. 70–71; C. H. Kraeling, *Ptolemais,
City of the Libyan Pentapolis* (Chicago, 1962), pp.
81–83.

37. Ward-Perkins, p. 363.

38. G. Downey (n. 20, above), pp. 174, 393–394,

477–478, 501, and 645.

39. Price and Trell, Fig. 443.

40. G. Susini, *The Roman Stonecutter* (Oxford, 1973),
pp. 23, 54.

41. On the use of streets and plazas as places of relaxa-
tion, see W. H. Whyte, *The Social Life of Small
Urban Spaces* (Washington, 1980), and *City Spaces,
Human Places* (Boston, 1981).

42. Vitruvius 5.3.8; cf. P.-A. Février et al., *La ville
antique* (Paris, 1980; = *Histoire de la France urbaine*
1), pp. 282–283, and H. Eschebach, "Die in-
nerstädtische Gebrauchswasserversorgung darge-
stellt am Beispiel Pompejis," *Journées d'études sur les
aqueducs romains* (Paris, 1983), pp. 81–132.

43. Perhaps 1000–1250 l. per day (250–300 gal.): T.
Ashby, *The Aqueducts of Ancient Rome* (Oxford,
1935), p. 30, and data supplied by the New En-
gland Waterworks Association; cf. E. M. Win-
slow, *A Libation to the Gods* (London, 1961), pp.
20–23.

44. R. Merrifield, *The Roman City of London* (London,
1965), pp. 146, 148; J. Wacher, *The Towns of
Roman Britain* (London, 1974), pp. 48, 100.

45. Sabratha: D. E. L. Haynes, *The Antiquities of Tripolitania* (Tripoli, 1965), p. 111. Ostia: Meiggs,
p. 90.

46. Frontinus 2.78.

47. Cf. Ward-Perkins, pp. 394 ("assorted fountains,
exedrae, statues, and shrines") and 489, n. 26 to
p. 394 ("arches were used indiscriminately across
streets or street-crossings").

48. Recent work here by D. Parapetti reported by
I. Browning, *Jerash and the Decapolis* (London,
1982), pp. 93, 149, 153.

49. Vitruvius 5.1.1.

50. Vitruvius 5.1.4–10.

51. J. H. Humphrey et al., "Aspects of the Circus
at Lepcis Magna," *Libya antiqua* 9–10 (1972–
1973), 29.

52. E. Makowiecka, *The Origin and Evolution of Architectural Form of Roman Library* (Warsaw, 1978),
pp. 78–84.

53. Vitruvius 5.1.2.

54. Population: Meiggs, pp. 532–534, 597–598.

55. Cf. Acts 19:28–41.

56. Vitruvius 5.3–8 (acoustics), 5.9 (refuge).

57. MacDonald, pp. 194–199.

58. A. H. M. Jones, *The Decline of the Ancient World*
(London, 1966), p. 239.

59. R. Duncan-Jones, *The Economy of the Roman Empire*
(Cambridge, 1974), pp. 89–93.

60. *Annals,* 14.53.

61. This and the following quotation are from J.

Wacher (n. 44, above), p. 109; cf. *PECS*, p. 191, and A. Sorrell, *Roman Towns in Britain* (London, 1976), pp. 49–50.

62. On cryptoporticos and height, see J. B. Ward-Perkins, "The Cryptoportico: A Practical Solution to Certain Problems of Roman Urban Design," in E. Etienne, ed., *Les cryptoportiques dans l'architecture romaine* (Rome, 1973), pp. 51–56.

63. Vitruvius 3.4.4.

64. Temples as museums: L. Casson, *Travel in the Ancient World* (London, 1974), pp. 249–251 and Fig. 18.

65. *PECS*, p. 918.

66. *Satyricon* 71. For love of status (*philotimia*) see Mac-Mullen (n. 18, above), pp. 125, 168.

67. For Roman funerary gardens, see Toynbee, pp. 94–100.

68. See for example J. S. Curl, *A Celebration of Death* (London, 1980), illustrations on pp. 211 and 267; in the latter (Mount Jerome Cemetery, Dublin), there are four- and ten-column tombs fortuitously similar to those of Dana north and the Tripolitanian wadis; cf. H. Gabelmann, *Römische Grabbauten der frühen Kaiserzeit* (Stuttgart, 1979) Abb. 39.

69. For example by Gabelmann (n. 68, above), esp. Abb. 41–44; G. Mansuelli in *EAA* 5 (1963), 184–199; and Toynbee, chaps. V and VI; cf. Ward-Perkins, p. 328.

70. Eurysaces: P. C. Rossetto, *Il sepolcro del fornaio Marco Virgilio Eurisace* (Rome, 1973), p. 30 and n. 19, and Fig. 28; cf. Toynbee, p. 255, and Coarelli, p. 212. Utica: P. Romanelli, *Topografia e archeologia dell'Africa romana* (Turin, 1970), Tav. 195. Portugal: Toynbee, p. 253 and Pl. 81.

71. Aula Regia: MacDonald, pp. 53–54 and Pl. 45. Marble halls: F. K. Yegül, "A Study in Architectural Iconography: *Kaisersaal* and the Imperial Cult," *AB* 64 (1982), 7–31. Cf. C. C. Vermeule, *Roman Imperial Art in Greece and Asia Minor* (Cambridge, Mass., 1968), p. 82: Philoppapos' monument is "more of a nymphaeum without water than a funerary monument in the Greco-Roman sense."

72. Ward-Perkins, pp. 329–334, gives a sensible summary of the problem.

73. Cf. the tomb plan on a marble slab found by the Via Labicana, illustrated in Toynbee, p. 99.

74. A. W. Lawrence, *Greek Architecture* (Harmondsworth, 1957), pp. 208–210; D. C. Kurz and J. Boardman, *Greek Burial Customs* (London, 1971), pp. 166–169.

75. N. Hannestad, "Über das Grabmal des Antinoos.

Topographische und thematische Studien im Canopus-Gebiet der Villa Adriana," *Analecta romana instituti danici* 11 (1982), 69–108.

76. Cf. Statius, *Silvae* 3.5.90: "countless columns".

77. For these running bands, see W. L. MacDonald, "Excavation, Restoration, and Italian Architecture of the 1930s," in H. Searing, ed., *In Search of Modern Architecture. A Tribute to H.-R. Hitchcock* (New York, 1982), pp. 300, 312–313.

78. MacDonald, pp. 14–19, 43–46, 71–74.

79. Vitruvius 7.5.5–6; these pages on Augustan imagery are based in part on the author's "Empire Imagery in Augustan Architecture," *Archaeologica transatlantica* 4 (1985; in press).

80. See Vitruvius 1.4.9, for example.

81. Frauds: Vitruvius 7.5.3–4.

82. Ward-Perkins, p. 310.

83. Cf. Vitruvius 5.6–7.

84. Apparently the only published measured plan is the provisional one by Harrison in *British School of Archaeology in Jerusalem* 7 (1925), Pl. I; the fanciful plan and elevation by E. M. Fiechter, reproduced in L. Crema, *L'architettura romana* (Turin, 1959), Fig. 520, were made before the stage was cleared.

85. In the genial restoration by I. Browning (n. 48, above), Fig. 65, these columns are brought too far forward from the wall surface (his upper story is hypothetical).

86. For the latter motif, see the discussion by P. W. Lehmann, *Samothrace* 5: *The Temenos* (Princeton, 1982), pp. 85–89.

87. Vitruvius 5.6.6.

88. Vitruvius 5.6.8.

89. See n. 71, above.

90. *Letters* 2.17.26.

91. The texts are collected in D. Krenker and F. Krüger, *Die Trierer Kaiserthermen* (Augsburg, 1929), pp. 320–337; see also F. K. Yegül, "The Small City Bath in Classical Antiquity and a Reconstruction Study of Lucian's 'Baths of Hippias'," *Archeologica classica* 31 (1979), 108–131.

92. See for example M. Marvin, "Freestanding sculpture from the Baths of Caracalla," *AJA* 87 (1983), 347–384; cf. W. Heinz, *Römische Thermen. Badewesen und Badeluxus* (Munich, 1983), and n. 64, above.

93. In addition to the archaeological evidence, see Pliny the Younger, *Letters* 1.3.1 and 5.6.26, and Vitruvius 5.10.5, for examples.

94. MacDonald, pp. 14–19.

95. Maintenance in late antiquity at Ostia: Meiggs, pp. 419–420.

96. K. Lehmann, "Piranesi as Interpreter of Roman

Architecture," *Piranesi* (Northampton, Mass., 1961), pp. 88–98; W. L. MacDonald, *Piranesi's Carceri: Sources of Invention* (Northampton, Mass., 1979).

97. A. Blunt, *Some Uses and Misuses of the Terms Baroque and Rococo as applied to Architecture* (London, 1973), p. 8.

98. R. Wittkower, *Art and Architecture in Italy 1600– 1750³* (Harmondsworth, 1973), p. 281.

99. H. Kähler, *Hadrian und seine Villa bei Tivoli* (Berlin, 1950), pp. 112–117 and Taf. 3–5.

100. Shown on p. 292 in P. Portoghesi, *Roma barocca* (Cambridge, Mass., 1970).

101. G. Picard, *Living Architecture: Roman* (New York, 1965), p. 182; A. Blunt (who connects the Conocchia not with Borromini's S. Andrea tower but with its drum and dome), *Borromini* (London, 1979), pp. 38–39, 196; the same, *Guide to Baroque Rome* (New York, 1982), pp. 8–9.

102. Price and Trell, Figs. 183–184.

103. Illustrated in M. Lyttelton, *Baroque Architecture in Classical Antiquity* (London, 1974), Pl. 95.

104. Blunt, *Borromini* (n. 101, above), pp. 41–43; P. Portoghesi, *Borromini* (London, 1968), pp. 6–7; cf. Blunt, *Some Uses* (n. 97, above), p. 32, and Ward-Perkins, p. 484, n. 28.

105. For this plan-pattern, see F. Rakob, *"Litus beatae veneris aureum*. Untersuchungen am 'Venustempel' in Baiae," *RM* 68 (1961), 114–149.

106. For this form see F. E. Brown, "Hadrianic Architecture," in L. F. Sandler, ed., *Essays in Memory of Karl Lehmann* (New York, 1964), pp. 55–58.

107. Borromini and Hadrian's villa: F. Borromini, *Opus architectonicum* (reprinted, London, 1965), p. 36; Blunt, *Borromini* (n. 101, above), pp. 70, 99, 116; Portoghesi (n. 104, above), pp. 8 and 9.

108. Successive plans in P. Chiolini, *I caratteri distributivi degli antichi edifici* (Milan, 1959), p. 107.

109. Plan in P. Portoghesi, "I monumenti borrominiani della basilica laterense," *Quaderni*, fasc. 11 (July, 1955), Fig. 54.

110. Literature on the subject can be traced via Ward-Perkins' notes: n. 22 to p. 236 on p. 478, n. 20 to p. 268 on p. 480, and n. 64 to p. 341 on p. 486.

111. See also J. Durm, *Die Baukunst der Etrusker. Die Baukunst der Römer* (Stuttgart, 1905), Fig. 544, and compare with Blunt, *Borromini* (n. 101, above), Fig. 25.

112. T. Heath, *A History of Greek Mathematics* 2 (reprinted, New York, 1981), chap. 20; J. Klein, *Greek Mathematical Thought and the Origins of Algebra.* (Cambridge, Mass., 1968), chap. 10.

113. Vitruvius 1.4.9, 7.5.3–4, and cf. 7.5.5.

114. Cf. E. Nash, "Hidden Visual Patterns in Roman Architecture and Ruins," in M. Healy, ed., *Vision and Artifact* (New York, 1976), pp. 95–103.

115. M. Heidegger, "Building, Dwelling, and Thinking," in *Poetry, Language and Thought* (New York, 1971), quoted by K. Frampton in *Modern Architecture: A Critical History* (London, 1980), p. 280.

116. Cf. R. Venturi, D. Scott Brown, S. Izenour, *Learning from Las Vegas²* (Cambridge, Mass., 1977), p. 54; H. Honour, *Neo-classicism* (Harmondsworth, 1968), p. 20; R. Jenkyns, *The Victorians and Ancient Greece* (Cambridge, Mass., 1980), pp. 11–12.

117. Ward-Perkins, p. 281, n. 10.

118. For example, *Jewish Antiquities* 14.76, 18.55, and *The Jewish War* 3.409, 7.23.

119. Artificial islands: Pliny the Younger, *Letters* 6.3.17.

120. Ward-Perkins, p. 309; Josephus, *The Jewish War* 3.36; E. Netzer, *Greater Herodium* (Jerusalem, 1981).

121. *The Jewish War* 1.408–415; cf. Vitruvius 5.12.1, and J. Finegan, *The Archeology of the New Testament* (Princeton, 1969), pp. 70–80.

122. J. Summerson, *The Classical Language of Architecture²* (London, 1980), p. 20.

123. Quoted by P. Collins, *Changing Ideals in Modern Architecture* (London, 1965), p. 290.

124. L. P. Richardson, "The Architecture of the Forum of Trajan," *Archaeological News* 6 (1977), 101–107.

125. See for example Collins (n. 123, above), pp. 91–93; cf. M. Finley, *The Legacy of Greece²* (Oxford, 1981), p. 5, and P. Kidson, in the same volume, pp. 389–391.

126. G. Goodwin, *A History of Ottoman Architecture* (London, 1971).

127. R. J. A. Wilson, *Piazza Armerina* (London, 1983), gives sensible views about this much-debated site and usefully summarizes others' opinions; A. Carandini et al., *Filosofiana. The Villa of Piazza Armerina*, 2 vols. (Palermo, 1982), is devoted chiefly to the mosaics; cf. K. M. D. Dunbabin, *The Mosaics of Roman North Africa. Studies in Iconography and Patronage* (Oxford, 1978), pp. 196–212, 243–245.

128. For example, N. Neuerburg, "Some Considerations on the Architecture of the Imperial Villa at Piazza Armerina," *Marsyas* 8 (1957–1959), 22–29; B. M. Boyle, "The Architecture of the Villa at Piazza Armerina," unpublished Yale University M.A. dissertation, 2 vols., 1962; Ward-Perkins, pp. 460–464; and Carandini (n. 127, above), I, pp. 384–393 (by M. Medri).

129. Plan in Ward-Perkins, p. 463. Cf. I. Lavin, "The

House of the Lord: Aspects of the Role of Palace *triclinia* in the Architecture of Antiquity and in the Early Middle Ages," *AB* 44 (1963), 1–27.

130. Other possibilities: The *ambulatio* or long walkway of Tiberius' Villa Iovis on Capri, with its centered, adjoining hall; the northwest portico at Val Catena; the corridor and basilica, set at right angles, at the Villa of Maxentius by the Via Appia; cf. the Ostian Round Temple's elongated, corridor-like porch.

131. Wilson (n. 127, above), pp. 73, 76–80, 82; Lavin (n. 129, above), p. 26; incipiently at Hadrian's Tivoli villa, ill. 199 (k), here.

132. Adapted from the Leone translation of the *Ten Books on Architecture*, ed. J. Rykwert (London, 1955), 1.9 (p. 13); cf. 5.14 (pp. 100–101).

133. *Letters* 2.17.27; cf. A. N. Sherwin-White, *The Letters of Pliny* (Oxford, 1966), pp. 186–199; and Z. Pavlovskis, *Man in an Artificial Landscape* (Leiden, 1973; = *Mnemosyne, Supp.* 25), pp. 25–33.

134. A. W. Van Buren, "Villa," *RE* XVI (1958; writers); A. G. McKay, *Houses, Villas and Palaces in the Roman World* (London, 1975), chap. 5 and references (paintings); T. Sarnowski, *Les représentations de villas sur les mosaïques africaines tardives* (Warsaw, 1978); M. I. Rostovtzeff, "Die hellenistische-römische Architekturlandschaft," *RM* 26 (1911), 1–185.

135. W. L. MacDonald and B. M. Boyle, "The Small Baths at Hadrian's Villa," *JSAH* 39 (1980), 5–27.

BIBLIOGRAPHY

With some exceptions, entries in *PECS,* as well as in *EAA* and *RE* (which include topics as well as sites), are omitted from this selection. For full titles, see the List of Abbreviations. The material is arranged as follows:

GENERAL WORKS

A. Boëthius, *Etruscan and Early Roman Architecture* (Harmondsworth, 1978).

———— *The Golden House of Nero* (Ann Arbor, 1960).

F. E. Brown, *Roman Architecture* (New York, 1961).

R. Chevallier, *Roman Roads* (London, 1976).

T. Cornell and J. Matthews, *Atlas of the Roman World* (London, 1982).

L. Crema, *L'architettura romana* (Turin, 1959).

———— *Significato della architettura romana. . .* (Rome, 1959; = *BollCentro,* 15).

Fototeca Unione, *Ancient Roman Architecture,* 2 vols. (Chicago, 1979, 1982); ca. 24,000 microfiches of Roman sites and buildings.

N. Lewis and M. Reinhold, *Roman Civilization. . . ,* vol. 2 (New York, 1955), chap. 5.

MacDonald.

W. L. MacDonald, "Roman Architects," in S. Kostof, ed., *The Architect. Chapters in the History of the Profession* (New York, 1977), pp. 28–58.

Mostra augustea della Romanità, 2 vols. 4th ed. (Rome, 1938).

H. Plommer, *Vitruvius and Later Roman Building Manuals* (Cambridge, 1973).

J. J. Pollitt, *The Art of Rome, c. 753 B.C.–337 A.D.,* (Englewood Cliffs, N.J., 1966).

Price and Trell.

F. Rakob, "Römische Architektur," in T. Kraus, ed., *Das römische Weltreich* (Berlin, 1967; = *Propyläen Kunstgeschichte,* 2).

D. S. Robertson, *A Handbook of Greek and Roman Architecture,* 2nd ed., revised (Cambridge, 1943; reprinted London, 1969).

J. Summerson, *The Classical Language of Architecture,* 2nd ed. (London, 1980).

Tabula imperii romani, 1934ff.; see *JRS* 74 (1984), 200–201.

Vitruvius, *De architectura,* trans. M. H. Morgan (Cambridge, Mass., 1914; reprinted New York, 1960). A translation and detailed commentary is being published, book by book, in the Budé collection (Paris, 1969ff.). See also F. E. Brown, "Vitruvius and the Liberal Art of Architecture," *Bucknell Review* 11.4 (1963), 99–107.

A. Von Gerkan, *Von Antiker Architektur und Topographie* (Stuttgart, 1959).

Ward-Perkins.

J. B. Ward-Perkins, *Roman Architecture* (New York, 1977).

URBANISM

S. Anderson, ed., *On Streets* (Cambridge, Mass., 1978).

E. Bacon, *Design of Cities,* rev. ed. (New York, 1974).

A. Boëthius, *Roman and Greek Town Architecture* (Göteborg, 1948; = *Göteborgs Högskolas Årsskrift,* 54.3).

A. Boëthius, "Urbanistica," *EAA* 7 (1966), 1062–1071.

L. Casson, *Ships and Seamanship in the Ancient World* (Princeton, 1971); ports, pp. 366–370.

F. Castagnoli, *Orthogonal Town Planning in Antiquity* (Cambridge, Mass., 1971).

———, ed., *Studi di urbanistica antica* (Rome, 1966).

R. Chevallier, bibliography in *Aufstieg und Niedergang der römischen Welt,* ed. H. Temporini, II.1 (1975), pp. 649–788.

C. J. Classen, *Die Stadt im Spiegel der Descriptiones und Laudes Urbium* (Munich, 1980).

D. Claude, *Die byzantinische Stadt im 6. Jahrhundert* (Munich, 1969).

M. Clavel and P. Lévêque, *Villes et structures urbains dans l'occident romain* (Paris, 1971).

M. Coppa, *Storia dell'urbanistica. Le età ellenistiche,* 2 vols. (Rome, 1981).

G. Cullen, *The Concise Townscape,* rev. ed. (London, 1971).

P.-M. Duval and E. Frézouls, *Thèmes de recherches sur les villes antiques d'occident* (Paris, 1977).

P.-A. Février and P. Leveau, *Villes et campagnes dans l'empire romain. Actes du colloque. . .* (Aix-en-Provence, 1982).

T. Frank, ed., *An Economic Survey of Ancient Rome,* 6 vols. (Baltimore, 1933–1940; reprinted, Paterson, N.J., 1959).

E. Frézouls, "Metodo per lo studio dell'urbanistica. Strutture e infrastrutture delle città antiche d'occidente," *Centro studi e documentazione sull'Italia romana, Atti* 3 (1970–1971; not seen).

P. Gould and R. White, *Mental Maps* (Harmondsworth, 1974).

P. Groth, "Streetgrids as Frameworks for Urban Variety," *Harvard Architecture Review* 2 (1981), 68–75.

G. Gullini, "Tre note di urbanistica antica," *Centro studi e documentazione sull'Italia romana, Atti* 5 (1973–1974), 183–198.

M. Hammond, *The City in the Ancient World* (Cambridge, Mass., 1972).

F. Haverfield, *Ancient Town-Planning* (Oxford, 1913).

K. Hopkins, "Economic Growth and Towns in Classical Antiquity," in M. Abrams, ed., *Towns in Societies* (Cambridge, 1978), pp. 35–77.

P. Lavedan and J. Hugueny, *Histoire de l'urbanisme. Antiquité* (Paris, 1966).

K. Lehmann-Hartleben, "Städtebau Italiens und des römischen Reiches," *RE* IIIA (1929), 2016–2124.

K. Lynch, *The Image of the City* (Cambridge, Mass., 1960).

W. L. MacDonald, "Connection and Passage in North African Architecture," in C. McClendon, ed., *Rome and the Provinces: Studies in the Transformation of Art and Architecture in the Mediterranean World* (in press).

R. MacMullen, *Roman Social Relations, 50 B.C. to A.D. 284* (New Haven, 1974), Chaps. 2 and 3 and appendices.

G. A. Mansuelli, *Architettura e città. Problemi del mondo classico* (Bologna, 1970).

——— *Studi sulla città antica* (Rome, 1982).

R. T. Marchese, ed., *Aspects of Greco-Roman Urbanism. Essays on the Classical City* (Oxford, 1983).

R. Martin, *L'urbanisme dans la Grèce antique,* 2nd ed. (Paris, 1974).

M. I. Rostovtzeff, *The Social and Economic History of the Roman Empire,* 2 vols. 2nd ed. (Oxford, 1957).

B. Rudofsky, *Streets for People* (New York, 1969).

J. Rykwert, *The Idea of a Town. The Anthropology of Urban Form in Rome, Italy and the Ancient World* (Princeton, 1976).

C. Sitte, *City Planning According to Artistic Principles,* trans. G. R. Collins and C. C. Collins (New York, 1965).

L. Storoni Mazzolani, *The Idea of the City in Roman Thought,* trans. S. O'Donnell (London, 1970).

J. B. Ward-Perkins, *Cities of Ancient Greece and Italy: Planning in Classical Antiquity* (New York, 1974).

W. H. Whyte, *City Spaces, Human Places* (Boston, 1981).

——— *The Social Life of Small Urban Spaces* (Washington, 1980).

PICTORIAL SOURCES

J. J. G. Alexander, "The Illustrated Manuscripts of the *Notitia Dignitatum,*" in R. Goodburn and P. Bartholomew, eds., *Aspects of the Notitia Dignitatum* (Oxford, 1976), pp. 11–50.

M. Avi-Yonah, *The Madaba Mosaic Map* (Jerusalem, 1954).

F. M. Biebel, "The Walled Cities of the Gerasa Mosaics," in C. Kraeling, ed., *Gerasa, City of the Decapolis* (New Haven, 1938), pp. 341–351.

E. Billig, *Spätantike Architekturdarstellungen* 1 (Stockholm, 1977; = *Acta Universitatis Stockholmiensis, Stockholm Studies in Classical Archaeology* 10.1).

K. Bulas, "Tabulae Iliacae," *EAA* 7 (1966), 579–580.

J. N. Carder, "Art Historical Problems of a Roman Land Surveying Manuscript. . . ," diss., Univ. of Pittsburgh (1978).

F. Castagnoli, "Gli edifici rappresentati in un relievo

del sepolcro degli Haterii," *BC* 69 (1941), 59–69.

R. Chevallier, above, under General Works.

La colonna traiana. Rilievi fotografici. . . (Rome, 1942).

J. W. Crowfoot, *Early Churches in Palestine* (London, 1941), pp. 128–131 and Plates XV and XVIII.

O. A. W. Dilke, *The Roman Land Surveyors. An Introduction to the Agrimensores* (Newton Abbot, 1971).

G. Downey, *A History of Antioch in Syria from Seleucus to the Arab Conquest* (Princeton, 1961), pp. 659–664.

K. M. D. Dunbabin, *The Mosaics of Roman North Africa. Studies in Iconography and Patronage* (Oxford, 1978), pp. 128–130.

I. Ehrensperger-Katz, "Les représentations de villes fortifiées dans l'art paléochrétien et leurs dérivées byzantines," *Cahiers archéologiques* 19 (1969), 1–27.

V. Fasolo, "Rappresentazioni architettoniche nella pittura romana," *Atti del terzo congresso nazionale di storia dell'architettura* 3 (1938), 207–213.

F. B. Florescu, *Die Trajanssäule—Grundfragen und Tafeln,* (Bucharest, 1969).

M. Frederiksen, *Campania* (Rome and London, 1984), pp. 351, 355.

G. Fuchs, *Architekturdarstellungen auf römischen Münzen der Republik und frühen Kaiserzeit* (Berlin, 1969).

R. Graefe, *Vela erunt. Die Zeltdächer der römischen Theater und ähnlicher Anlangen. Tafelband* (Mainz, 1979), Taf. 99–131.

H. Küthmann et al., *Bauten Roms auf Münzen und Medaillen* (Munich, 1973).

J. Lassus, "Antioch en 459, d'après la mosaïque de Yakto," in J. Balty, ed., *Apamée de Syrie. Bilan des recherches archéologiques 1965–1968* (Brussels, 1969), pp. 137–146.

A. & M. Levi.

G. Mansuelli, "La rappresentazione della città nell'arte tardo-romana e bizantina," *Corsi di cultura sull'arte ravennate e bizantina* 19 (1972), 239–244.

S. E. Ostrow in *Puteoli* 3 (Naples, 1979), 77–111.

Price and Trell.

I. A. Richmond, *Trajan's Army on Trajan's Column* (London, 1982); an augmented reprint of *PBSR* 13 (1935), 1–40.

M. I. Rostovtzeff, "Die hellenistische-römische Architekturlandschaft," *RM* 26 (1911), 1–185.

T. Sarnowski, *Les représentations de villas sur les mosaïques africaines tardives* (Warsaw, 1978).

E. B. Smith, *Architectural Symbolism of Imperial Rome and the Middle Ages* (Princeton, 1956).

H.-G. Thümmel, "Zur Deutung der Mosaikkarte

von Madaba," *Zeitschrift des deutschen Palästina-Vereins* 89 (1973), 66–79.

B. L. Trell, "Architectura numismatica orientalis. A Short Guide to . . . Numismatic Formulae," *Numismatic Chronicle* 10 (1970), 29–50.

———— "Architecture on Ancient Coins," *Archaeology* 29.1 (1976), 6–13.

M. Turcan-Déléani, "Les monuments représentés sur la colonne Trajane. Schématisme et réalisme," *MEFRA* 70 (1958), 149–176.

BUILDING TYPES AND ELEMENTS

P. Arias, "Teatro e Odeon," *EAA* 7 (1966), 640–650.

M. Bieber, *The History of the Greek and Roman Theater,* 2nd ed. (Princeton, 1961).

D. F. Brown, "The Arcuated Lintel. . . ," *AJA* 46 (1942), 389–399.

F. C. Brown et al., *Study of the Orders,* rev. ed. (Chicago, 1948).

M. Cagiano de Azavedo, "I 'Capitolia' dell'impero romano," *Atti della pontificia accademia romana di archeologia, Memorie* 5 (1940), 1–76.

C. Callmer, "Antike Bibliotheken," *Acta instituti romani regni Sueciae* 10 (1944), 145–193.

G. Carettoni, "Palestra," *EAA* 5 (1963), 882–887.

F. Castagnoli, "Capitolium," *EAA* 2 (1959), 326–330.

P. Chiolini, *I caratteri distributivi degli antichi edifici* (Milan, 1959).

E. Coche de la Ferté, "Basilica," *EAA* 2 (1959), 2–15.

J. J. Coulton, *The Architectural Development of the Greek Stoa* (Oxford, 1976), Chap. 9 (porticos, peristyles, streets, basilicas).

L. Crema (Turin, 1959), above, under General Works, is arranged typologically within broad chronological divisions.

A. De Franciscis and R. Pane, *Mausolei romani in Campania,* (Naples, 1957).

S. De Maria, "Metodologia per una rilettura dei fornici di Roma antica," *Parametro* 20 (Oct. 1973), 36–40.

E. Etienne, ed., *Les cryptoportiques dans l'architecture romaine* (Rome, 1973).

G. Forni, "Anfiteatro," *EAA* 1 (1958), 374–390.

———— "Circo e Ippodoromo," *EAA* 2 (1959), 647–655.

———— "Teatro," *EAA, Supplemento* (1973), 772–789.

E. Forssman, *Säule und Ornament* (Munich, 1961).

A. Frazer, "Modes of European Courtyard Design before the Medieval Cloister," *Gesta* 12 (1973), 1–12.

H. Gabelmann, *Römische Grabbauten der frühen Kaiserzeit* (Stuttgart, 1979).

P. Gazzola, *Ponti romani,* 2 vols. (Florence, 1963).

G. Girri, *La taberna nel quadro urbanistica . . . di Ostia* (Rome, 1956).

B. Götze, "Antike Bibliotheken," *JDAI* 52 (1937), 225–247.

R. Graefe, above, under Pictorial Sources.

P. Grimal, *Les jardins romains,* 3rd ed. (Paris, 1984).

R. Günter, *Wand, Fenster und Licht in der spätantik-frühchristlichen Architektur* (Herford, 1965).

J. A. Hanson, *Roman Theater-Temples* (Princeton, 1959).

W.-D. Heilmeyer, *Korinthische Normalkapitelle: Studien zur Geschichte der römischen Architekturdekoration, RM,* Ergänzungsheft 16 (1970).

W. Heinz, *Römische Thermen. Badewesen und Badeluxus* (Munich, 1983).

G. Hornbostel-Hüttner, *Studien zur römischen Nischenarchitektur* (Leiden, 1979).

J. Humphrey, *Roman Circuses* (in press).

H. Kähler, "Biblioteca," *EAA* 2 (1959), 93–99.

———— *Die römische Tempel* (Berlin, 1970).

———— "Terme," *EAA* 7 (1966), 715–719.

———— "Triumphbogen (Ehrenbogen)," *RE* VIIA (1939), 373–493.

D. Krencker and F. Krüger, *Die Trierer Kaiserthermen* (Augsburg, 1929).

K. Lehmann-Hartleben, above, under Urbanism.

G. Lugli, "Torre," *EAA,* Supplemento (1973), 854–861.

MacDonald, chap. 1 (vaults).

E. Makowiecka, *The Origin and Evolution of Architectural Form of Roman Library* (Warsaw, 1978).

G. A. Mansuelli, "El arco honorifico en el desarrollo de la arquitectura romana," *Archivo español de arqueologia* 27 (1954), 93–178.

———— "Il monumento commemorativo romano," *BollCentro* 12 (1958), 3–23.

———— "Monumento funerario," *EAA* 5 (1963), 170–202.

————, ed., *Studi sull'arco onorario romano* (Rome, 1979).

A. G. McKay, *Houses, Villas and Palaces in the Roman World* (London, 1975).

N. Neuerburg, "Greek and Roman Pyramids," *Archaeology* 22 (1969), 106–115.

———— *L'architettura delle fontane e dei ninfei nell'Italia antica* (Naples, 1965; = *Memorie dell'accademia di archeologia lettere e belle arti di Napoli* 5).

F. Noack, "Triumph und Triumphbogen," *Vorträge der Bibliotek Warburg 1925/1926* (Berlin, 1928).

M. Pallottino, "Arco onorario e trionfale," *EAA* 1 (1958), 588–598.

Z. Pavlovskis, *Man in an Artificial Landscape* (Leiden, 1973; = *Mnemosyne, Supplement* 25) (villas and palaces).

F. Rakob, "Der Bauplan einer kaiserlichen Villa," *Festschrift Klaus Langheit* (Cologne, 1973), 113–125.

G. Rickman, *Roman Granaries and Store Buildings* (Cambridge, 1971).

G. Rohde, *Die Bedeutung der Tempelgründungen im Staatsleben der Römer* (Marburg, 1932).

D. W. Rupp, "Greek Altars of the Northeastern Peloponnese . . . '" diss., Bryn Mawr (1974) (use of tetrastyla over altars, pp. 381–396; cf. *AJA* 78.2 [1974] 176).

C. de Ruyt, *Macellum. Marché alimentaire des romains* (Louvain, 1983).

D. Scagliarini and E. Salza Prina Ricotti, "Villa," *EAA, Supplemento* (1973), 911–916.

S. Settis, " 'Esedra' e 'ninfeo' nella terminologia architettonica del mondo romano . . . ," in *Aufstieg und Niedergang der römischen Welt,* ed. H. Temporini, I.4 (Berlin, 1973), pp. 661–745.

R. A. Staccioli, "Magazzino (horreum)," *EAA* 4 (1961), 767–772.

D. E. Strong, "Some Early Examples of the Composite Capital," *JRS* 50 (1960), 119–128.

———— "Some Observations on Early Roman Corinthian," *JRS* 53 (1963), 73–84.

K. M. Swoboda, *Römische und romanische Paläste,* 3rd ed. (Vienna, 1969) (villas).

B. Tamm, *Auditorium and Palatium* (Stockholm, 1963; = *Stockholm Studies in Classical Archaeology* 2).

J. Tønsberg, *Offentlige Biblioteker i Romerriget i det 2. århundrede e. Chr.* (Copenhagen, 1976).

Toynbee.

G. Traversari, *Gli spettacoli in acqua nel teatro tardo-antico,* (Rome, 1960).

N. Venuti, "Urbiche, porte," *EAA* 7 (1966), 1072–1074.

J. B. Ward-Perkins, "Constantine and the Origins of the Christian Basilica," *PBSR* 22 (1954), 69–90.

J. B. Ward-Perkins and M. H. Ballance, "The Caesareum at Cyrene and the Basilica at Cremna," *PBSR* 26 (1958), 137–194.

J. B. Ward-Perkins and S. Gibson, "The Market-Theatre at Cyrene," *Libya antiqua* 13/14 (1976/1977), 331–375.

S. Weinstock, "Templum," *RM* 47 (1932), 95–121.

R. J. A. Wilson, *Piazza Armerina* (London, 1983) (late villas).

F. K. Yegül, "The Small City Bath in Classical Antiquity and a Reconstruction Study of Lucian's 'Baths of Hippias'," *Archeologia classica* 31 (1979), 108–131.

———— "A Study in Architectural Iconography: *Kaisersaal* and the Imperial Cult," *AB* 64 (1982), 7–31.

P. Zucker, *Town and Square* (New York, 1959).

MATERIALS AND TECHNOLOGY

J.-P. Adam, *La construction romaine* (Paris, 1984).

T. Ashby, *The Aqueducts of Ancient Rome* (Oxford, 1935; reprinted 1971).

M. E. Blake, *Ancient Roman Construction in Italy from the Prehistoric Period to Augustus* (Washington, 1947).

———— *Roman Construction in Italy from Tiberius through the Flavians* (Washington, 1959).

———— *Roman Construction in Italy from Nerva through the Antonines,* ed. D. T. Bishop (Philadelphia, 1973).

H. Bloch, *I bolli laterizi e la storia edilizia romana* (Rome, 1947; reprinted from *BC* 64, 65, and 66 [1936–1938]); see also *AJA* 63 (1959), 225–240.

———— "The Roman Brick Industry and Its Relationship to Roman Architecture," *JSAH* 1 (1941), 3–8.

L. Crema, "La volta nell'architettura romana," *L'Ingegnere* 16 (1942), 941–952.

G. De Angelis d'Ossat, "La forma e la costruzione della cupola nell'architettura romana," *Atti del terzo congresso nazionale di storia dell'architettura* 3 (1938), 223–250.

O. A. W. Dilke, above, under Pictorial Sources.

G. Giovannoni, *La tecnica della costruzione presso i romani,* (Rome, 1925).

———— "Building and Engineering," in C. Bailey, ed., *The Legacy of Ancient Rome* (Oxford, 1951), pp. 429–474.

R. Gnoli, *Marmora romana* (Rome, 1971).

M. Hainzmann, "Untersuchungen zur Geschichte und Verwaltung der stadtrömischen Wasserleitung," diss., Vienna, 1975.

W. Heinz, above, under Building Types and Elements.

T. Helen, *Organization of Roman Brick Production in the First and Second Centuries A.D.* (Helsinki, 1975).

A. T. Hodge, "A Plain Man's Guide to Roman Plumbing," *Classical views/Echos du monde classique* 17 (1983), 311–328.

———— "Siphons in Roman Aqueducts," *PBSR* 51 (1983), 174–221.

Journées d'etudes sur les acqueducs romains, Lyon (26–28 mai 1977) (Paris, 1983).

H. Kammerer-Grothaus, "Der Deus Rediculus . . . Ziegelarchitektur des 2. Jahrhunderts n. Chr. in Latium" *RM* 81 (1974), 130–252.

D. Krencker and F. Krüger, above, under Building Types and Elements.

F. Kretzschmer, *Bilddokumente römischer Technik,* 3rd ed. (Düsseldorf, 1967).

J. G. Landels, *Engineering in the Ancient World* (Berkeley, 1978).

G. Lugli, *La tecnica edilizia romana con particulare riguardo a Roma e Lazio,* 2 vols. (Rome, 1957; reprinted 1968).

MacDonald, chap. 7.

W. L. MacDonald, "Some Implications of Later Roman Construction," *JSAH* 17 (1952), 2–8.

W. L. MacDonald and B. M. Boyle, "The Small Baths at Hadrian's Villa," *JSAH* 39 (1980), 5–27.

R. Mainstone, *Developments in Structural Form* (London, 1975).

I marmi italiani (Rome, 1939).

R. Meiggs, *Trees and Timber in the Ancient Mediterranean World* (Oxford, 1982).

D. Monna and P. Pensabene, *Marmi dell'Asia Minore* (Rome, 1977).

C. Rocatelli, "Brick in Antiquity," in C. G. Mars, ed., *Brickwork in Italy* (Chicago, 1925), pp. 1–46.

M. Steinby, "Ziegelstempel von Rom und Umgebung," *RE, Supp.* 15 (1978), 1489–1531.

E. D. Thatcher, "The Open Rooms of the Terme del Foro at Ostia," *Memoirs of the American Academy in Rome* 24 (1956), 167–264.

E. B. Van Deman, *The Building of the Roman Aqueducts* (Washington, 1934).

H. Walda and S. Walker, "The Art and Architecture of Lepcis Magna: Marble Origins by Isotopic Analysis," *Libyan Studies* 15 (1984), 81–92.

J. B. Ward-Perkins, "Dalmatia and the Marble Trade," *Disputationes Salonitanae, 1970* (1975), 38–44.

———— "The Marble Trade and its Organization: Evidence from Nicomedia," *Memoirs of the American Academy in Rome* 36 (1980), 325–338.

———— "Nicomedia and the Marble Trade," *PBSR* 48 (1980), 23–69.

———— "Notes on the Structure and Building Methods of Early Byzantine Architecture," in D. T. Rice, ed., *The Great Palace of the Byzantine Emperors, Second Report* (Edinburgh, 1958), pp. 52–104.

———— "Quarrying in Antiquity: Technology, Tradition, and Social Change," *Proceedings of the British Academy* 57 (1972), 1–24.

J. B. Ward Perkins, "Tripolitania and the Marble Trade," *JRS* 41 (1951), 89–104.

K. D. White, *Greek and Roman Technology* (Ithaca, N.Y., 1984).

STYLE AND MEANING

A. Bammer, *Architektur und Gesellschaft*, 2nd ed. (Vienna, 1985).

M. Berucci, "Esperienze costruttive ed estetiche dall'architettura romana," *BollCentro* 6 (1952), 3–5.

———— "Ragioni statiche ed estetiche delle proporzione degli ambiente coperte a volta," *BollCentro* 12 (1958), 25–34.

S. Bettini, *Lo spazio architettonico da Roma a Bizanzio* (Bari, 1978).

A. Blunt, review of Lyttelton (see below), *Burlington Magazine* 118 (1976), 320–324.

O. Brendel in *JSAH* 29 (1970), 264.

F. E. Brown, above, under General Works.

C. Ceschi, *Barocco romano d'oriente e barocco italiano del seicento* (Genoa, 1941).

D. S. Corlàita, "La situazione urbanistica degli archi onorari nella prima età imperiale," in G. A. Mansuelli, ed., *Studi sull'arco onorario romano* (Rome, 1979), pp. 29–72.

A. De Franciscis and R. Pane, above, under Building Types and Elements.

A. Frazer, above, under Building Types and Elements.

———— "From Column to Wall: The Peribolos of the Mausoleum of Maxentius," *In Memoriam Otto J. Brendel. Essays in Archaeology and the Humanities* (Mainz, 1975), pp. 185–190.

———— "The Iconography of the Emperor Maxentius' Buildings in Via Appia," *AB* 48 (1966), 385–392.

H. Gabelmann, above, under Building Types and Elements.

E. Hubala, "Roma sotterranea, Andachtsstätten in Rom und ihre Bedeutung für die barocke Baukunst," *Das Münster* 18 (1965), 157–173.

J. Le Gall, "Les romaines et l'orientation solaire," *MEFRA* 87 (1975), 287–320.

K. Lehmann, "The Dome of Heaven," *AB* 27 (1945), 1–27.

———— "Piranesi as Interpreter of Roman Architecture," *Piranesi* (Northampton, Mass., 1961), pp. 88–98.

H. P. L'Orange, *Art Forms and Civic Life*, 2nd ed. (Princeton, 1985).

M. Lyttelton, *Baroque Architecture in Classical Antiquity* (London, 1974).

MacDonald, chaps. 8 and 9.

W. L. MacDonald, "Empire Imagery in Augustan Architecture," *Archaeologica transatlantica* 4 (1985), 137–48.

W. L. MacDonald and B. M. Boyle, above, under Materials and Technology.

A. Maśliński, *Architektura antyku w interpretacji baroku,* (Lublin, 1962) (French résumé).

R. Pane, "Barocco antico," *Rassegna d'architettura* 7 (1935), 37–41.

G. C. Picard, *La civilisation de l'afrique romain* (Paris, 1959), chap. 6.

F. Rakob, "*Litus beatae veneris aurem.* Untersuchungen am 'Venustempel' in Baiae," *RM* 68 (1961), 114–149.

K. Schefold, *Römische Kunst als religiöses Phänomen* (Hamburg, 1964).

E. B. Smith, *Architectural Symbolism of Imperial Rome and the Middle Ages* (Princeton, 1956).

———— *The Dome* (Princeton, 1950).

Toynbee.

G. Von Kaschnitz-Weinberg, *Die Mittelmeerischen Grundlagen der antiken Kunst* (Frankfurt, 1944).

———— "Vergleichende Studien zur italisch-römischen Struktur, I, Baukunst," *RM* 59 (1944, pub. 1948), 89–128.

J. B. Ward-Perkins, review of Lyttelton (see above), *AJA* 80 (1976), 322–324.

F. K. Yegül, above, under Building Types and Elements (1982).

REGIONS

WESTERN EUROPE
(for Italy, see also above, under both General Works and Urbanism)

J. de Alarcão, *Portugal romano* (Lisbon, 1973).

G. Alföldy, *Noricum* (London, 1974).

A. Balil, *Casa y urbanismo en la España antigua,* 4 vols. (Valladolid, 1972–1974).

O. Brogan, *Roman Gaul* (Cambridge, Mass., 1953).

C. Carducci, "L'architettura in piemonte nell'antichità," *Atti del X congresso di storia dell'architettura* (1959), 152–186.

J.-P. Clébert, *Provence antique,* 2: *L'époque gallo-romaine,* (Paris, 1970).

R. G. Collingwood and I. A. Richmond, *The Archae-*

ology of Roman Britain, rev. ed. (London, 1969), chaps. 6, 8, 9.

A. Degrassi, *Porti romani dell'Istria* (1955; not seen).

F. Ertl, *Topografia norici* (Kremsmünster, 1965).

P.-A. Février, "The Origin and Growth of the Cities of Southern Gaul to the Third Century A.D.," *JRS* 63 (1973), 1–28.

P.-A. Février et al., *Histoire de la France urbaine,* 1: *La ville antique* (1980).

E. Frézouls, ed., *Les villes antiques de la France, Belgique 1* (Strasbourg, 1982).

A. Garcia y Bellido, *Arte romano,* 2nd ed. (Madrid, 1972).

Germania romana: Römerstadt in Deutschland, 1 and 2 (Heidelberg, 1960, 1965; = *Gymnasium,* Beihefte 1, 5).

A. Grenier, *Manuel d'archéologie gallo-romaine,* III, *L'architecture,* 2 vols. (Paris, 1958); IV, *Les monuments des eaux,* 2 vols. (Paris, 1960).

M. J. T. Lewis, *Temples in Roman Britain* (Cambridge, 1966).

P. MacKendrick, *The Iberian Stones Speak* (New York, 1969).

———— *Roman France* (London, 1971).

———— *Romans on the Rhine* (New York, 1970).

F. Staehelin, *Der Schweiz in römischer Zeit,* 3rd ed. (Basel, 1948).

J. Von Elbe, *Roman Germany. A Guide to Sites and Museums,* (Mainz, 1975).

H. Von Petrikovits, *Das römische Rheinland* (Cologne, 1960).

J. Wacher, *The Towns of Roman Britain* (London, 1975).

Ward-Perkins.

R. J. A. Wilson, *Roman Sicily* (forthcoming).

F. J. Wiseman, *Roman Spain* (London, 1956).

EASTERN EUROPE

A. Giuliano, *La cultura artistica delle province della Grecia nell'età romana* (Rome, 1965).

R. Hoddinott, *Bulgaria in Antiquity* (London, 1975).

I. Ivanov, "Der Städtebau in Ober- und Untermoesien und Thrakien in der Römerzeit und der Spätantike," *Actes du 1er congrès international des études balkaniques et sud-est européennes* (Sofia, 1969), pp. 491–502.

P. MacKendrick, *The Dacian Stones Speak* (Chapel Hill, 1975).

A. Mócsy, *Pannonia and Upper Moesia* (London, 1974).

K. Sz. Póczy, *Städte in Pannonien* (Budapest, 1976).

A. G. Poulter, ed., *Ancient Bulgaria,* 2 vols. (Nottingham, 1983).

E. B. Thomas, *Römische Villen in Pannonien* (Budapest, 1964).

V. Velkov, *Cities in Thrace and Dacia in Late Antiquity* (Amsterdam, 1977).

———— *Roman Cities in Bulgaria* (Amsterdam, 1980).

Ward-Perkins.

J. J. Wilkes, *Dalmatia* (London, 1969).

AFRICA

A. Adriani, *Repertorio d'arte dell'Egitto greco-romano, Serie C (Architettura e topografia),* 2 vols. (Palermo, 1963–1966).

U. M. De Villard, *La Nubia romana* (Rome, 1941).

A. Di Vita, *Tripolitania ellenistica e romana* (forthcoming).

N. Ferchiou, *Architecture romaine de Tunisie. L'ordre: Rythmes et proportions dans le Tell* (Tunis, 1975).

P.-A. Février, "Notes sur le développement urbain en Afrique du Nord. Les exemples comparés de Djemila et de Sétif," *Cahiers archéologiques* 14 (1964), 1–47.

E. Frézouls, "Teatri romani dell'Africa francese," *Dionisio* 15 (1952), 90–103.

R. G. Goodchild, *Libyan Studies,* ed. J. Reynolds (London, 1976).

S. Gsell, *Les monuments antiques de l'Algérie,* 2 vols. (Paris, 1901).

D. E. L. Haynes, *The Antiquities of Tripolitania* (Tripoli, 1965).

J.-C. Lachaux, *Théâtres et amphithéâtres d'Afrique proconsulaire* (Aix-en-Provence, ca. 1980).

C. Lepelley, *Les cités de l'Afrique romaine au bas-empire* (Paris, 1979).

A. Lézine, *Architecture romaine d'Afrique* (Tunis, 1963).

———— *Carthage. Utique. Etudes d'architecture et d'urbanisme* (Paris, 1968).

W. L. MacDonald, above, under Urbanism.

P. MacKendrick, *The North African Stones Speak* (Chapel Hill, 1980).

G. C. Picard, above, under Style and Meaning.

P. Romanelli, *Topografia e archeologia dell'Africa romana* (Turin, 1970).

S. Stucchi, *Architettura cirenaica* (Rome, 1975).

Ward-Perkins.

B. H. Warmington, *The North African Provinces from Diocletian to the Vandal Conquest* (Cambridge, 1954; reprinted 1971).

THE EAST

E. Akurgal, *Ancient Civilizations and Ruins of Turkey,* trans. J. Whybrow and M. Emre, 5th ed. (Istanbul, 1983).

G. E. Bean, *Aegean Turkey* (London, 1966).

―――― *Lycian Turkey* (London, 1978).

―――― *Turkey beyond the Maeander* (London, 1971).

―――― *Turkey's Southern Shore* (London, 1968).

G. Bowersock, *Roman Arabia* (Cambridge, Mass., 1983).

H. C. Butler, *Architecture and Other Arts* (New York, 1903) (Syria).

―――― *Syria*, Division II, *Architecture*, Section A, *Southern Syria* (Leiden, 1906–1919), and Section B, *Northern Syria* (Leiden, 1907–1920; = *Princeton University Archaeological Expeditions to Syria in 1904–05 and 1909*).

D. De Bernardi Ferrero, *Teatri classici in Asia Minore*, 4 vols. (Turin, 1966–1974).

E. Frézouls, "Recherches sur les théâtres de l'orient Syrien," *Syria* 36 (1959), 202–227; 38 (1961), 54–86.

G. L. Harding, *The Antiquities of Jordan*, rev. ed. (New York, 1967).

A. H. M. Jones, *The Cities of the Eastern Roman Provinces*, 2nd ed. (Oxford, 1971).

―――― *The Greek City from Alexander to Justinian* (Oxford, 1940).

D. M. Krencker and W. Zschietzschmann, *Römische Tempel in Syrien*, 2 vols. (Berlin, 1938).

K. Lanckoronski, *Städte Pamphyliens und Pisidiens*, 2 vols. (Vienna, 1890–1892).

D. Magie, *Roman Rule in Asia Minor*, 2 vols. (Princeton, 1950).

E. Rosenbaum et al., *A Survey of Coastal Cities in Western Cilicia* (Ankara, 1967).

G. Tchalenko, *Villages antiques de la Syrie du nord*, 3 vols. (Paris, 1953–1958).

Ward-Perkins.

J. B. Ward-Perkins (1958), above, under Materials and Technology.

SITES

This selection is limited to places and buildings emphasized in the text. For additional citations and other sites, see the regional works listed above and *EAA, PECS,* and *RE.*

ANTIOCH ON THE ORONTES

Antioch-on-the-Orontes. The Excavations, 5 vols. (Princeton, 1934–1972).

G. Downey and J. Lassus, above, under Pictorial Sources.

APAMEA

J. C. Balty, ed., *Apamée de Syrie. Bilan des recherches archéologiques 1965–1968* (Brussels, 1969).

J. Balty and J. C. Balty, eds., *Apamée de Syrie. Bilan des recherches archéologiques 1969–1971* (Brussels, 1972).

J. C. Balty, *Guide d'Apamée* (Brussels, 1981).

APHRODISIAS

K. T. Erim, *Aphrodisias* (New York, 1985).

ATHENS

J. Day, *A History of Athens under Roman Domination* (New York, 1942), pp. 183–251.

I. T. Hill, *The Ancient City of Athens* (London, 1953), chap. 19.

J. Travlos, *Pictorial Dictionary of Ancient Athens* (London, 1971).

T. L. Shear, Jr., "Athens: From City-State to Provincial Town," *Hesperia* 50 (1981), 356–377.

BAALBEK

T. Wiegand, ed., *Baalbek*, 3 vols. (Berlin, 1921–1925).

F. Ragette, *Baalbek* (Park Ridge, N.J., 1980).

BOSRA

S. Cerulli, "Bosra: Il sistemo viario della città romana," *Felix Ravenna* 115 (1978), 140–158.

M. Sartre, *Bostra, des origines à l'Islam* (forthcoming).

BULLA REGIA

A. Beschaouch et al., *Les ruines de Bulla Regia* (Rome, 1977).

Recherches archéologiques franco-tunisiennes à Bulla Regia 1. Miscellanea, 1 (Rome, 1983).

BU NGEM

D. E. L. Haynes, above, under Regions (Africa), pp. 140–142.

R. Rebuffat et al., "Bu Njem 1967," *Libya antiqua* 3–4 (1966–1967), 49–137; "Bu Njem 1971," *Libya antiqua* 11–12 (1974–1975), 189–241.

CAESAREA MARITIMA

A. Frova, *Caesarea Maritima: Rapporto preliminare* (Milan, 1959).

―――― *Scavi di Caesarea Maritima* (Rome, 1966).

A. Raban and R. L. Hohlfelder, "The Ancient Harbors of Caesarea Maritima," *Archaeology* 34 (1981), 56–60.

CAPERA

J. M. Blazquez, *Caparra* (Madrid, 1965).

CONSTANTINOPLE

R. Janin, *Constantinople byzantine,* 2nd ed. (Paris, 1964).

G. Dagron, *Naissance d'une capitale. Constantinople et ses institutions de 330 à 451* (Paris, 1974).

CORINTH

Corinth. Results of the Excavations conducted by the American School of Classical Studies at Athens (begun in 1932).

Ancient Corinth. A Guide to the Excavations, 6th ed. (Athens, 1954).

H. S. Robinson, *The Urban Development of Ancient Corinth* (Athens, 1965).

CYRENE

R. G. Goodchild, *Cyrene and Apollonia,* 2nd ed. (London, 1963).

_____ *Kyrene und Apollonia* (Zürich, 1971).

S. Stucchi, above, under Regions (Africa).

J. B. Ward-Perkins and M. H. Ballance, above, under Building Types and Elements.

DJEMILA

P.-A. Février, above, under Regions (Africa).

P.-A. Février, *Djemila* (Algiers, 1968).

Y. Allais, "Le quartier occidental de Djemila (Cuicul)," *Antiquités africaines* 5 (1971), 95–120.

DOUGGA

C. Poinssot, *Les ruines de Dougga* (Tunis, 1958).

A. Golfetto, *Dougga* (Basel, 1961).

EPHESUS

Forschungen in Ephesos, veröffentlicht vom Österreichischen Archäologischen Institut in Wien (begun in 1906).

F. Miltner, *Ephesos, Stadt der Artemis und des Johannes,* (Vienna, 1958).

F. Fasolo, *L'architettura romana di Efeso* (Rome, 1962 = *BollCentro* 18).

J. Keil, *Führer durch Ephesos,* 5th ed. (Vienna, 1964).

W. Alzinger, *Die Ruinen von Ephesos* (Berlin and Vienna, 1972).

_____ "Augusteische Architektur in Ephesos," *Sonderschriften des Österreichischen Archäologischen Instituts* 16 (1974).

C. Foss, *Ephesus after Antiquity: A Late Antique, Byzantine and Turkish City* (Cambridge, 1979).

GERASA

C. Kraeling, ed., *Gerasa, City of the Decapolis* (New Haven, 1938).

I. Browning, *Jerash and the Decapolis* (London, 1982).

GHIRZA: See Wadi settlements, below

HERCULANEUM

A. Maiuri, *I nuovi scavi di Ercolano,* 2 vols. (Rome, 1958).

HIPPO REGIUS

E. Marec, *Hippone la royale,* 2nd ed. (Algiers, 1954).

S. Dahmani, *Hippo Regius* (Algiers, 1973).

JERUSALEM

K. M. Kenyon, *Digging Up Jerusalem* (London, 1974).

Y. Tsafrir, "Jerusalem," *Reallexikon zur byzantinischen Kunst* 3 (1978), 525–615.

KHAMISSA

S. Gsell and C. A. Joly, *Khamissa* (Paris, 1914).

LAMBAESIS

M. Janon, "Recherches a Lambèse," *Antiquités africaines* 7 (1973), 193–254.

F. Rakob, "Die Principia des römischen Legionslagers in Lambaesis," *RM* 81 (1974), 41–89.

_____ "Das Groma-Nymphaeum im Legionslager von Lambaesis," *RM* 86 (1979), 375–397.

LEPCIS MAGNA

R. Bartoccini, *Le terme di Lepcis* (Bergamo, 1929).

_____ "L'arco quadrifronte dei Severi a Lepcis," *Africa italiana* 4 (1931), 32–152.

J. B. Ward-Perkins, "Severan Art and Architecture at Lepcis Magna," *JRS* 38 (1948), 59–80.

J. B. Ward-Perkins and J. M. C. Toynbee, "The Hunting Baths at Lepcis Magna," *Archaeologia* 93 (1949), 165–195.

R. Bartoccini, *Il porto romano di Leptis Magna, Supp.* 13 to *BollCentro* (1960).

R. Bianchi Bandinelli et al., *Leptis Magna* (Verona, 1964).

H. Walda and S. Walker, above, under Materials and Technology.

LONDON

R. Merrifield, *London, City of the Romans* (London, 1983).

MAKTAR

G. C. Picard, *Civitas Mactaritana* (Paris, 1957; = *Karthago* 8).

MERIDA

M. Almagro, *Mérida. Guide de la Ville* (Merida, 1959).

A. Blanco Freijeiro, ed., *Augusta Emerita* (Madrid, 1976).

MEROË

W. S. Smith, *The Art and Architecture of Ancient Egypt* (Harmondsworth, 1958).

L. P. Kirwan, *Rome beyond the Southern Egyptian Frontier,* (London, 1977; a separate publication from the *Proceedings of the British Academy* 63).

MILAN

A. Calderini, *Storia di Milano,* 1 (Milan, 1953).

R. Krautheimer, *Three Christian Capitals* (Berkeley, 1983).

M. Mirabella Roberti, *Milano romana* (Milan, 1984).

MILETUS

Milet. Ergebnisse der Ausgrabungen und Untersuchungen seit dem Jahre 1899 (begun in 1906).

G. Kleiner, *Die Ruinen von Milet* (Berlin, 1968).

———— *Das römische Milet* (Wiesbaden, 1970; = *Sitzungsberichte der Wissenschaftlichen Gesellschaft an der J. W. Goethe-Universität* 8).

MUSTI

A. Beschaouch, "Municipium Iulium Aurelium Mustitanum," *Cahiers de Tunisie* 15 (1967), 85–102.

NAGA: See Meroë, above

NICOPOLIS AD ISTRUM

Price and Trell, p. 246.

Ward-Perkins, pp. 249–251.

NICOPOLIS IN EPIRUS

Price and Trell, p. 250.

NÎMES

R. Naumann, *Die Quellbezirk von Nîmes* (Berlin, 1937).

R. Amy and P. Gros, *La Maison Carrée* (Paris, 1979; = *Supp.* 38 to *Gallia*).

OLYMPIA

H. Schleif and H. Weber, "Das Nymphaion des Her-

odes Atticus," *Olympische Forschungen* 1 (Berlin, 1944), 53–82.

C. Tiberi, "L'Esedra di Erode Attico a Olimpia e il Canopo della Villa di Adriano presso Tivoli," *Quaderni* 31–48 (1961), 35–48.

A. Mallwitz, *Olympia und seine Bauten* (Munich, 1972).

ORANGE

R. Amy et al., *L'arc d'Orange* (Paris, 1962, = *Supp.* 15 to *Gallia*).

OSTIA

Scavi di Ostia (begun in 1953).

Meiggs.

G. Girri, above, under Building Types and Elements.

C. Pavolini, *Ostia* (Rome and Bari, 1983).

PALMYRA

K. Michalowski et al., *Palmyre. Fouilles polonaises,* 1–7 (Warsaw-Paris, 1960–1977).

Palmyre. Bilan et perspectives (Strasbourg, 1976).

I. Browning, *Palmyra* (London, 1979).

PERGAMON

Altertümer von Pergamon (begun in 1912; vol. XI covers the Asklepieion).

E. Boehringer, "Pergamon," in *Neue deutsche Ausgrabungen im Mittelmeergebiet und im vorderen Orient* (Berlin, 1959), pp. 121–171.

B. Schlüter and K. Nohlen, *Topographische Karte von Pergamon, 1 : 2500* . . . (Bonn, 1973).

M. Le Glay, "Hadrien et l'Asklépieion de Pergame," *Bulletin de correspondance hellénique* 100 (1976), 347–372.

PERGE

K. Lanckoronski, above, under Regions (The East), vol. 1, pp. 33–63.

G. E. Bean, above, under Regions (The East), 1968 vol., pp. 45–58.

PETRA

R. E. Brünnow and A. von Domaszewski, *Die Provincia Arabia* 1 (Strassburg, 1904).

G. R. H. Wright, "The Khazne at Petra: A Review," *Annual of the Department of Antiquities of Jordan* 6–7 (1962), 24–54.

I. Browning, *Petra* (London, 1973).

G. W. Bowersock, above, under Regions (The East).

PIAZZA ARMERINA

N. Neuerburg, "Some Considerations on the Architecture of the Imperial Villa at Piazza Armerina," *Marsyas* 8 (1959), 22–29.

C. Ampolo et al., "La villa del Casale a Piazza Armerina. Problemi, saggi stratigrafici ed altre ricerche," *MEFRA* 83 (1971), 141–281.

J. Polzer, "The Villa at Piazza Armerina and the Numismatic Evidence," *AJA* 77 (1973), 139–150.

A. Carandini et al., *Filosofiana. The Villa of Piazza Armerina*, 2 vols. (Palermo, 1982).

R. J. A. Wilson, *Piazza Armerina* (London, 1983).

POLA

G. Traversari, *L'arco dei Sergi* (Padua, 1971).

POMPEII

A. Maiuri, *L'ultima fase edilizia di Pompeii* (Rome, 1942).

H. Eschebach, *Stadtplan von Pompeji, RM,* Ergänzungsheft 17 (1970).

E. La Rocca et al., *Guida archeologica di Pompeii* (Verona, 1976).

V. Kockel, *Die Grabbauten vor dem Herkulaner Tor in Pompeji,* (Mainz, 1983).

L. Richardson Jr., *Pompeii: An Architectural History* (forthcoming).

PRIENE

M. Schede, *Die Ruinen von Priene* (Berlin, 1964).

PTOLEMAIS IN CYRENAICA

G. Pesce, *Il "Palazzo delle Colonne" in Tolemaide di Cirenaica* (Rome, 1950; = *Monografie di archeologia libica* 2).

C. H. Kraeling, *Ptolemais, City of the Libyan Pentapolis* (Chicago, 1962).

RIMINI

S. De Maria, "La porta augustea di Rimini. . . ," pp. 73–91 in G. A. Mansuelli, ed., above, under Building Types and Elements.

G. A. Mansuelli, "Il monumento augusteo del 27 a. C. Nuove ricerche sull'arco di Rimini," *Arte antica e moderna* 8 (1959), 363–391; 9 (1960), 16–39.

ROME

Nash.

MacDonald.

Toynbee.

Coarelli.

S. B. Platner and T. Ashby, *A Topographical Dictionary of Ancient Rome* (Oxford, 1919).

G. Lugli, *Roma antica. Il centro monumentale* (Rome, 1946).

D. R. Dudley, *Urbs Roma. A Source Book of Classical Texts . . .* (London, 1967).

F. Castagnoli, *Topografica e urbanistica di Roma antica,* (Bologna, 1969).

S. Quilici Gigli, *Roma fuori le mura. Guida al monumenti . . .* (Rome, 1980).

F. Coarelli, *Dintorni di Roma* (Rome-Bari, 1981).

SABRATHA

D. E. L. Haynes, above, under Regions (Africa).

G. Caputo, *Il teatro di Sabratha e l'architettura teatrale africana* (Rome, 1959; = *Monografie di archeologia libica* 6).

ST.-CHAMAS

F. Berard, "Note sur le Pont Flavien," *Rhodania* (1969, No. 2), 3–6.

ST.-RÉMY

H. Rolland, *Fouilles de Glanum,* 2 vols. (Paris, 1946, 1958; = Supp. 1 and 11 to *Gallia*).

SAMARIA/SEBASTE

J. W. Crowfoot et al., *The Buildings at Samaria* (London, 1942).

S. MARIA CAPUA VETERE

A. De Franciscis and R. Pane, pp. 76–87; see above, under Building Types and Elements.

Toynbee, pp. 128–130.

SARDIS

G. M. A. Hanfmann and J. C. Waldbaum, *A Survey of Sardis,* (Cambridge, Mass., 1975).

C. Foss, *Byzantine and Turkish Sardis* (Cambridge, Mass., 1976).

F. Yegül, "The Marble Court at Sardis and Historical Reconstruction," *Journal of Field Archaeology* 3 (1976), 169–194.

G. M. A. Hanfmann, *Sardis from Prehistoric to Roman Times* (Cambridge, Mass., 1983).

SBEITLA

N. Duval, "Histoire et bibliographie du site de Sbeitla, 1724–1970," *Recherches archéologiques à Sbeitla* 1 (Paris, 1971), 393–443.

N. Duval and F. Baratte, *Les ruines de Sufetula: Sbeitla,* (Tunis, 1973).

SIDE

A. Müfid Mansel, *Die Ruinen von Side* (Berlin, 1963).

P. Knoblauch, *Die Hafenanlagen und die anschliessenden Seemauern von Side* (Ankara, 1977).

SOLI-POMPEIOPOLIS

A. A. Boyce, "The Harbor of Pompeiopolis. A Study in Roman Ports and Dated Coins," *AJA* 62 (1958), 66–78.

SPLIT

B. Schulz, "Die Porta Aurea in Spalato," *JDAI* 24 (1909), 46–52.

G. Niemann, *Der Palast Diokletians in Spalato* (Vienna, 1910).

E. Hebrard and J. Zeiller, *Spalato. Le palais de Dioclétien* (Paris, 1911).

N. Duval, "La place de Split dans l'architecture du Bas-Empire," *Urbs* (1961–1962), 67–95.

J. and T. Marasović, *Dioklecijanova Palača* (Zagreb, 1968).

Diocletian's Palace. Reports on Joint Excavations . . . (Univeristy of Minnesota, Urbanistički zavod Dalmacije; begun 1972).

STOBI

J. Wiseman, et al., eds., *Studies in the Antiquities of Stobi,* 3 vols. (Belgrade, 1973–1981).

THENAE

D. Krencker and F. Krüger, pp. 224–225; see above, under Building Types and Elements.

THUBURBO MAIUS

A. Merlin, *Le forum de Thuburbo Maius* (Tunis-Paris, 1922).

A. Lézine (1963), pp. 91–142; see above, under Regions (Africa).

——— *Thuburbo Majus* (Tunis, 1968).

TIDDIS

A. Berthier, *Tiddis, antique Castellum Tidditanorum* (Algiers, 1972).

TIGZIRT

Reports in *MEFRA* 65–69 (1953–1957).

TIMGAD

A. Ballu, *Les ruines de Timgad,* 3 vols. (Paris, 1897–1911).

E. Boeswillwald et al., *Timgad, une cité africaine sous l'empire romain* (Paris, 1904).

S. Gsell, above, under Regions (Africa).

J. Lassus, *Visite à Timgad* (Algiers, 1969).

TIPASA

S. Lancel, *Tipasa de Maurétanie* (Algiers, 1966).

——— "Tipasitana IV: La necropole romaine orientale de la porte de Césarée—Rapport préliminaire," *Bulletin d'archéologie algérienne* 4 (1970), 149–266.

P. Aubert, *Le nymphée de Tipasa et les nymphées et "Septizonia" nord-africains* (Paris-Rome, 1974).

TIVOLI (HADRIAN'S VILLA)

H. Kähler, *Hadrian und seine Villa bei Tivoli* (Berlin, 1950).

W. L. MacDonald and B. M. Boyle, above, under Materials and Technology.

TRIER

D. Krencker and F. Krüger, above, under Building Types and Elements.

E. M. Wightmann, *Trier and the Treveri* (London, 1970).

LA TURBIE

J. Formige, *Le trophée des Alpes* (Paris, 1949; = *Supp.* 2 to *Gallia*).

TURIN

I. A. Richmond, "Augustan Gates at Torino and Spello," *PBSR* 12 (1932), 52–62.

VAISON-LA-ROMAINE

J. Sautel, *Vaison dans l'antiquité,* 3 vols. (Avignon, 1941–1942; Lyon, 1942).

——— *Sites, histoire et monuments de Vaison-la-romaine,* (Lyon, 1955).

Reports in *Gallia* from 1960 onward.

VERONA

L. Beschi, "Verona romana e i monumenti," in *Verona e il suo territorio* I (Verona, 1960; not seen).

G. Tosi, *L'arco dei Gavi a Verona* (Rome, 1983).

VERULAMIUM

S. Frere, *Verulamium Excavations,* 2 vols. (Oxford, 1972, 1983).

J. Wacher, above, under Regions (Western Europe).

VIENNE

A. Pelletier, *Vienne antique* (Roanne, 1982).

VOLUBILIS

R. Thouvenot, *Volubilis* (Paris, 1949).

R. Etienne, *Le quartier nord-est de Volubilis,* 2 vols. (Paris, 1960).

R. Rebuffat, "Le développement urbain de Volubilis au second siècle de notre ère," *Bulletin archéologique du Comité des travaux historiques et archéologiques* (1965–1966), 231–240.

WADI SETTLEMENTS AND MONUMENTS IN TRIPOLITANIA

D. E. L. Haynes, pp. 135–169; see above, under Regions (Africa).

O. Brogan, "Henscir el-Ausāf by Tigi (Tripolitania) and Some Related Tombs in the Tunisian Gefara," *Libya antiqua* 2 (1965), 47–56.

O. Brogan and D. Smith, "The Roman Frontier Settlement at Ghirza: An Interim Report," *JRS* 47 (1957), 173–184.

LIST OF PRINCIPAL EMPERORS

Augustus	27 B.C.–A.D. 14		Probus	276–282
Tiberius	14–37		Diocletian	284–305
Caligula	37–41		Galerius	293–311
Claudius	41–54		Licinius	311–323
Nero	54–68		Maxentius	306–312
Vespasian	69–79		Constantine I	306–337
Titus	79–81		Constantius II	337–361
Domitian	81–96		Julian	361–363
Nerva	96–98		Valentinian I	364–375 (west)
Trajan	98–117		Valens	364–378 (east)
Hadrian	117–138		Theodosius I	379–395
Antoninus Pius	138–161		Arcadius	395–408 (east)
Marcus Aurelius	161–180		Honorius	395–423 (west)
Commodus	181–193		Theodosius II	408–450 (east)
Septimus Severus	193–211		Leo I	457–474 (east)
Caracalla	211–217		Zeno	474–491 (east)
Elagabalus	218–222		Romulus Augustulus	475–476 (west)
Severus Alexander	222–235			
Gordian III	238–244		Anastasius	491–518
Philip	244–249		Justin I	518–527
Valerian	253–260		Justinian I	527–565
Gallienus	253–268			
Aurelian	270–275			

SOURCES OF ILLUSTRATIONS

Drawings not otherwise credited were made by Peter C. Papademetriou (when a student), Sarah Calkins, and Michael Lawrence, after the sources given below. Illustrations not listed were made from the author's photographs. Costs were defrayed in part by a grant from the William L. Bryant Foundation.

James Addiss: 71, 82, 138

Alinari/Art Resource, NY: 80, 88 (the arch), 91, 93, 136, 182, 186 (the tower), 190, 194, 196

Wilhelm Alzinger, *Die Ruinen von Ephesos* (Berlin and Vienna, 1972), p. 72: 104

Massimo Amodei: 120, 126

Bruno M. Apollonj: *Il foro e la basilica severiana di Leptis Magna* (Rome, 1936), Tavv. I–II: 57

Athens, Third Archaeological District: 178 (photograph)

Edmund N. Bacon, *Design of Cities*, rev. ed. (New York, 1974), pp. 84, 90–91: 206, 210

B. T. Batsford, Ltd., publishers of John Wacher, *The Towns of Roman Britain* (London, 1975), Fig. 47: 33

Ranuccio Bianchi Bandinelli et al., *Leptis Magna* (Verona, 1964), Fig. 241: 51

Bernard M. Boyle: 176, 177, 208, 209

Iain Browning, *Palmyra* (London, 1979), Map 4: 16

Chatto & Windus, publishers of Iain Browning, *Jerash and the Decapolis* (London, 1982), Fig. 38: 13

La colonna di Traiano. Rilievi fotografici . . . (Rome, 1942): 58, 174

Christian Courtois, *Timgad, antique Thamugadi*, Algiers, 1951, plans: 21, 23

Deutsches archäologisches Institut, Rome: 141, 181, 211, 212

Glanville Downey, *A History of Antioch in Syria from Seleucus to the Arab Conquest* (Princeton, 1961), ill. 11: 18

Paul-Albert Février, *Djemila* (Algiers, 1968), map: 1, 4

Fototeca Unione, at the American Academy in Rome: 2, 5, 14, 24, 25, 29, 37, 40, 43, 45–48, 54, 56, 59, 60, 63 (Athens), 64, 70, 74–78, 86, 89, 90, 98–100, 103, 106, 108–112, 114, 116, 119, 121, 127, 130, 131, 137, 139, 142, 143, 146, 149, 151, 158 (Herculaneum), 168, 169, 172, 173, 174 (Thuburbo Maius), 175, 180, 189, 198, 201, 202

Gabinetto Fotografico Nazionale: 26, 42, 122, 125, 133, 157 (model), 192, 213

Gino V. Gentili, *The Imperial Villa of Piazza Armerina*, 4th ed. (Rome, 1970), plan: 207

Walter de Gruyter & Co., publishers of Arif Müfid Mansel, *Die Ruinen von Side* (Berlin, 1963), Frontispiece: 20

D. E. L. Haynes, *The Antiquities of Tripolitania* (Tripoli, 1965), plan of Lepcis Magna and Fig. 21: 36, 140

Margaret Henry: 147

R. Janin, *Constantinople byzantine* (Paris, 1964), maps I and V: 19

Heinz Kähler, *Hadrian und seine Villa bei Tivoli* (Berlin, 1950), Taf. 3: 185

Carl Kraeling, ed., *Gerasa, City of the Decapolis* (New Haven, 1938) Plan I: 35

Daniel Krencker and F. Krüger, *Die Trierer Kaiserthemen* (Augsburg, 1929), Abb. 2, 317, 412: 34, 179, 170

Thomas Lyman: 6

Phyllis Dearborn Massar: 188

Christian Norberg-Schulz, *Baroque Architecture* (New York, 1971), Pl. 156: 183

Andrew Oliver, Jr.: 41, 113

Claude Poinssot, *Les ruines de Dougga* (Tunis, 1958), Fig. 2: 65

Proceedings of the British Academy 37 (1951), p. 273, Fig. 2: 52

Friedrich Ragette, *Baalbek* (Park Ridge, N.J., 1980), p. 55: 156

Eugenio La Rocca et al., *Guida archeologica di Pompeii* (Verona, 1976), p. 122: 150

Scavi di Ostia, I, *Topografia generale* (Rome, 1953), Plan, and Fig. 32: 44, 203, 197

B. Schlüter and K. Nohlen, *Topographische Karte von*

Pergamon 1:2500 . . . (Bonn, 1973; published by the Deutsches archäologisches Institut): 200

S.P.A.D.E.M./Arch. Phot. Paris: 73, 92 (Martin-Sabon)

Jocelyn Toynbee and John Ward Perkins, *The Shrine of St. Peter and the Vatican Excavations* (London, 1956), Fig. 6: 148

Verlag Ernst Wasmuth, copyright holders of John Travlos, *Pictorial Dictionary of Ancient Athens* (London, 1971), Fig. 247: 178 (plan)

INDEX

Ancient site names, if different from those used in the text, are given in parentheses.